ko Takahashi

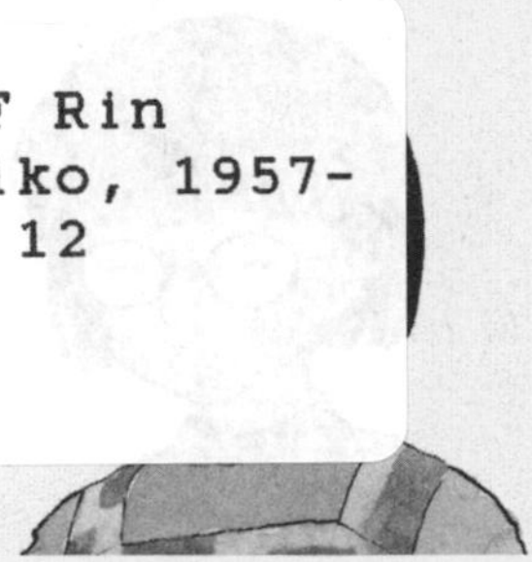

The spotlight on Rumiko Takahashi's career began in 1978 when she won an honorable mention in Shogakukan's annual New Comic Artist Contest for *Those Selfish Aliens*. Later that same year, her boy-meets-alien comedy series, *Urusei Yatsura*, was serialized in *Weekly Shonen Sunday*. This phenomenally successful manga series was adapted into anime format and spawned a TV series and half a dozen theatrical-release movies, all incredibly popular in their own right. Takahashi followed up the success of her debut series with one blockbuster hit after another—*Maison Ikkoku* ran from 1980 to 1987, *Ranma ½* from 1987 to 1996, and *Inuyasha* from 1996 to 2008. Other notable works include *Mermaid Saga*, *Rumic Theater*, and *One-Pound Gospel*.

Takahashi won the prestigious Shogakukan Manga Award twice in her career, once for *Urusei Yatsura* in 1981 and the second time for *Inuyasha* in 2002. A majority of the Takahashi canon has been adapted into other media such as anime, live-action TV series, and film. Takahashi's manga, as well as the other formats her work has been adapted into, have continued to delight generations of fans around the world. Distinguished by her wonderfully endearing characters, Takahashi's work adeptly incorporates a wide variety of elements such as comedy, romance, fantasy, and martial arts. While her series are difficult to pin down into one simple genre, the signature style she has created has come to be known as the "Rumic World." Rumiko Takahashi is an artist who truly represents the very best from the world of manga.

RIN-NE
VOLUME 12
Shonen Sunday Edition

STORY AND ART BY
RUMIKO TAKAHASHI

KYOKAI NO RINNE Vol. 12
by Rumiko TAKAHASHI
© 2009 Rumiko TAKAHASHI
All rights reserved.
Original Japanese edition published by SHOGAKUKAN.
English translation rights in the United States of America,
Canada, the United Kingdom and Ireland arranged with
SHOGAKUKAN.

Translation/Christine Dashiell
Touch-up Art & Lettering/Evan Waldinger
Design/Shawn Carrico
Editor/Mike Montesa

Printed in Canada

Published by VIZ Media, LLC
P.O. Box 77010
San Francisco, CA 94107

10 9 8 7 6 5 4 3 2 1
First printing, July 2013

www.viz.com   WWW.SHONENSUNDAY.COM

Story and Art by
Rumiko Takahashi

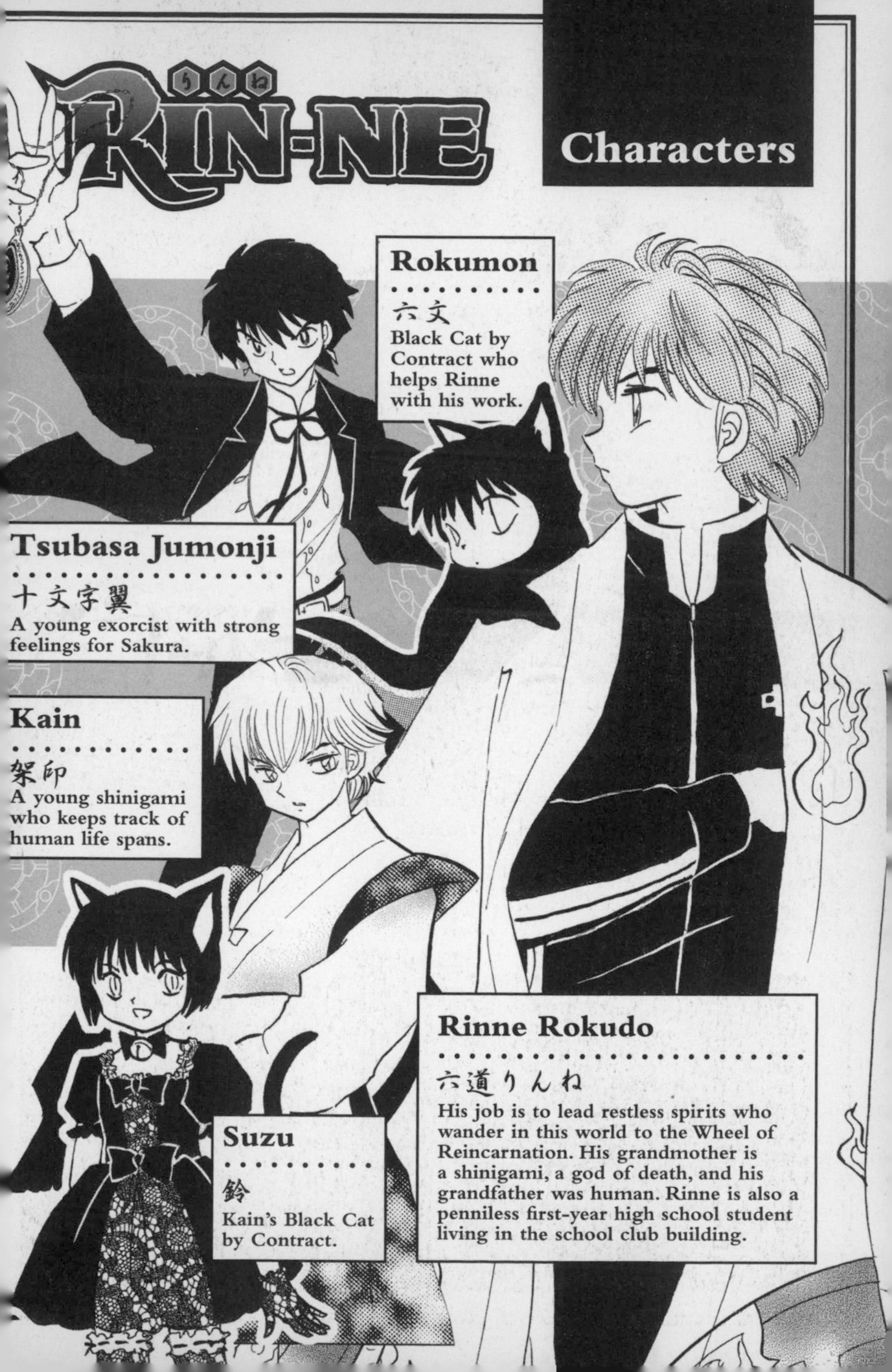
りんね
RIN-NE

Characters

Rokumon

六文

Black Cat by Contract who helps Rinne with his work.

Tsubasa Jumonji

十文字翼

A young exorcist with strong feelings for Sakura.

Kain

架印

A young shinigami who keeps track of human life spans.

Rinne Rokudo

六道りんね

His job is to lead restless spirits who wander in this world to the Wheel of Reincarnation. His grandmother is a shinigami, a god of death, and his grandfather was human. Rinne is also a penniless first-year high school student living in the school club building.

Suzu

鈴

Kain's Black Cat by Contract.

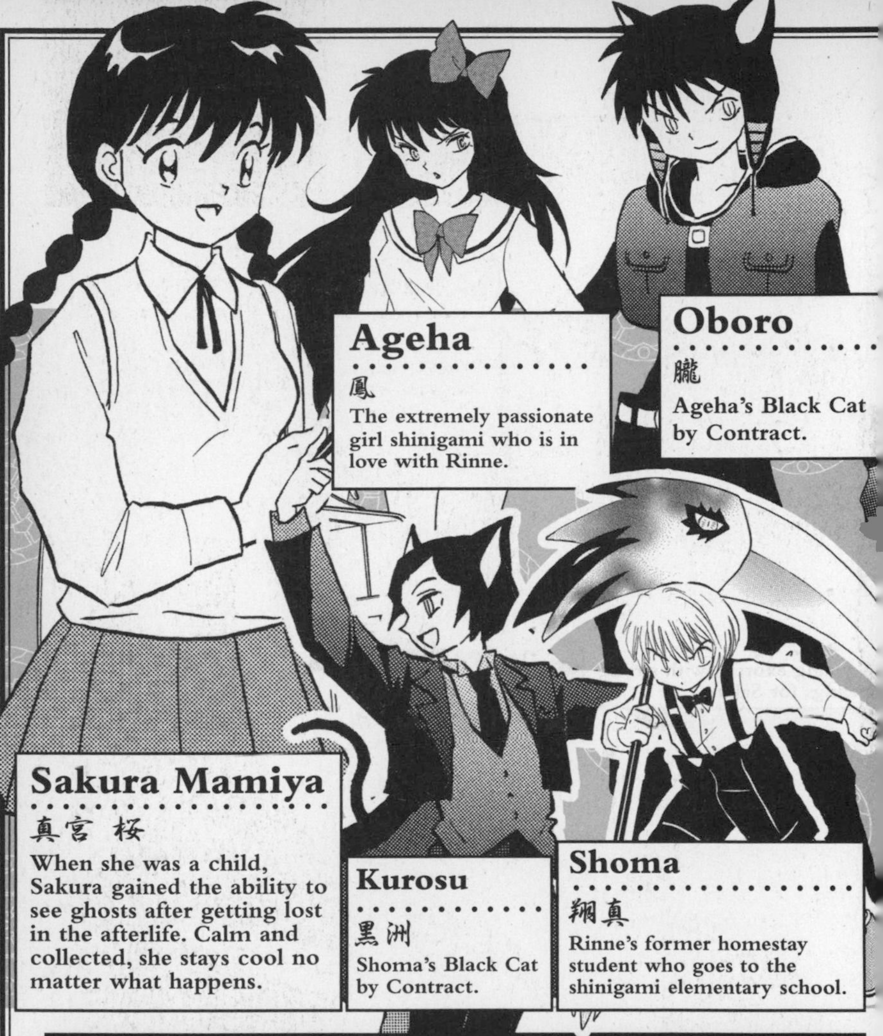

Sakura Mamiya

真宮 桜

When she was a child, Sakura gained the ability to see ghosts after getting lost in the afterlife. Calm and collected, she stays cool no matter what happens.

Ageha

鳳

The extremely passionate girl shinigami who is in love with Rinne.

Oboro

朧

Ageha's Black Cat by Contract.

Kurosu

黒洲

Shoma's Black Cat by Contract.

Shoma

翔真

Rinne's former homestay student who goes to the shinigami elementary school.

The Story So Far

Together, Sakura, the girl who can see ghosts, and Rinne the shinigami (sort of) spend their days helping spirits that can't pass on reach the afterlife, and deal with all kinds of strange phenomena at their school.

One day, after eating some candy that makes her blind to seeing ghosts, Sakura becomes the target of a pack of evil spirits taking part in the A1 Grand Prix. Rinne has to go all out to protect Sakura, even though she can't see what he's doing! Then Shoma and his Black Cat Kurosu appear again, making sure Rinne's shinigami to-do list is kept full!

Contents

CHAPTER 109: THE ATTENTION-GRABBING EVENT

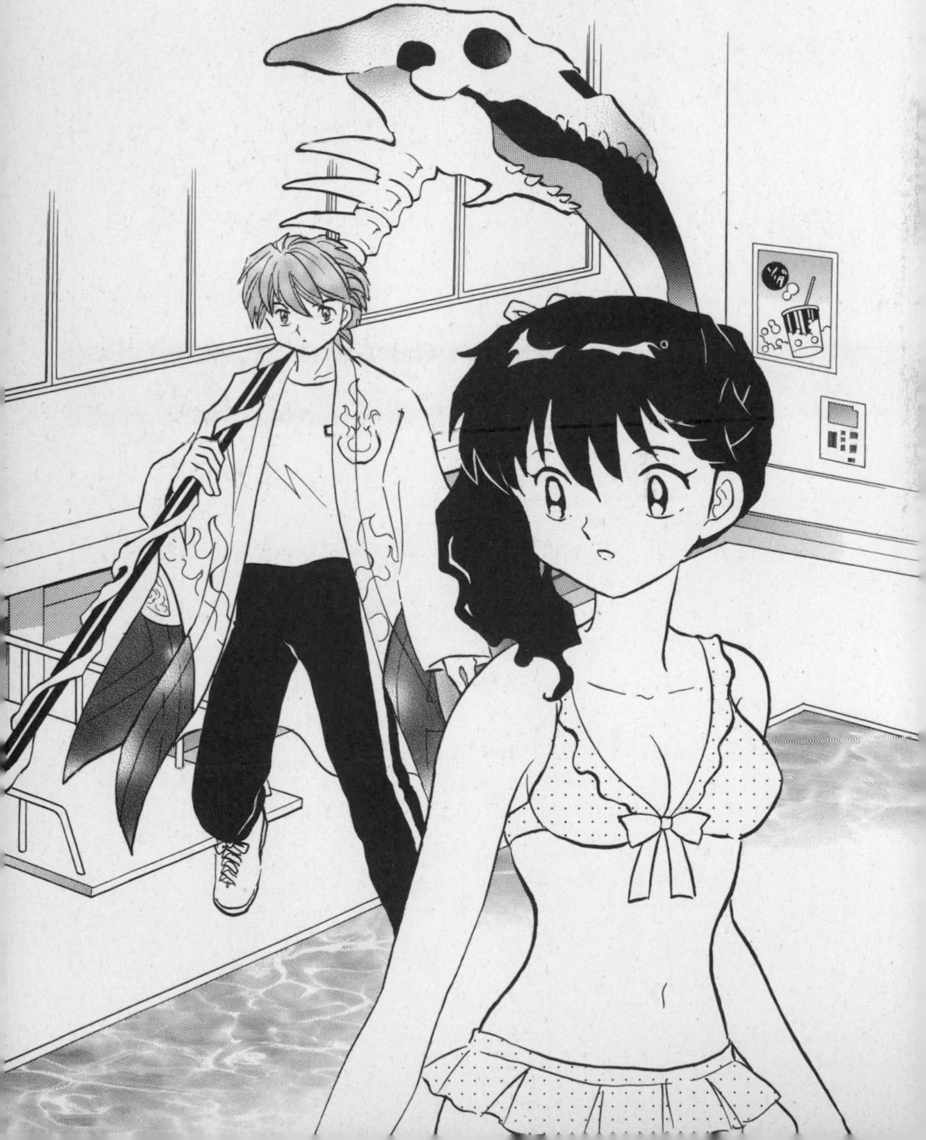

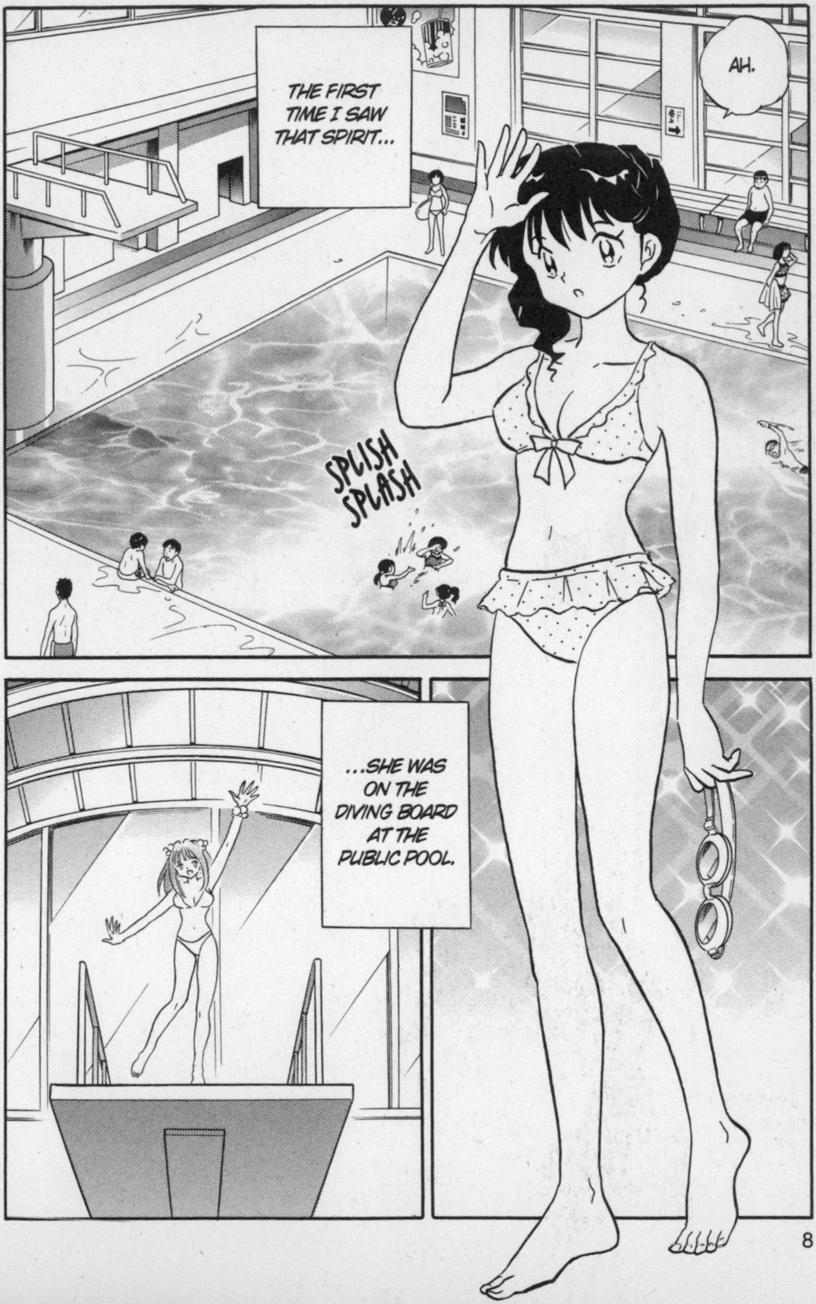
AH.
THE FIRST TIME I SAW THAT SPIRIT...
SPLISH SPLASH
...SHE WAS ON THE DIVING BOARD AT THE PUBLIC POOL.

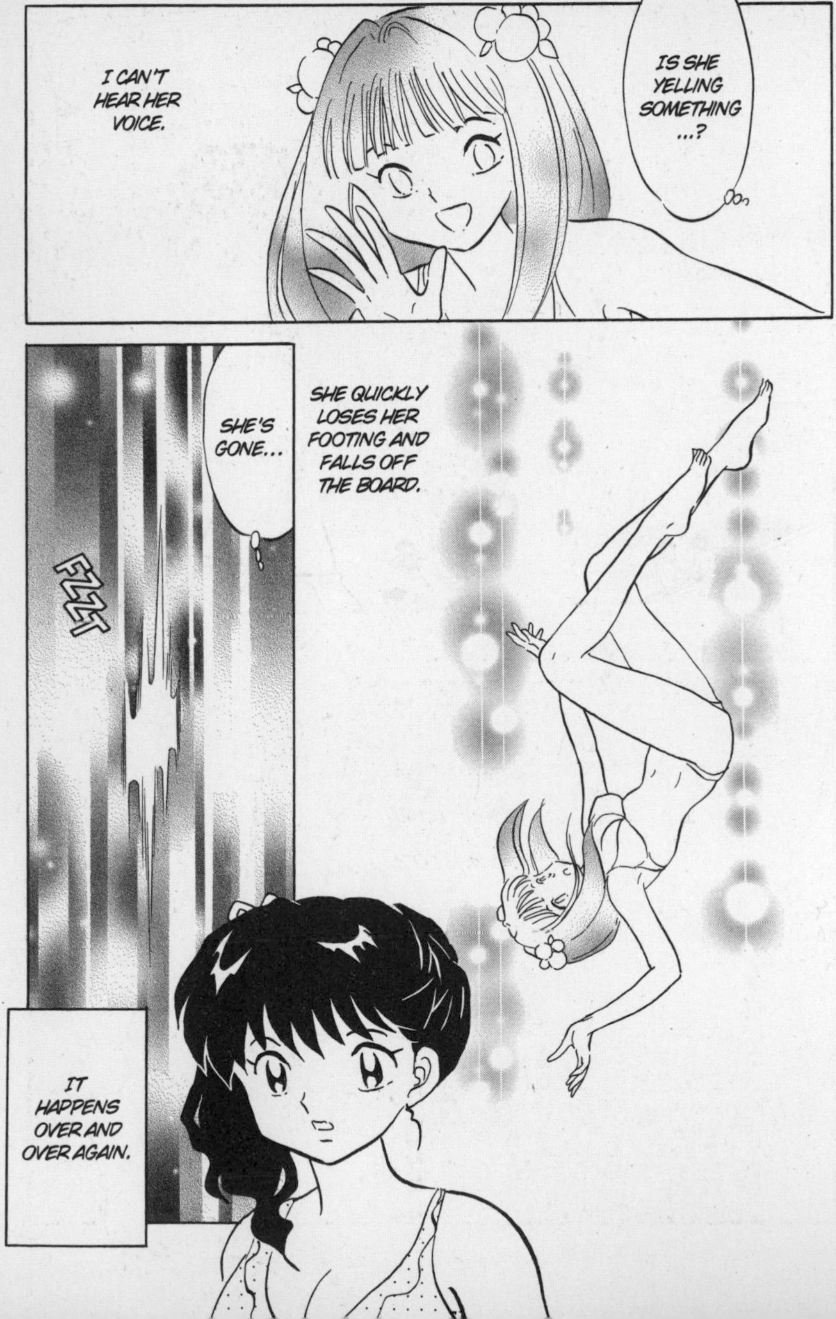
IS SHE YELLING SOMETHING ...?
I CAN'T HEAR HER VOICE.
SHE QUICKLY LOSES HER FOOTING AND FALLS OFF THE BOARD.
SHE'S GONE...
FZZT
IT HAPPENS OVER AND OVER AGAIN.

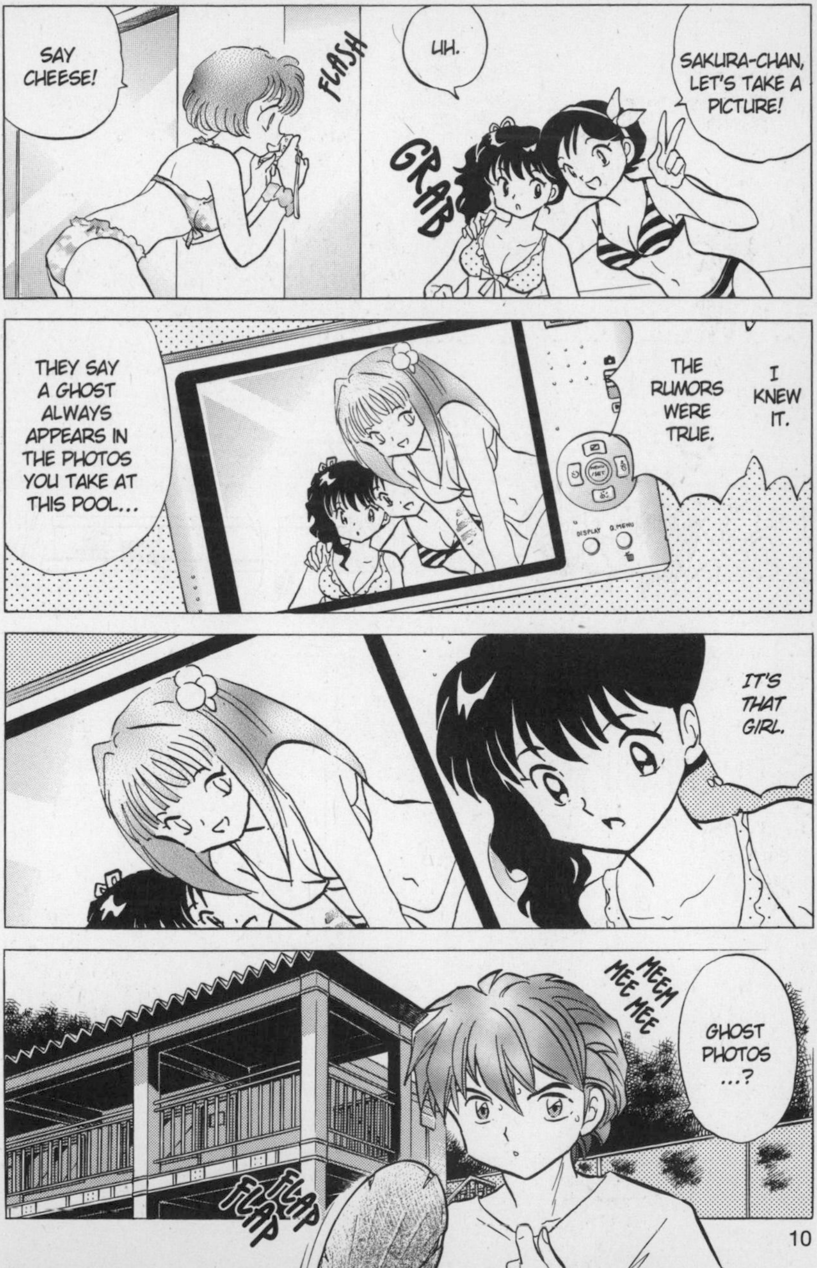
SAKURA-CHAN, LET'S TAKE A PICTURE!
GRAB
UH.
FLASH
SAY CHEESE!
I KNEW IT.
THE RUMORS WERE TRUE.
THEY SAY A GHOST ALWAYS APPEARS IN THE PHOTOS YOU TAKE AT THIS POOL...
DISPLAY
Q.MENU
IT'S THAT GIRL.
MEEM MEE MEE
GHOST PHOTOS ...?
FLAP FLAP

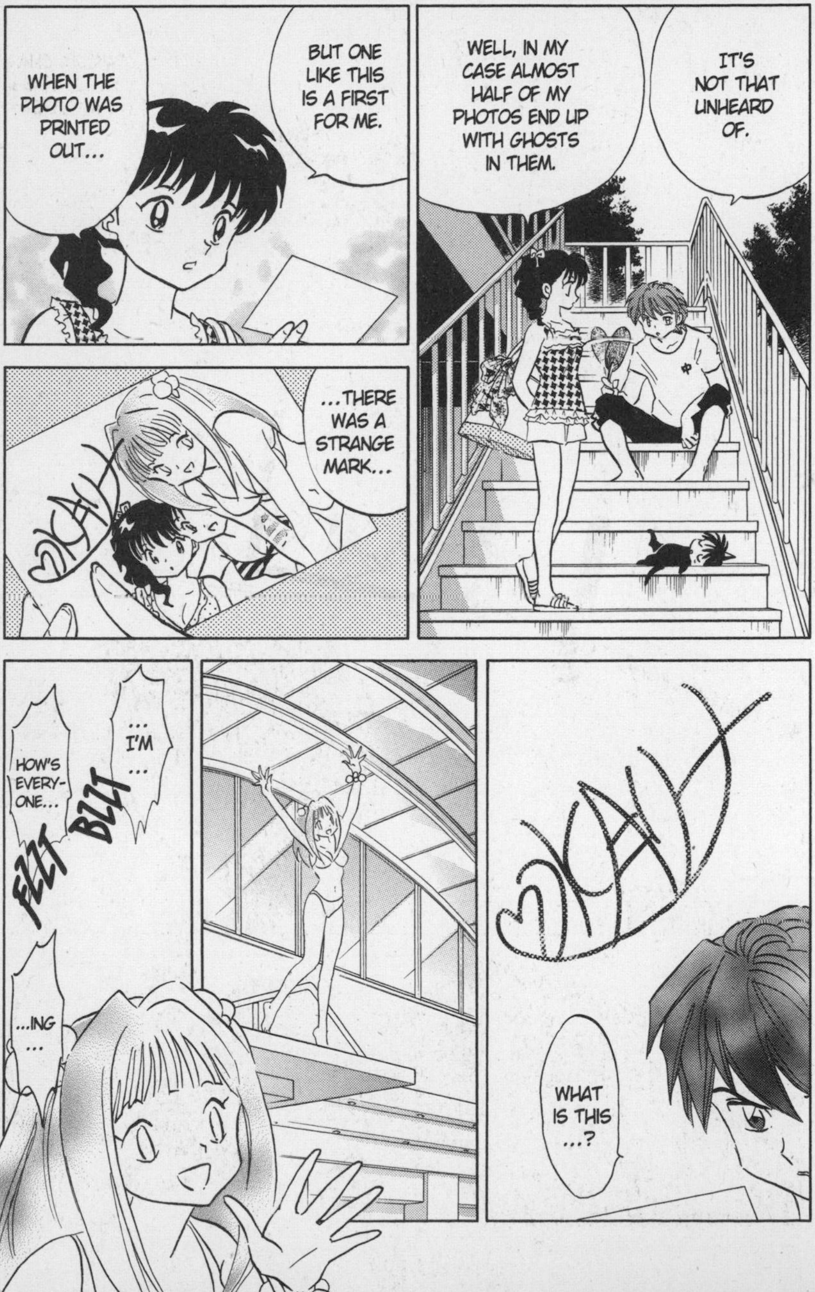
IT'S NOT THAT UNHEARD OF.
WELL, IN MY CASE ALMOST HALF OF MY PHOTOS END UP WITH GHOSTS IN THEM.
BUT ONE LIKE THIS IS A FIRST FOR ME.
WHEN THE PHOTO WAS PRINTED OUT...
...THERE WAS A STRANGE MARK...
WHAT IS THIS ...?
... I'M ...
HOW'S EVERY-ONE...
BLZT
FZZT
...ING ...

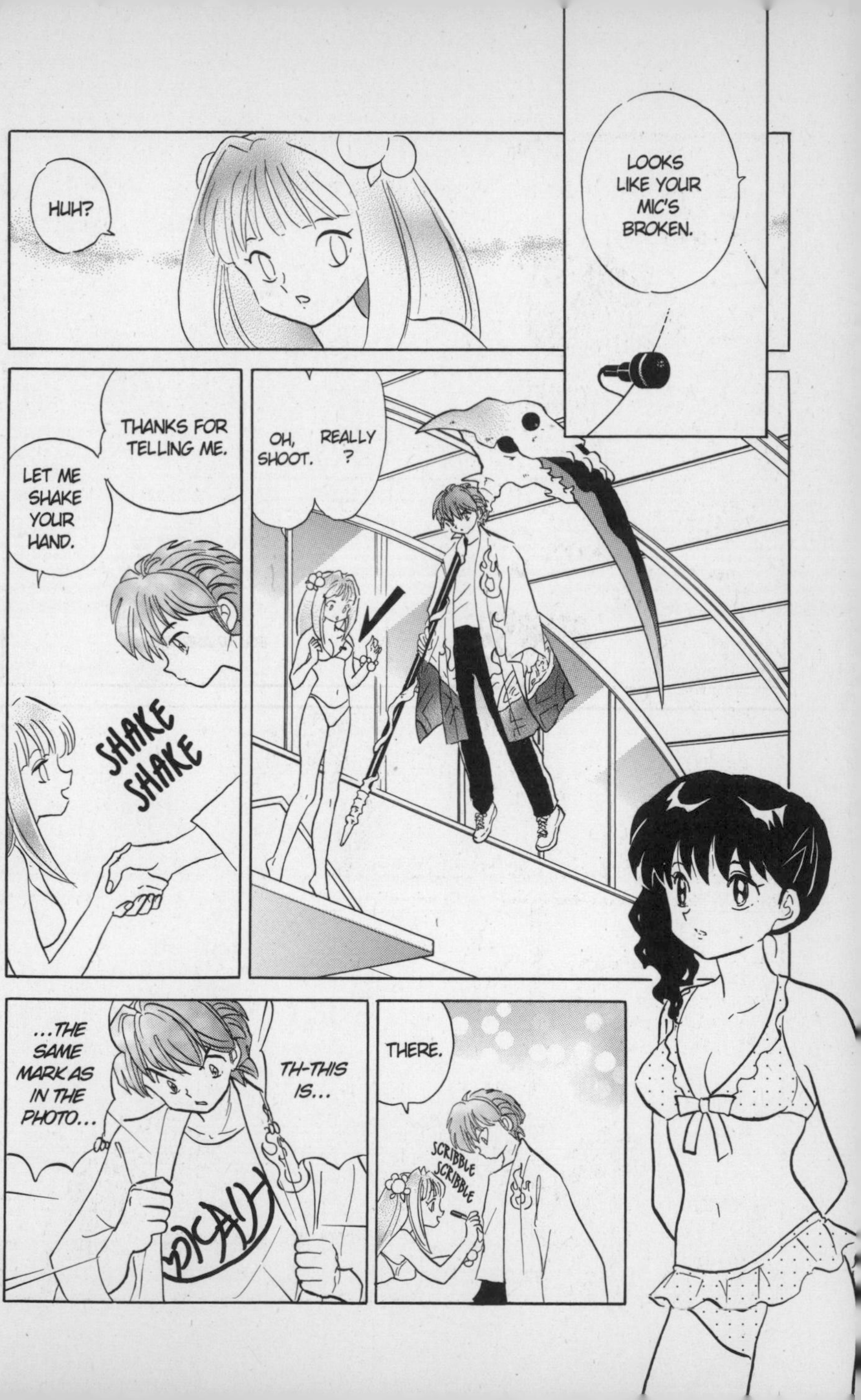
LOOKS LIKE YOUR MIC'S BROKEN.
HUH?
REALLY ?
OH, SHOOT.
THANKS FOR TELLING ME.
LET ME SHAKE YOUR HAND.
SHAKE SHAKE
THERE.
SCRIBBLE SCRIBBLE
TH-THIS IS...
...THE SAME MARK AS IN THE PHOTO...

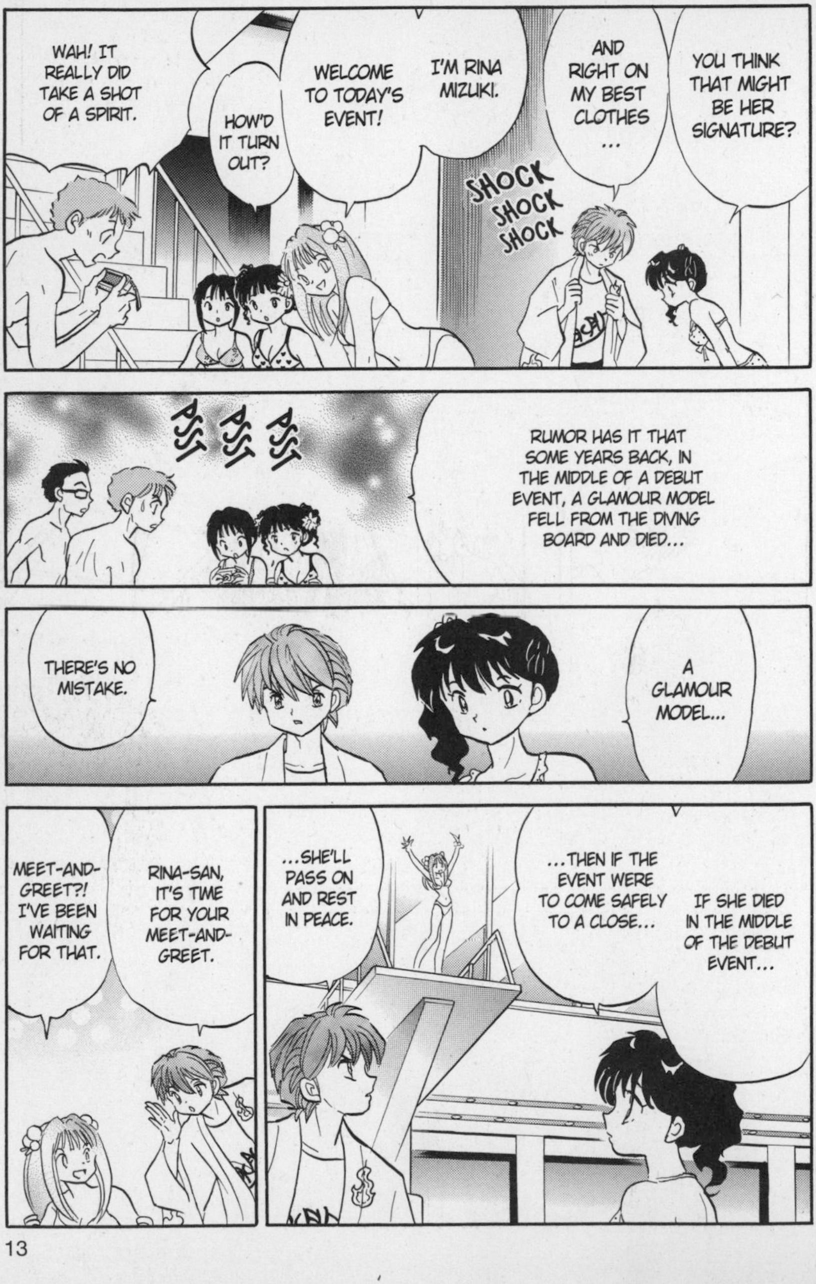
YOU THINK THAT MIGHT BE HER SIGNATURE?
AND RIGHT ON MY BEST CLOTHES ...
SHOCK SHOCK SHOCK
I'M RINA MIZUKI.
WELCOME TO TODAY'S EVENT!
HOW'D IT TURN OUT?
WAH! IT REALLY DID TAKE A SHOT OF A SPIRIT.
RUMOR HAS IT THAT SOME YEARS BACK, IN THE MIDDLE OF A DEBUT EVENT, A GLAMOUR MODEL FELL FROM THE DIVING BOARD AND DIED...
PSST PSST PSST
A GLAMOUR MODEL...
THERE'S NO MISTAKE.
IF SHE DIED IN THE MIDDLE OF THE DEBUT EVENT...
...THEN IF THE EVENT WERE TO COME SAFELY TO A CLOSE...
...SHE'LL PASS ON AND REST IN PEACE.
RINA-SAN, IT'S TIME FOR YOUR MEET-AND-GREET.
MEET-AND-GREET?! I'VE BEEN WAITING FOR THAT.

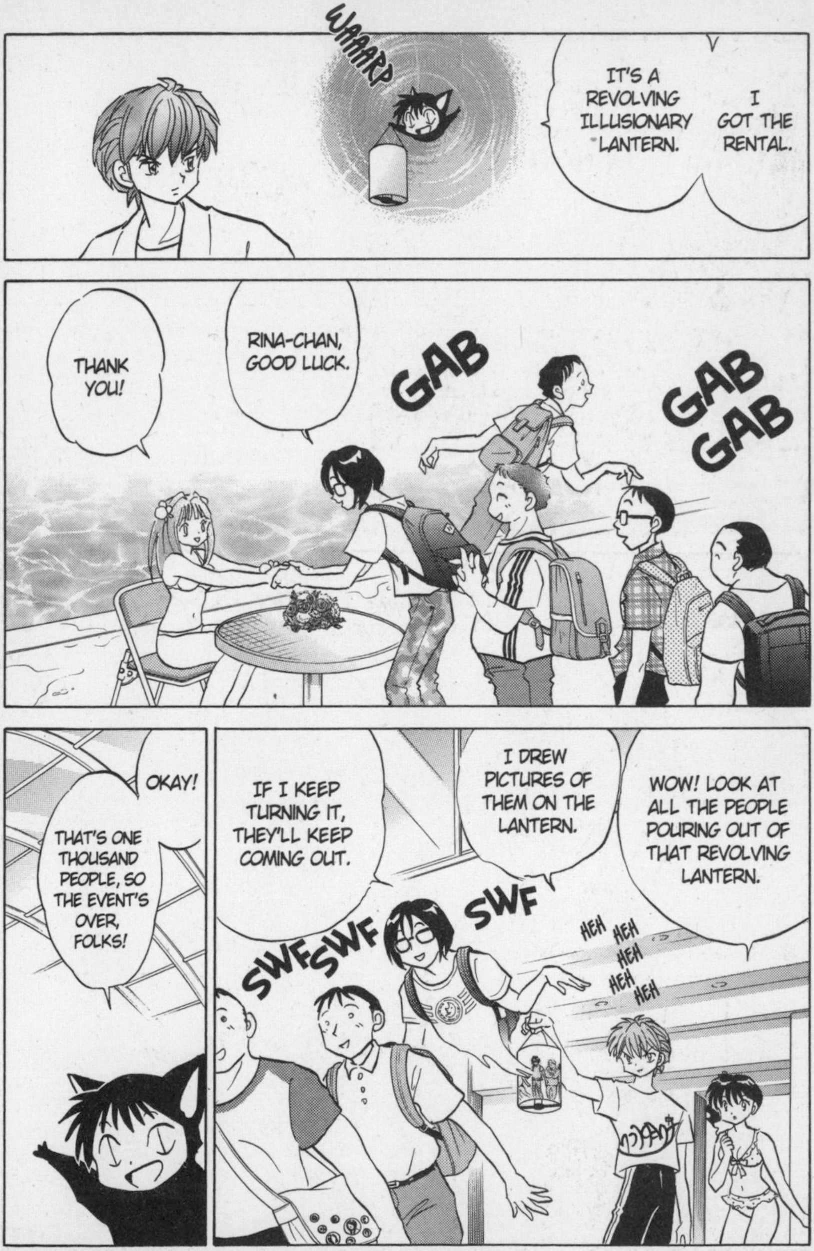
I GOT THE RENTAL.
IT'S A REVOLVING ILLUSIONARY LANTERN.
WAAARP
GAB GAB
RINA-CHAN, GOOD LUCK.
GAB
THANK YOU!
WOW! LOOK AT ALL THE PEOPLE POURING OUT OF THAT REVOLVING LANTERN.
I DREW PICTURES OF THEM ON THE LANTERN.
IF I KEEP TURNING IT, THEY'LL KEEP COMING OUT.
SWF
HEH HEH HEH HEH HEH HEH
SWF SWF
OKAY!
THAT'S ONE THOUSAND PEOPLE, SO THE EVENT'S OVER, FOLKS!

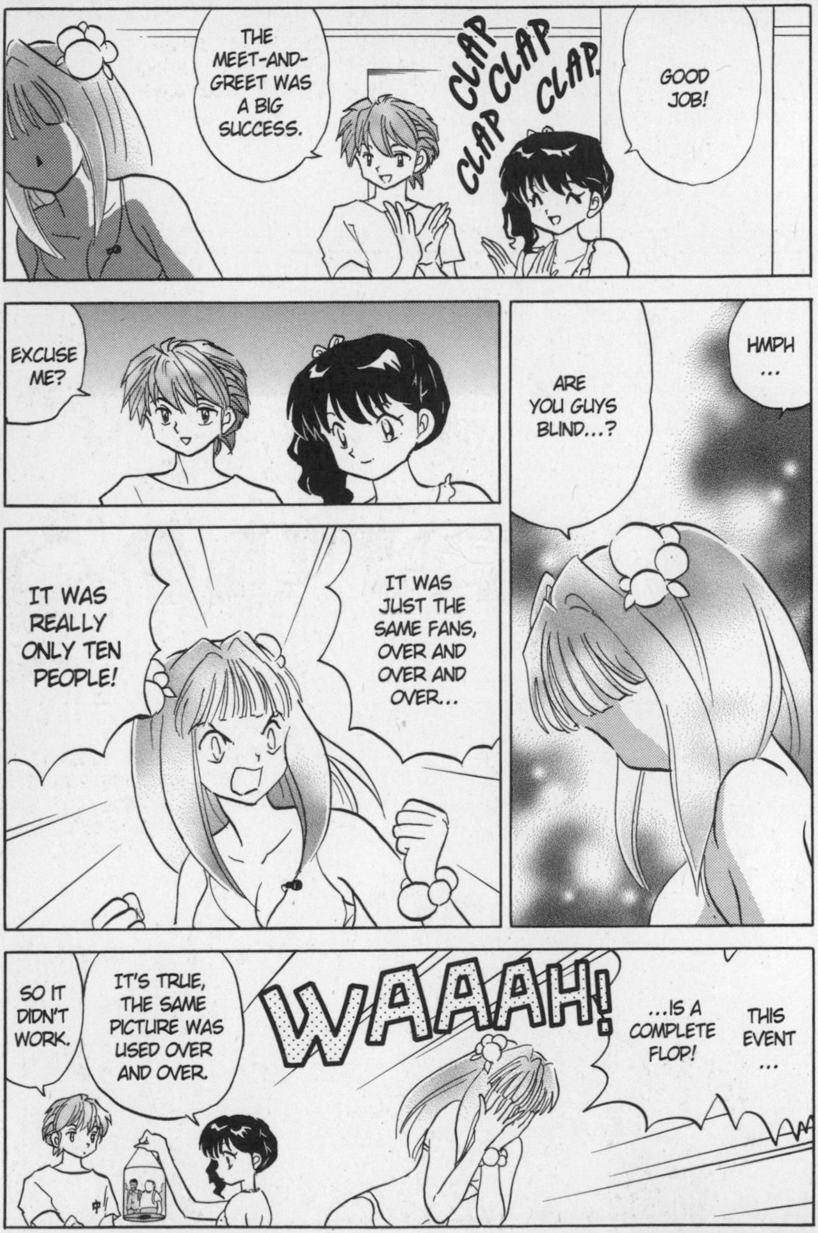
GOOD JOB!
CLAP CLAP CLAP CLAP
THE MEET-AND-GREET WAS A BIG SUCCESS.
HMPH ...
ARE YOU GUYS BLIND...?
EXCUSE ME?
IT WAS JUST THE SAME FANS, OVER AND OVER AND OVER...
IT WAS REALLY ONLY TEN PEOPLE!
THIS EVENT ...
...IS A COMPLETE FLOP!
WAAAH!
IT'S TRUE, THE SAME PICTURE WAS USED OVER AND OVER.
SO IT DIDN'T WORK.

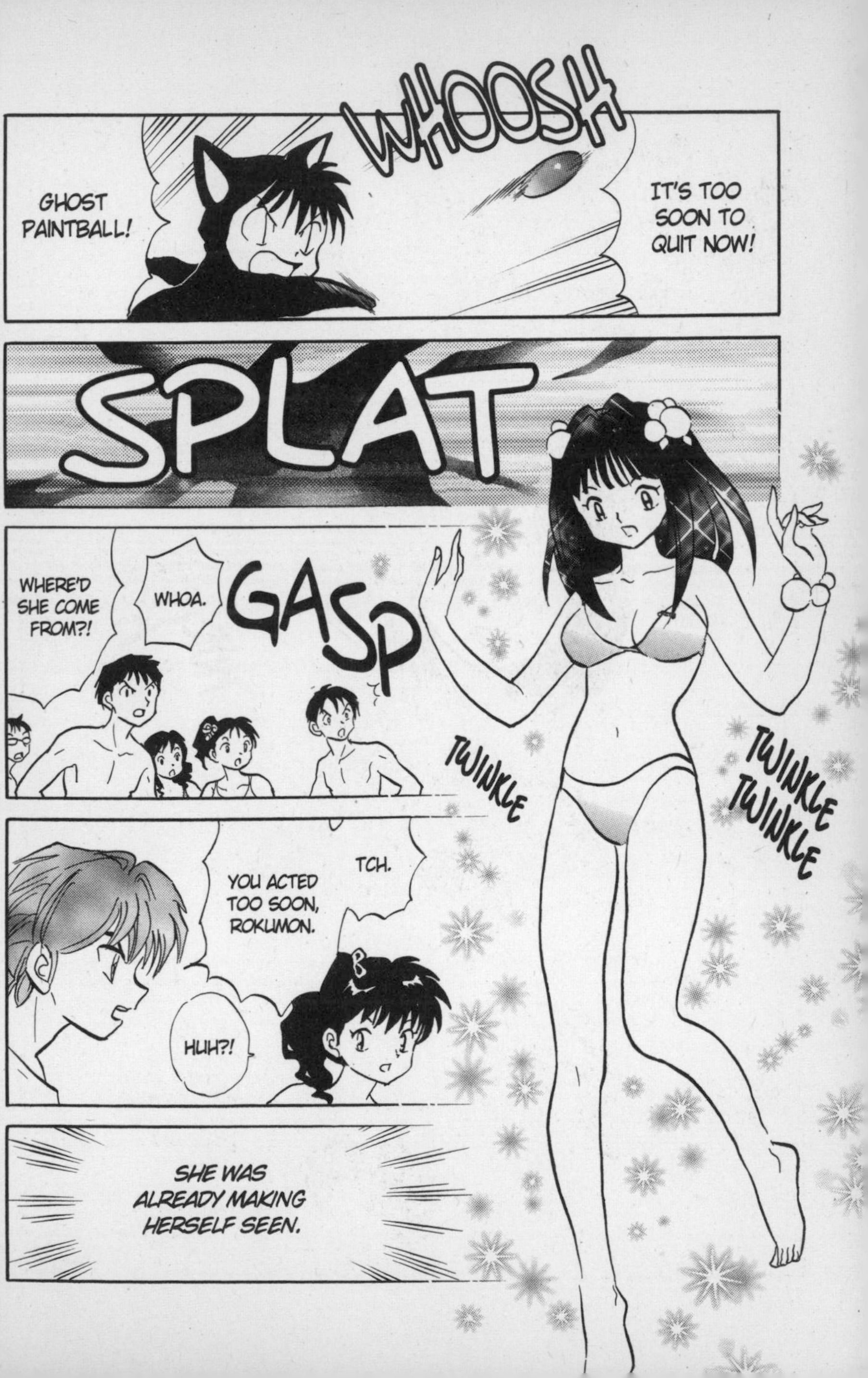
IT'S TOO SOON TO QUIT NOW!
WHOOSH
GHOST PAINTBALL!
SPLAT
TWINKLE TWINKLE
TWINKLE
GASP
WHOA.
WHERE'D SHE COME FROM?!
TCH.
YOU ACTED TOO SOON, ROKUMON.
HUH?!
SHE WAS ALREADY MAKING HERSELF SEEN.

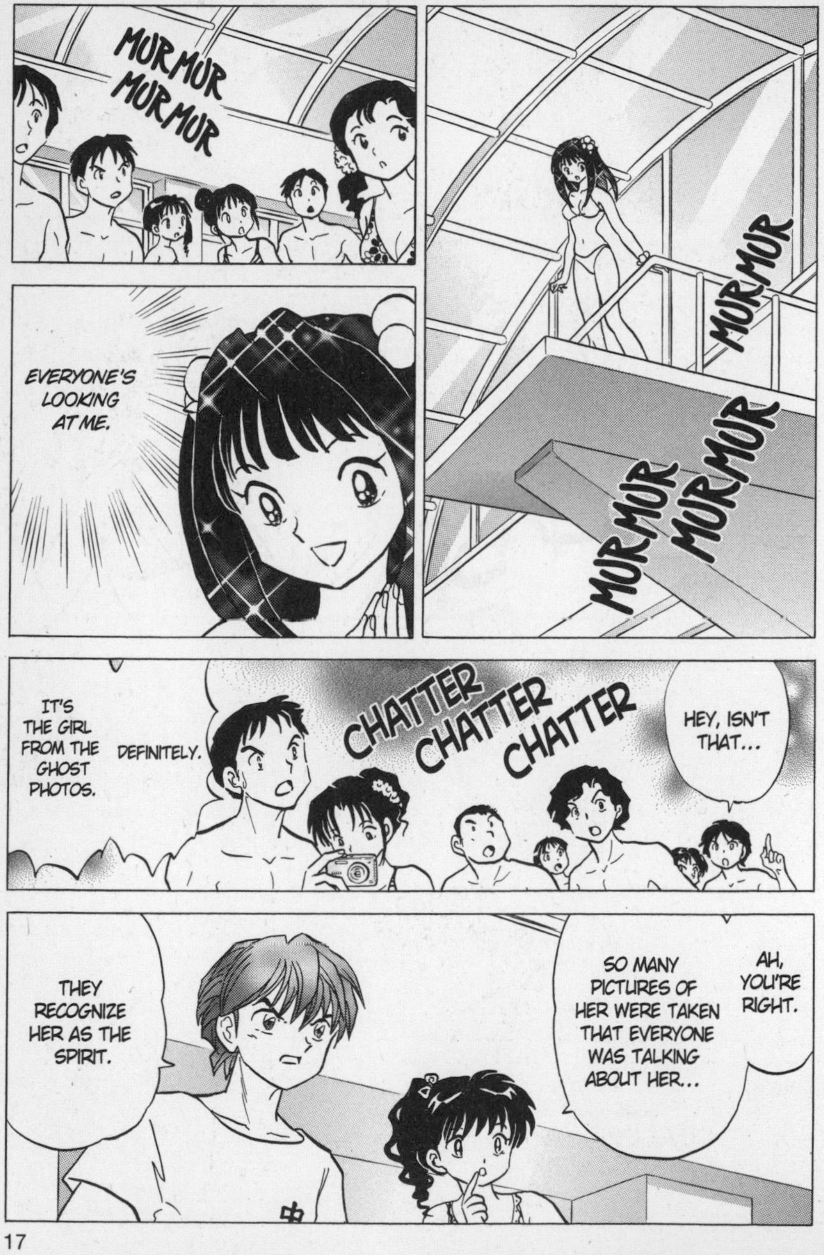
MURMUR
MURMUR MURMUR
MURMUR MURMUR
EVERYONE'S LOOKING AT ME.
HEY, ISN'T THAT...
CHATTER CHATTER CHATTER
DEFINITELY.
IT'S THE GIRL FROM THE GHOST PHOTOS.
AH, YOU'RE RIGHT.
SO MANY PICTURES OF HER WERE TAKEN THAT EVERYONE WAS TALKING ABOUT HER...
THEY RECOGNIZE HER AS THE SPIRIT.

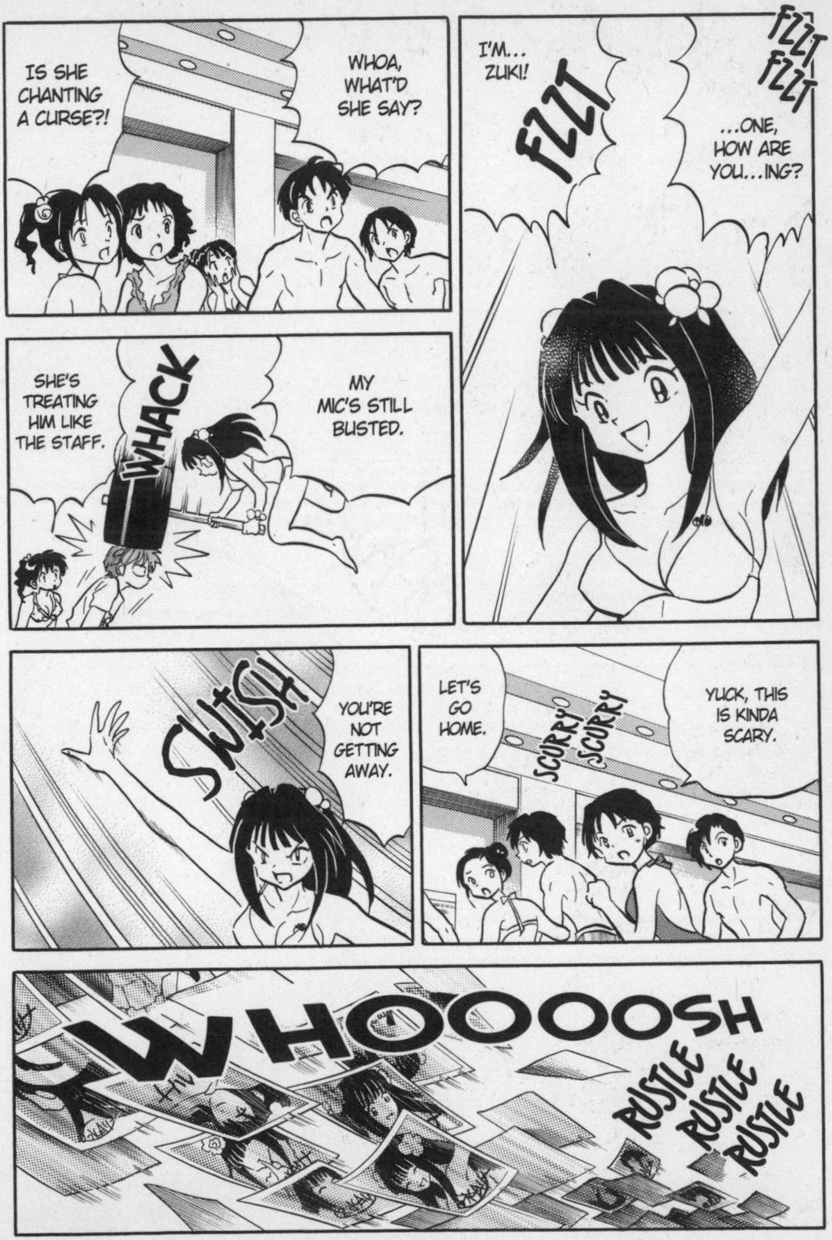
FZZT FZZT
...ONE, HOW ARE YOU...ING?
FZZT
I'M... ZUKI!
WHOA, WHAT'D SHE SAY?
IS SHE CHANTING A CURSE?!
MY MIC'S STILL BUSTED.
WHACK
SHE'S TREATING HIM LIKE THE STAFF.
YUCK, THIS IS KINDA SCARY.
SCURRY SCURRY
LET'S GO HOME.
YOU'RE NOT GETTING AWAY.
SWISH
WHOOOOSH
RUSTLE RUSTLE RUSTLE

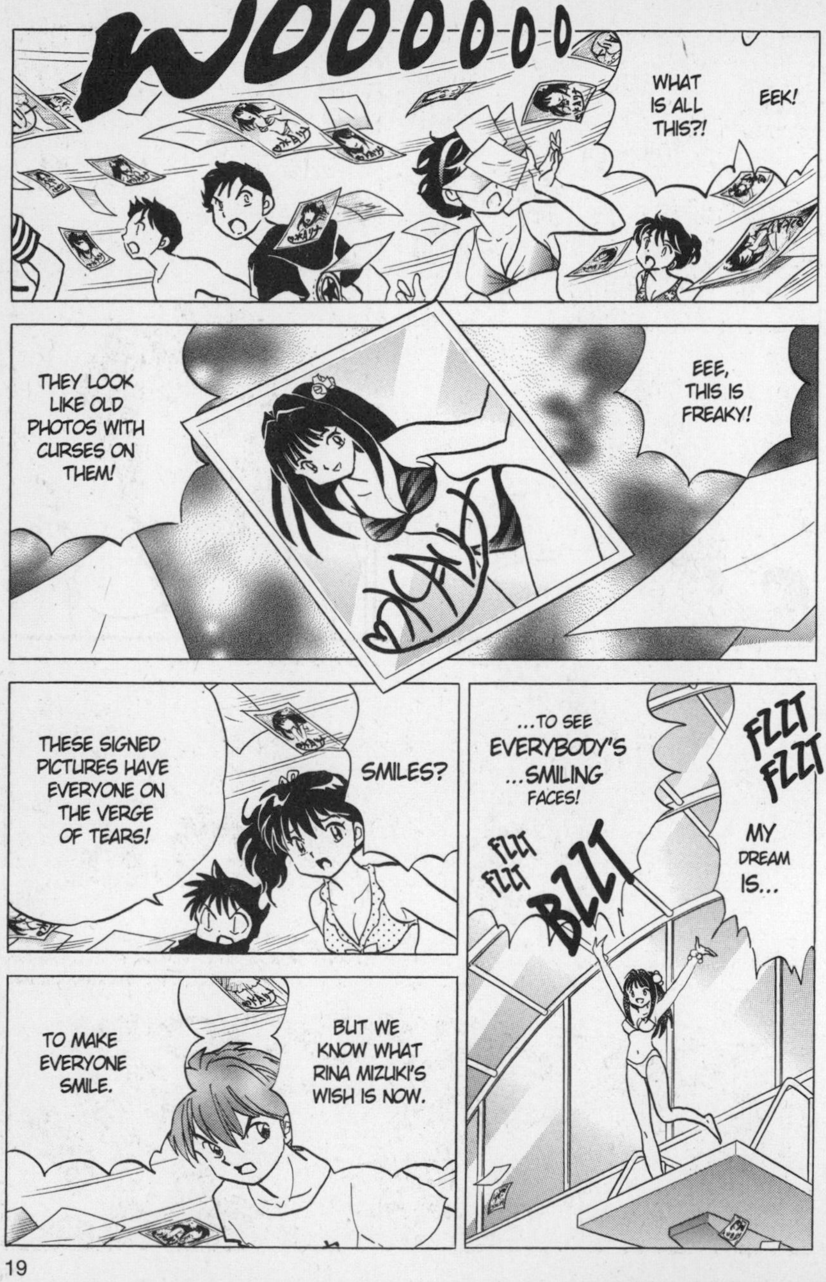
WOOOOOO
EEK!
WHAT IS ALL THIS?!
EEE, THIS IS FREAKY!
THEY LOOK LIKE OLD PHOTOS WITH CURSES ON THEM!
FZZT FZZT
MY DREAM IS...
...TO SEE EVERYBODY'S ...SMILING FACES!
FZZT FZZT
BZZT
SMILES?
THESE SIGNED PICTURES HAVE EVERYONE ON THE VERGE OF TEARS!
BUT WE KNOW WHAT RINA MIZUKI'S WISH IS NOW.
TO MAKE EVERYONE SMILE.

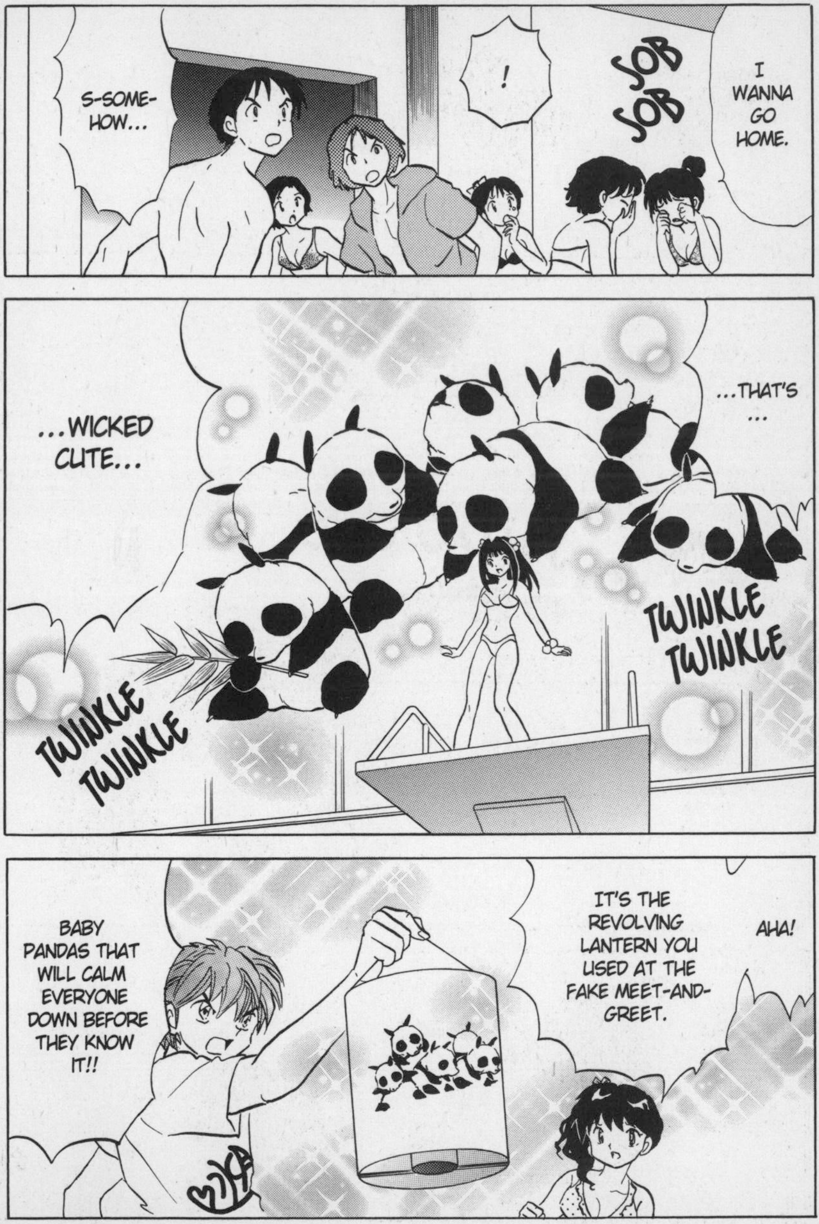
I WANNA GO HOME.
JOB JOB
!
S-SOME-HOW...
...THAT'S ...
TWINKLE TWINKLE
...WICKED CUTE...
TWINKLE TWINKLE
AHA!
IT'S THE REVOLVING LANTERN YOU USED AT THE FAKE MEET-AND-GREET.
BABY PANDAS THAT WILL CALM EVERYONE DOWN BEFORE THEY KNOW IT!!

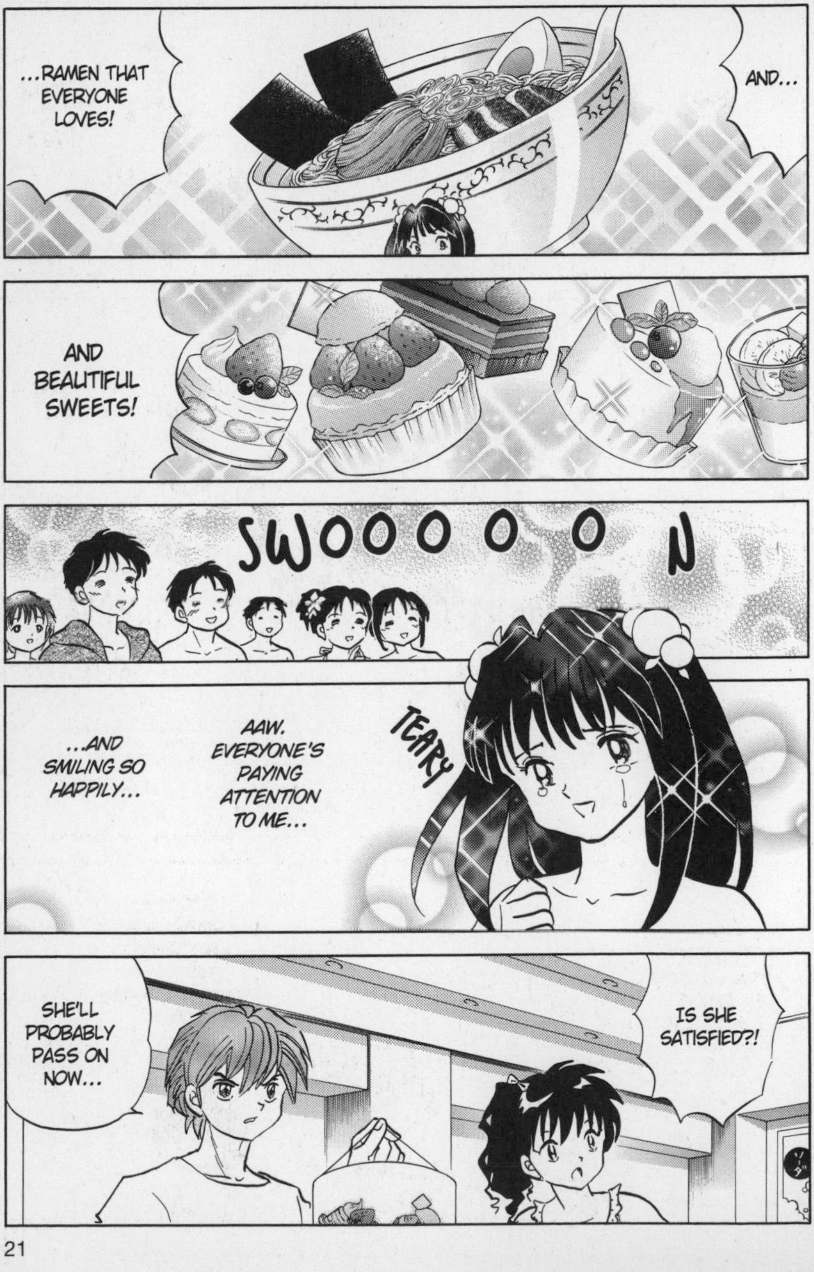
AND...
...RAMEN THAT EVERYONE LOVES!
AND BEAUTIFUL SWEETS!
SWOOOOON
TEARY
AAW. EVERYONE'S PAYING ATTENTION TO ME...
...AND SMILING SO HAPPILY...
IS SHE SATISFIED?!
SHE'LL PROBABLY PASS ON NOW...

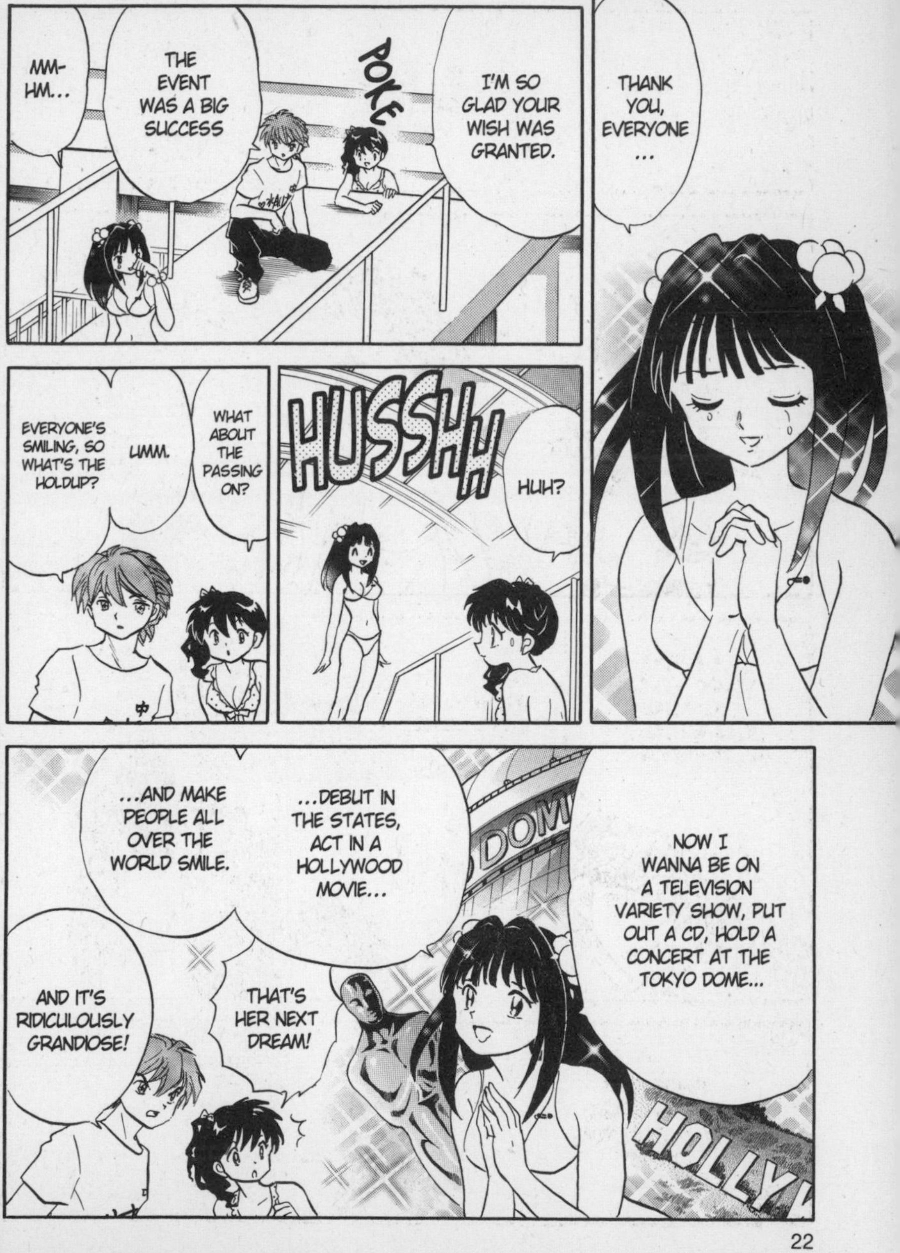
THANK YOU, EVERYONE ...
I'M SO GLAD YOUR WISH WAS GRANTED.
POKE
THE EVENT WAS A BIG SUCCESS
MM-HM...
HUSSHH
HUH?
WHAT ABOUT THE PASSING ON?
UMM.
EVERYONE'S SMILING, SO WHAT'S THE HOLDUP?
NOW I WANNA BE ON A TELEVISION VARIETY SHOW, PUT OUT A CD, HOLD A CONCERT AT THE TOKYO DOME...
...DEBUT IN THE STATES, ACT IN A HOLLYWOOD MOVIE...
...AND MAKE PEOPLE ALL OVER THE WORLD SMILE.
THAT'S HER NEXT DREAM!
AND IT'S RIDICULOUSLY GRANDIOSE!

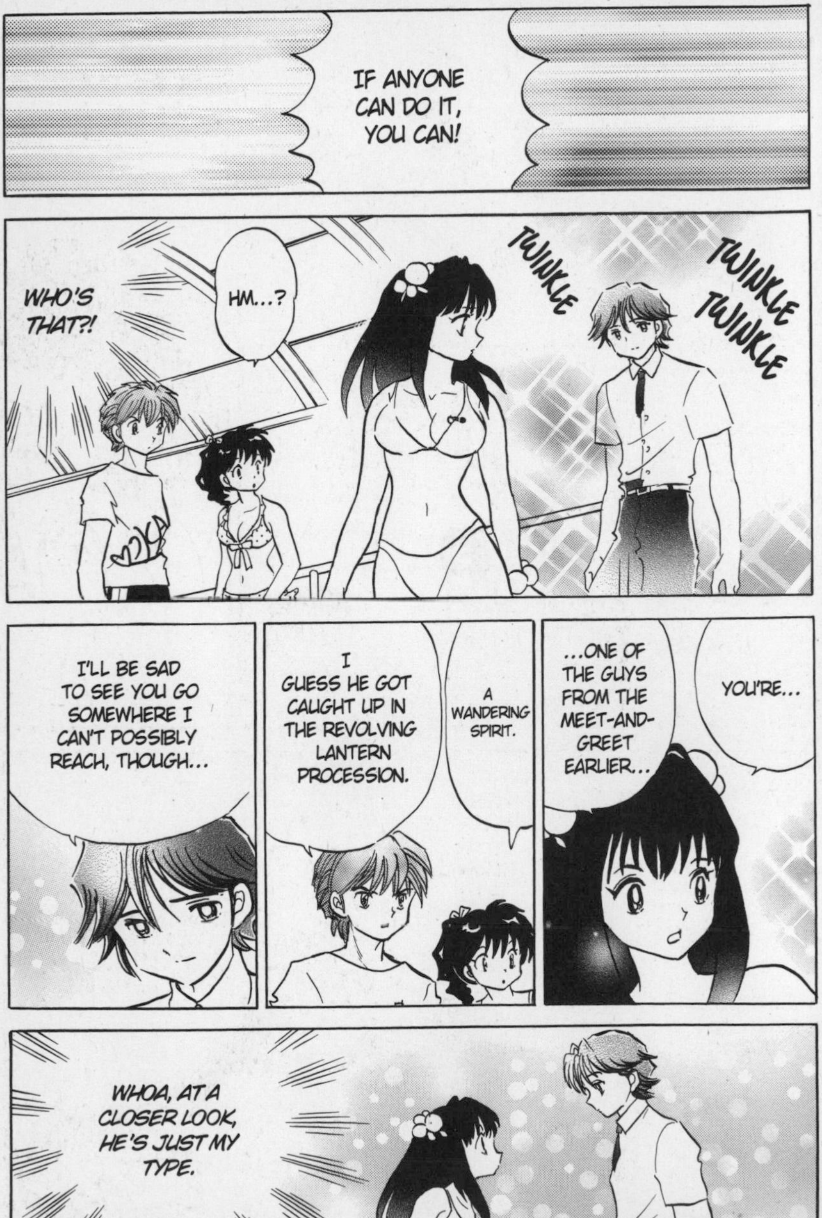
IF ANYONE CAN DO IT, YOU CAN!
TWINKLE TWINKLE
TWINKLE
TWINKLE
HM...?
WHO'S THAT?!
YOU'RE...
...ONE OF THE GUYS FROM THE MEET-AND-GREET EARLIER...
A WANDERING SPIRIT.
I GUESS HE GOT CAUGHT UP IN THE REVOLVING LANTERN PROCESSION.
I'LL BE SAD TO SEE YOU GO SOMEWHERE I CAN'T POSSIBLY REACH, THOUGH...
WHOA, AT A CLOSER LOOK, HE'S JUST MY TYPE.

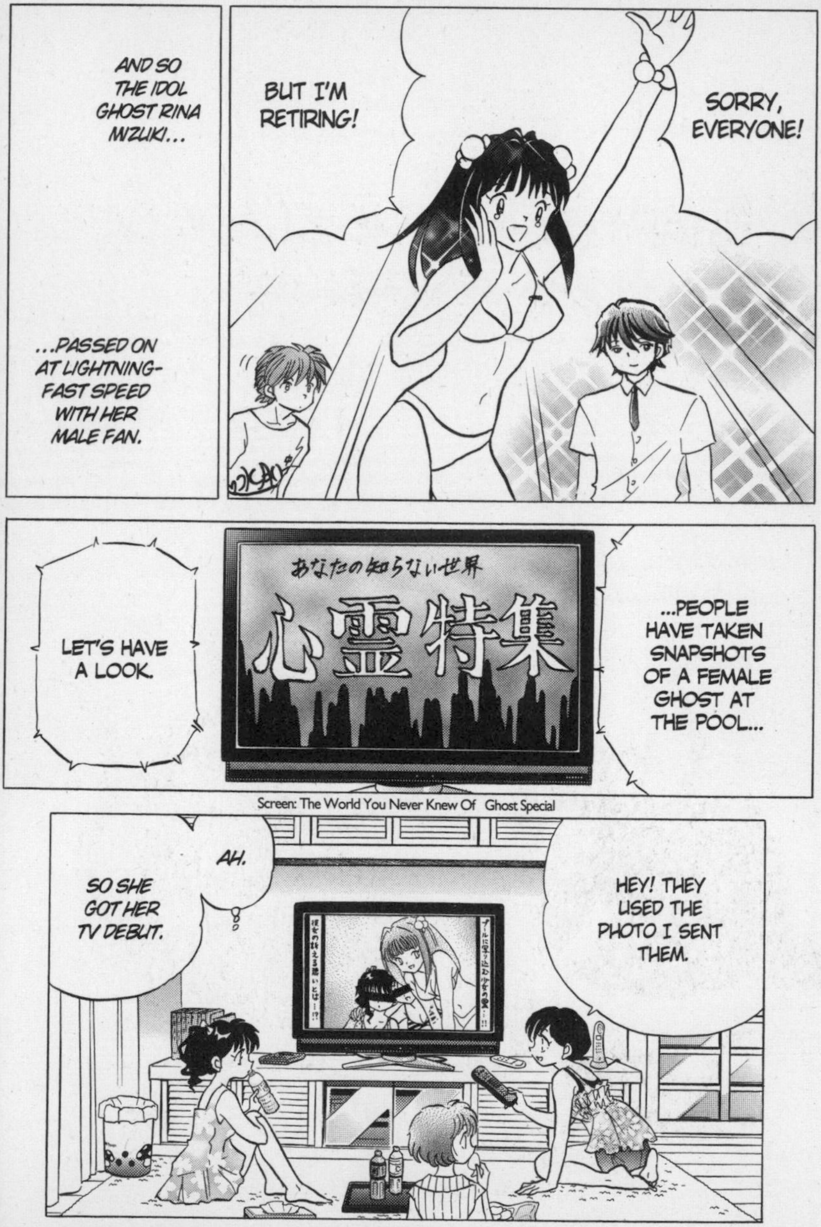
SORRY, EVERYONE!
BUT I'M RETIRING!
AND SO THE IDOL GHOST RINA MIZUKI...
...PASSED ON AT LIGHTNING-FAST SPEED WITH HER MALE FAN.
...PEOPLE HAVE TAKEN SNAPSHOTS OF A FEMALE GHOST AT THE POOL...
あなたの知らない世界
心霊特集
LET'S HAVE A LOOK.
Screen: The World You Never Knew Of Ghost Special
HEY! THEY USED THE PHOTO I SENT THEM.
AH.
SO SHE GOT HER TV DEBUT.

CHAPTER 110: THE BLACK CAT RANKING EXAM

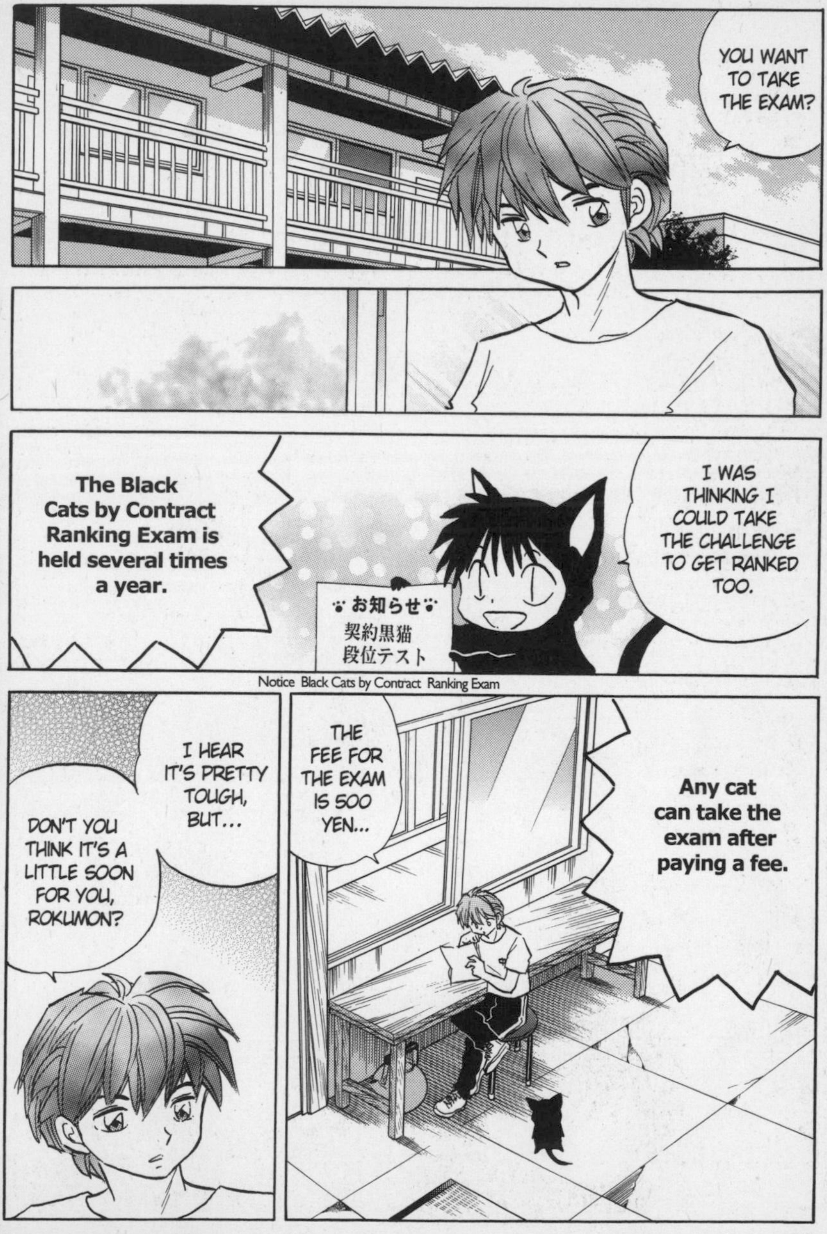
YOU WANT TO TAKE THE EXAM?
I WAS THINKING I COULD TAKE THE CHALLENGE TO GET RANKED TOO.
The Black Cats by Contract Ranking Exam is held several times a year.
お知らせ
契約黒猫
段位テスト
Notice Black Cats by Contract Ranking Exam
Any cat can take the exam after paying a fee.
THE FEE FOR THE EXAM IS 500 YEN...
I HEAR IT'S PRETTY TOUGH, BUT…
DON'T YOU THINK IT'S A LITTLE SOON FOR YOU, ROKUMON?

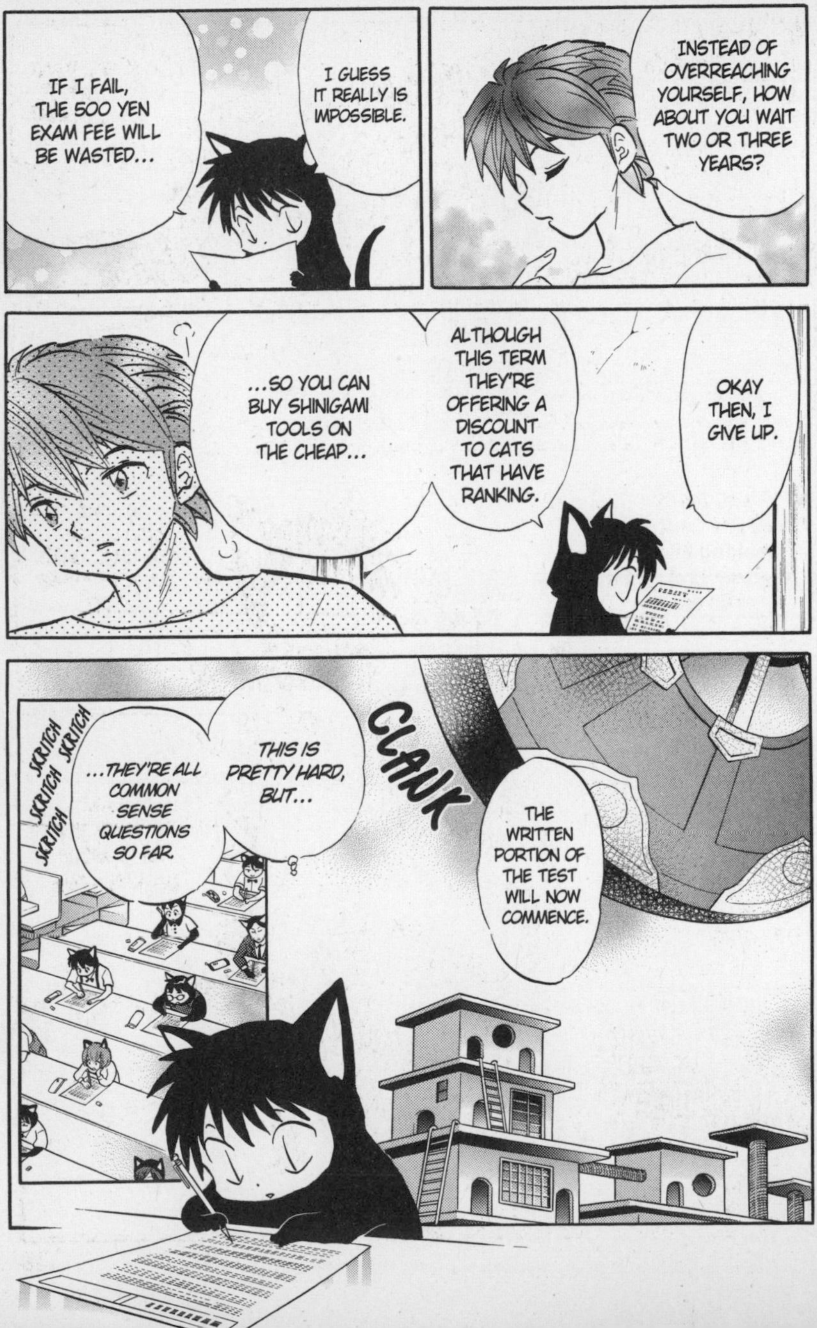
INSTEAD OF OVERREACHING YOURSELF, HOW ABOUT YOU WAIT TWO OR THREE YEARS?
I GUESS IT REALLY IS IMPOSSIBLE.
IF I FAIL, THE 500 YEN EXAM FEE WILL BE WASTED...
OKAY THEN, I GIVE UP.
ALTHOUGH THIS TERM THEY'RE OFFERING A DISCOUNT TO CATS THAT HAVE RANKING.
...SO YOU CAN BUY SHINIGAMI TOOLS ON THE CHEAP...
THE WRITTEN PORTION OF THE TEST WILL NOW COMMENCE.
CLAUNK
THIS IS PRETTY HARD, BUT...
...THEY'RE ALL COMMON SENSE QUESTIONS SO FAR.
SKRITCH SKRITCH
SKRITCH SKRITCH

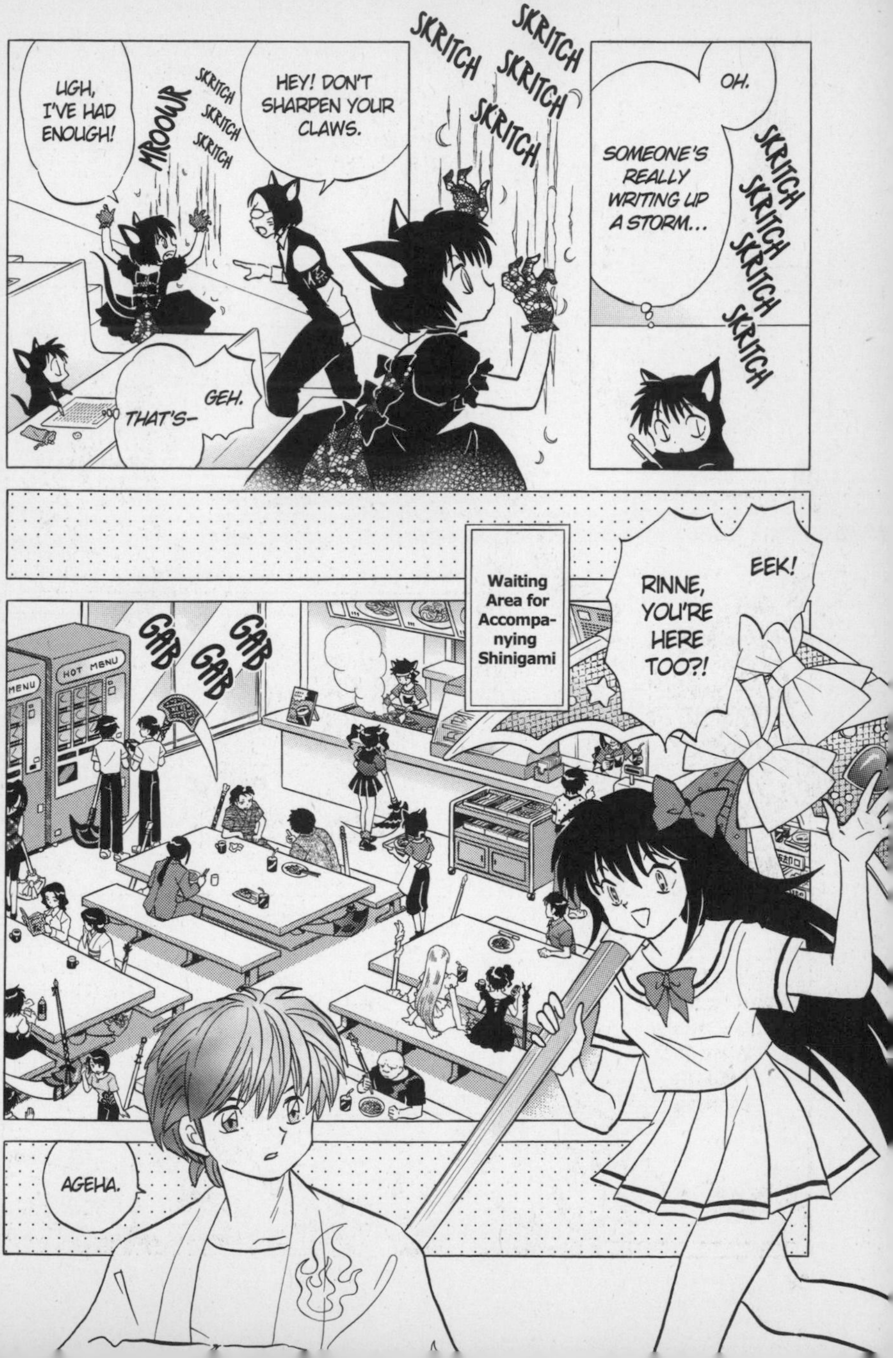
OH.
SOMEONE'S REALLY WRITING UP A STORM...
SKRITCH SKRITCH SKRITCH SKRITCH
SKRITCH SKRITCH SKRITCH SKRITCH
HEY! DON'T SHARPEN YOUR CLAWS.
UGH, I'VE HAD ENOUGH!
SKRITCH SKRITCH SKRITCH
MROOWR
GEH.
THAT'S-
EEK!
RINNE, YOU'RE HERE TOO?!
Waiting Area for Accompanying Shinigami
GAB GAB GAB
HOT MENU
MENU
AGEHA.

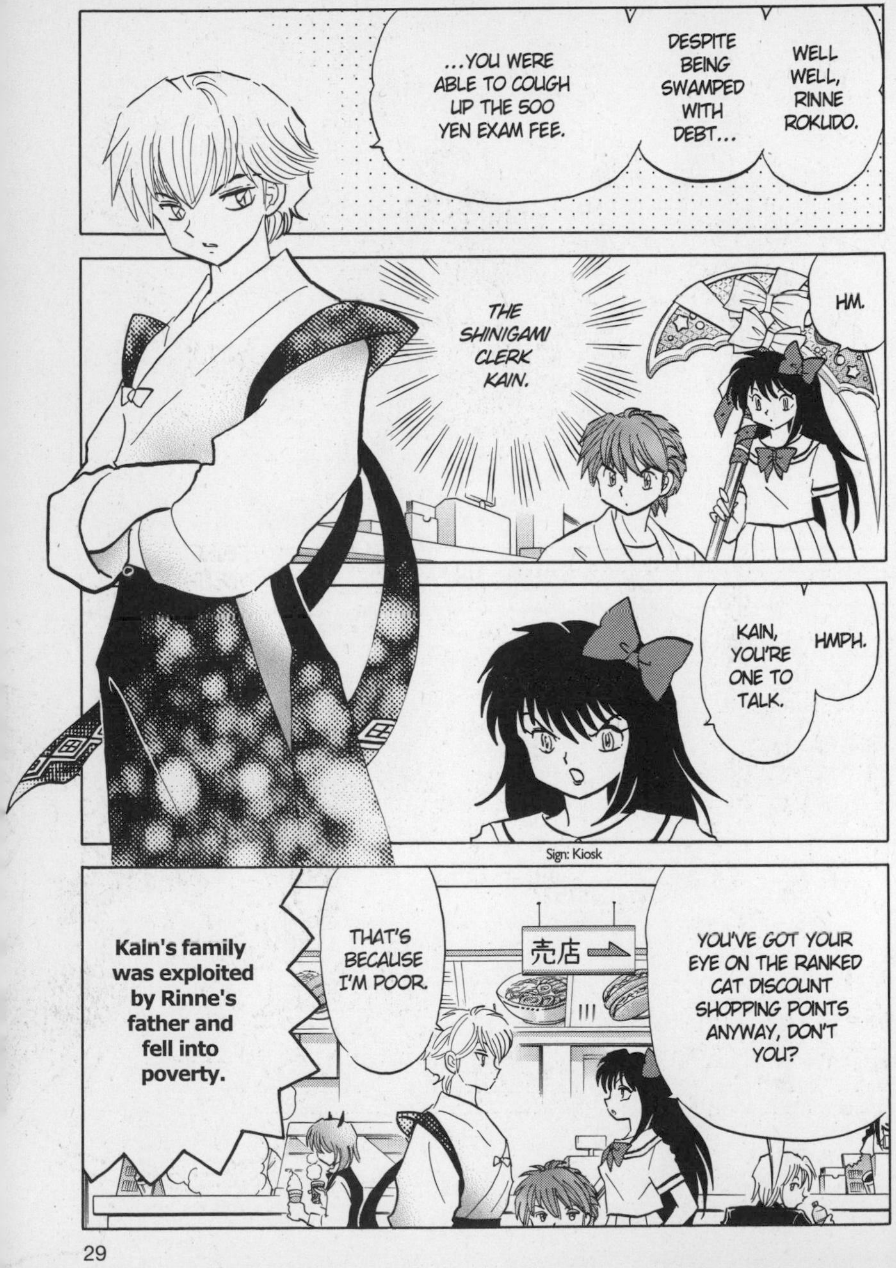
WELL WELL, RINNE ROKUDO.
DESPITE BEING SWAMPED WITH DEBT...
...YOU WERE ABLE TO COUGH UP THE 500 YEN EXAM FEE.
HM.
THE SHINIGAMI CLERK KAIN.
HMPH.
KAIN, YOU'RE ONE TO TALK.
Sign: Kiosk
売店
YOU'VE GOT YOUR EYE ON THE RANKED CAT DISCOUNT SHOPPING POINTS ANYWAY, DON'T YOU?
THAT'S BECAUSE I'M POOR.
Kain's family was exploited by Rinne's father and fell into poverty.

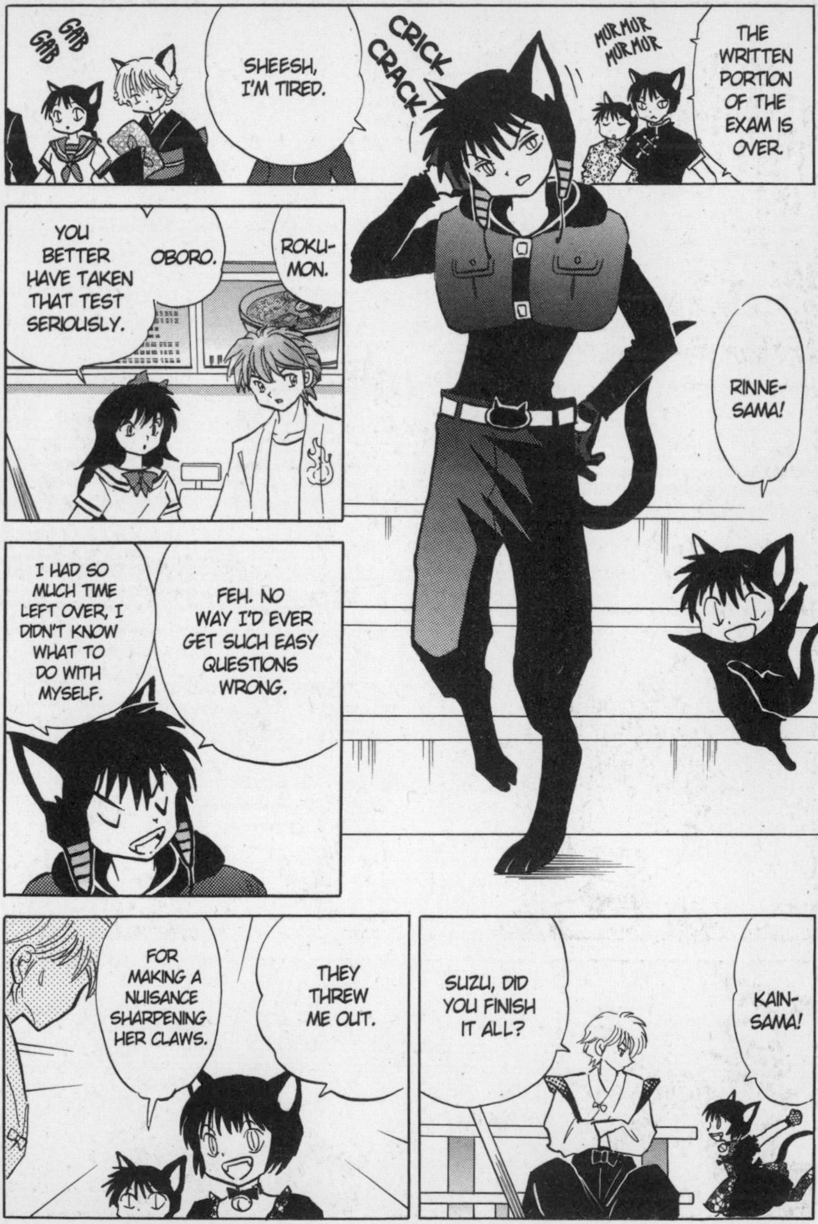
THE WRITTEN PORTION OF THE EXAM IS OVER.
MURMUR MURMUR
CRICK CRACK
SHEESH, I'M TIRED.
GAB GAB
RINNE-SAMA!
ROKU-MON.
OBORO.
YOU BETTER HAVE TAKEN THAT TEST SERIOUSLY.
FEH. NO WAY I'D EVER GET SUCH EASY QUESTIONS WRONG.
I HAD SO MUCH TIME LEFT OVER, I DIDN'T KNOW WHAT TO DO WITH MYSELF.
KAIN-SAMA!
SUZU, DID YOU FINISH IT ALL?
THEY THREW ME OUT.
FOR MAKING A NUISANCE SHARPENING HER CLAWS.

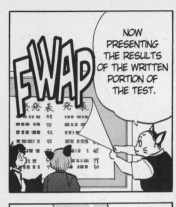

HO HO HO HO HO, KAIN!
LOOKS LIKE YOUR 500 YEN EXAM FEE JUST WENT DOWN THE DRAIN!
HOW'D KAIN END UP WITH SUCH A STUPID BLACK CAT?
NOW PRESENTING THE RESULTS OF THE WRITTEN PORTION OF THE TEST.
FWAP
I DID IT! 80 OUT OF 100.
YOU'RE AMAZING.
OBORO, YOU GOT ZERO...
WHAT GIVES!
YOU FORGOT TO WRITE YOUR NAME.
I...
...WROTE MY NAME!
SO LONG AS YOU WRITE YOUR NAME DOWN, THAT'S FIVE POINTS.
YAAAY! FIVE POINTS! FIVE POINTS!
HMPH, WE WON.
YOU IDIOT!
BONK

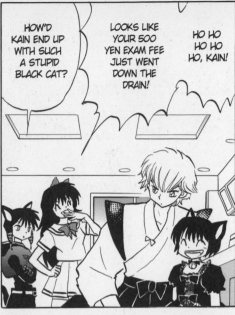

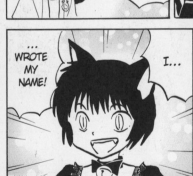

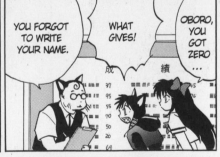

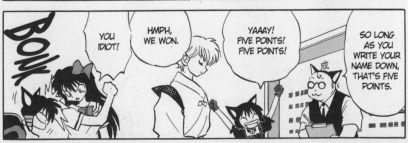

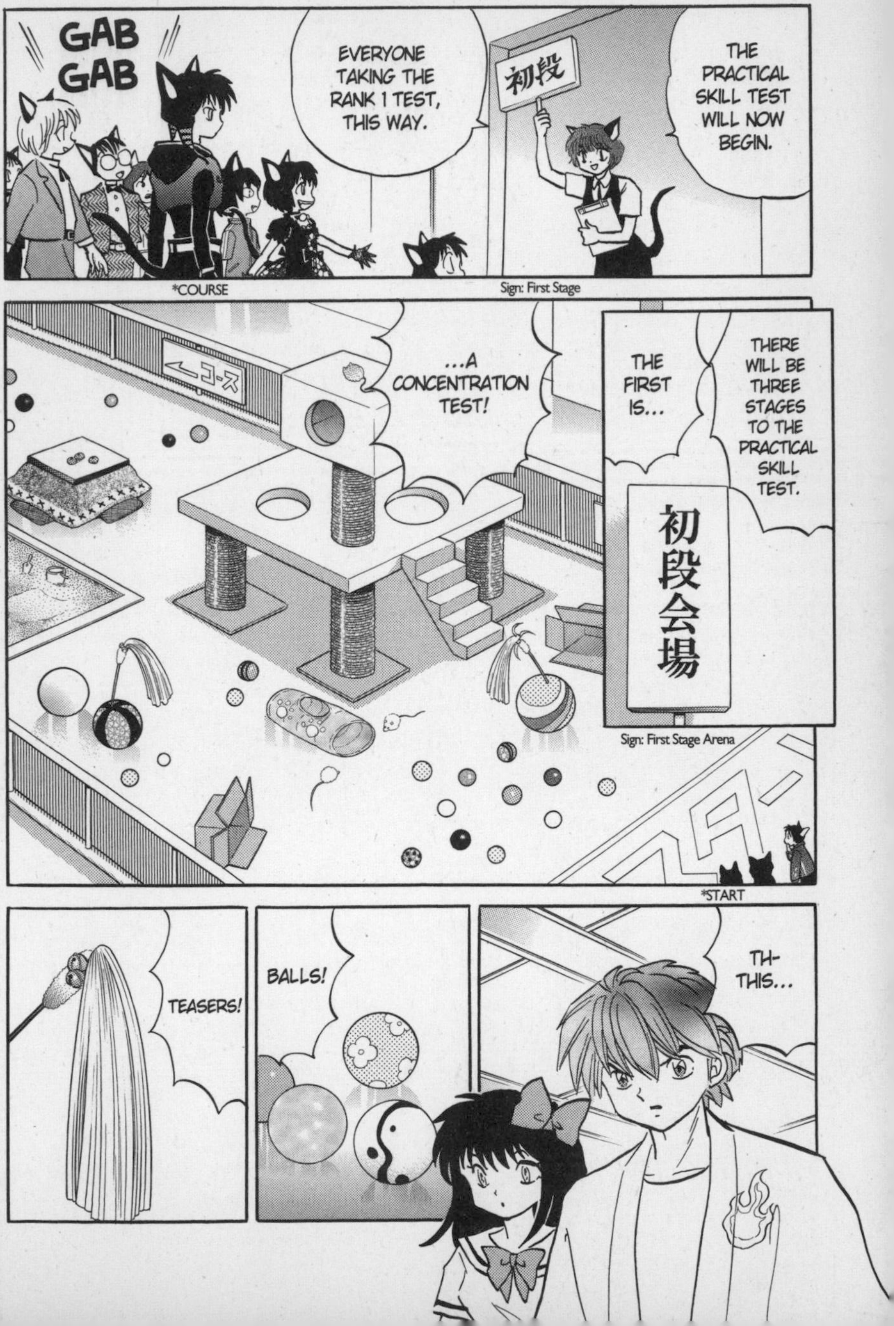
THE PRACTICAL SKILL TEST WILL NOW BEGIN.
初段
EVERYONE TAKING THE RANK 1 TEST, THIS WAY.
GAB GAB
Sign: First Stage
*COURSE
THERE WILL BE THREE STAGES TO THE PRACTICAL SKILL TEST.
THE FIRST IS...
初段会場
...A CONCENTRATION TEST!
←コース
Sign: First Stage Arena
*START
TH- THIS...
BALLS!
TEASERS!

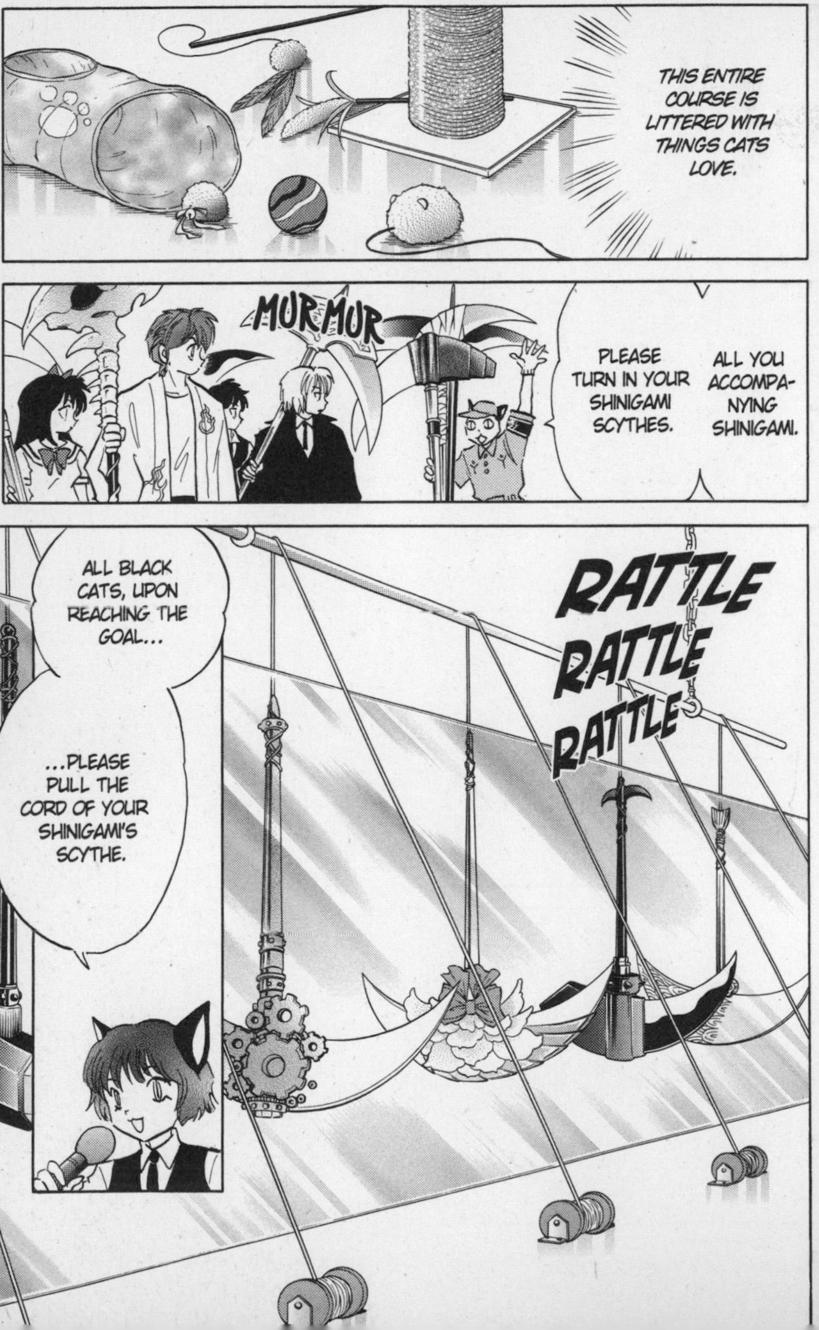
THIS ENTIRE COURSE IS LITTERED WITH THINGS CATS LOVE.
ALL YOU ACCOMPA-NYING SHINIGAMI.
PLEASE TURN IN YOUR SHINIGAMI SCYTHES.
MURMUR
RATTLE
RATTLE
RATTLE
ALL BLACK CATS, UPON REACHING THE GOAL...
...PLEASE PULL THE CORD OF YOUR SHINIGAMI'S SCYTHE.

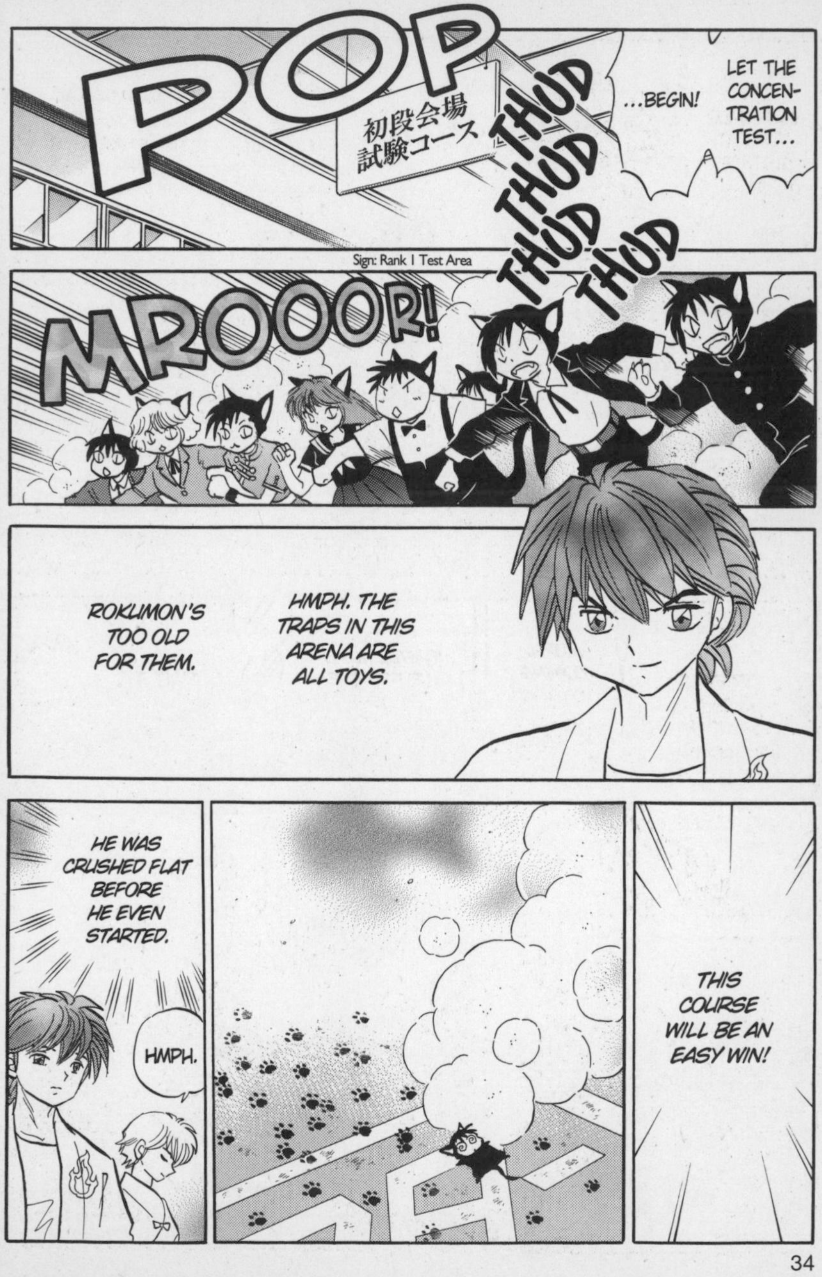
LET THE CONCEN-TRATION TEST…
…BEGIN!
THUD THUD THUD THUD
初段会場
試験コース
POP
Sign: Rank 1 Test Area
MROOOR!
HMPH. THE TRAPS IN THIS ARENA ARE ALL TOYS.
ROKUMON'S TOO OLD FOR THEM.
THIS COURSE WILL BE AN EASY WIN!
HE WAS CRUSHED FLAT BEFORE HE EVEN STARTED.
HMPH.

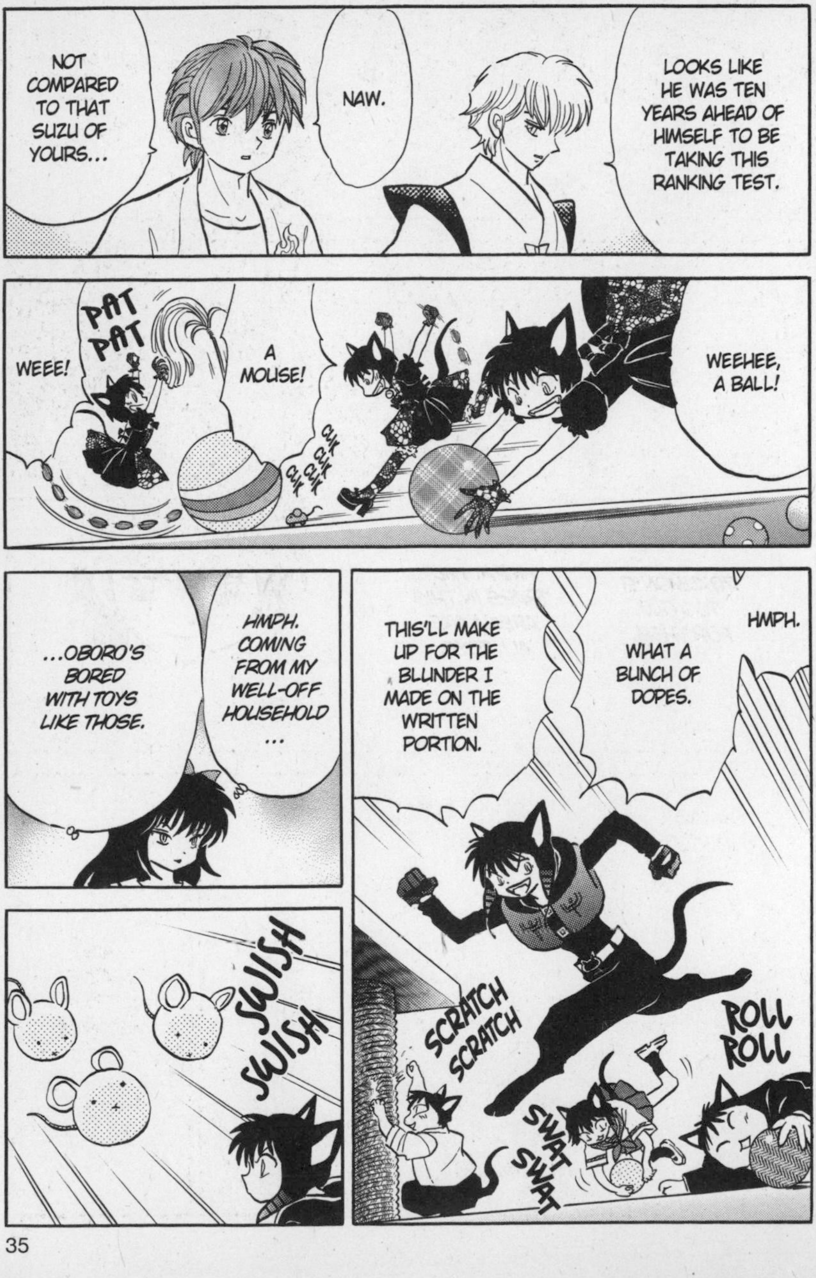
LOOKS LIKE HE WAS TEN YEARS AHEAD OF HIMSELF TO BE TAKING THIS RANKING TEST.
NAW.
NOT COMPARED TO THAT SUZU OF YOURS...
WEEHEE, A BALL!
CUK CUK CUK CUK
A MOUSE!
PAT PAT
WEEE!
HMPH.
WHAT A BUNCH OF DOPES.
THIS'LL MAKE UP FOR THE BLUNDER I MADE ON THE WRITTEN PORTION.
ROLL ROLL
SCRATCH SCRATCH
SWAT SWAT
HMPH. COMING FROM MY WELL-OFF HOUSEHOLD ...
...OBORO'S BORED WITH TOYS LIKE THOSE.
SWISH SWISH

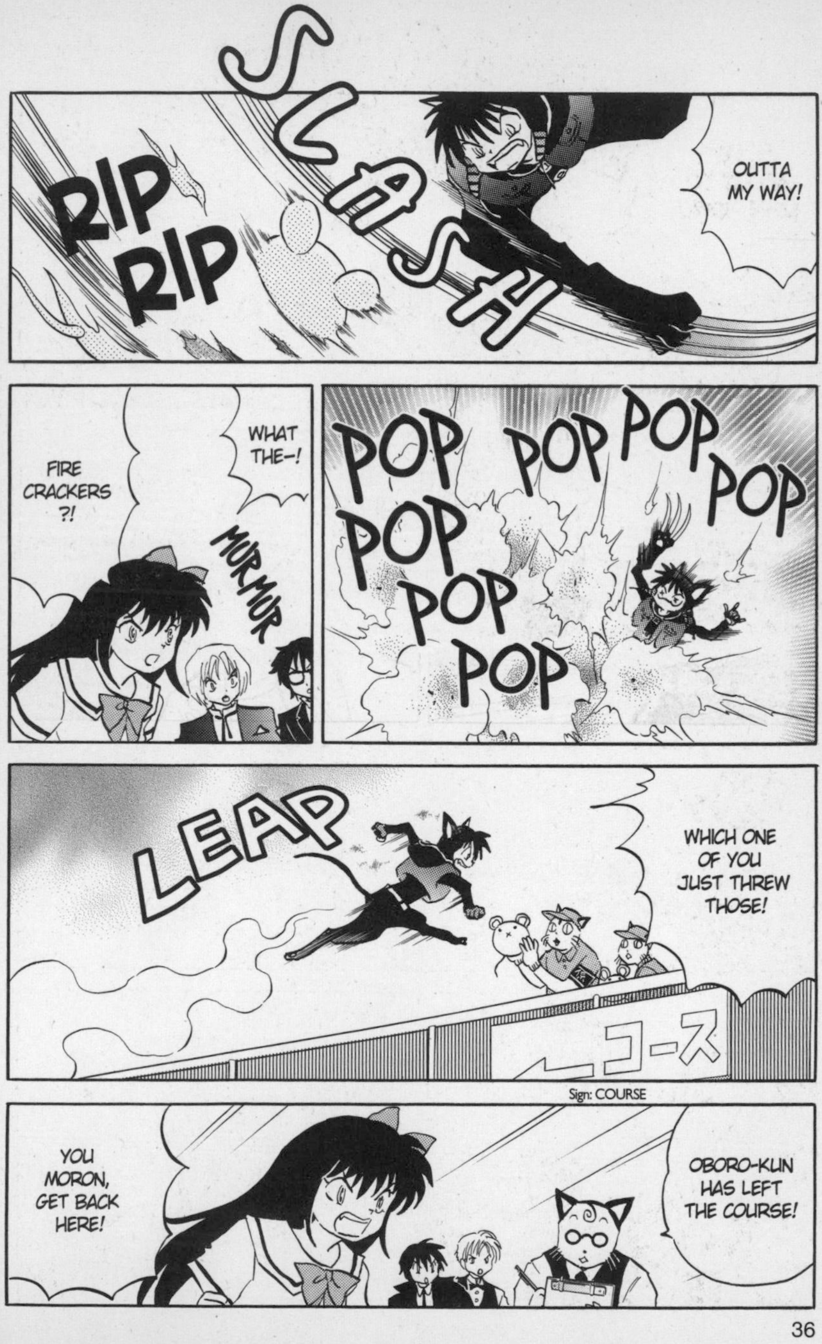
SLASH
OUTTA MY WAY!
RIP RIP
POP POP POP POP POP POP POP POP
WHAT THE-!
FIRE CRACKERS ?!
MURMUR
WHICH ONE OF YOU JUST THREW THOSE!
LEAP
コース
Sign: COURSE
OBORO-KUN HAS LEFT THE COURSE!
YOU MORON, GET BACK HERE!

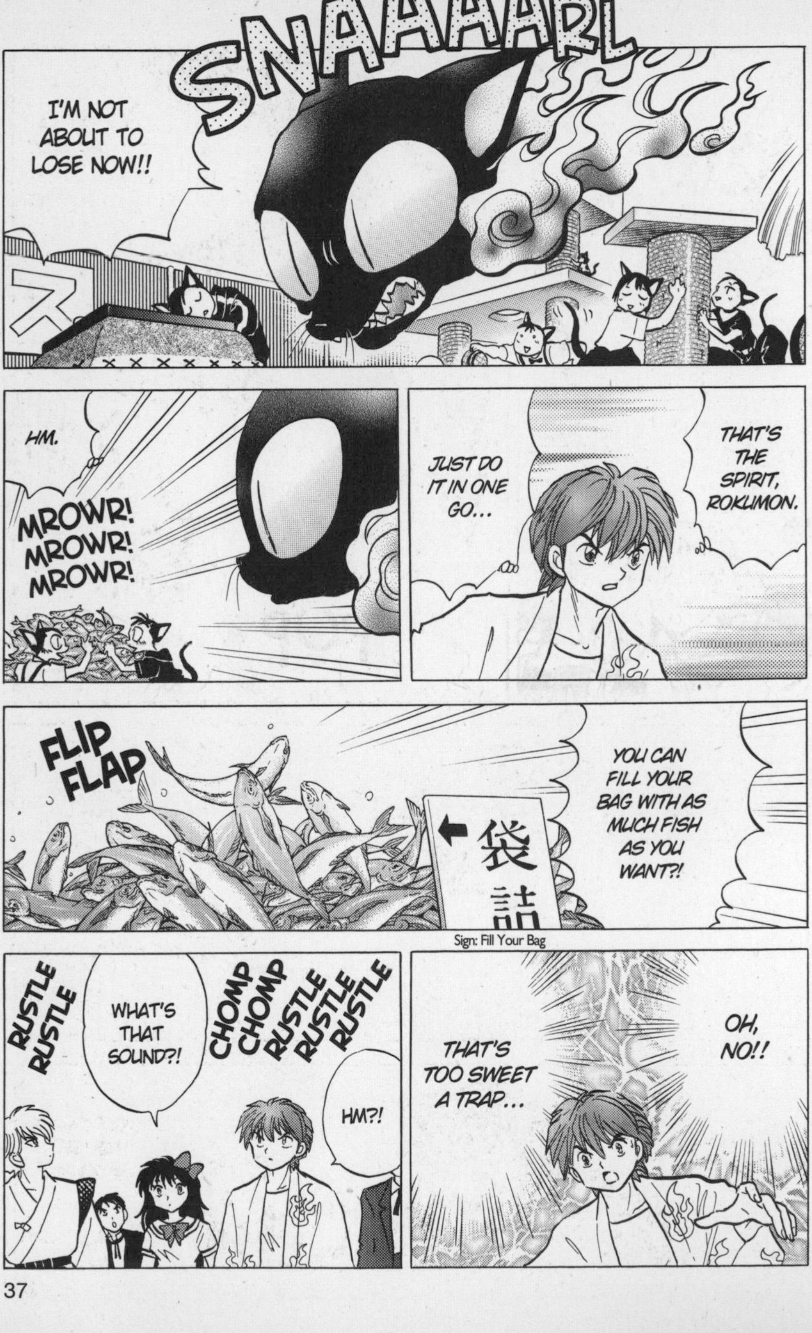
SNAAAARL
I'M NOT ABOUT TO LOSE NOW!!
THAT'S THE SPIRIT, ROKUMON.
JUST DO IT IN ONE GO...
HM.
MROWR! MROWR! MROWR!
YOU CAN FILL YOUR BAG WITH AS MUCH FISH AS YOU WANT?!
袋詰
FLIP FLAP
OH, NO!!
THAT'S TOO SWEET A TRAP...
CHOMP CHOMP RUSTLE RUSTLE RUSTLE
HM?!
WHAT'S THAT SOUND?!
RUSTLE RUSTLE
Sign: Fill Your Bag

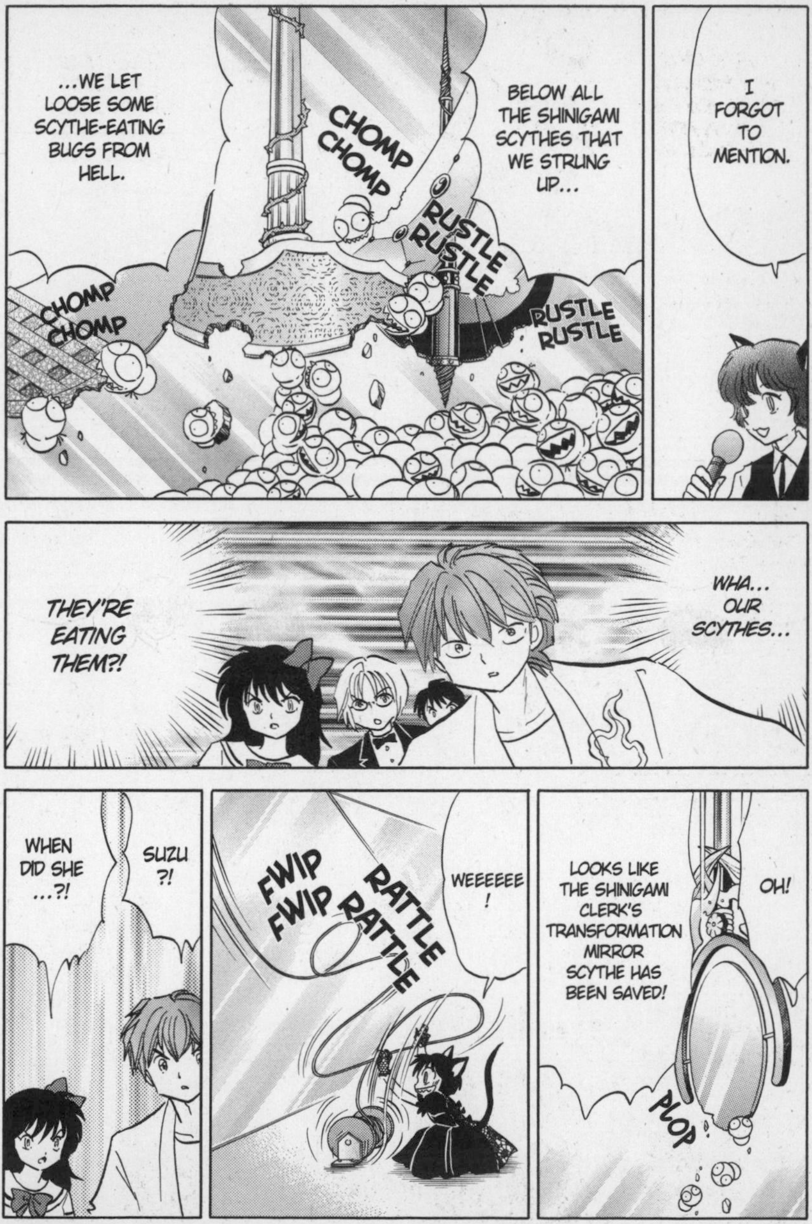

I FORGOT TO MENTION.
BELOW ALL THE SHINIGAMI SCYTHES THAT WE STRUNG UP...
CHOMP CHOMP
RUSTLE RUSTLE
...WE LET LOOSE SOME SCYTHE-EATING BUGS FROM HELL.
RUSTLE RUSTLE
CHOMP CHOMP
WHA... OUR SCYTHES...
THEY'RE EATING THEM?!
OH!
LOOKS LIKE THE SHINIGAMI CLERK'S TRANSFORMATION MIRROR SCYTHE HAS BEEN SAVED!
PLOP
WEEEEEE!
RATTLE RATTLE
FWIP FWIP
SUZU?!
WHEN DID SHE ...?!

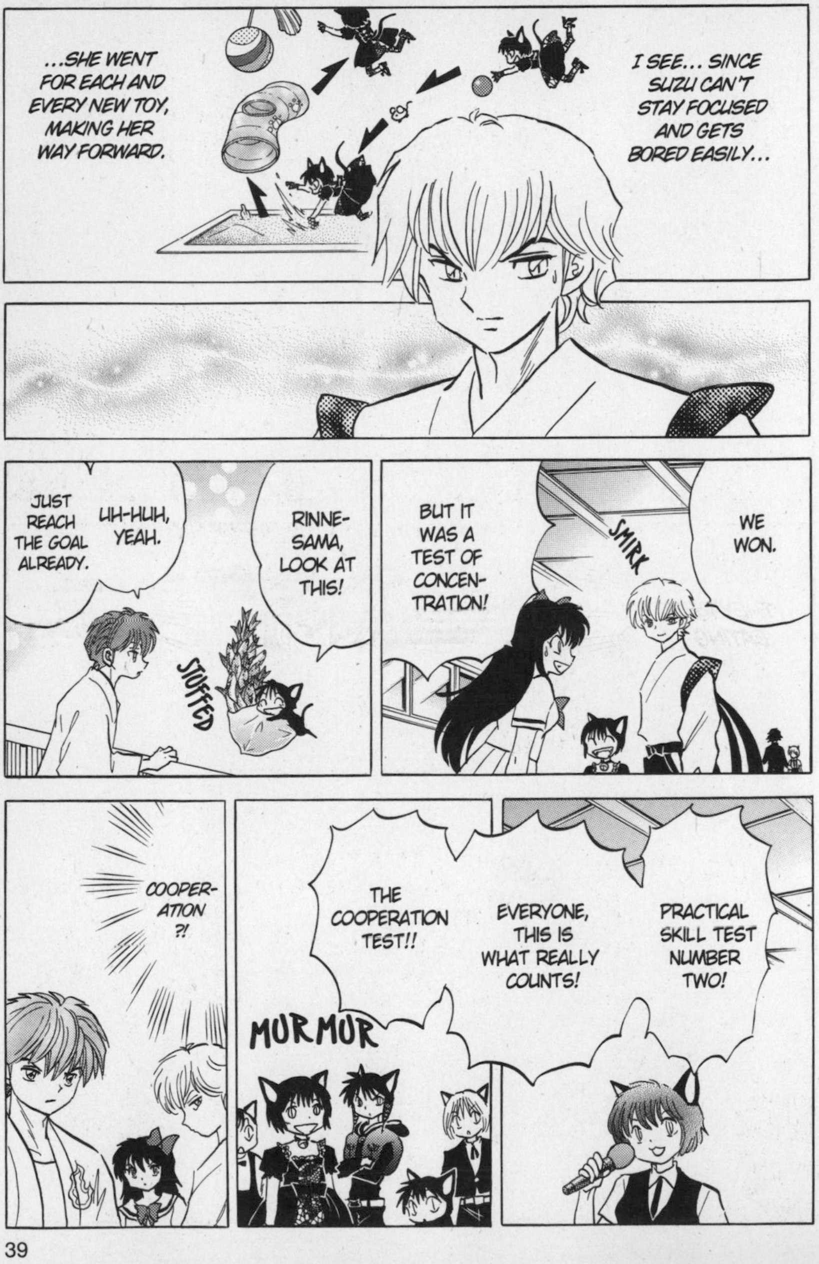
I SEE... SINCE SUZU CAN'T STAY FOCUSED AND GETS BORED EASILY...
...SHE WENT FOR EACH AND EVERY NEW TOY, MAKING HER WAY FORWARD.
WE WON.
SMIRK
BUT IT WAS A TEST OF CONCEN-TRATION!
RINNE-SAMA, LOOK AT THIS!
STUFFED
UH-HUH, YEAH.
JUST REACH THE GOAL ALREADY.
PRACTICAL SKILL TEST NUMBER TWO!
EVERYONE, THIS IS WHAT REALLY COUNTS!
THE COOPERATION TEST!!
MURMUR
COOPER-ATION?!

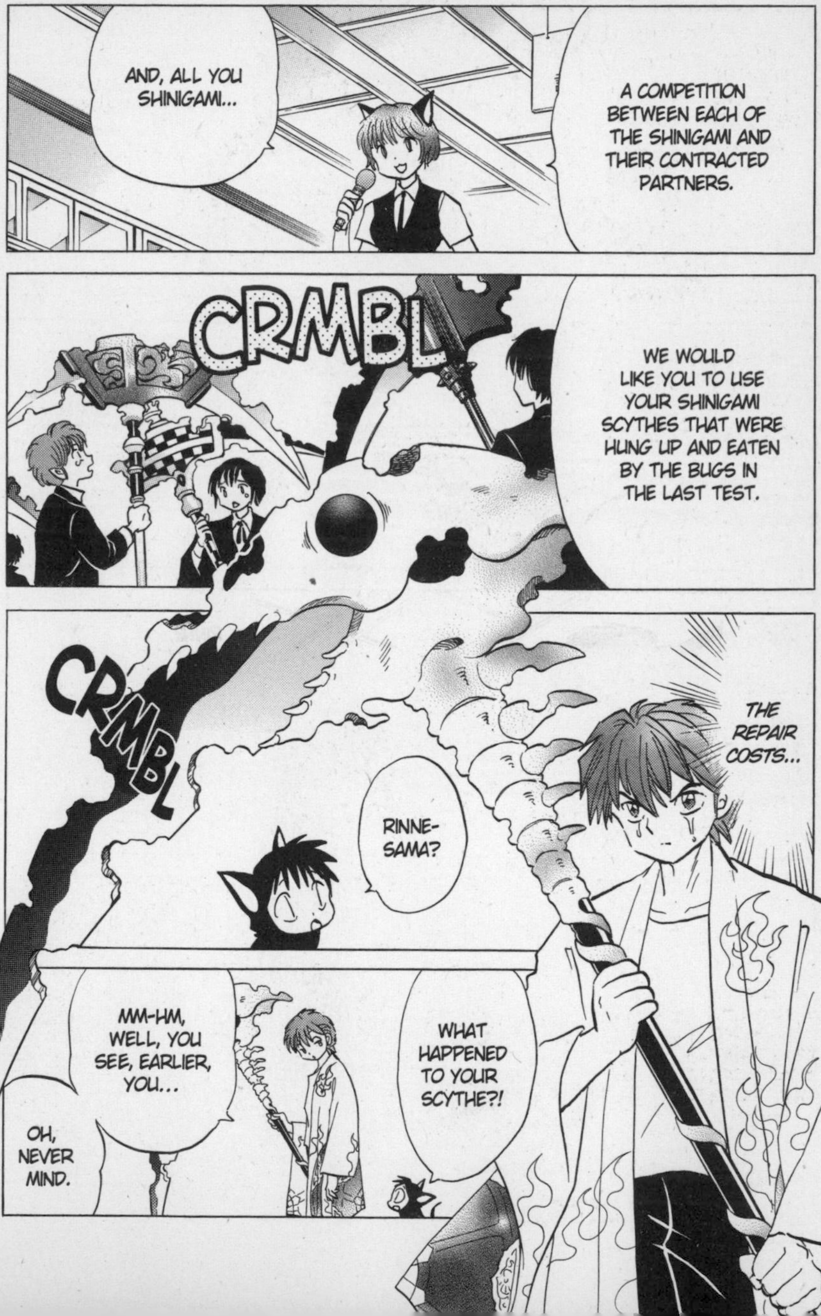
A COMPETITION BETWEEN EACH OF THE SHINIGAMI AND THEIR CONTRACTED PARTNERS.
AND, ALL YOU SHINIGAMI...
WE WOULD LIKE YOU TO USE YOUR SHINIGAMI SCYTHES THAT WERE HUNG UP AND EATEN BY THE BUGS IN THE LAST TEST.
CRMBL
THE REPAIR COSTS...
CRMBL
RINNE-SAMA?
WHAT HAPPENED TO YOUR SCYTHE?!
MM-HM, WELL, YOU SEE, EARLIER, YOU...
OH, NEVER MIND.

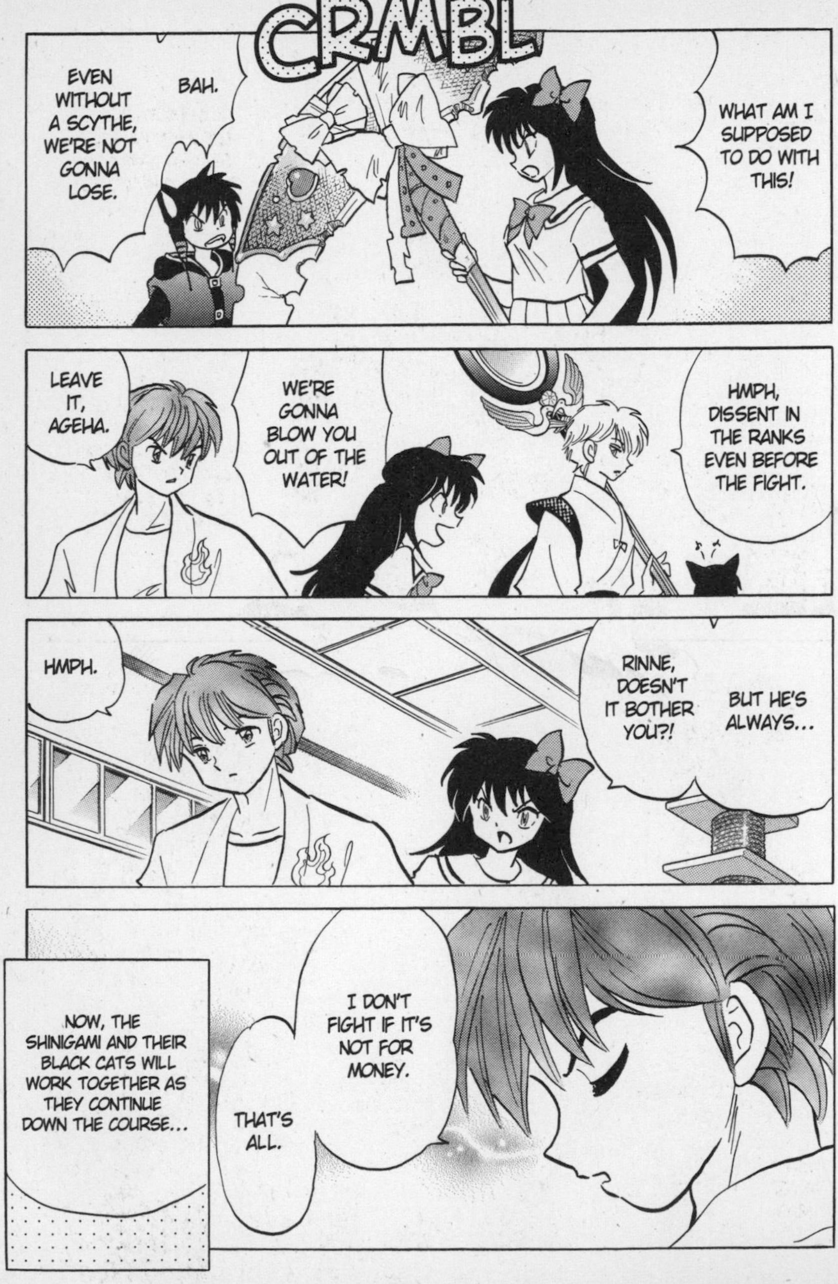
CRMBL
WHAT AM I SUPPOSED TO DO WITH THIS!
BAH.
EVEN WITHOUT A SCYTHE, WE'RE NOT GONNA LOSE.
HMPH, DISSENT IN THE RANKS EVEN BEFORE THE FIGHT.
WE'RE GONNA BLOW YOU OUT OF THE WATER!
LEAVE IT, AGEHA.
RINNE, DOESN'T IT BOTHER YOU?!
BUT HE'S ALWAYS…
HMPH.
I DON'T FIGHT IF IT'S NOT FOR MONEY.
THAT'S ALL.
NOW, THE SHINIGAMI AND THEIR BLACK CATS WILL WORK TOGETHER AS THEY CONTINUE DOWN THE COURSE…

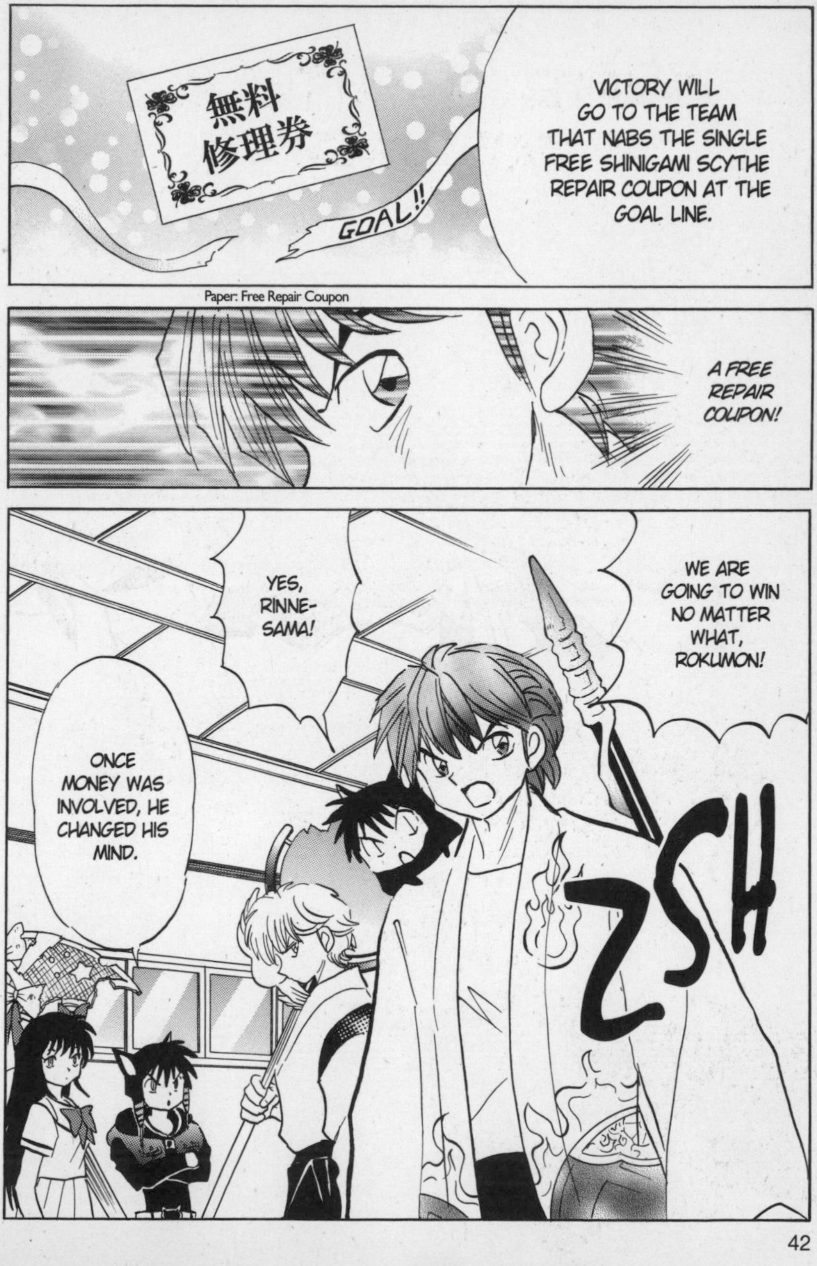
VICTORY WILL GO TO THE TEAM THAT NABS THE SINGLE FREE SHINIGAMI SCYTHE REPAIR COUPON AT THE GOAL LINE.
無料修理券
GOAL!!
Paper: Free Repair Coupon
A FREE REPAIR COUPON!
WE ARE GOING TO WIN NO MATTER WHAT, ROKUMON!
YES, RINNE-SAMA!
ZSH
ONCE MONEY WAS INVOLVED, HE CHANGED HIS MIND.

CHAPTER 111: BATTLE AT CAT TOWER

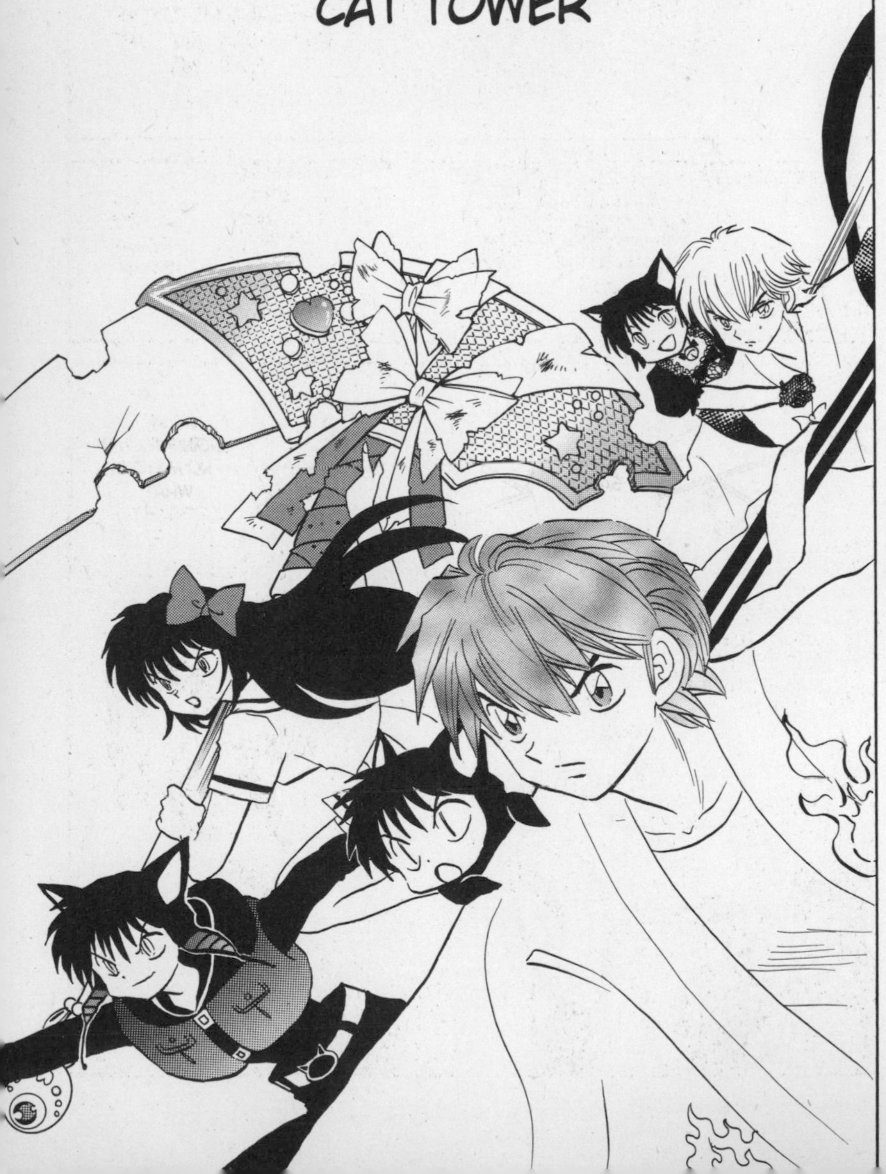

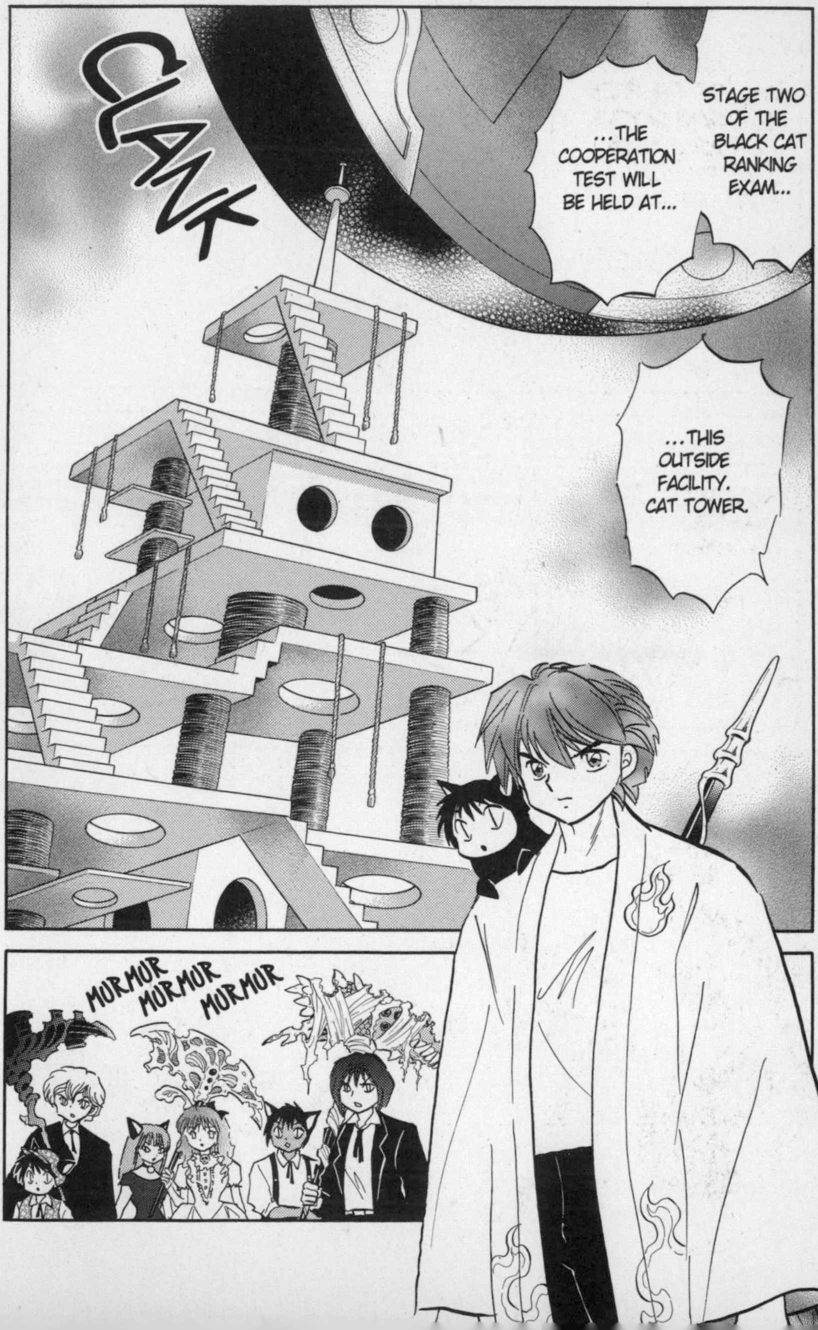
STAGE TWO OF THE BLACK CAT RANKING EXAM...
...THE COOPERATION TEST WILL BE HELD AT...
CLANK
...THIS OUTSIDE FACILITY. CAT TOWER.
MURMOR MURMOR MURMOR

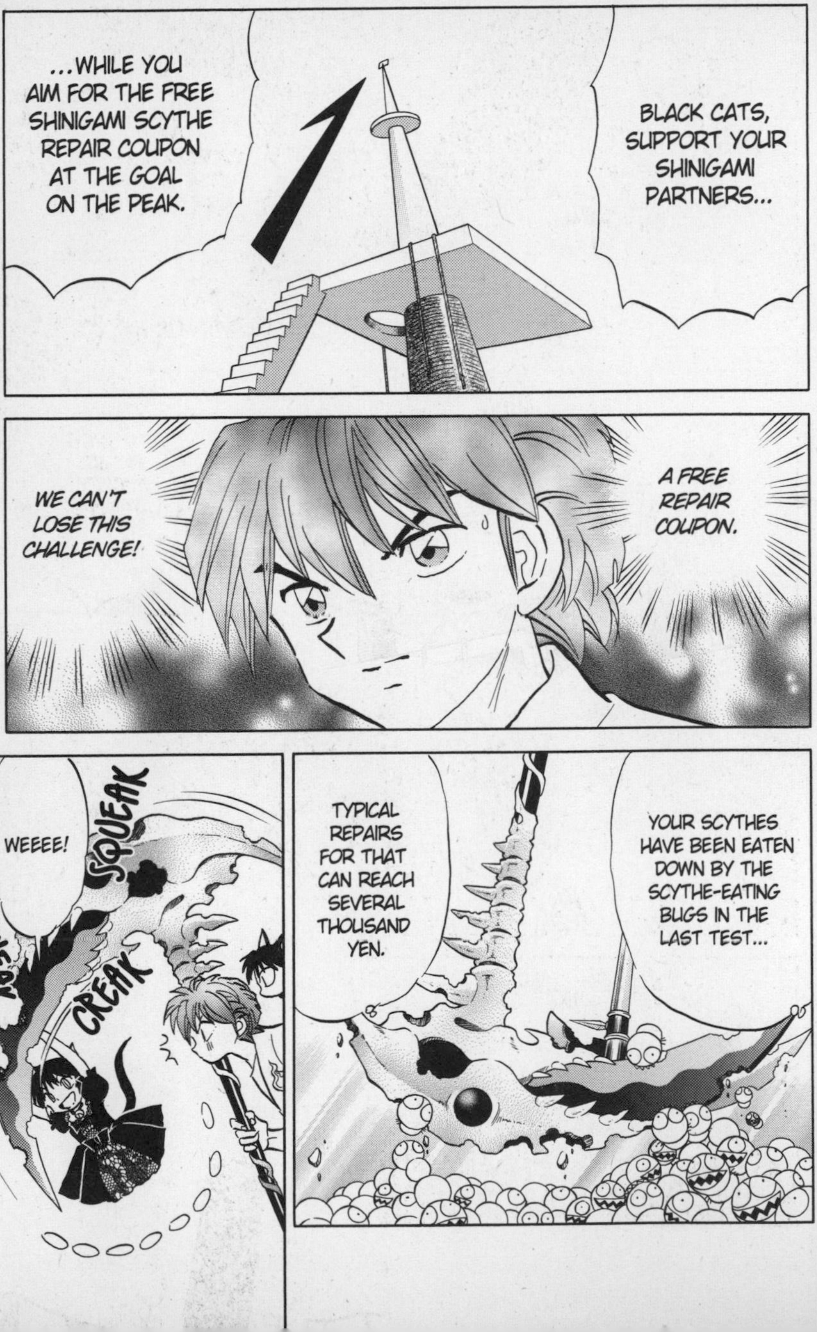
BLACK CATS, SUPPORT YOUR SHINIGAMI PARTNERS...
...WHILE YOU AIM FOR THE FREE SHINIGAMI SCYTHE REPAIR COUPON AT THE GOAL ON THE PEAK.
A FREE REPAIR COUPON.
WE CAN'T LOSE THIS CHALLENGE!
YOUR SCYTHES HAVE BEEN EATEN DOWN BY THE SCYTHE-EATING BUGS IN THE LAST TEST...
TYPICAL REPAIRS FOR THAT CAN REACH SEVERAL THOUSAND YEN.
SQUEAK
WEEEE!
SQUEAK
CREAK

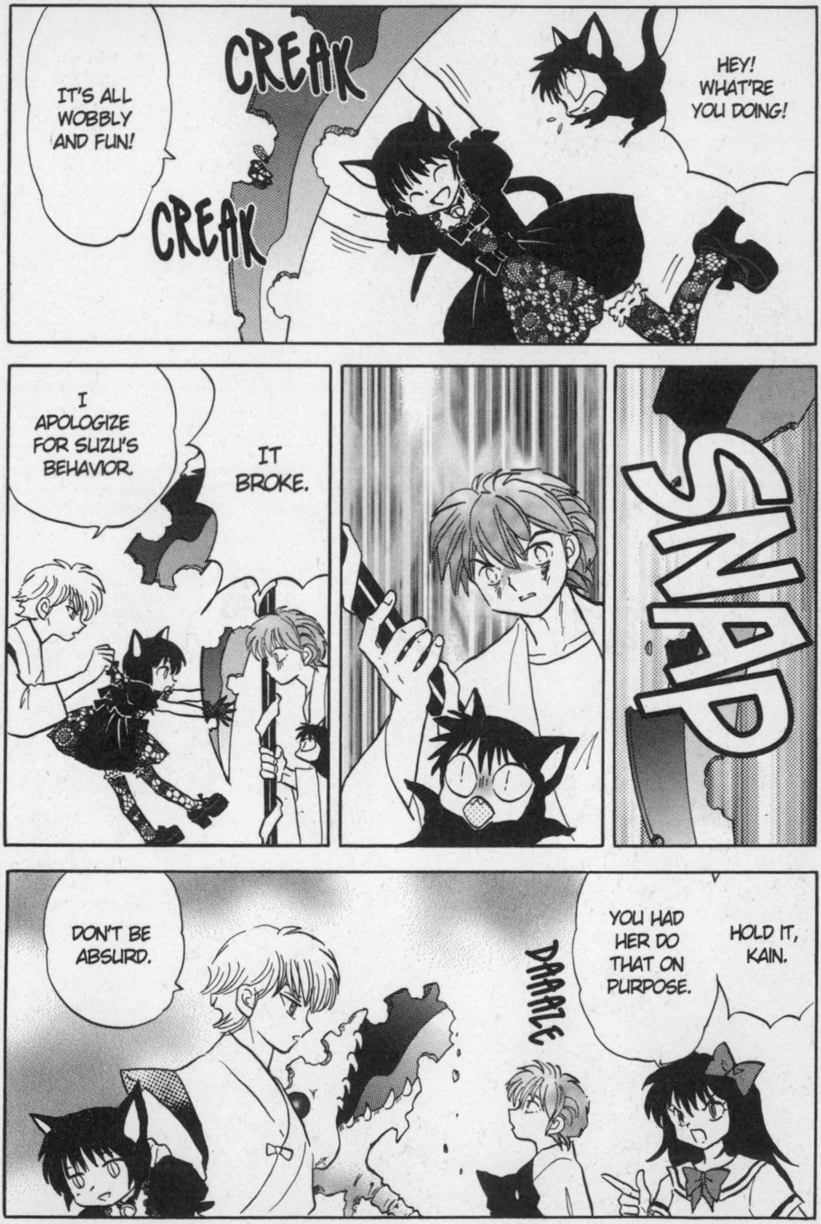
HEY! WHAT'RE YOU DOING!
CREAK
IT'S ALL WOBBLY AND FUN!
CREAK
SNAP
IT BROKE.
I APOLOGIZE FOR SUZU'S BEHAVIOR.
HOLD IT, KAIN.
YOU HAD HER DO THAT ON PURPOSE.
DON'T BE ABSURD.

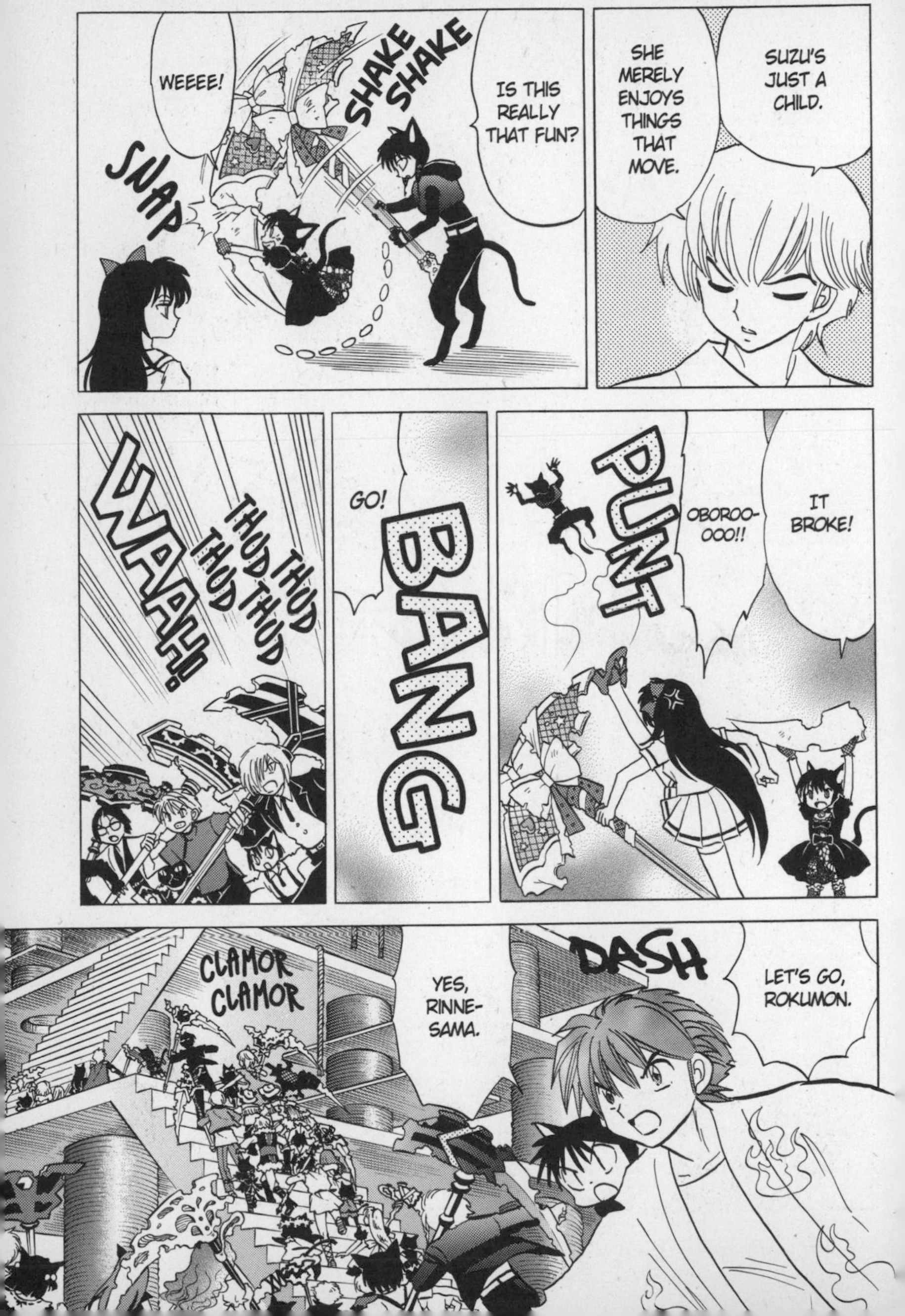
SUZU'S JUST A CHILD.
SHE MERELY ENJOYS THINGS THAT MOVE.
IS THIS REALLY THAT FUN?
SHAKE SHAKE
WEEEE!
SNAP
IT BROKE!
OBOROO-OOO!!
PUNT
GO!
BANG
THUD THUD THUD THUD
WAAH!!
LET'S GO, ROKUMON.
DASH
YES, RINNE-SAMA.
CLAMOR CLAMOR

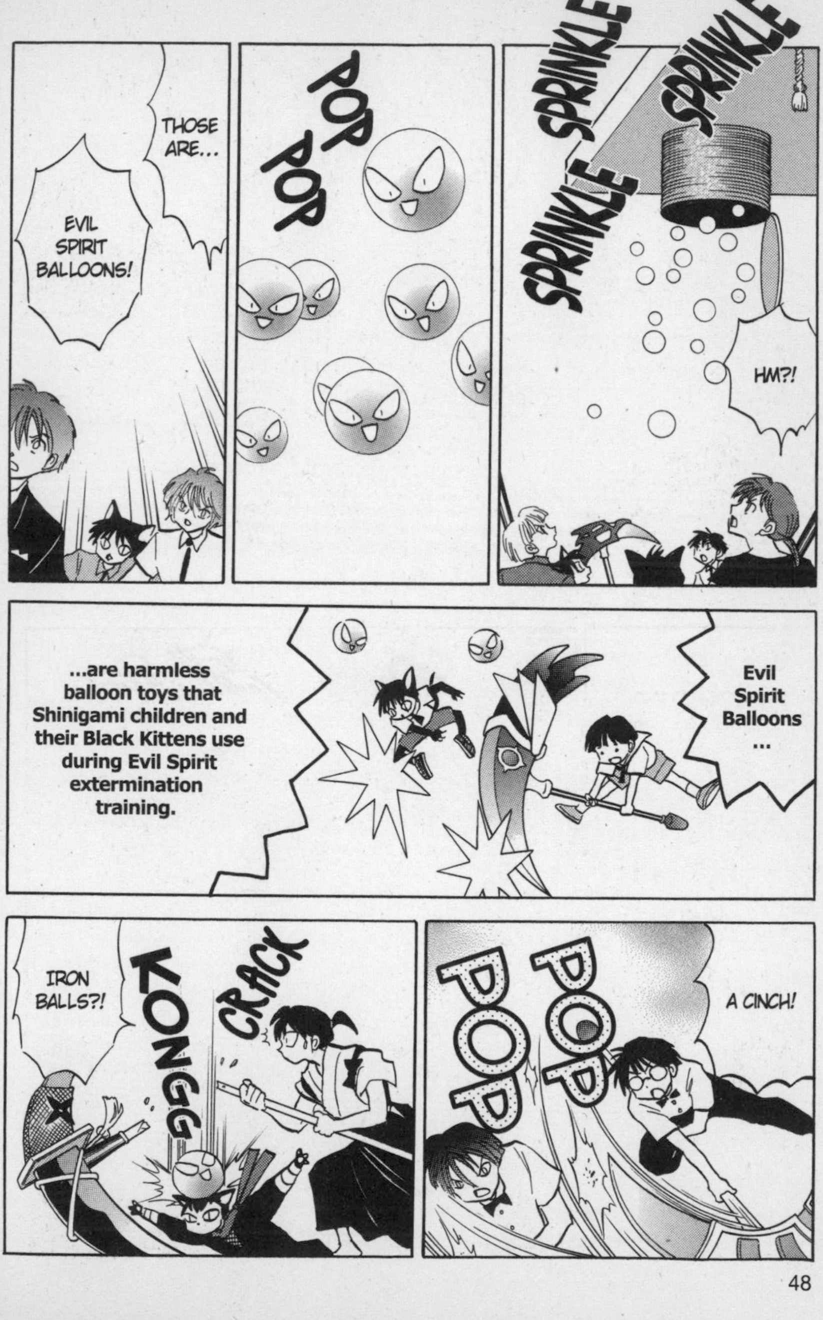

SPRINKLE
SPRINKLE
SPRINKLE
HM?!
POP
POP
THOSE ARE...
EVIL SPIRIT BALLOONS!
Evil Spirit Balloons ...
...are harmless balloon toys that Shinigami children and their Black Kittens use during Evil Spirit extermination training.
POP
POP
A CINCH!
CRACK
KONGG
IRON BALLS?!

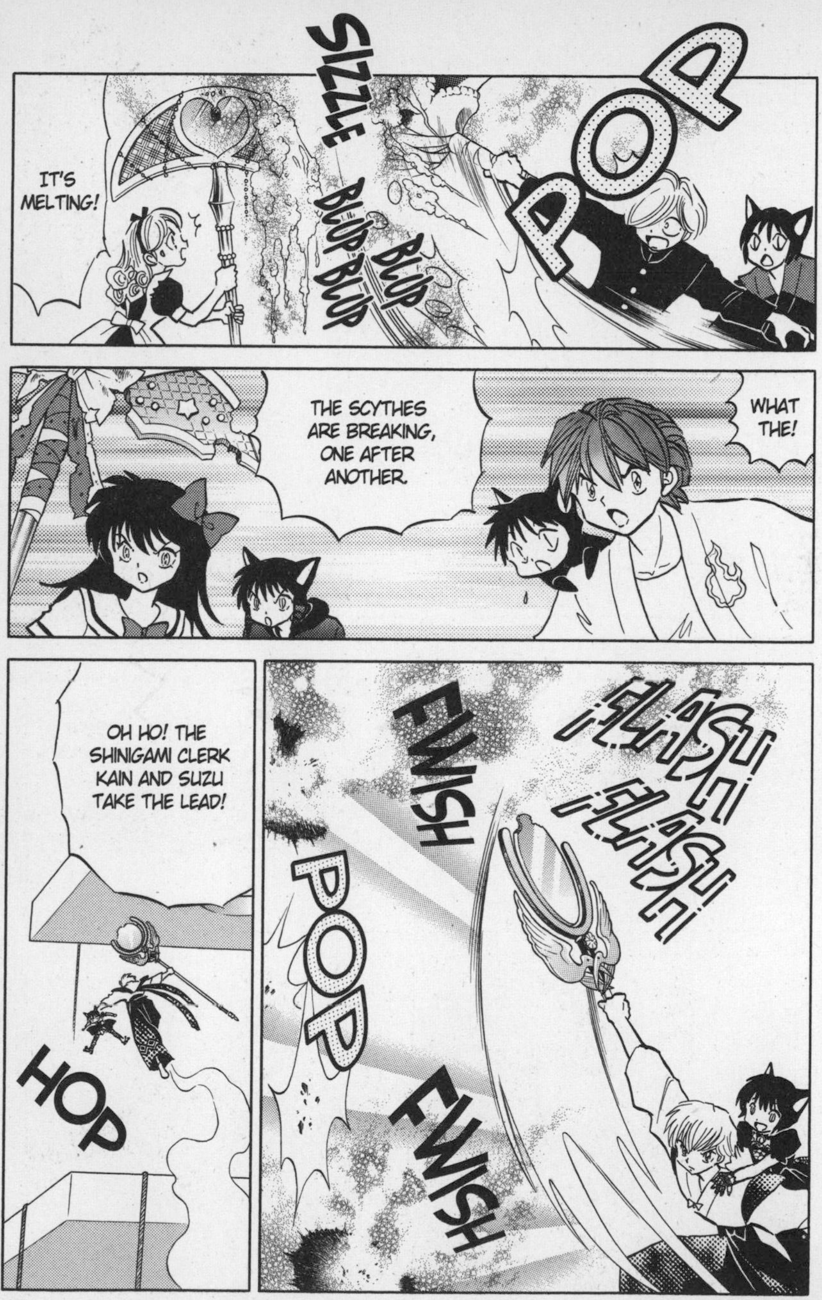
POP
SIZZLE
BLUP BLUP
BLUP BLUP
IT'S MELTING!
WHAT THE!
THE SCYTHES ARE BREAKING, ONE AFTER ANOTHER.
FLASH FLASH
FWISH
POP
FWISH
OH HO! THE SHINIGAMI CLERK KAIN AND SUZU TAKE THE LEAD!
HOP

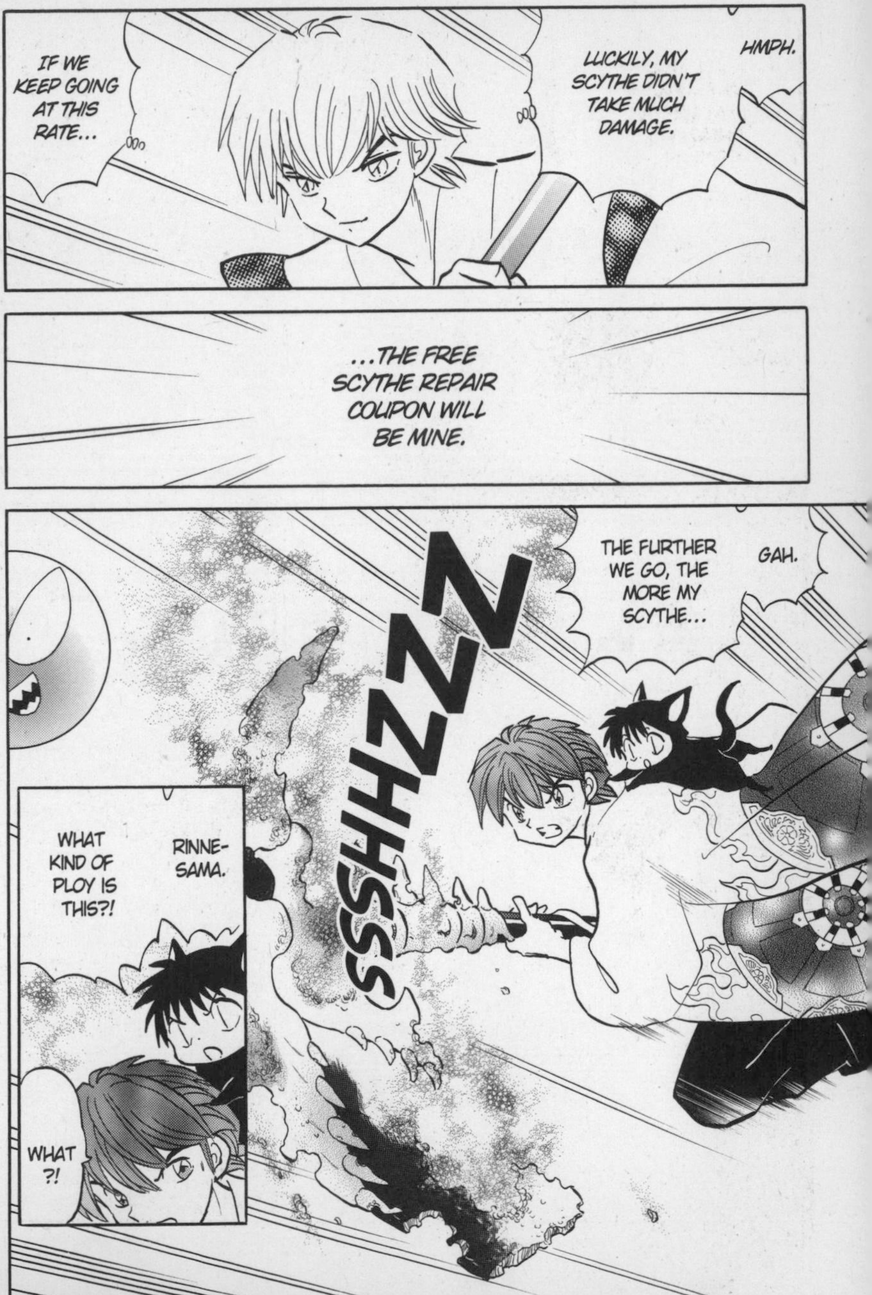
HMPH.
LUCKILY, MY SCYTHE DIDN'T TAKE MUCH DAMAGE.
IF WE KEEP GOING AT THIS RATE...
...THE FREE SCYTHE REPAIR COUPON WILL BE MINE.
GAH.
THE FURTHER WE GO, THE MORE MY SCYTHE...
SSSHHZZZ
RINNE-SAMA.
WHAT KIND OF PLOY IS THIS?!
WHAT ?!

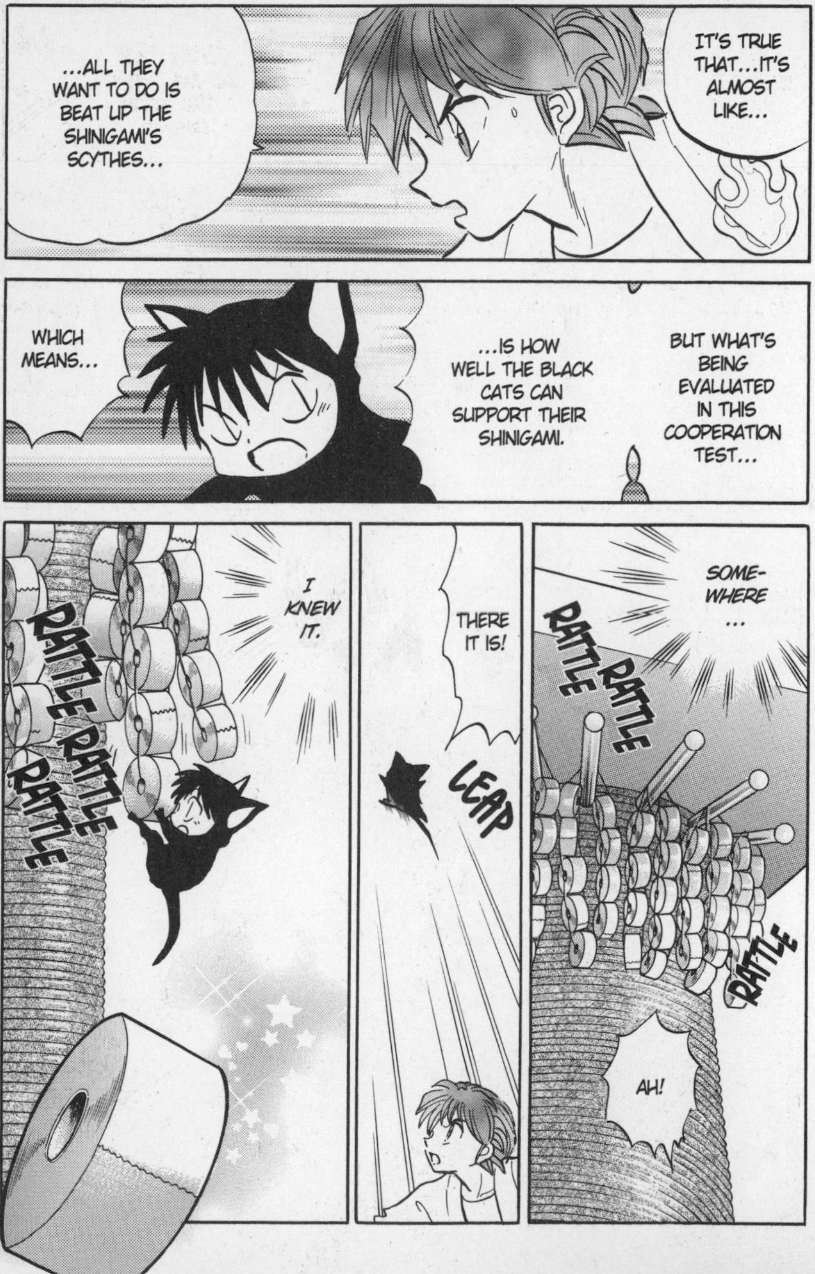
IT'S TRUE THAT...IT'S ALMOST LIKE...
...ALL THEY WANT TO DO IS BEAT UP THE SHINIGAMI'S SCYTHES...
BUT WHAT'S BEING EVALUATED IN THIS COOPERATION TEST...
...IS HOW WELL THE BLACK CATS CAN SUPPORT THEIR SHINIGAMI.
WHICH MEANS...
SOME-WHERE ...
RATTLE RATTLE
RATTLE
AH!
THERE IT IS!
LEAP
I KNEW IT.
RATTLE RATTLE
RATTLE RATTLE

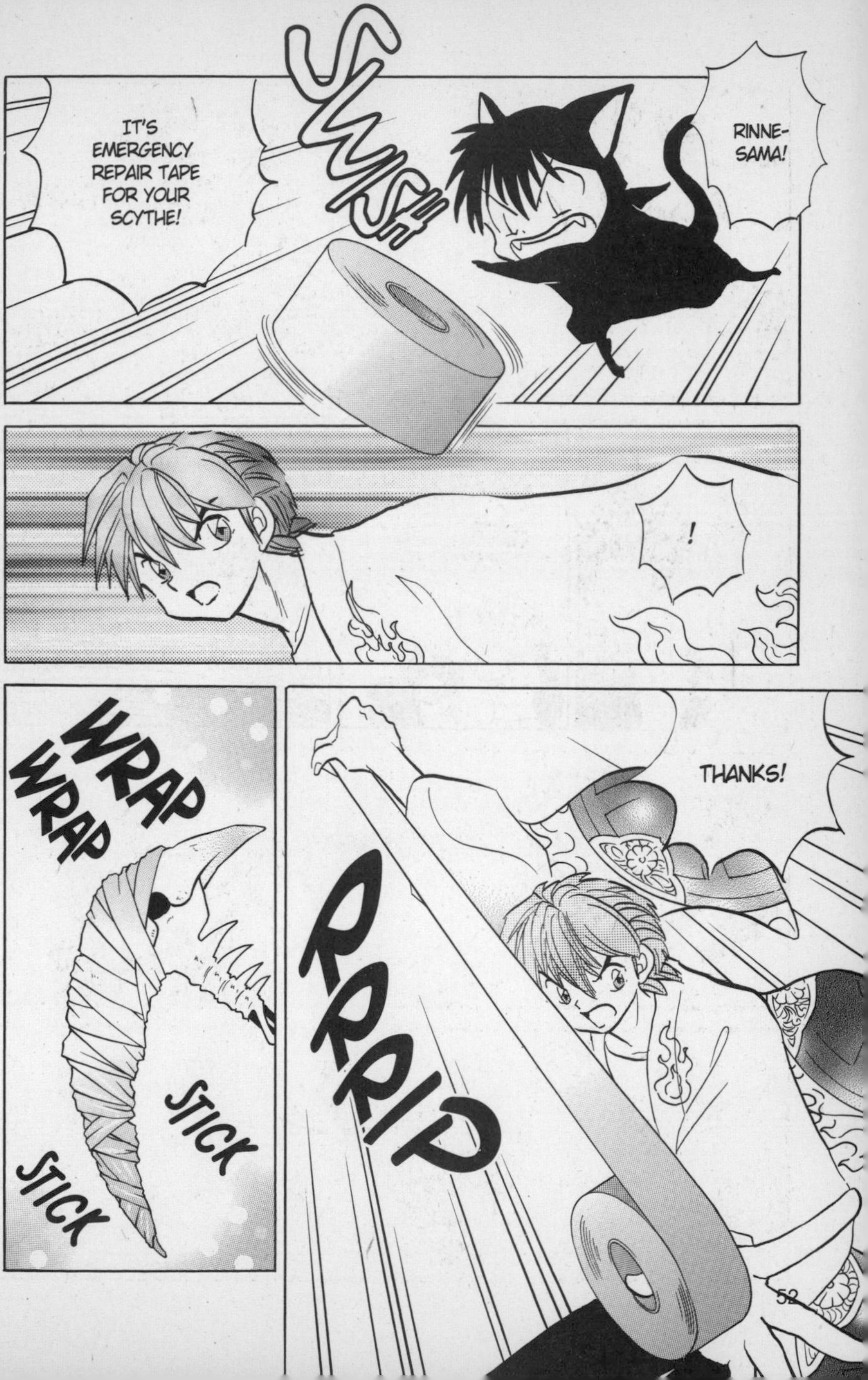
RINNE-SAMA!
SWISH
IT'S EMERGENCY REPAIR TAPE FOR YOUR SCYTHE!
!
THANKS!
RRRIP
WRAP WRAP
STICK STICK

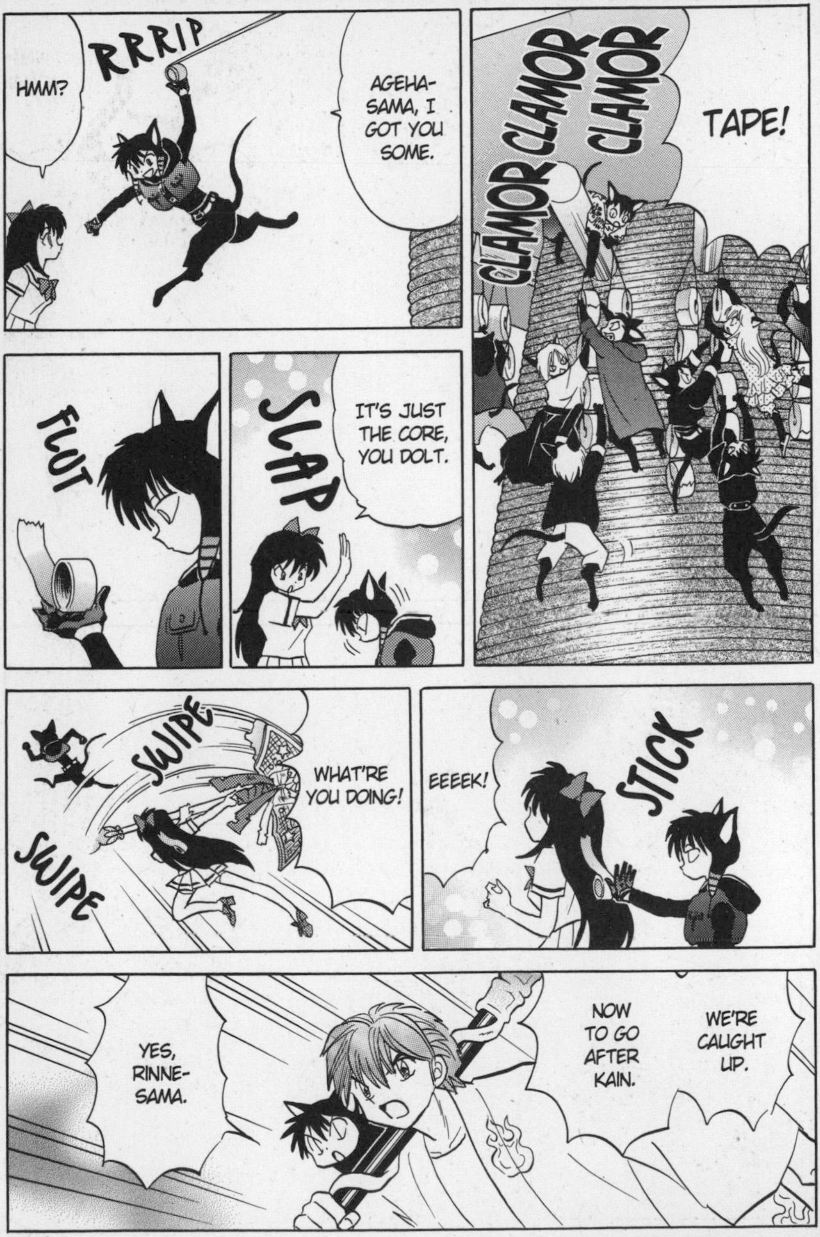
TAPE!
CLAMOR CLAMOR CLAMOR
AGEHA-SAMA, I GOT YOU SOME.
RRRIP
HMM?
IT'S JUST THE CORE, YOU DOLT.
SLAP
FLUT
STICK
EEEEK!
WHAT'RE YOU DOING!
SWIPE
SWIPE
WE'RE CAUGHT UP.
NOW TO GO AFTER KAIN.
YES, RINNE-SAMA.

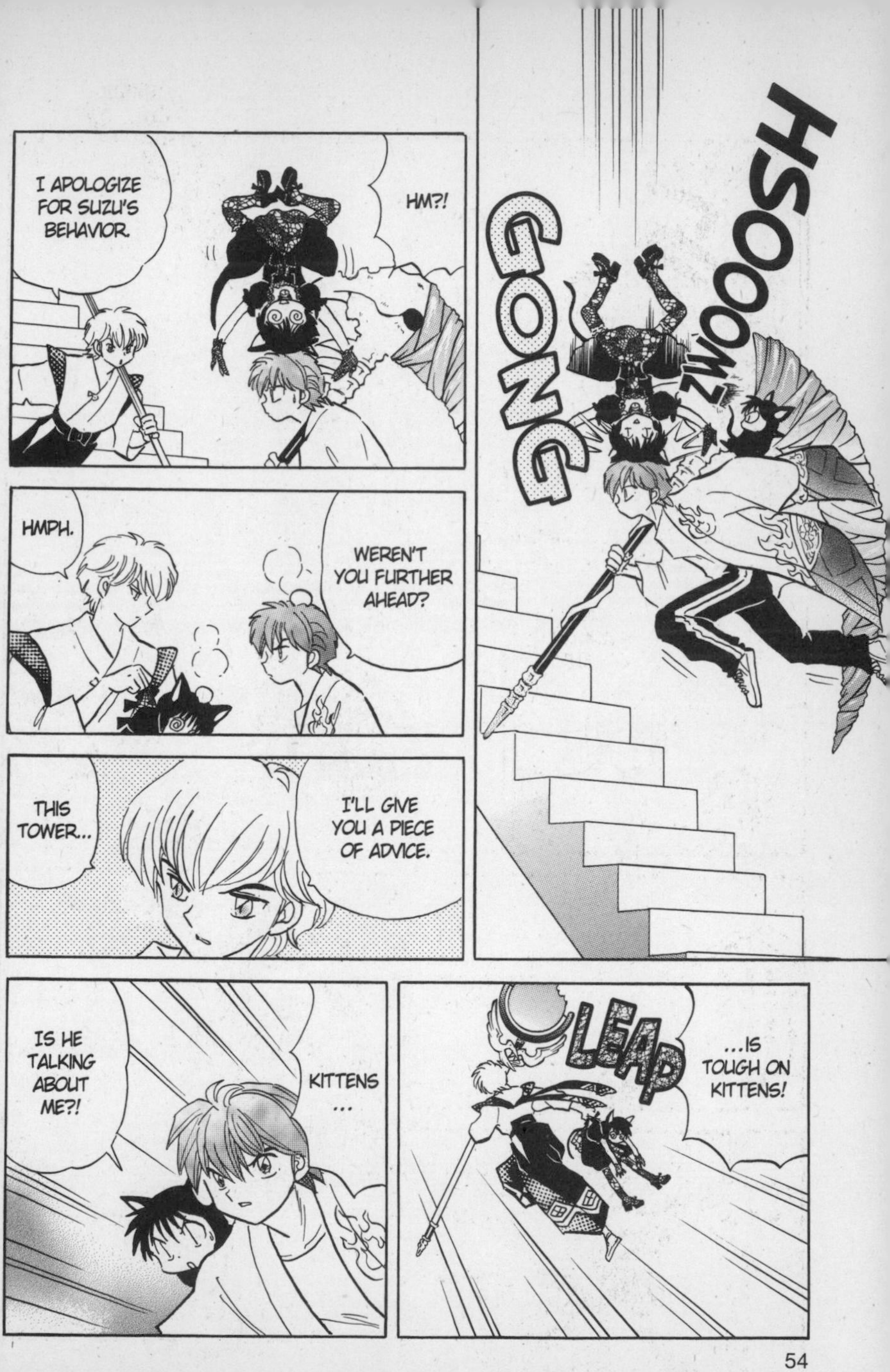
ZWOOOSH
GONG
HM?!
I APOLOGIZE FOR SUZU'S BEHAVIOR.
WEREN'T YOU FURTHER AHEAD?
HMPH.
I'LL GIVE YOU A PIECE OF ADVICE.
THIS TOWER...
...IS TOUGH ON KITTENS!
LEAP
KITTENS...
IS HE TALKING ABOUT ME?!

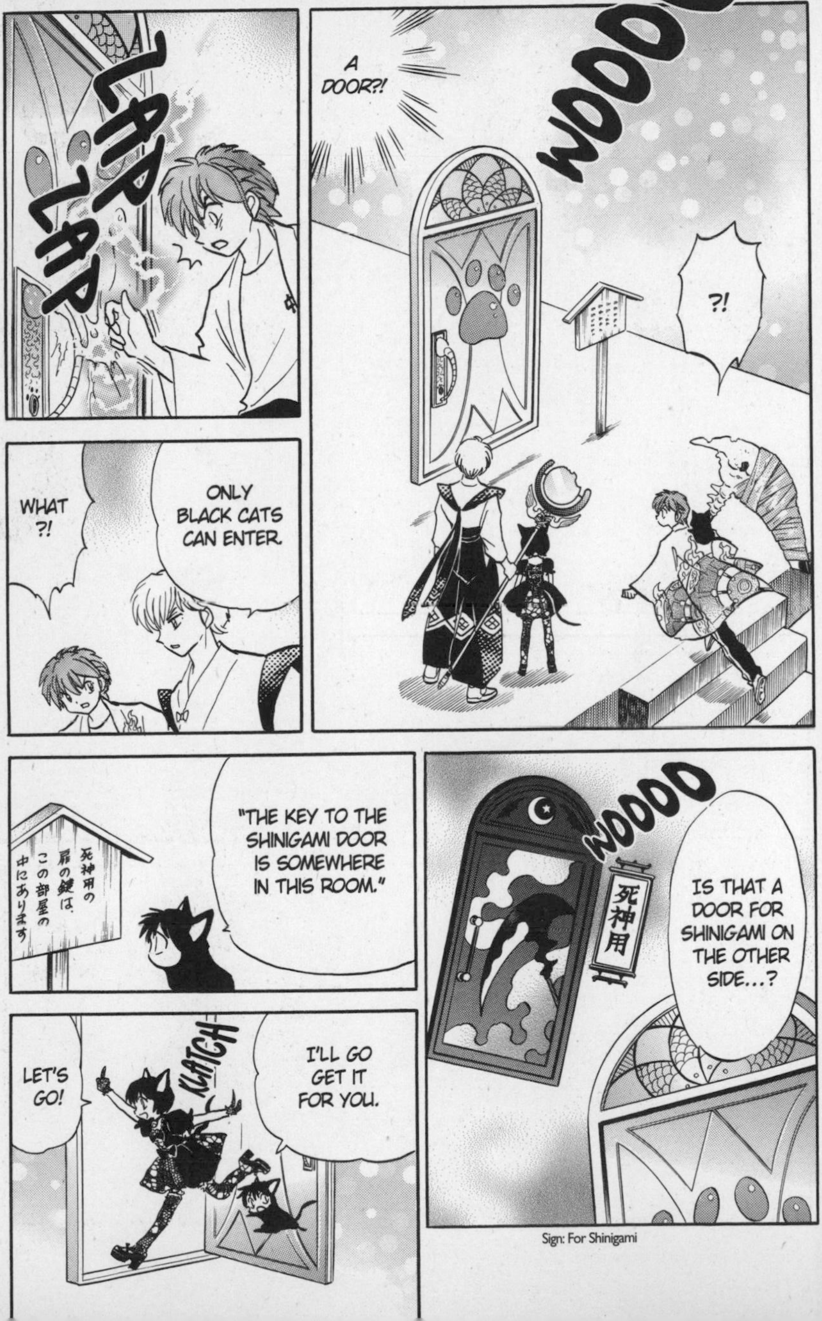
WOOOO
A DOOR?!
?!
ZAP ZAP
ONLY BLACK CATS CAN ENTER.
WHAT ?!
WOOOO
死神用
IS THAT A DOOR FOR SHINIGAMI ON THE OTHER SIDE...?
"THE KEY TO THE SHINIGAMI DOOR IS SOMEWHERE IN THIS ROOM."
死神用の扉の鍵はこの部屋の中にあります
I'LL GO GET IT FOR YOU.
KLATCH
LET'S GO!

Sign: For Shinigami

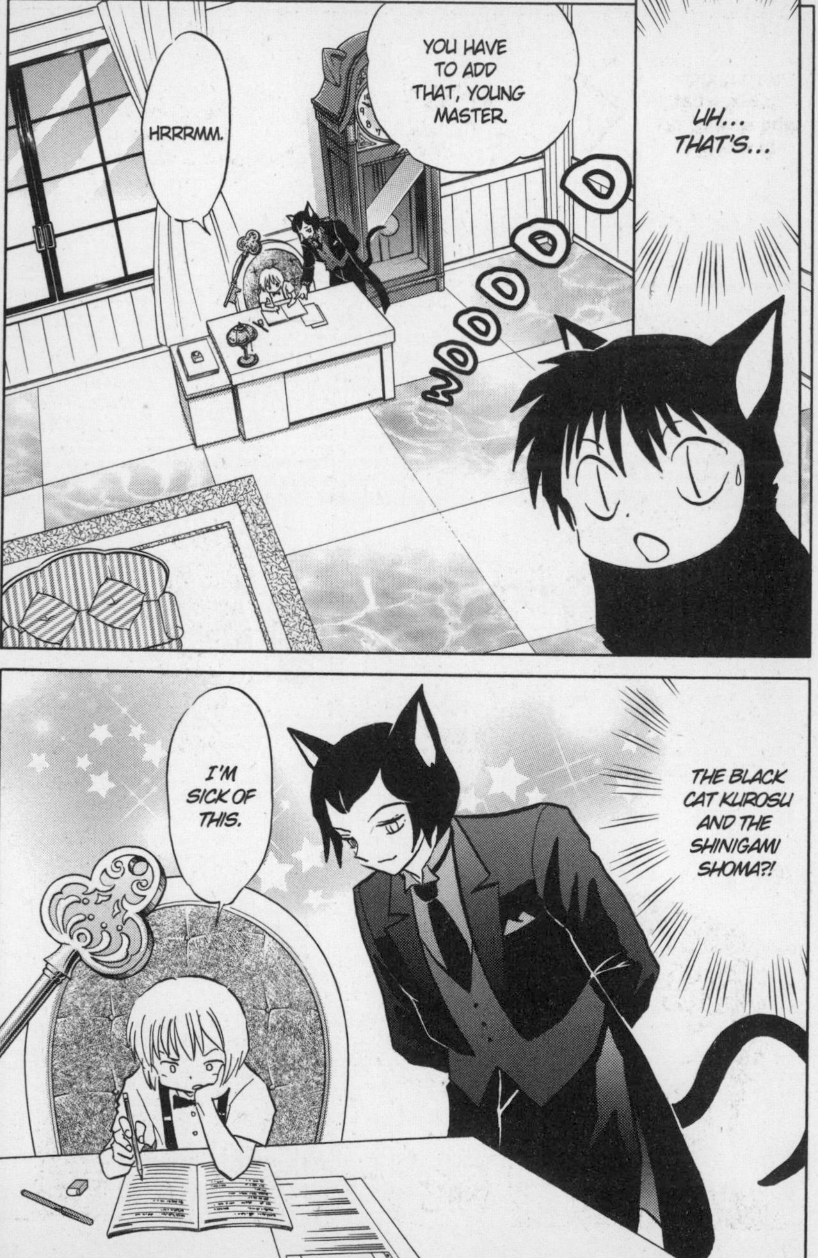
UH... THAT'S...
WOOOOO
YOU HAVE TO ADD THAT, YOUNG MASTER.
HRRRMM.
THE BLACK CAT KUROSU AND THE SHINIGAMI SHOMA?!
I'M SICK OF THIS.

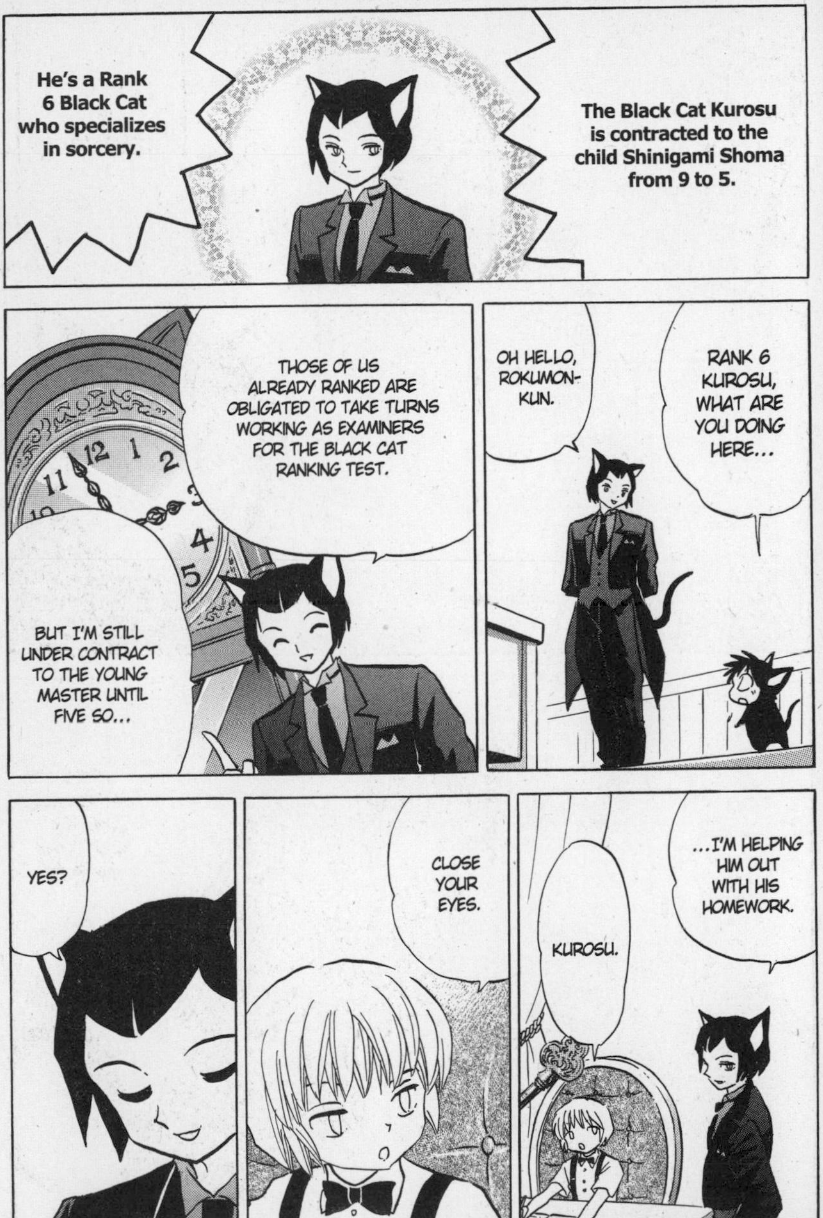
The Black Cat Kurosu is contracted to the child Shinigami Shoma from 9 to 5.
He's a Rank 6 Black Cat who specializes in sorcery.
RANK 6 KUROSU, WHAT ARE YOU DOING HERE...
OH HELLO, ROKUMON-KUN.
THOSE OF US ALREADY RANKED ARE OBLIGATED TO TAKE TURNS WORKING AS EXAMINERS FOR THE BLACK CAT RANKING TEST.
BUT I'M STILL UNDER CONTRACT TO THE YOUNG MASTER UNTIL FIVE SO...
...I'M HELPING HIM OUT WITH HIS HOMEWORK.
KUROSU.
CLOSE YOUR EYES.
YES?

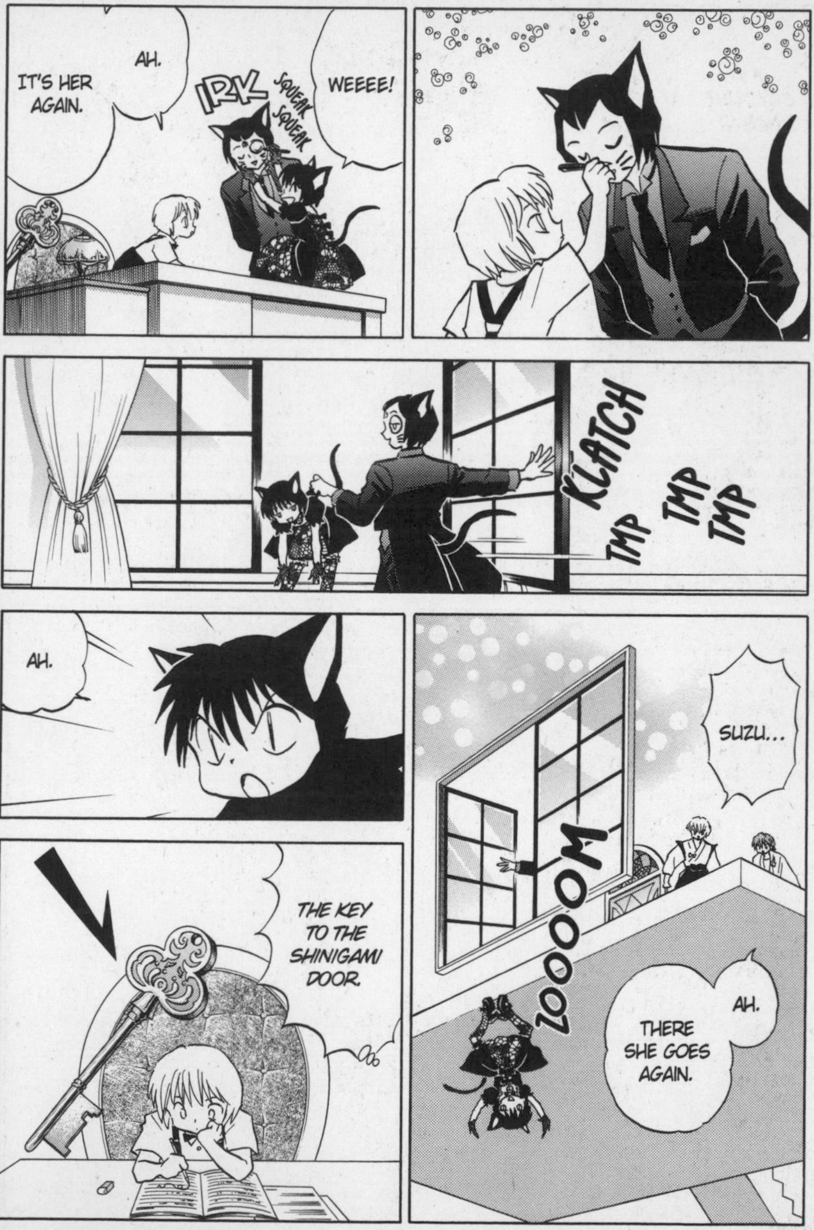
WEEEE!
SQUEAK SQUEAK
IRK
AH.
IT'S HER AGAIN.
KLATCH
TMP TMP TMP TMP
SUZU...
ZOOOOOM
AH.
THERE SHE GOES AGAIN.
AH.
THE KEY TO THE SHINIGAMI DOOR.

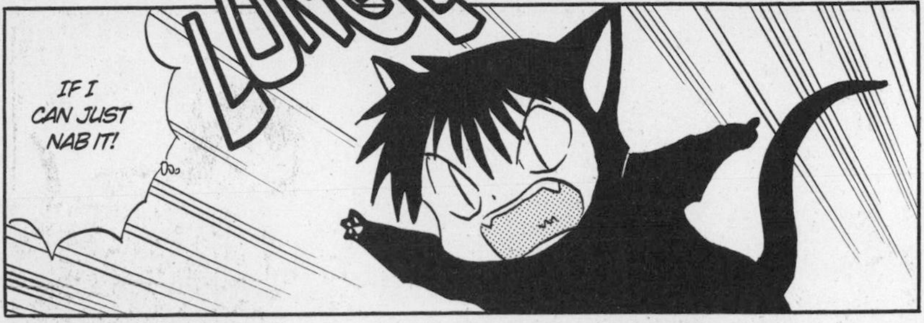
LUNGE
IF I CAN JUST NAB IT!

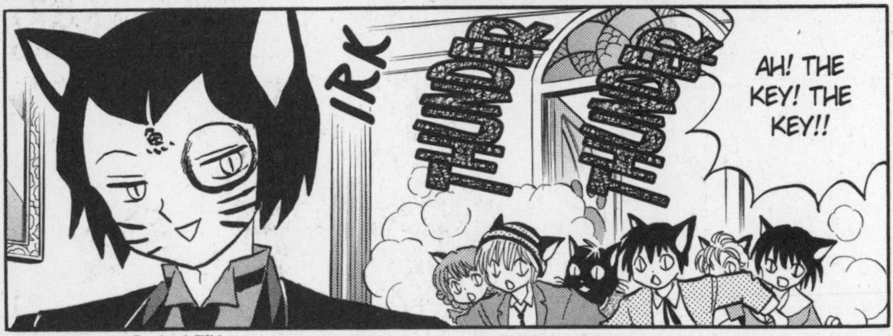
AH! THE KEY! THE KEY!!
THUNDER
THUNDER
IRK

Forehead: FISH

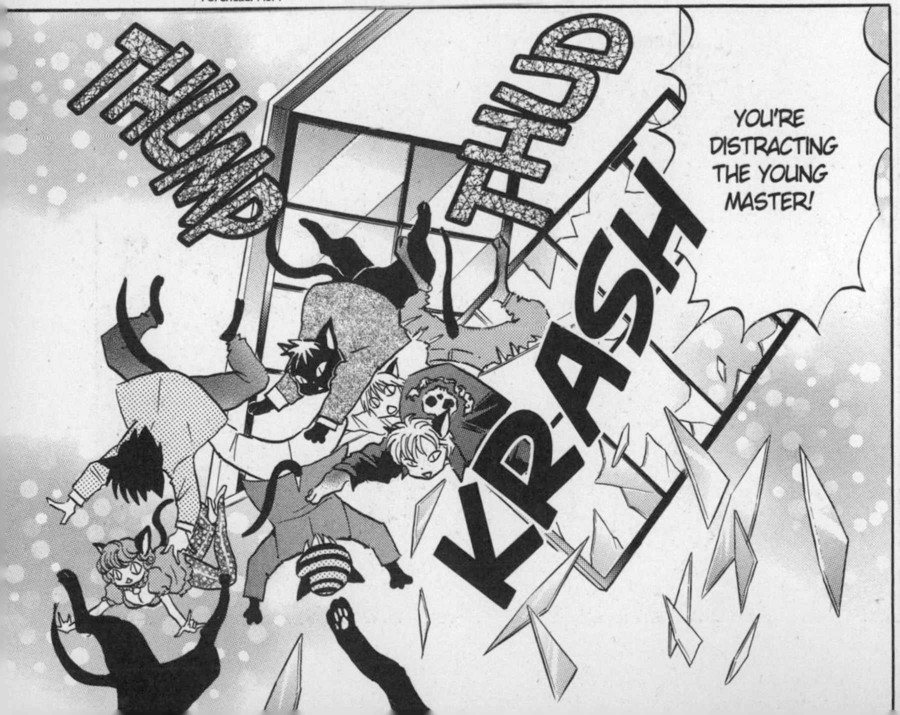
YOU'RE DISTRACTING THE YOUNG MASTER!
THUD
THUMP
KRASH

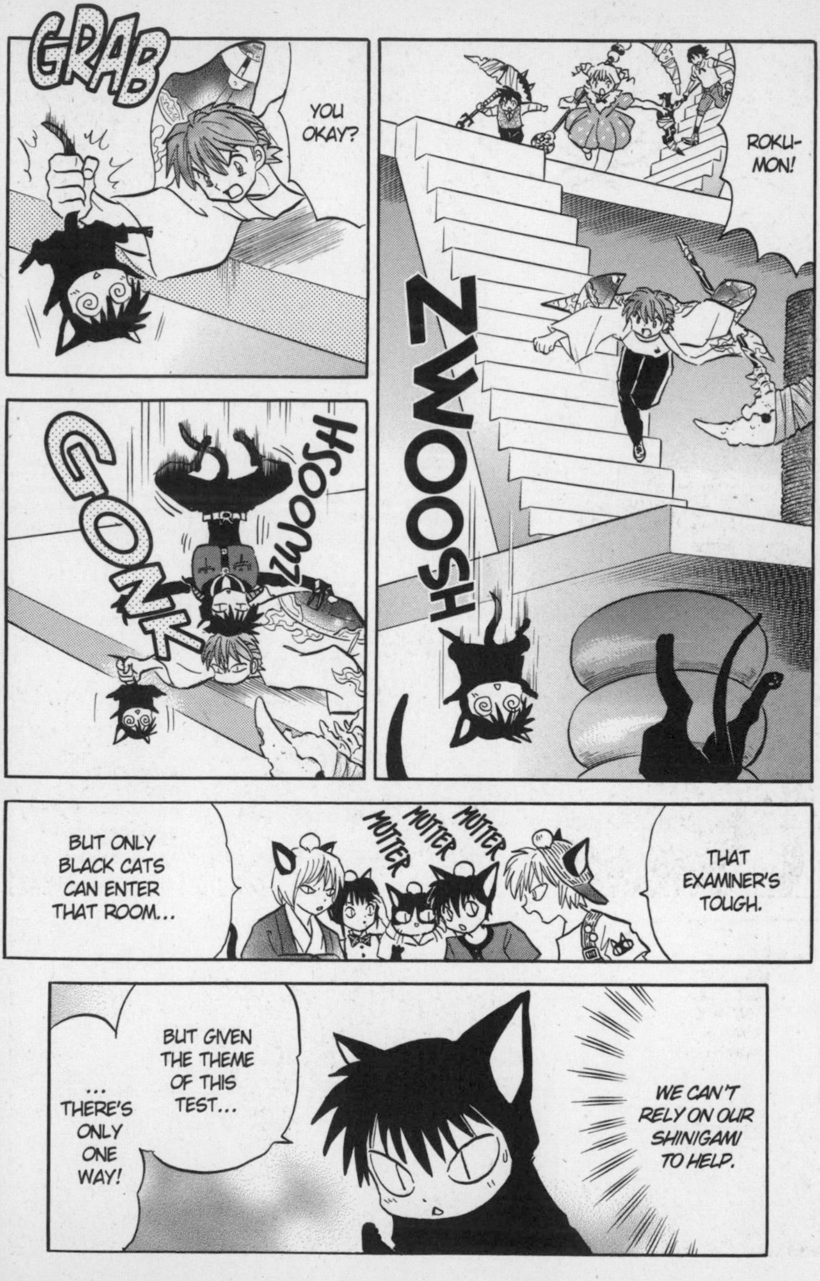
ROKU-MON!
ZWOOSH
GRAB
YOU OKAY?
ZWOOSH
GONK
THAT EXAMINER'S TOUGH.
MUTTER
MUTTER
MUTTER
BUT ONLY BLACK CATS CAN ENTER THAT ROOM...
WE CAN'T RELY ON OUR SHINIGAMI TO HELP.
BUT GIVEN THE THEME OF THIS TEST...
...THERE'S ONLY ONE WAY!

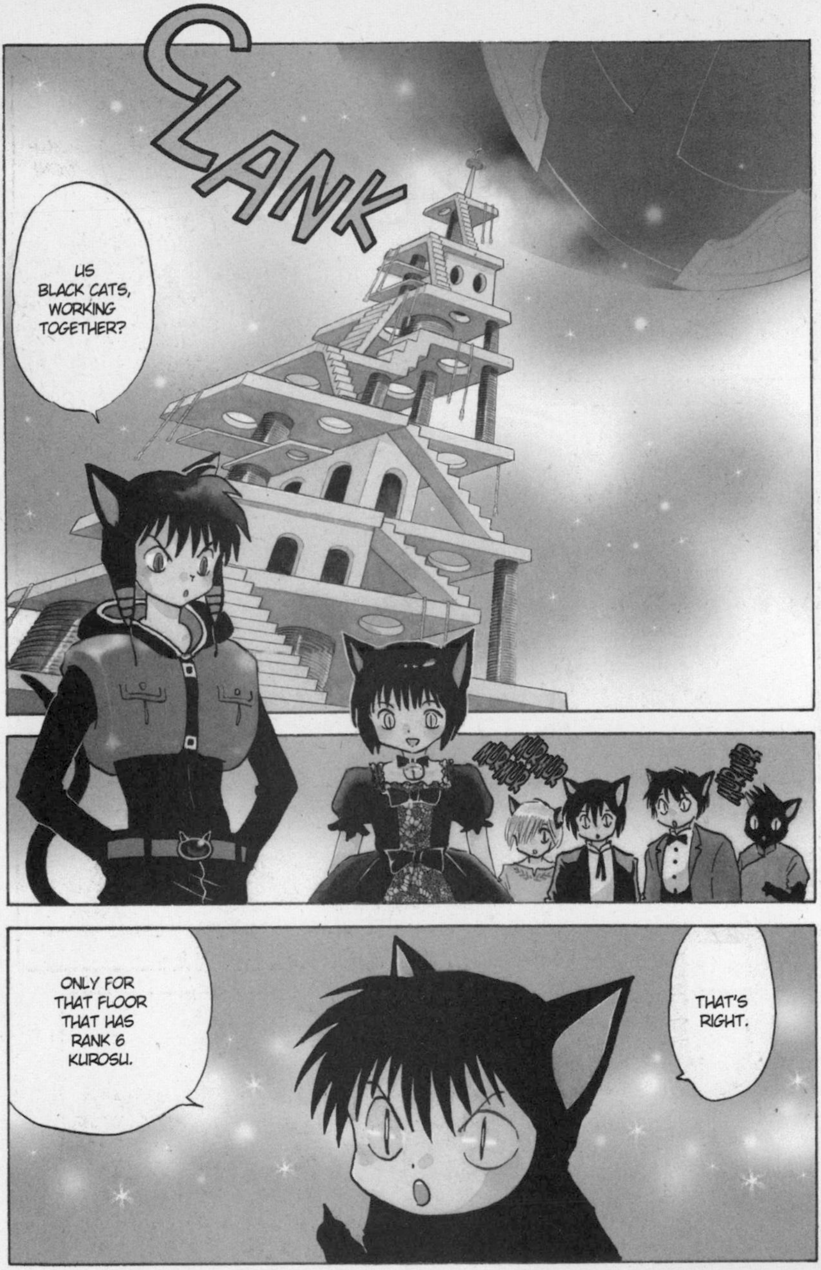
CLANK
US BLACK CATS, WORKING TOGETHER?
THAT'S RIGHT.
ONLY FOR THAT FLOOR THAT HAS RANK 6 KUROSU.

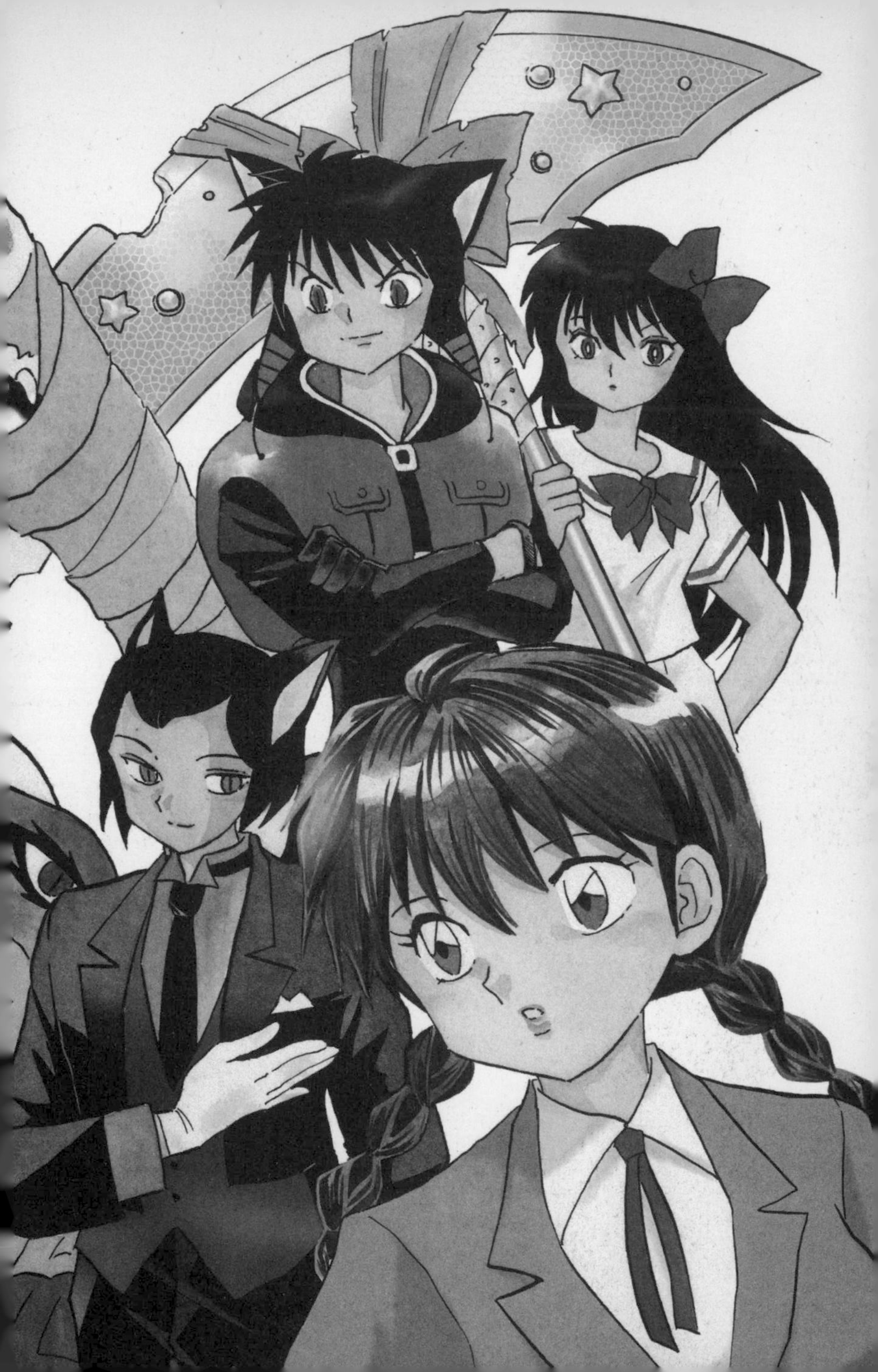

CHAPTER 112: LET'S WORK TOGETHER!

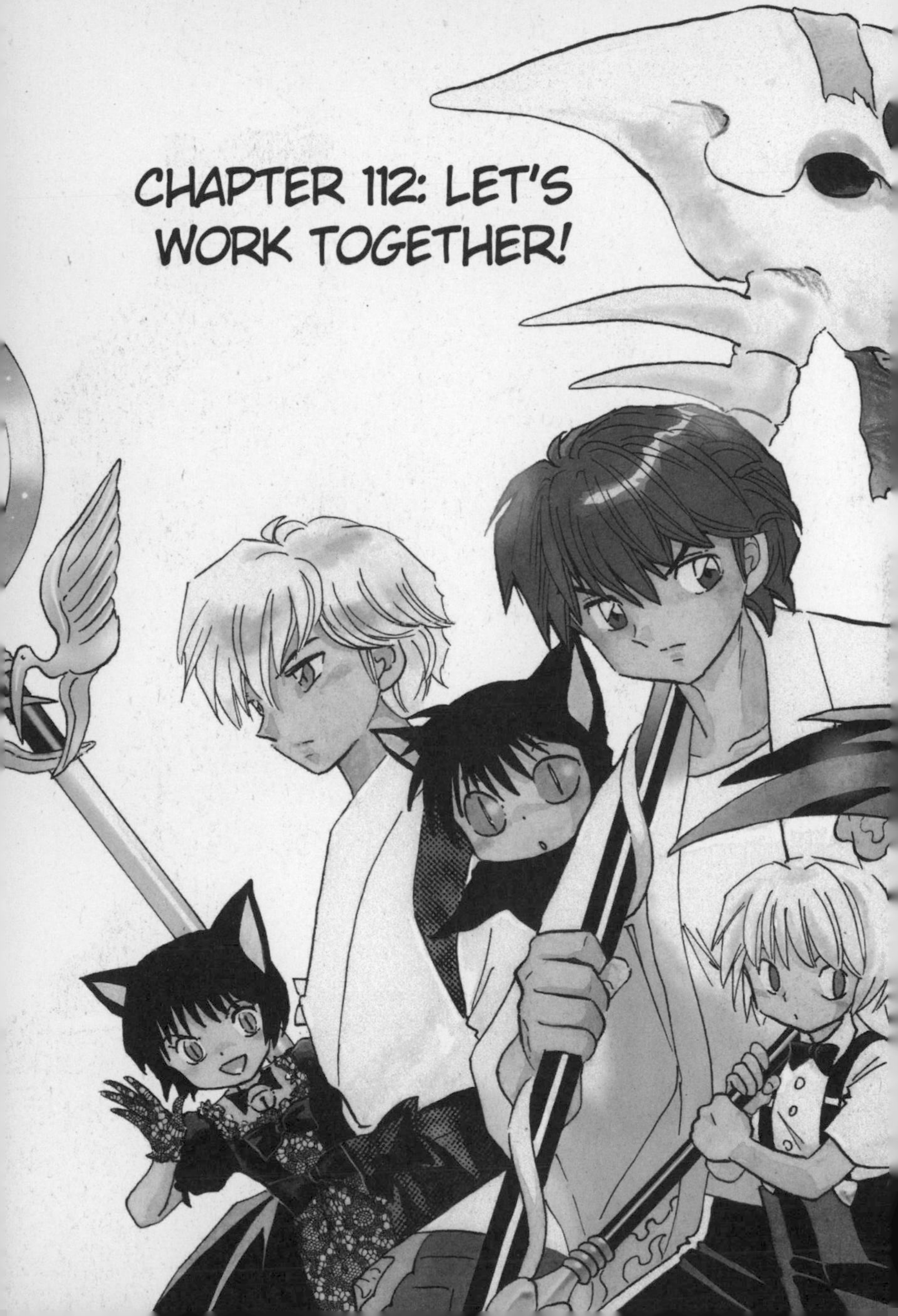

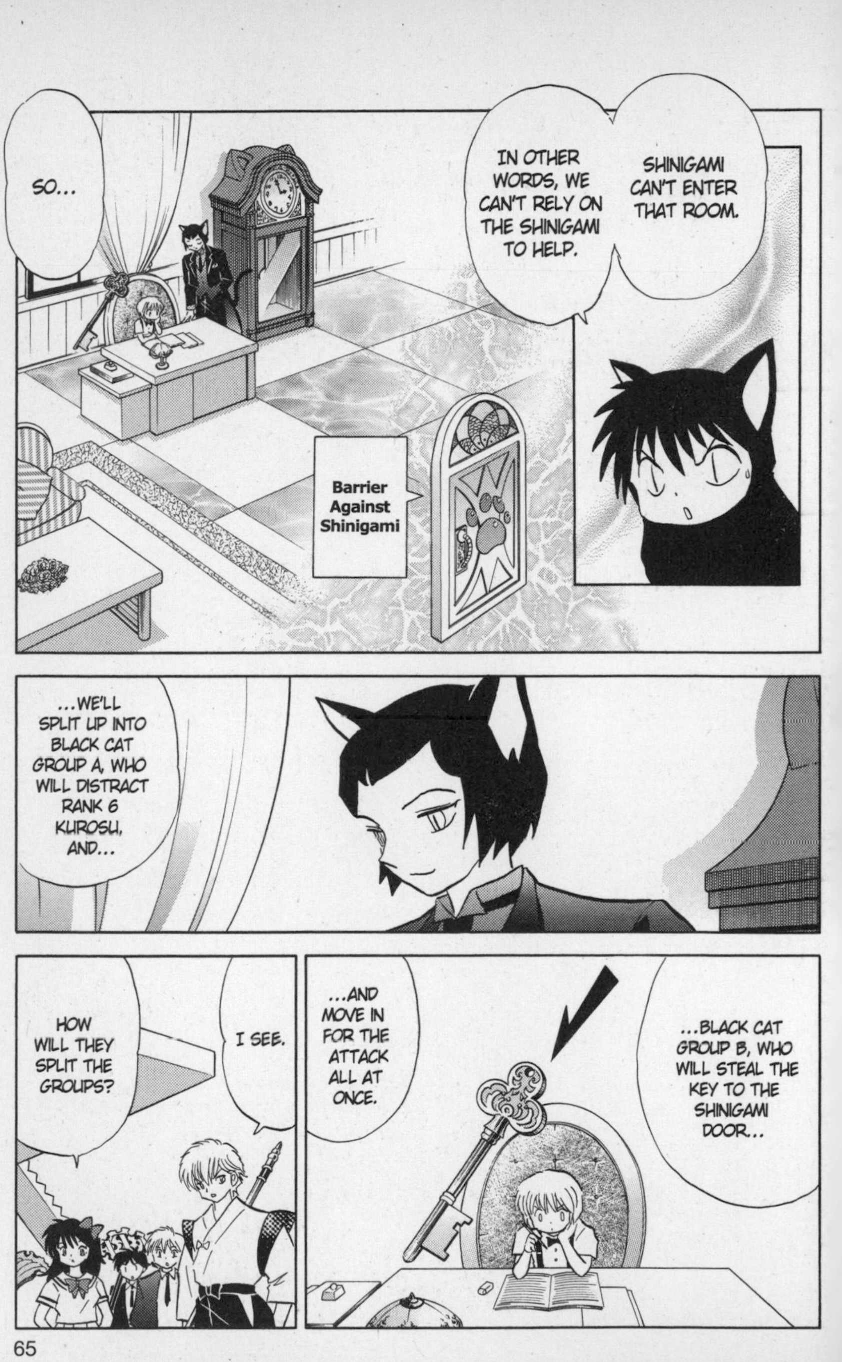
SHINIGAMI CAN'T ENTER THAT ROOM.
IN OTHER WORDS, WE CAN'T RELY ON THE SHINIGAMI TO HELP.
Barrier Against Shinigami
SO...
...WE'LL SPLIT UP INTO BLACK CAT GROUP A, WHO WILL DISTRACT RANK 6 KUROSU, AND...
...BLACK CAT GROUP B, WHO WILL STEAL THE KEY TO THE SHINIGAMI DOOR...
...AND MOVE IN FOR THE ATTACK ALL AT ONCE.
I SEE.
HOW WILL THEY SPLIT THE GROUPS?

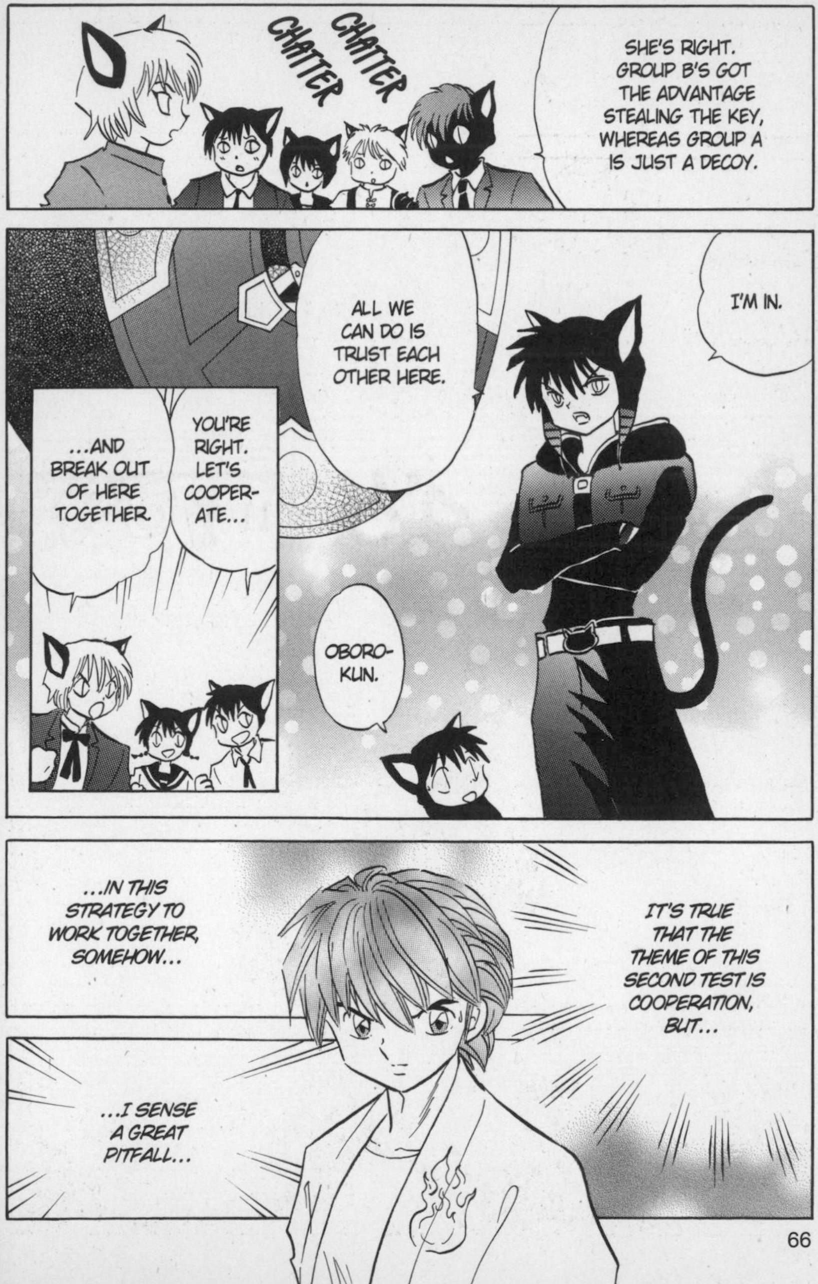
SHE'S RIGHT. GROUP B'S GOT THE ADVANTAGE STEALING THE KEY, WHEREAS GROUP A IS JUST A DECOY.
CHATTER
CHATTER
I'M IN.
ALL WE CAN DO IS TRUST EACH OTHER HERE.
OBORO-KUN.
YOU'RE RIGHT. LET'S COOPER-ATE...
...AND BREAK OUT OF HERE TOGETHER.
IT'S TRUE THAT THE THEME OF THIS SECOND TEST IS COOPERATION, BUT...
...IN THIS STRATEGY TO WORK TOGETHER, SOMEHOW...
...I SENSE A GREAT PITFALL...

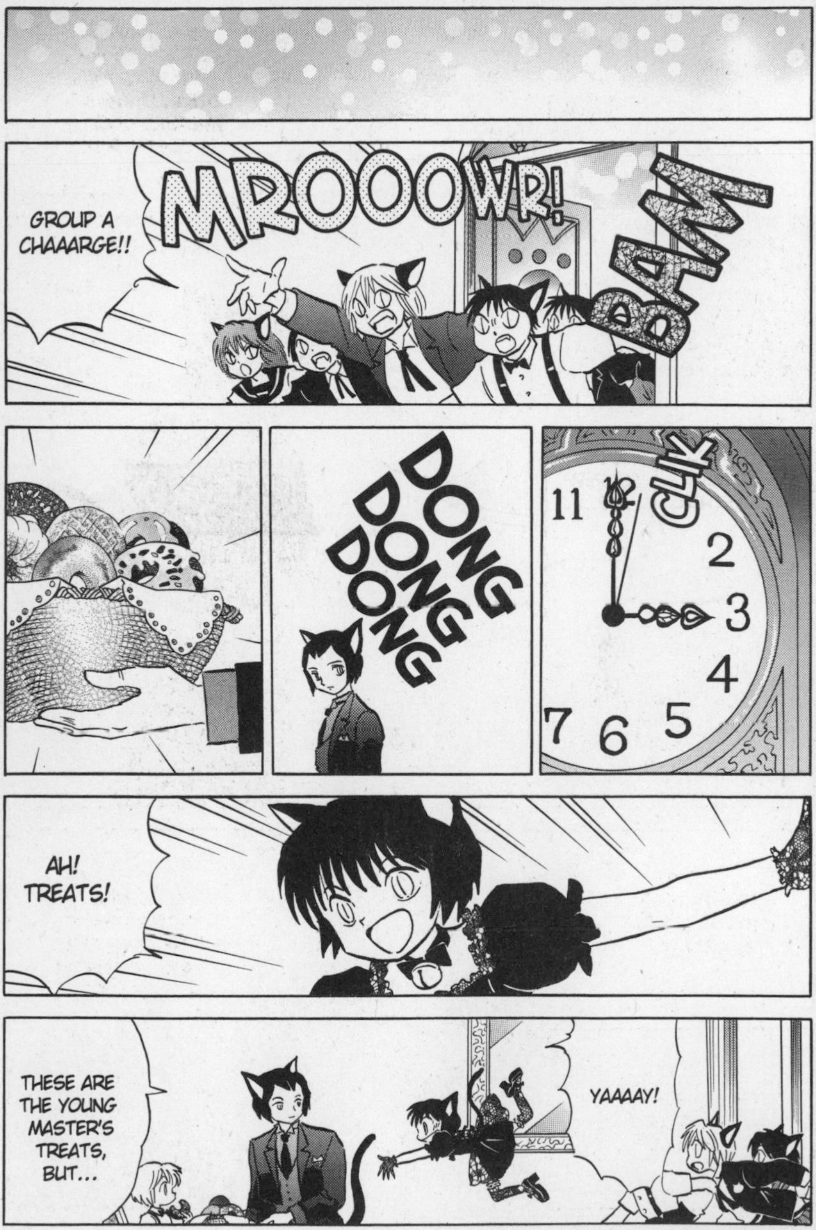
BAM
MROOOWR!
GROUP A CHAAARGE!!
CLIK
DONG DONG DONG
AH! TREATS!
YAAAAY!
THESE ARE THE YOUNG MASTER'S TREATS, BUT...

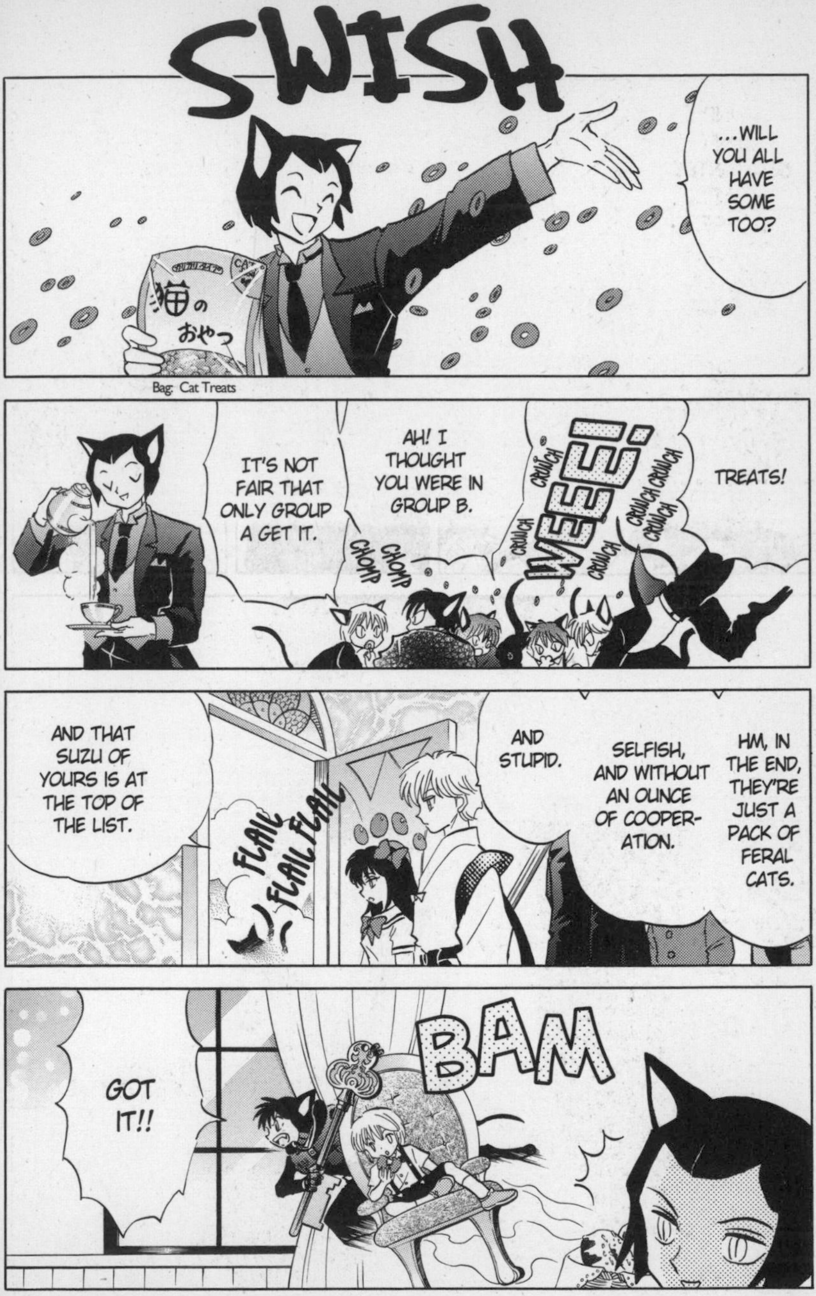
SWISH
...WILL YOU ALL HAVE SOME TOO?
猫のおやつ
TREATS!
CRUNCH CRUNCH CRUNCH CRUNCH
WEEE!
CRUNCH CRUNCH
AH! I THOUGHT YOU WERE IN GROUP B.
CHOMP CHOMP
IT'S NOT FAIR THAT ONLY GROUP A GET IT.
HM, IN THE END, THEY'RE JUST A PACK OF FERAL CATS.
SELFISH, AND WITHOUT AN OUNCE OF COOPER-ATION.
AND STUPID.
FLAIL FLAIL FLAIL
AND THAT SUZU OF YOURS IS AT THE TOP OF THE LIST.
BAM
GOT IT!!
Bag: Cat Treats

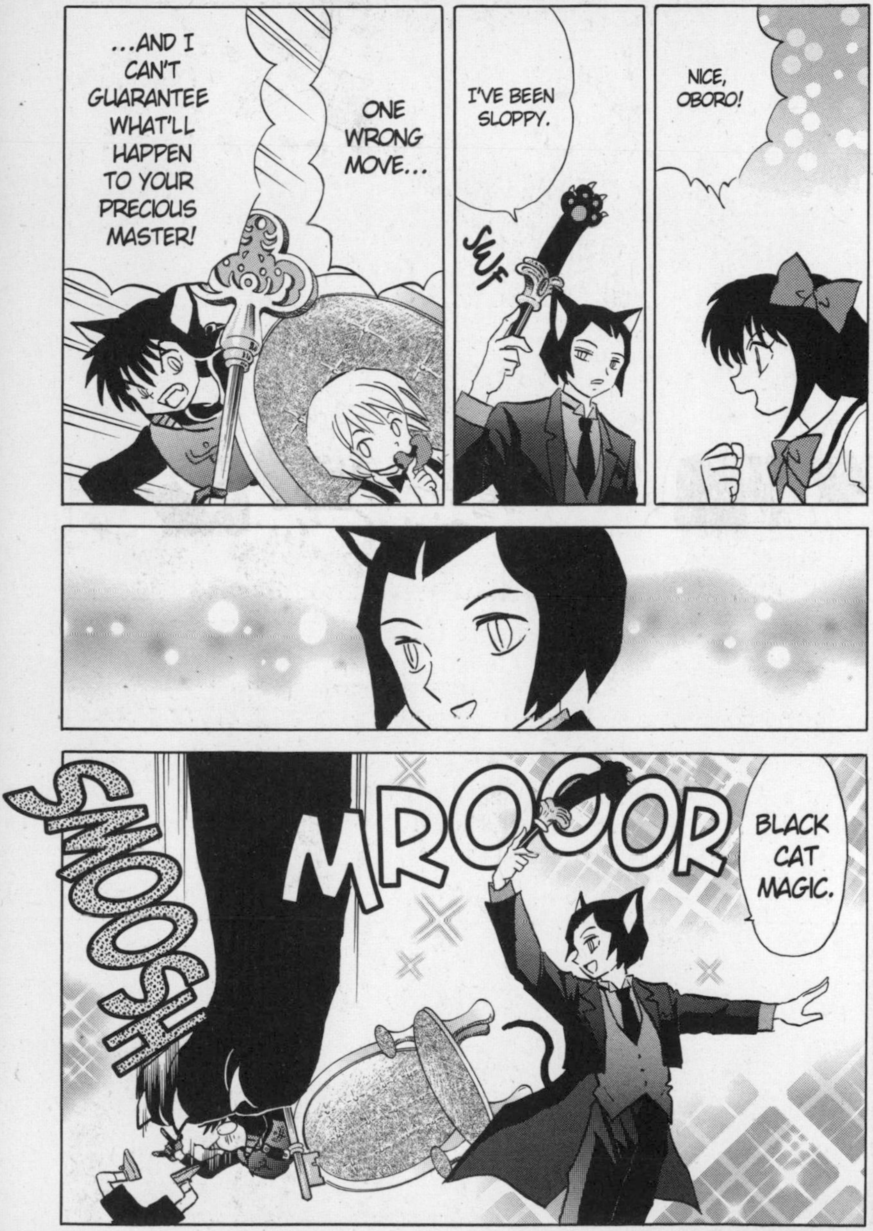
NICE, OBORO!
I'VE BEEN SLOPPY.
SWF
ONE WRONG MOVE...
...AND I CAN'T GUARANTEE WHAT'LL HAPPEN TO YOUR PRECIOUS MASTER!
BLACK CAT MAGIC.
MROOOR
SMOOSH

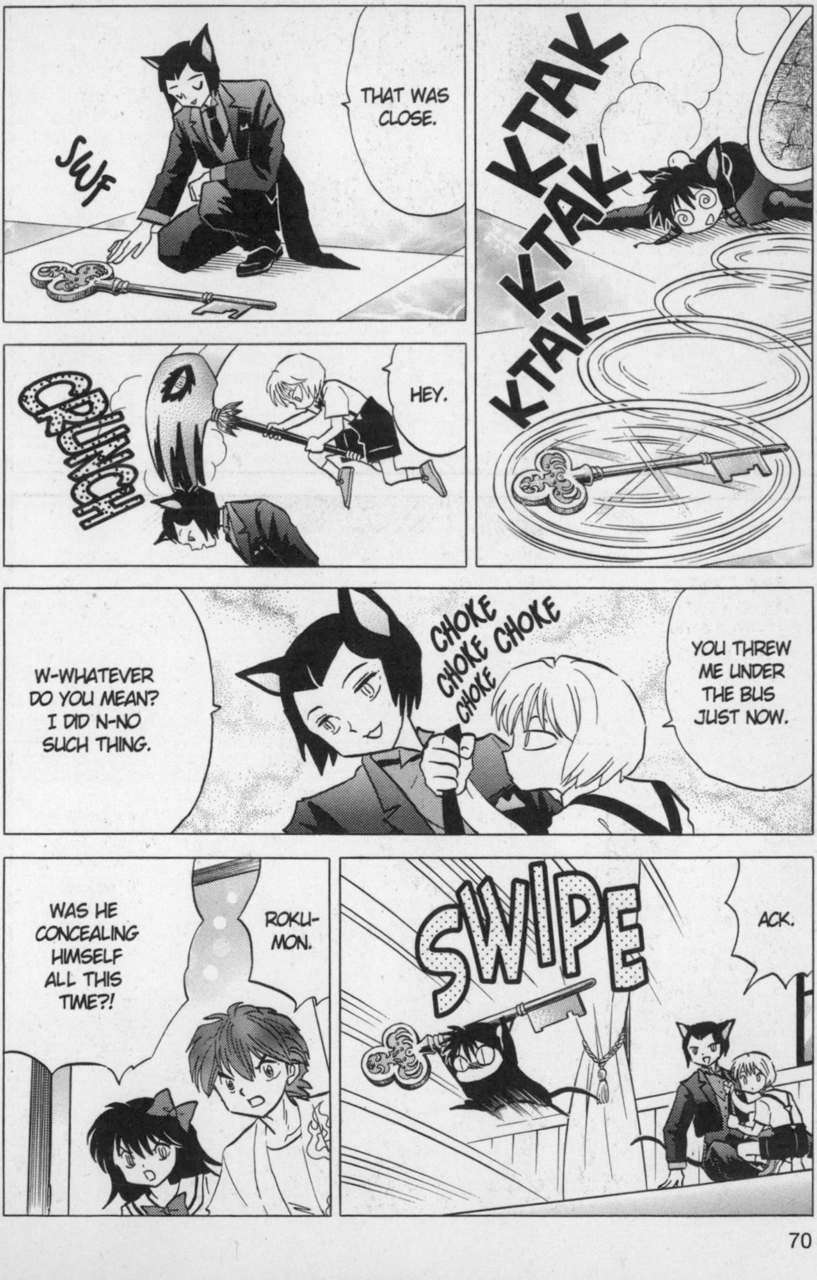
KTAK KTAK KTAK KTAK
THAT WAS CLOSE.
SWF
HEY.
CRUNCH
YOU THREW ME UNDER THE BUS JUST NOW.
CHOKE CHOKE CHOKE CHOKE
W-WHATEVER DO YOU MEAN? I DID N-NO SUCH THING.
ACK.
SWIPE
ROKU-MON.
WAS HE CONCEALING HIMSELF ALL THIS TIME?!

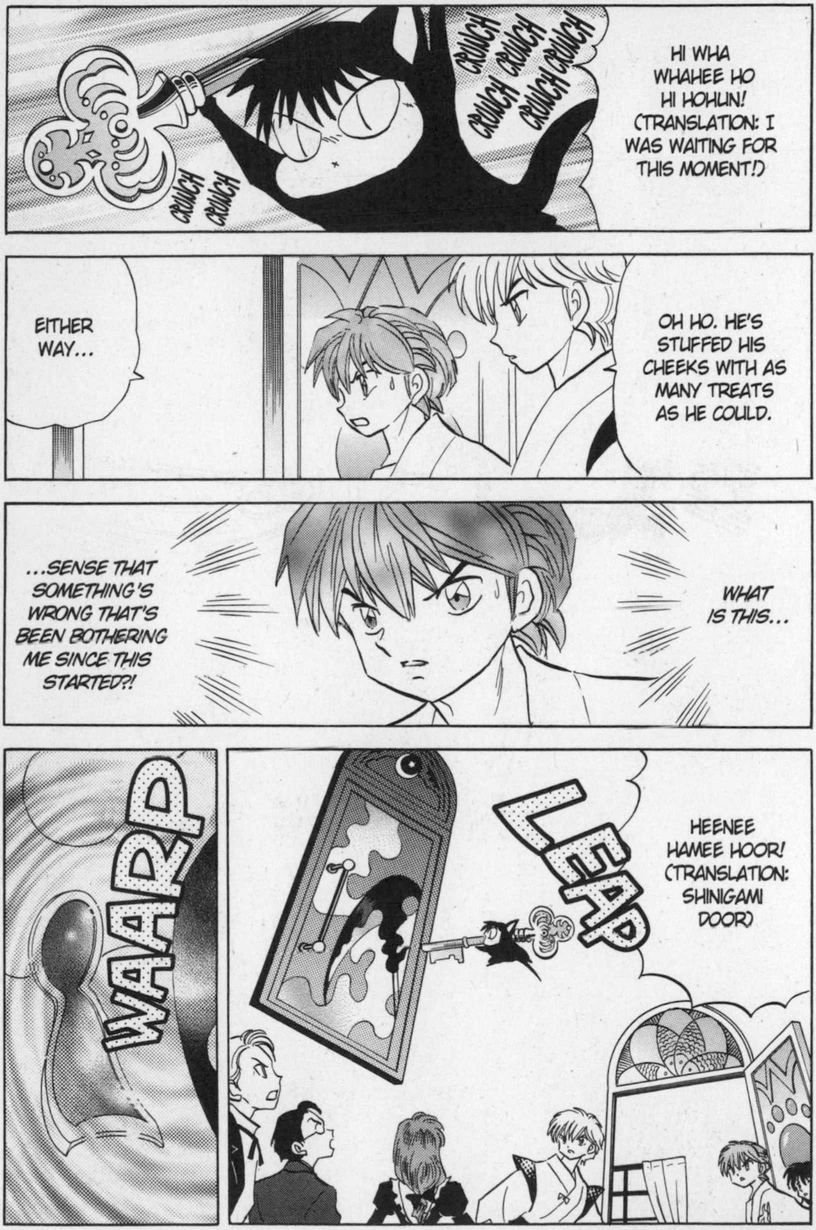
HI WHA WHAHEE HO HI HOHUN! (TRANSLATION: I WAS WAITING FOR THIS MOMENT!)
CRUNCH CRUNCH CRUNCH CRUNCH CRUNCH CRUNCH
CRUNCH CRUNCH
OH HO. HE'S STUFFED HIS CHEEKS WITH AS MANY TREATS AS HE COULD.
EITHER WAY...
WHAT IS THIS...
...SENSE THAT SOMETHING'S WRONG THAT'S BEEN BOTHERING ME SINCE THIS STARTED?!
HEENEE HAMEE HOOR! (TRANSLATION: SHINIGAMI DOOR)
LEAP
WAARP

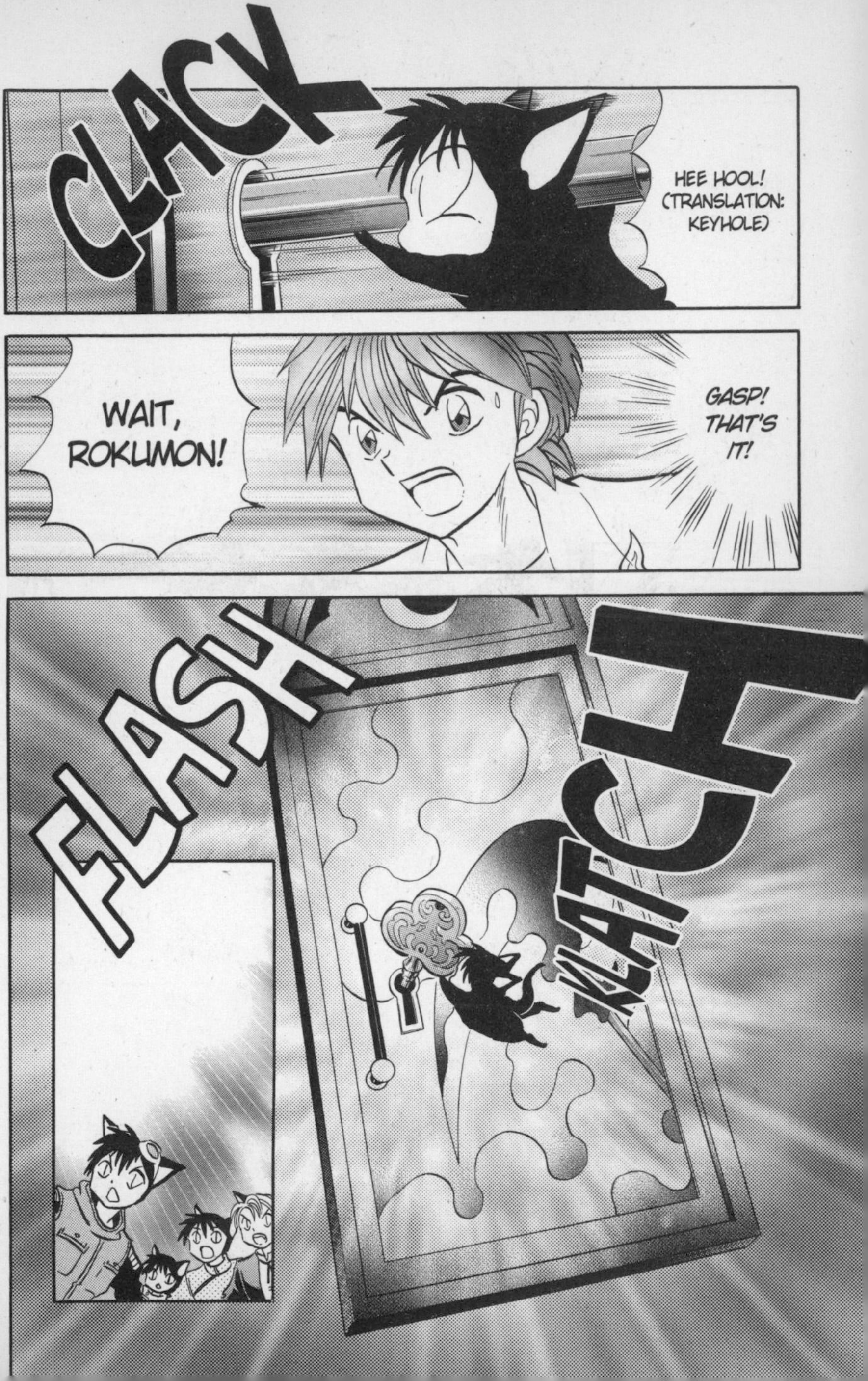
CLACK
HEE HOOL! (TRANSLATION: KEYHOLE)
GASP! THAT'S IT!
WAIT, ROKUMON!
KLATCH
FLASH

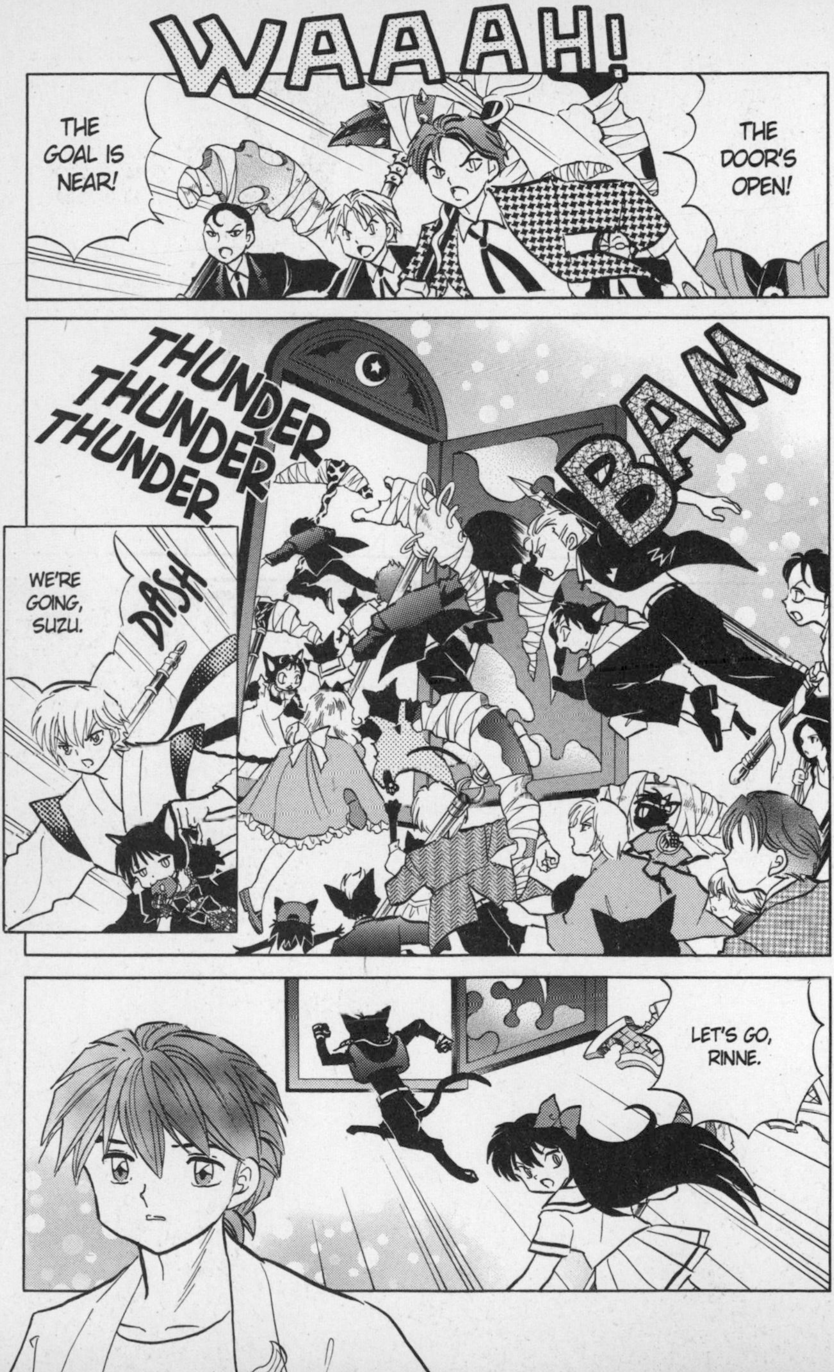
WAAAH!
THE DOOR'S OPEN!
THE GOAL IS NEAR!
BAM
THUNDER THUNDER THUNDER
WE'RE GOING, SUZU.
DASH
LET'S GO, RINNE.

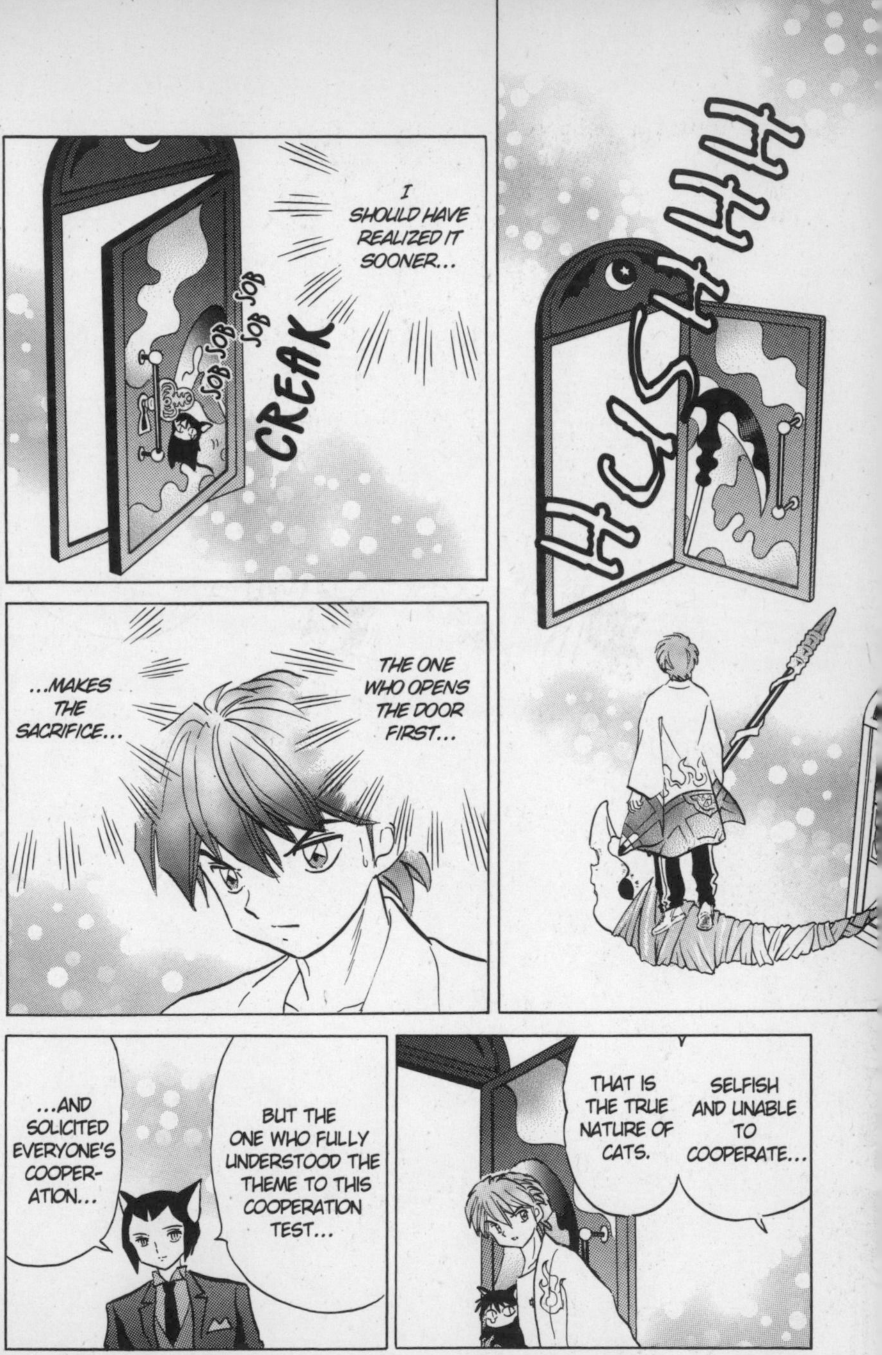
I SHOULD HAVE REALIZED IT SOONER...
CREAK
SOB SOB SOB SOB
THE ONE WHO OPENS THE DOOR FIRST...
...MAKES THE SACRIFICE...
SELFISH AND UNABLE TO COOPERATE...
THAT IS THE TRUE NATURE OF CATS.
BUT THE ONE WHO FULLY UNDERSTOOD THE THEME TO THIS COOPERATION TEST...
...AND SOLICITED EVERYONE'S COOPER-ATION...

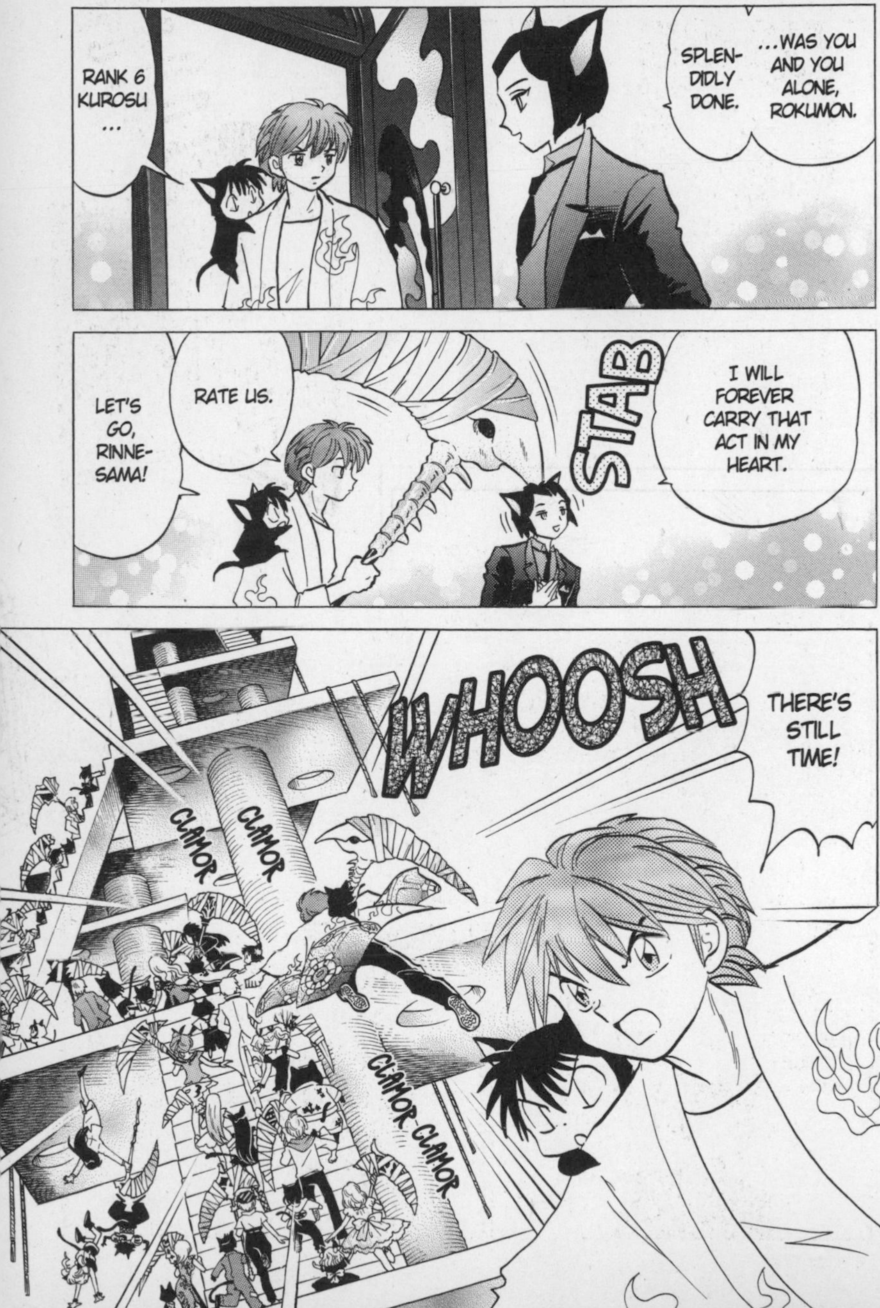
SPLEN-DIDLY DONE. ...WAS YOU AND YOU ALONE, ROKUMON.
RANK 6 KUROSU ...
I WILL FOREVER CARRY THAT ACT IN MY HEART.
STAB
RATE US.
LET'S GO, RINNE-SAMA!
THERE'S STILL TIME!
WHOOSH
CLAMOR
CLAMOR
CLAMOR-CLAMOR

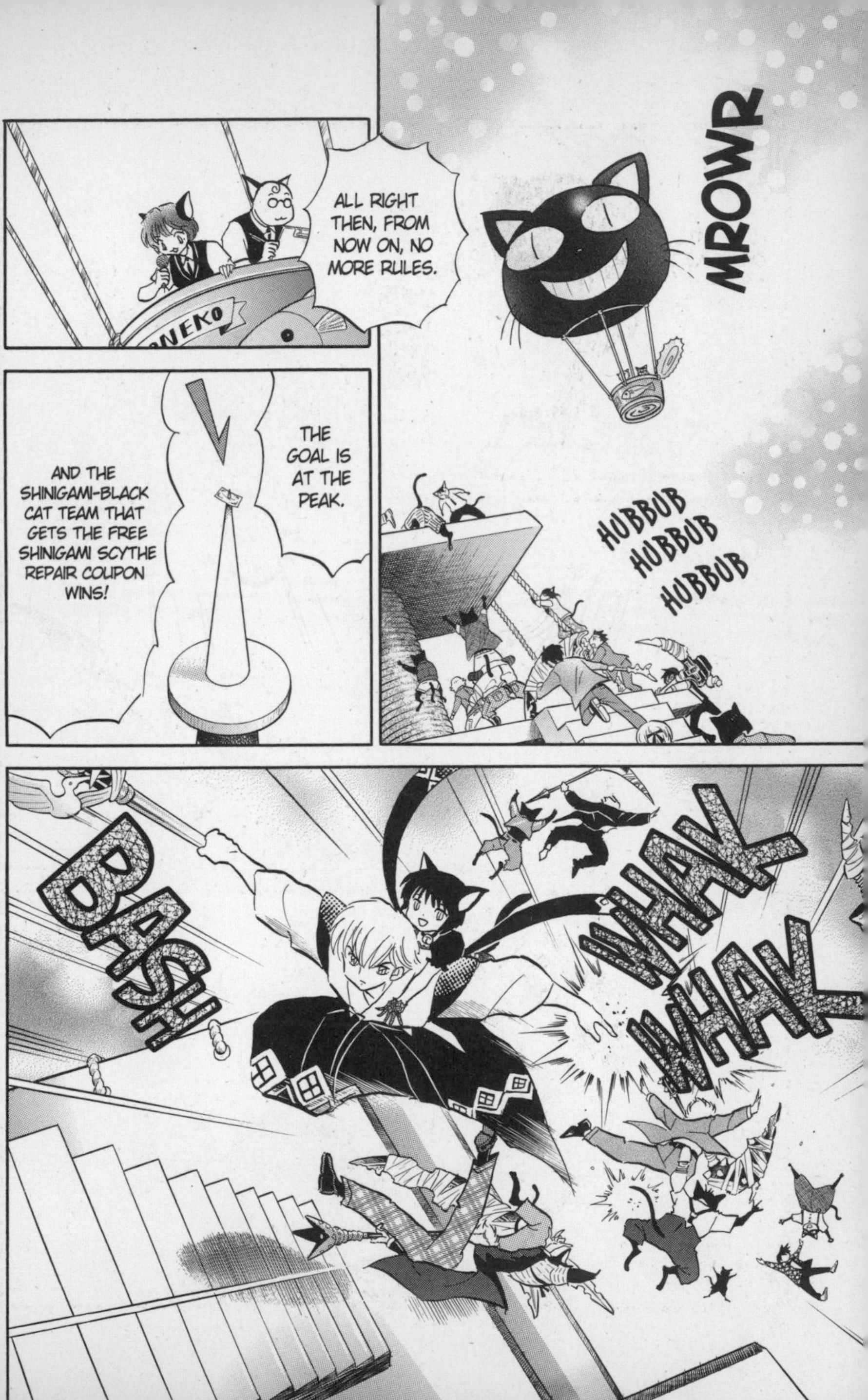
MROWR
HUBBUB HUBBUB HUBBUB
ALL RIGHT THEN, FROM NOW ON, NO MORE RULES.
NEKO
THE GOAL IS AT THE PEAK.
AND THE SHINIGAMI-BLACK CAT TEAM THAT GETS THE FREE SHINIGAMI SCYTHE REPAIR COUPON WINS!
WHAK WHAK
BASH

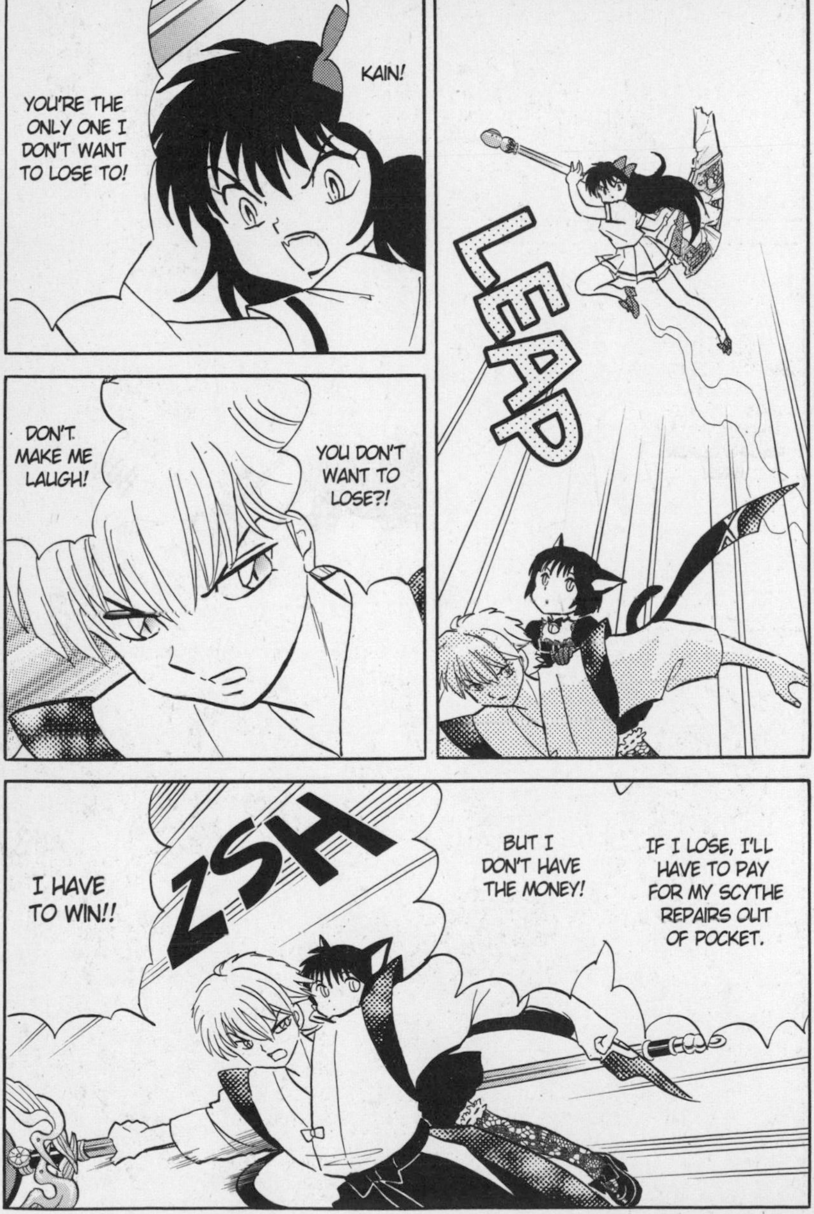
LEAP
KAIN!
YOU'RE THE ONLY ONE I DON'T WANT TO LOSE TO!
YOU DON'T WANT TO LOSE?!
DON'T. MAKE ME LAUGH!
IF I LOSE, I'LL HAVE TO PAY FOR MY SCYTHE REPAIRS OUT OF POCKET.
BUT I DON'T HAVE THE MONEY!
ZSH
I HAVE TO WIN!!

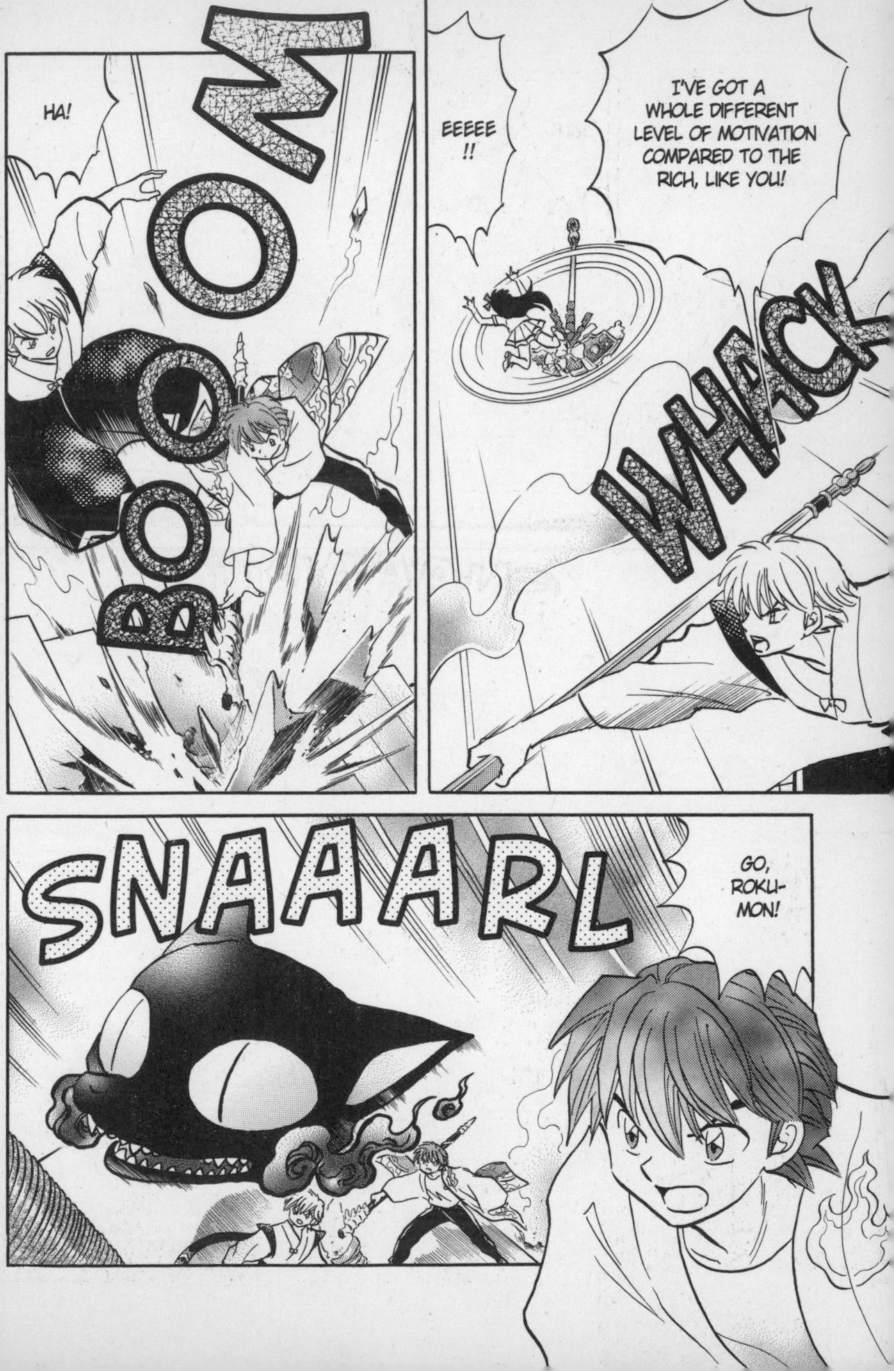
I'VE GOT A WHOLE DIFFERENT LEVEL OF MOTIVATION COMPARED TO THE RICH, LIKE YOU!
EEEEE !!
WHACK
BOOM
HA!
GO, ROKU-MON!
SNAAARL

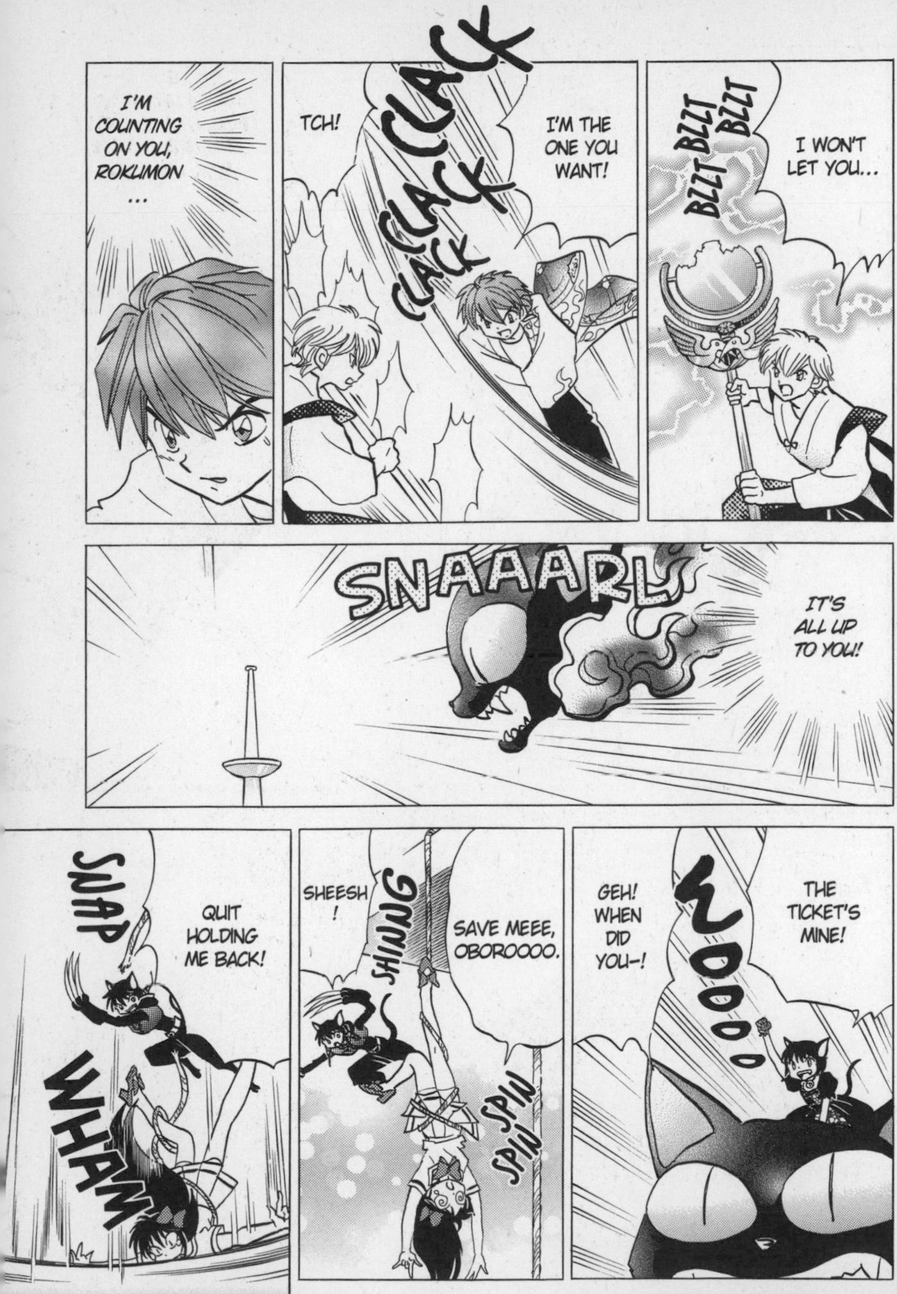
I WON'T LET YOU...
BZZT BZZT BZZT BZZT
I'M THE ONE YOU WANT!
CLACK CLACK CLACK CLACK
TCH!
I'M COUNTING ON YOU, ROKUMON ...
IT'S ALL UP TO YOU!
SNAAARL
THE TICKET'S MINE!
WOOOOO
GEH! WHEN DID YOU-!
SAVE MEEE, OBOROOOO.
SHIIING
SHEESH!
SPIN SPIN
QUIT HOLDING ME BACK!
SNAP
WHAM

BOOM
BOOM
THAT HURT, YOU IDIOT!
THE TICKET!
IT'S MIIIINE!
KONNNG
LOOOOM
RIP
VICTORY IN THE COOPERATION TEST GOES TO THE AGEHA-OBORO TEAM!
SHRED
SHRED
SHRED
HERE'S WHAT I THINK OF THIS TICKET!
I DON'T NEED IT ANYWAY!
AND NOW FOR THE FINAL TEST!

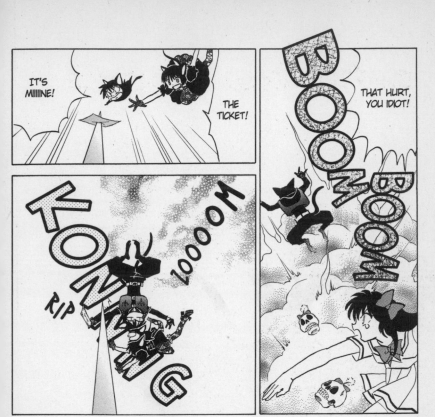

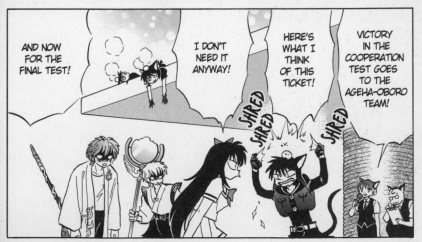

CHAPTER 113: BATTLE ROYALE

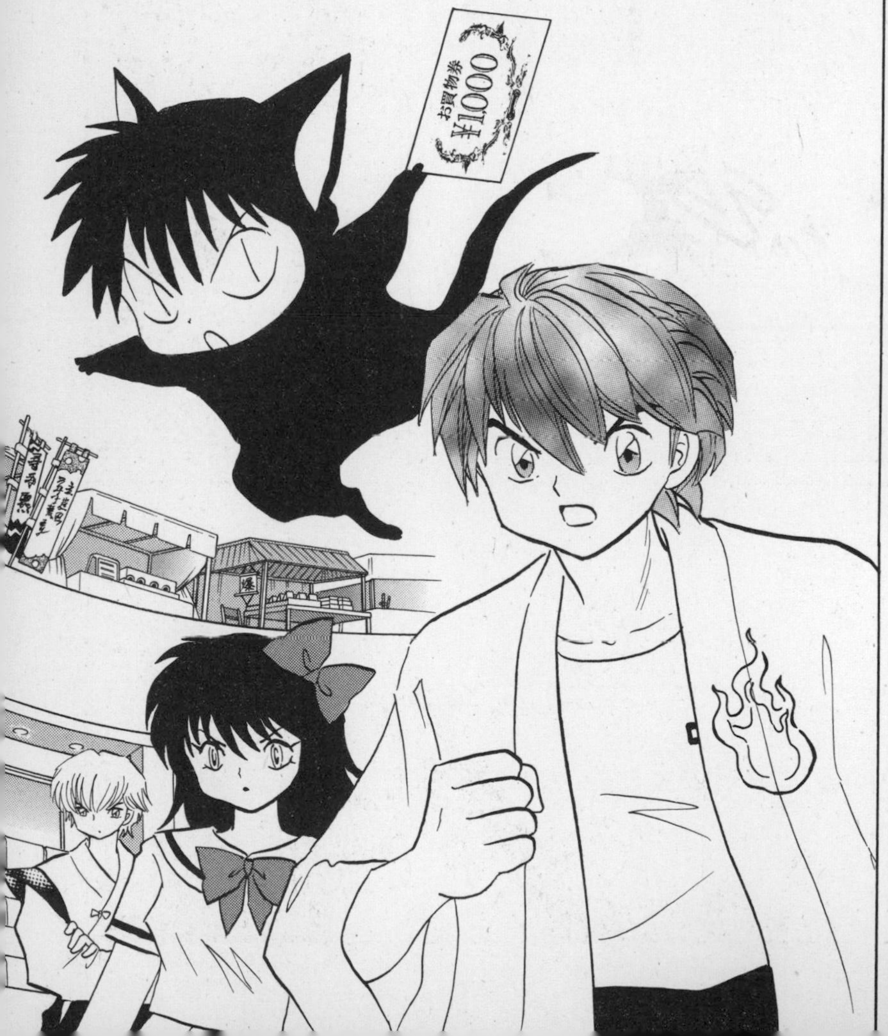
お買物券
¥1000

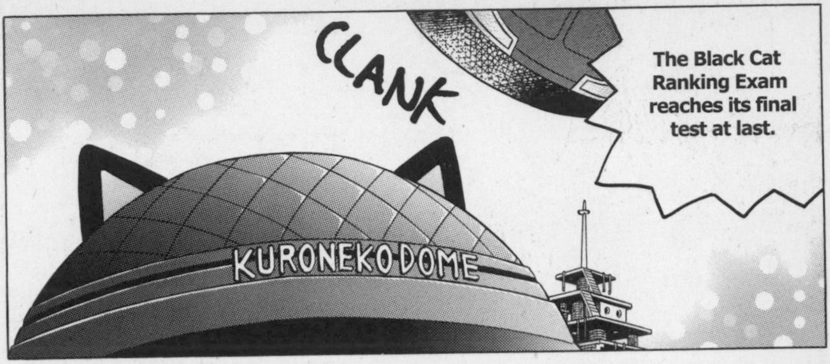
The Black Cat Ranking Exam reaches its final test at last.
CLANK
KURONEKODOME

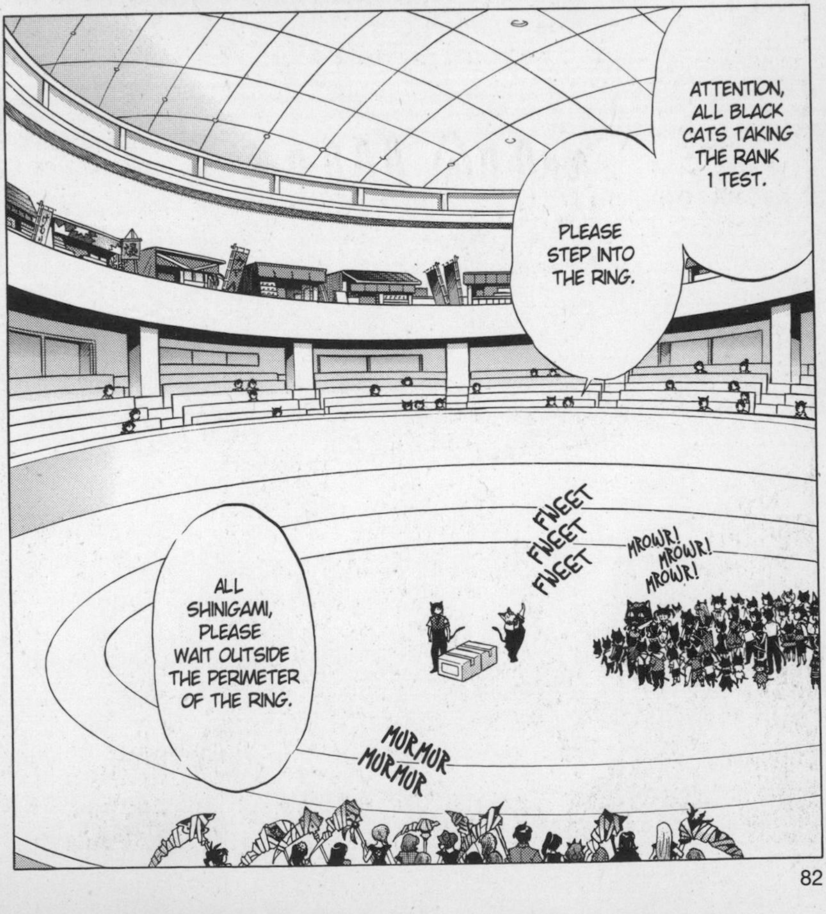
ATTENTION, ALL BLACK CATS TAKING THE RANK 1 TEST.
PLEASE STEP INTO THE RING.
MROWR! MROWR! MROWR!
FWEET FWEET FWEET
ALL SHINIGAMI, PLEASE WAIT OUTSIDE THE PERIMETER OF THE RING.
MURMUR MURMUR

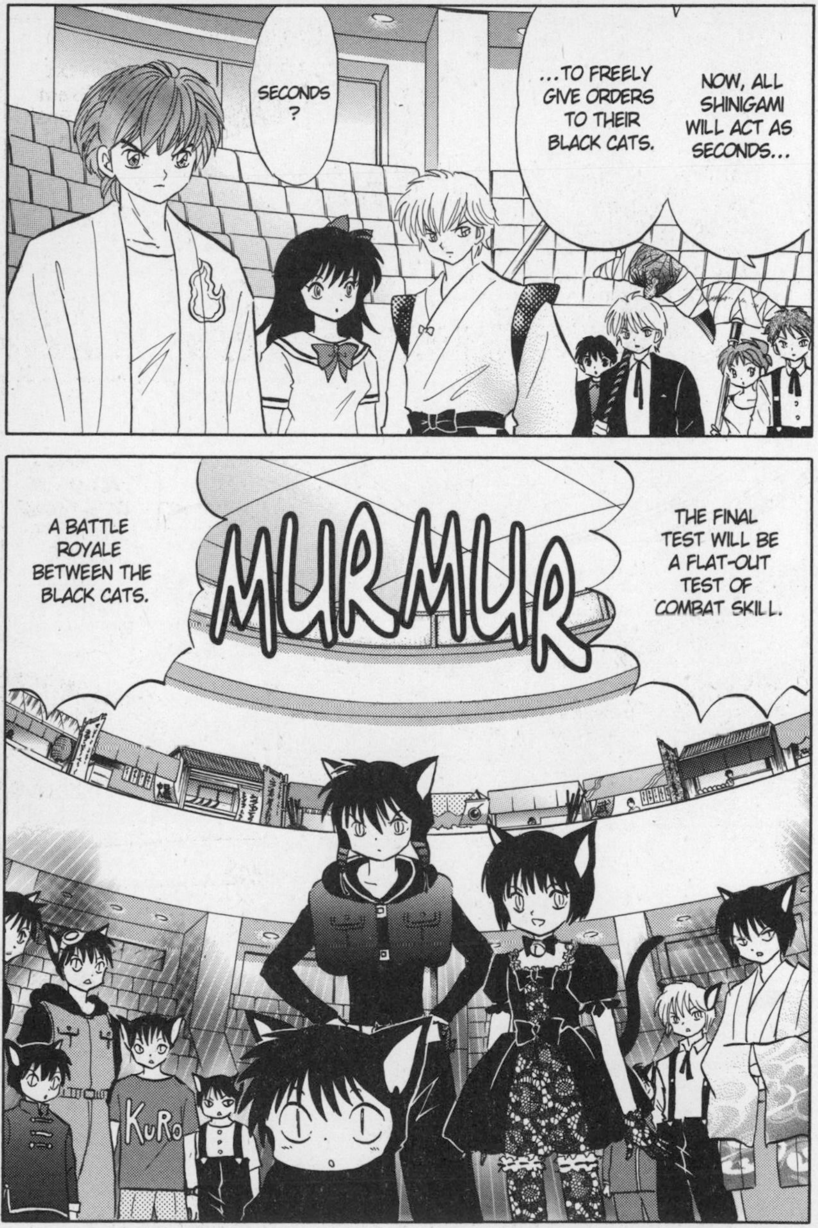
NOW, ALL SHINIGAMI WILL ACT AS SECONDS...
...TO FREELY GIVE ORDERS TO THEIR BLACK CATS.
SECONDS?
THE FINAL TEST WILL BE A FLAT-OUT TEST OF COMBAT SKILL.
MURMUR
A BATTLE ROYALE BETWEEN THE BLACK CATS.
KuRo

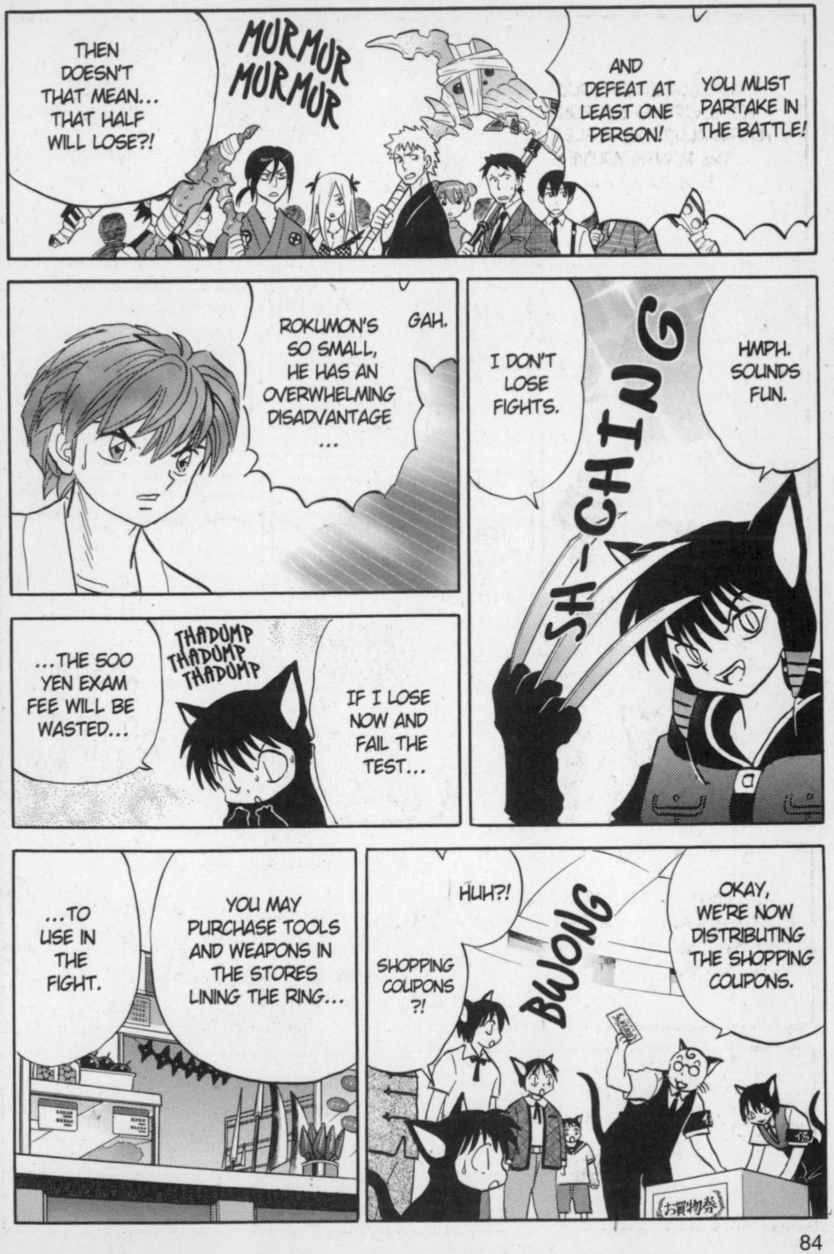
YOU MUST PARTAKE IN THE BATTLE!
AND DEFEAT AT LEAST ONE PERSON!
MURMUR MURMUR
THEN DOESN'T THAT MEAN... THAT HALF WILL LOSE?!
HMPH. SOUNDS FUN.
SH-CHING
I DON'T LOSE FIGHTS.
GAH.
ROKUMON'S SO SMALL, HE HAS AN OVERWHELMING DISADVANTAGE ...
IF I LOSE NOW AND FAIL THE TEST...
THADUMP THADUMP THADUMP
...THE 500 YEN EXAM FEE WILL BE WASTED...
OKAY, WE'RE NOW DISTRIBUTING THE SHOPPING COUPONS.
BWONG
HUH?!
SHOPPING COUPONS ?!
お買物券
YOU MAY PURCHASE TOOLS AND WEAPONS IN THE STORES LINING THE RING...
...TO USE IN THE FIGHT.

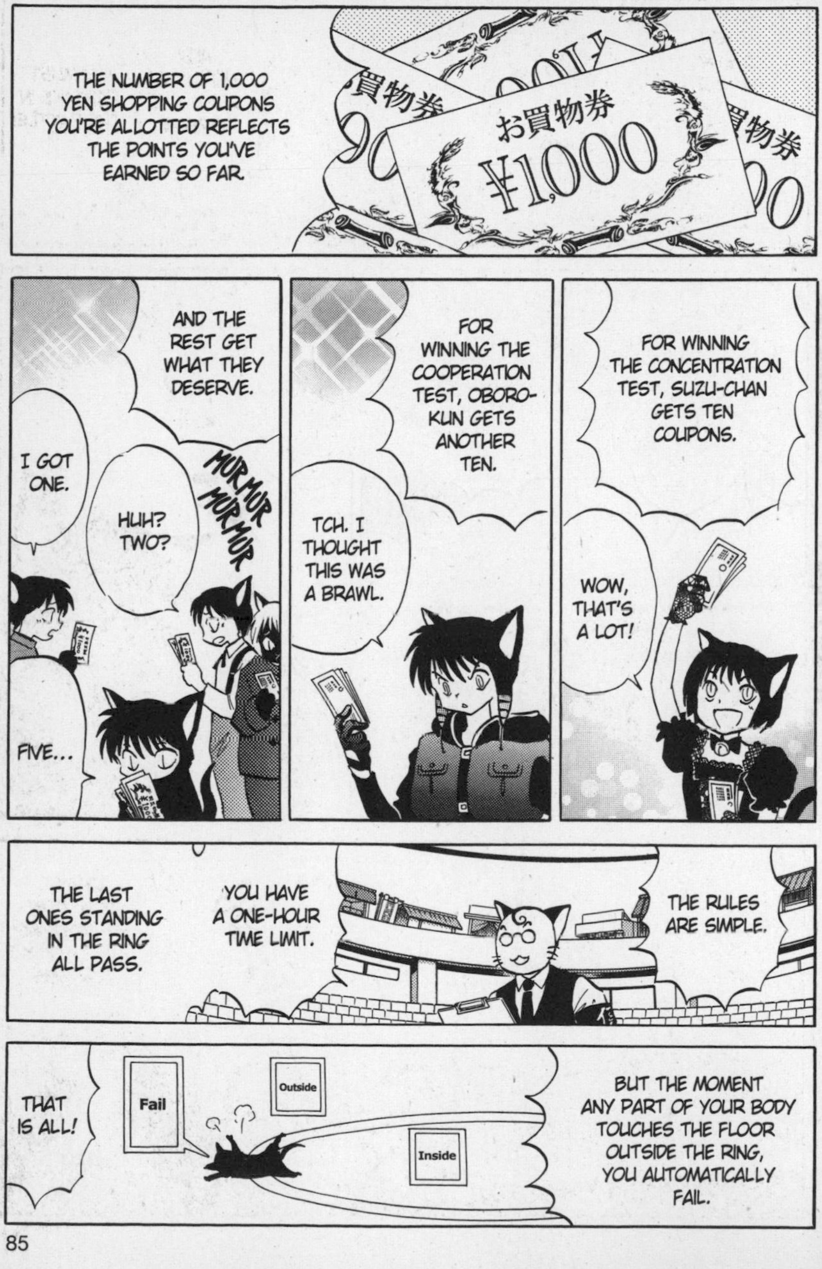
THE NUMBER OF 1,000 YEN SHOPPING COUPONS YOU'RE ALLOTTED REFLECTS THE POINTS YOU'VE EARNED SO FAR.
お買物券
¥1,000
FOR WINNING THE CONCENTRATION TEST, SUZU-CHAN GETS TEN COUPONS.
WOW, THAT'S A LOT!
FOR WINNING THE COOPERATION TEST, OBORO-KUN GETS ANOTHER TEN.
TCH. I THOUGHT THIS WAS A BRAWL.
AND THE REST GET WHAT THEY DESERVE.
MUR MUR MUR MUR
HUH? TWO?
I GOT ONE.
FIVE...
THE RULES ARE SIMPLE.
YOU HAVE A ONE-HOUR TIME LIMIT.
THE LAST ONES STANDING IN THE RING ALL PASS.
BUT THE MOMENT ANY PART OF YOUR BODY TOUCHES THE FLOOR OUTSIDE THE RING, YOU AUTOMATICALLY FAIL.
Inside
Outside
Fail
THAT IS ALL!

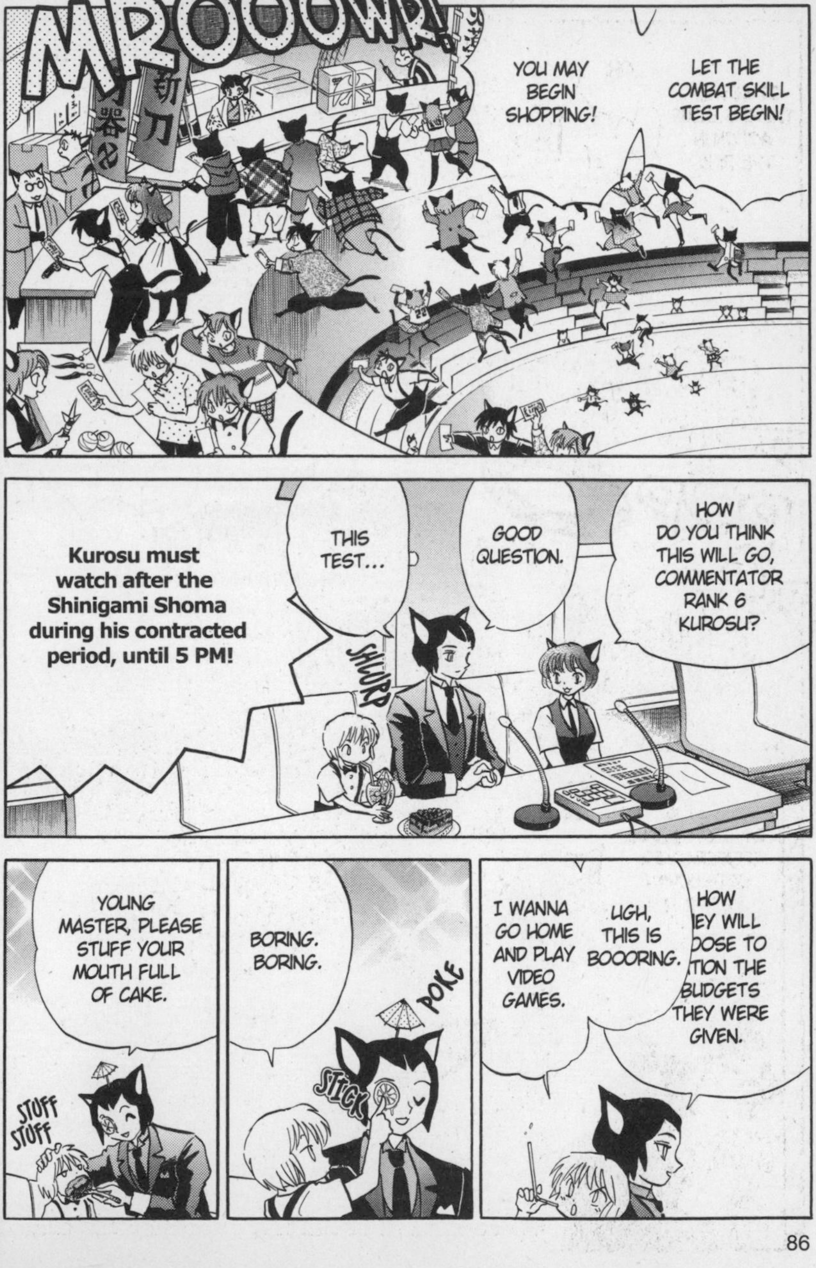

LET THE COMBAT SKILL TEST BEGIN!
YOU MAY BEGIN SHOPPING!
MROOOWR!
HOW DO YOU THINK THIS WILL GO, COMMENTATOR RANK 6 KUROSU?
GOOD QUESTION.
THIS TEST…
SHLURP
Kurosu must watch after the Shinigami Shoma during his contracted period, until 5 PM!
HOW EY WILL OOSE TO TION THE BUDGETS THEY WERE GIVEN.
UGH, THIS IS BOOORING.
I WANNA GO HOME AND PLAY VIDEO GAMES.
BORING. BORING.
POKE
STICK
YOUNG MASTER, PLEASE STUFF YOUR MOUTH FULL OF CAKE.
STUFF STUFF

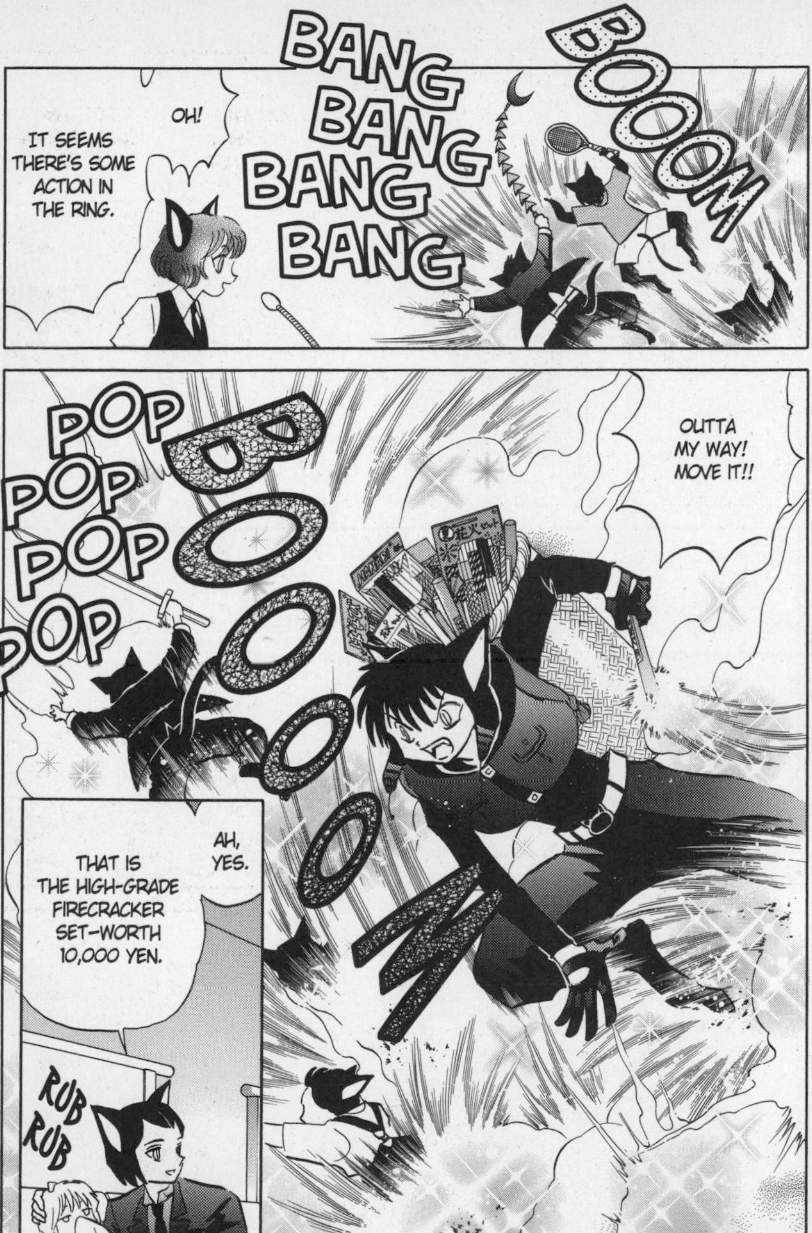
BOOOOM
BANG BANG BANG BANG
OH!
IT SEEMS THERE'S SOME ACTION IN THE RING.
OUTTA MY WAY! MOVE IT!!
BOOOOOM
POP POP POP POP
AH, YES.
THAT IS THE HIGH-GRADE FIRECRACKER SET—WORTH 10,000 YEN.
RUB RUB

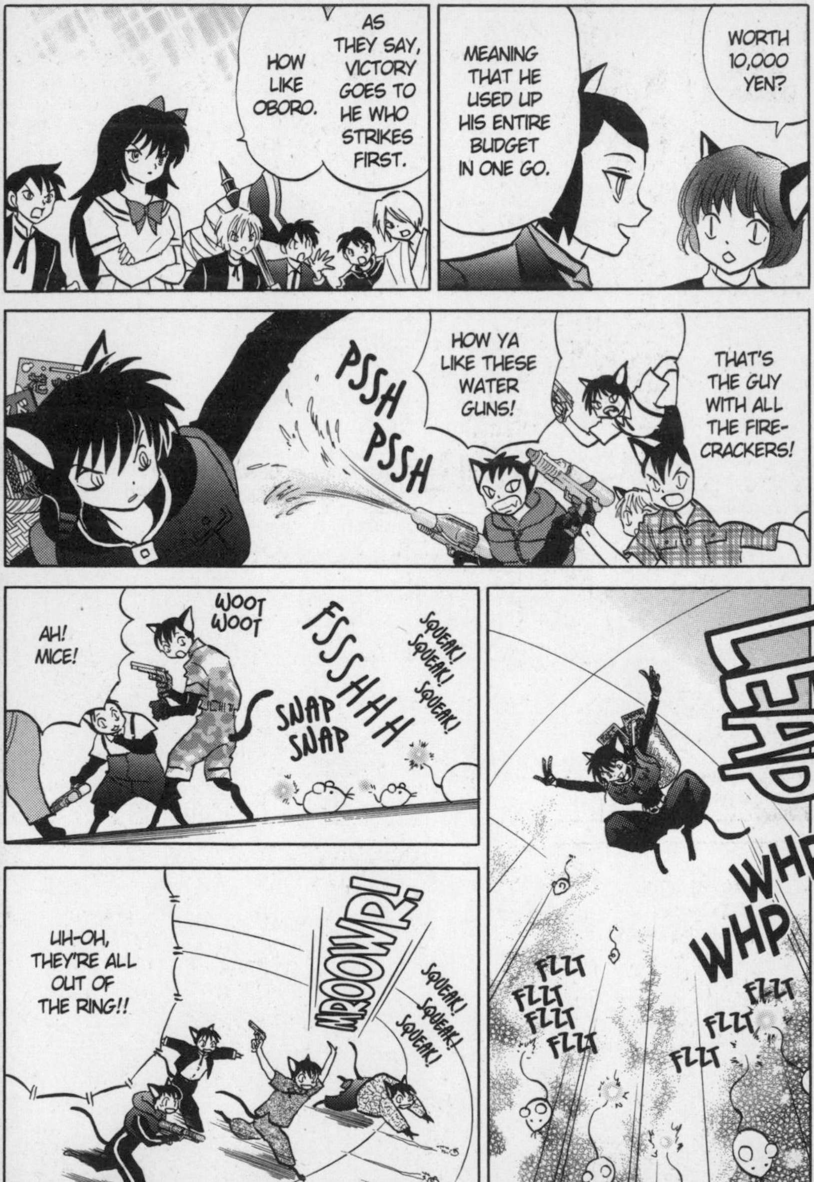
WORTH 10,000 YEN?
MEANING THAT HE USED UP HIS ENTIRE BUDGET IN ONE GO.
AS THEY SAY, VICTORY GOES TO HE WHO STRIKES FIRST.
HOW LIKE OBORO.
THAT'S THE GUY WITH ALL THE FIRE-CRACKERS!
HOW YA LIKE THESE WATER GUNS!
PSSH PSSH
LEAP
WHP WHP
FZZT FZZT
FZZT FZZT FZZT FZZT
SQUEAK! SQUEAK! SQUEAK!
FSSSHHH
WOOT WOOT
SNAP SNAP
AH! MICE!
SQUEAK! SQUEAK! SQUEAK!
MROOWR!
UH-OH, THEY'RE ALL OUT OF THE RING!!

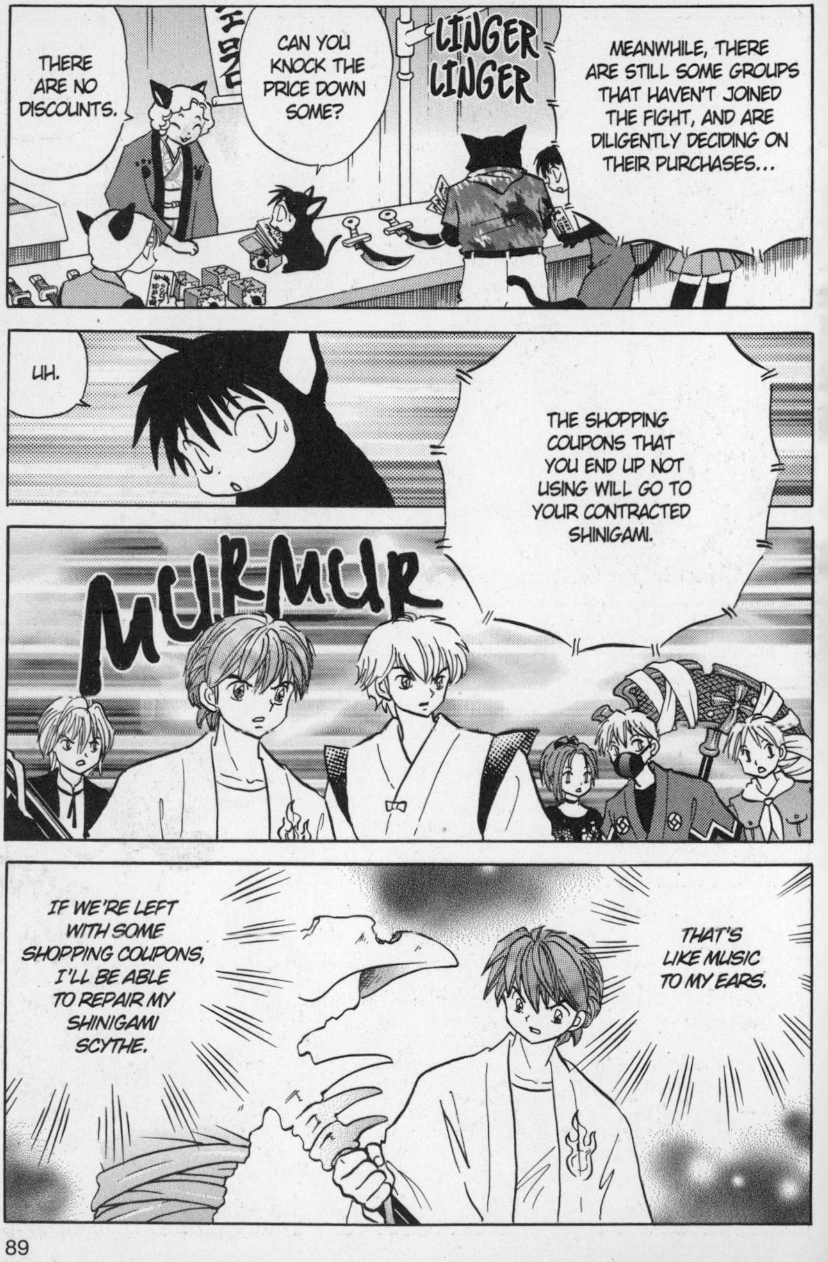
MEANWHILE, THERE ARE STILL SOME GROUPS THAT HAVEN'T JOINED THE FIGHT, AND ARE DILIGENTLY DECIDING ON THEIR PURCHASES...
LINGER LINGER
CAN YOU KNOCK THE PRICE DOWN SOME?
THERE ARE NO DISCOUNTS.
THE SHOPPING COUPONS THAT YOU END UP NOT USING WILL GO TO YOUR CONTRACTED SHINIGAMI.
UH.
MURMUR
IF WE'RE LEFT WITH SOME SHOPPING COUPONS, I'LL BE ABLE TO REPAIR MY SHINIGAMI SCYTHE.
THAT'S LIKE MUSIC TO MY EARS.

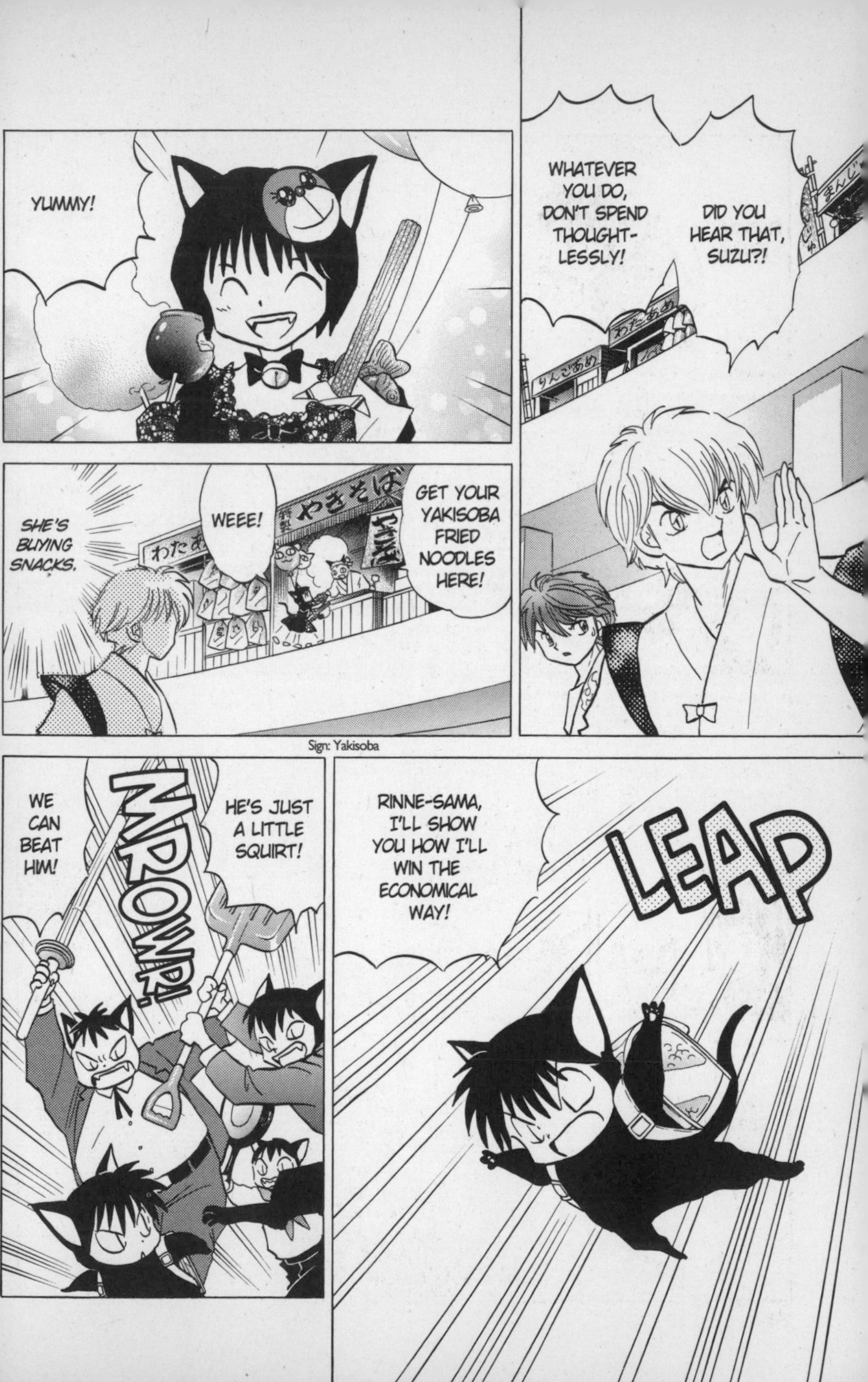
DID YOU HEAR THAT, SUZU?!
WHATEVER YOU DO, DON'T SPEND THOUGHT-LESSLY!
YUMMY!
GET YOUR YAKISOBA FRIED NOODLES HERE!
WEEE!
SHE'S BUYING SNACKS.
RINNE-SAMA, I'LL SHOW YOU HOW I'LL WIN THE ECONOMICAL WAY!
LEAP
HE'S JUST A LITTLE SQUIRT!
MROWR!
WE CAN BEAT HIM!

Sign: Yakisoba

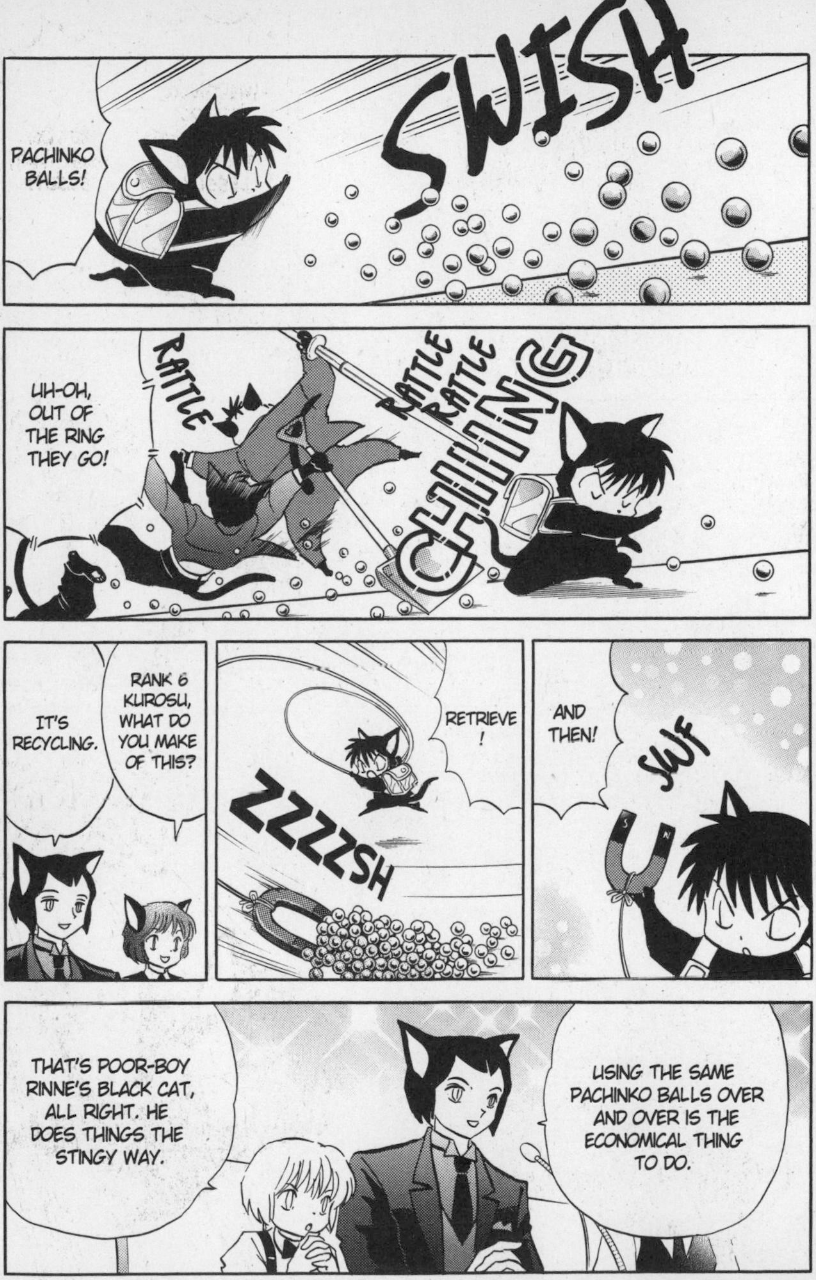
SWISH
PACHINKO BALLS!
RATTLE RATTLE
CHIIING
RATTLE
UH-OH, OUT OF THE RING THEY GO!
AND THEN!
SWF
RETRIEVE!
ZZZZZSH
RANK 6 KUROSU, WHAT DO YOU MAKE OF THIS?
IT'S RECYCLING.
USING THE SAME PACHINKO BALLS OVER AND OVER IS THE ECONOMICAL THING TO DO.
THAT'S POOR-BOY RINNE'S BLACK CAT, ALL RIGHT. HE DOES THINGS THE STINGY WAY.

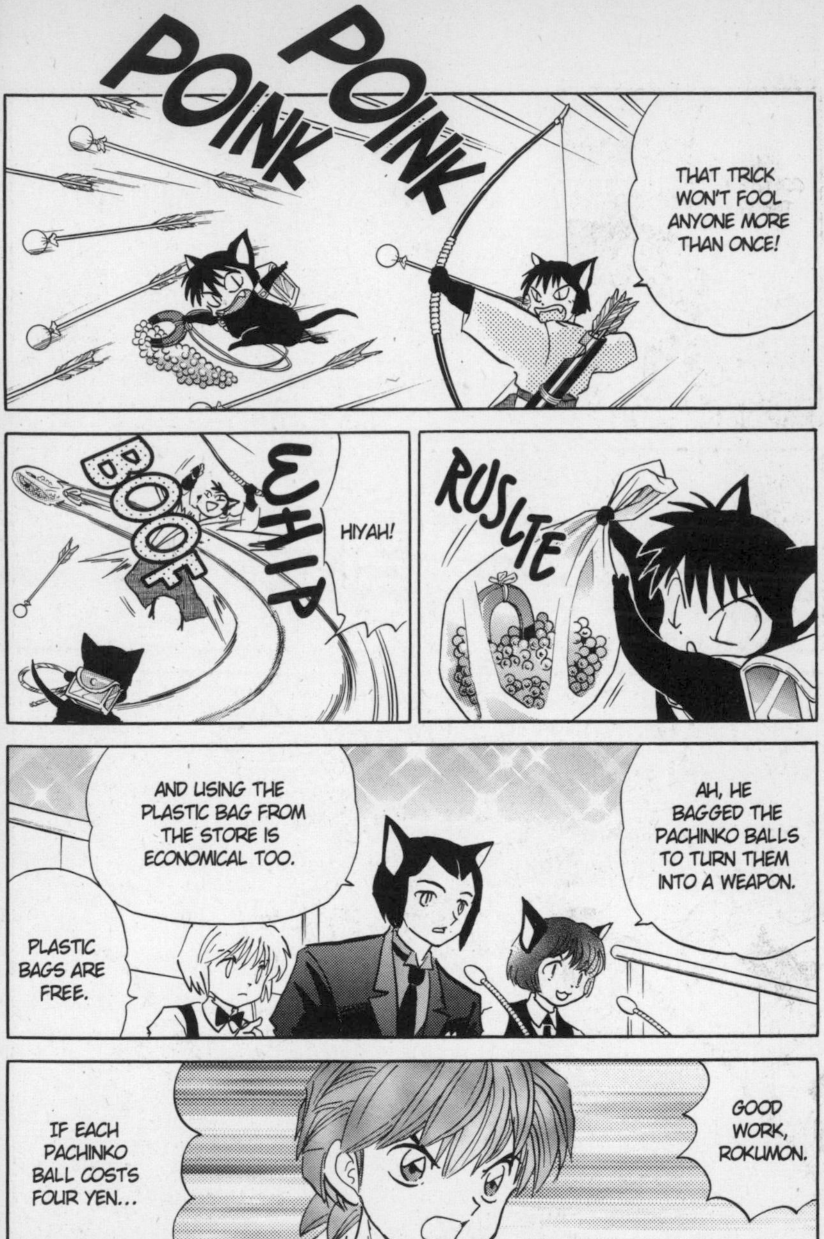
THAT TRICK WON'T FOOL ANYONE MORE THAN ONCE!
POINK
POINK
RUSLTE
HIYAH!
WHIP
BOOF
AH, HE BAGGED THE PACHINKO BALLS TO TURN THEM INTO A WEAPON.
AND USING THE PLASTIC BAG FROM THE STORE IS ECONOMICAL TOO.
PLASTIC BAGS ARE FREE.
GOOD WORK, ROKUMON.
IF EACH PACHINKO BALL COSTS FOUR YEN...

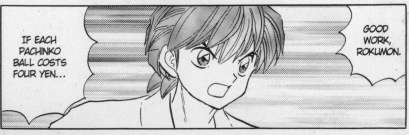

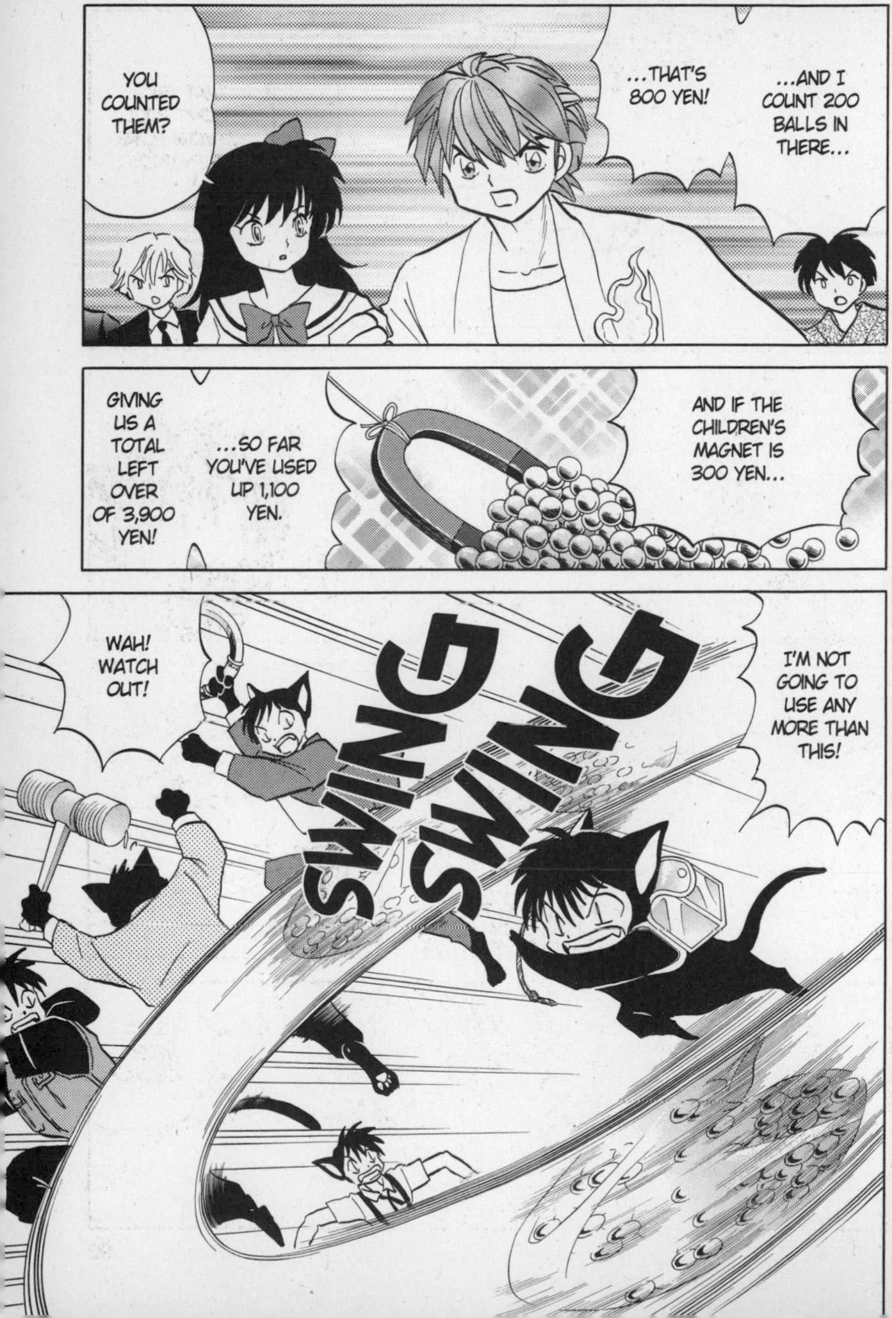
...AND I COUNT 200 BALLS IN THERE...
...THAT'S 800 YEN!
YOU COUNTED THEM?
AND IF THE CHILDREN'S MAGNET IS 300 YEN...
...SO FAR YOU'VE USED UP 1,100 YEN.
GIVING US A TOTAL LEFT OVER OF 3,900 YEN!
I'M NOT GOING TO USE ANY MORE THAN THIS!
SWING
SWING
WAH! WATCH OUT!

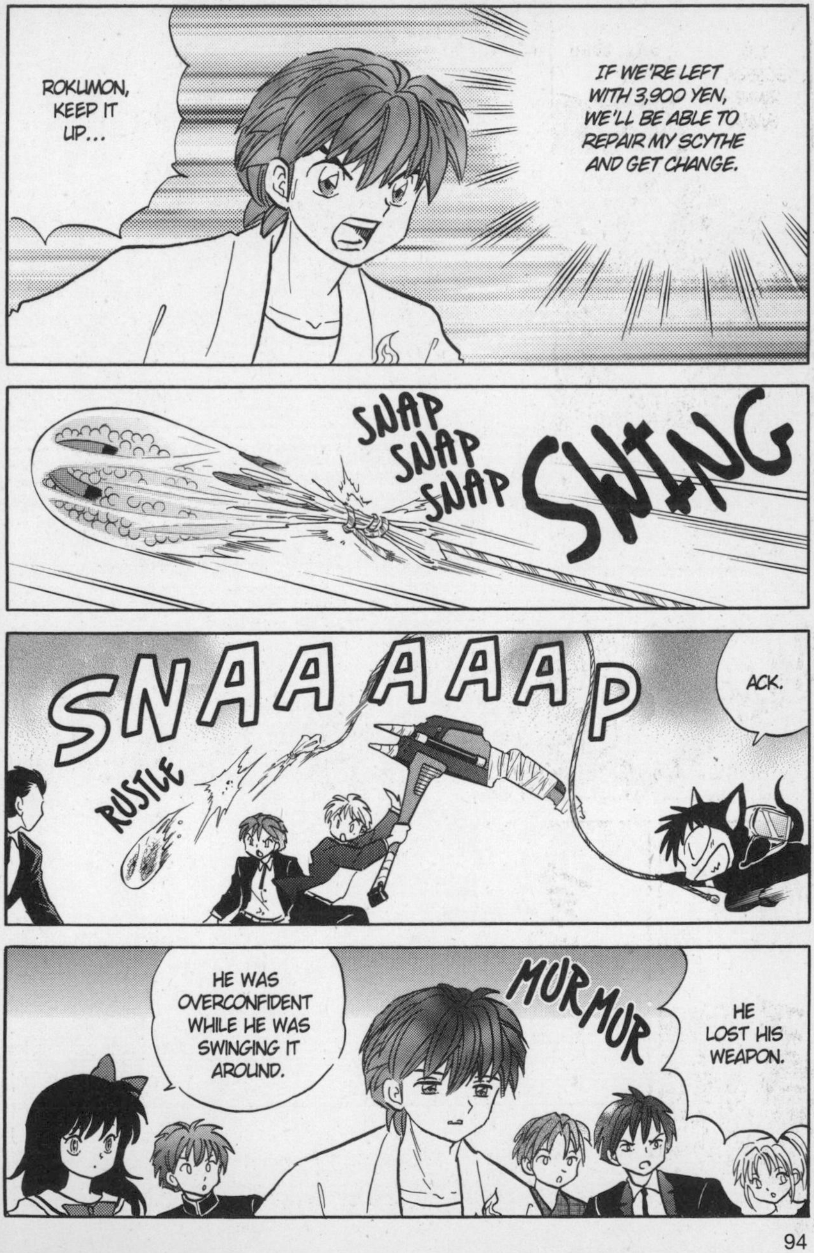
IF WE'RE LEFT WITH 3,900 YEN, WE'LL BE ABLE TO REPAIR MY SCYTHE AND GET CHANGE.
ROKUMON, KEEP IT UP...
SWING
SNAP SNAP SNAP
ACK.
SNAAAAAAP
RUSTLE
HE LOST HIS WEAPON.
MURMUR
HE WAS OVERCONFIDENT WHILE HE WAS SWINGING IT AROUND.

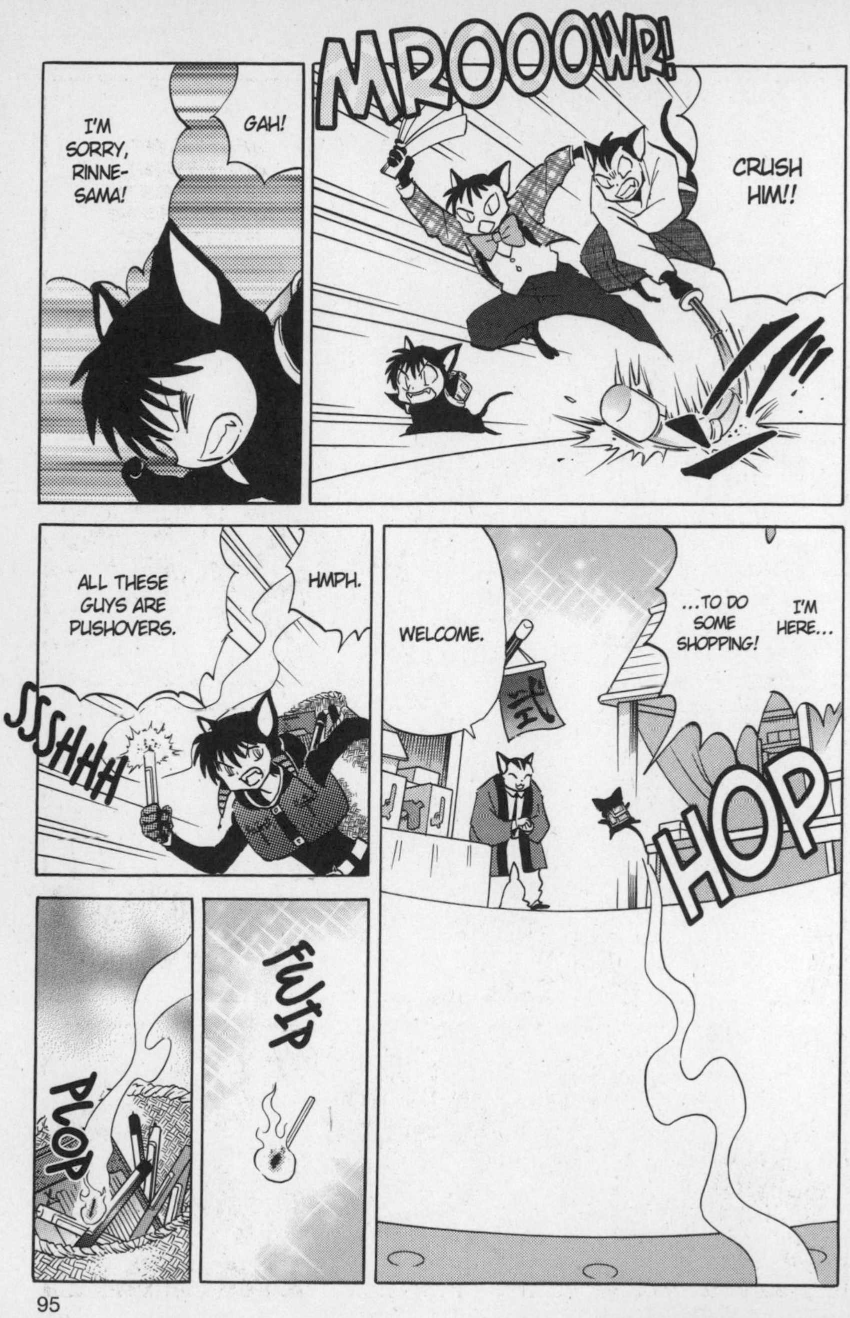
MROOOWR!
CRUSH HIM!!
GAH!
I'M SORRY, RINNE-SAMA!
I'M HERE...
...TO DO SOME SHOPPING!
WELCOME.
HOP
HMPH.
ALL THESE GUYS ARE PUSHOVERS.
SSSHHH
FWIP
PLOP

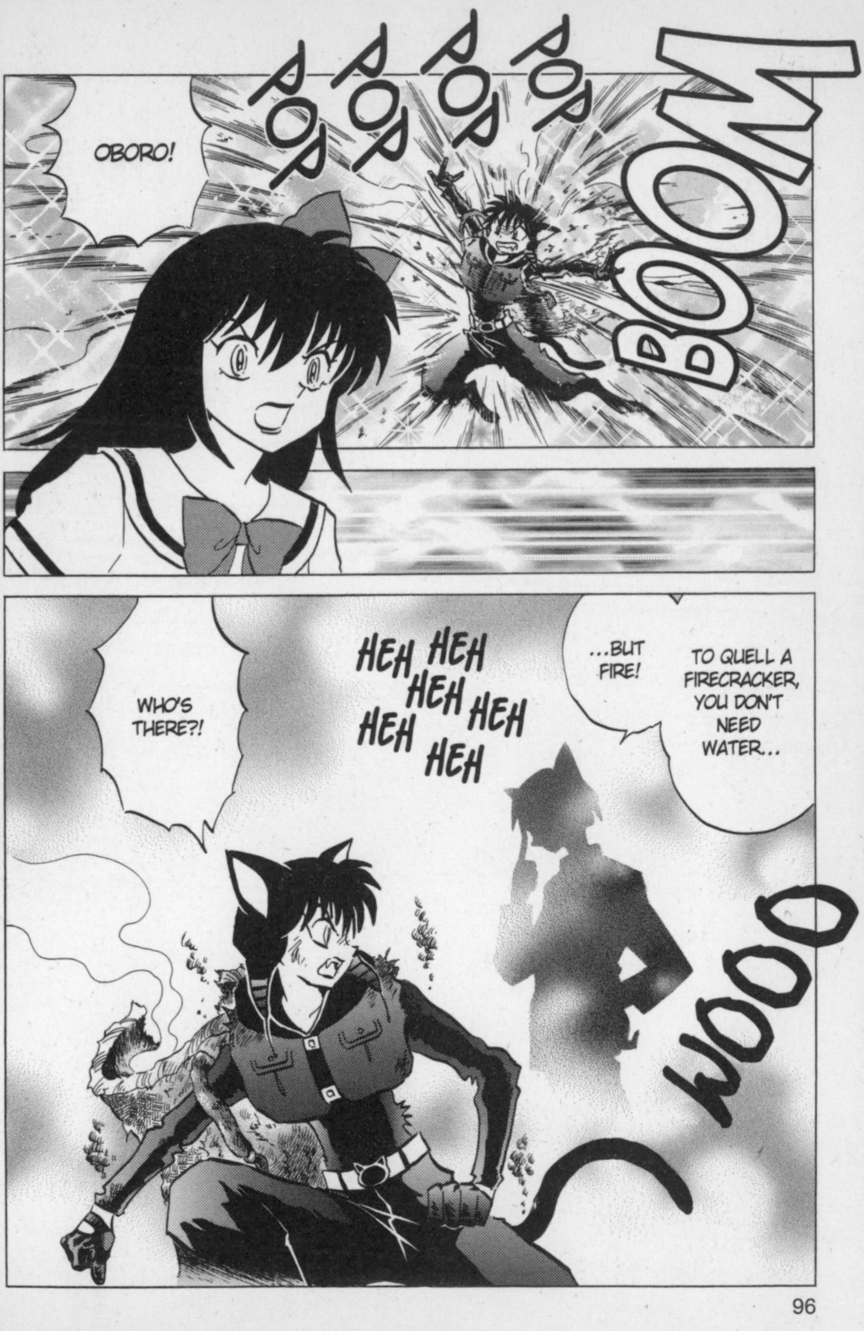
BOOM
POP POP POP POP
OBORO!
TO QUELL A FIRECRACKER, YOU DON'T NEED WATER...
...BUT FIRE!
HEH HEH HEH HEH HEH HEH
WHO'S THERE?!
WOOOM

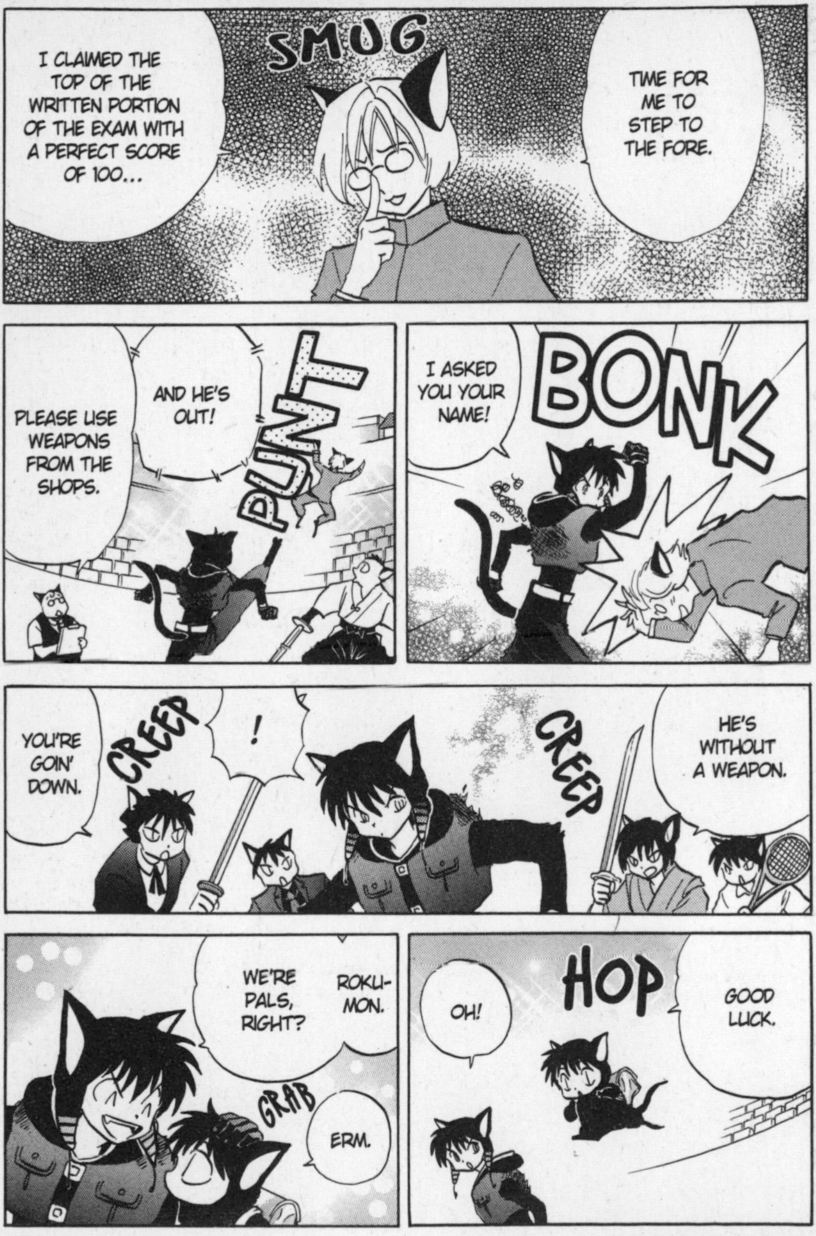
SMUG
I CLAIMED THE TOP OF THE WRITTEN PORTION OF THE EXAM WITH A PERFECT SCORE OF 100...
TIME FOR ME TO STEP TO THE FORE.
BONK
I ASKED YOU YOUR NAME!
PUNT
AND HE'S OUT!
PLEASE USE WEAPONS FROM THE SHOPS.
HE'S WITHOUT A WEAPON.
CREEP
!
CREEP
YOU'RE GOIN' DOWN.
GOOD LUCK.
HOP
OH!
ROKU-MON.
WE'RE PALS, RIGHT?
GRAB
ERM.

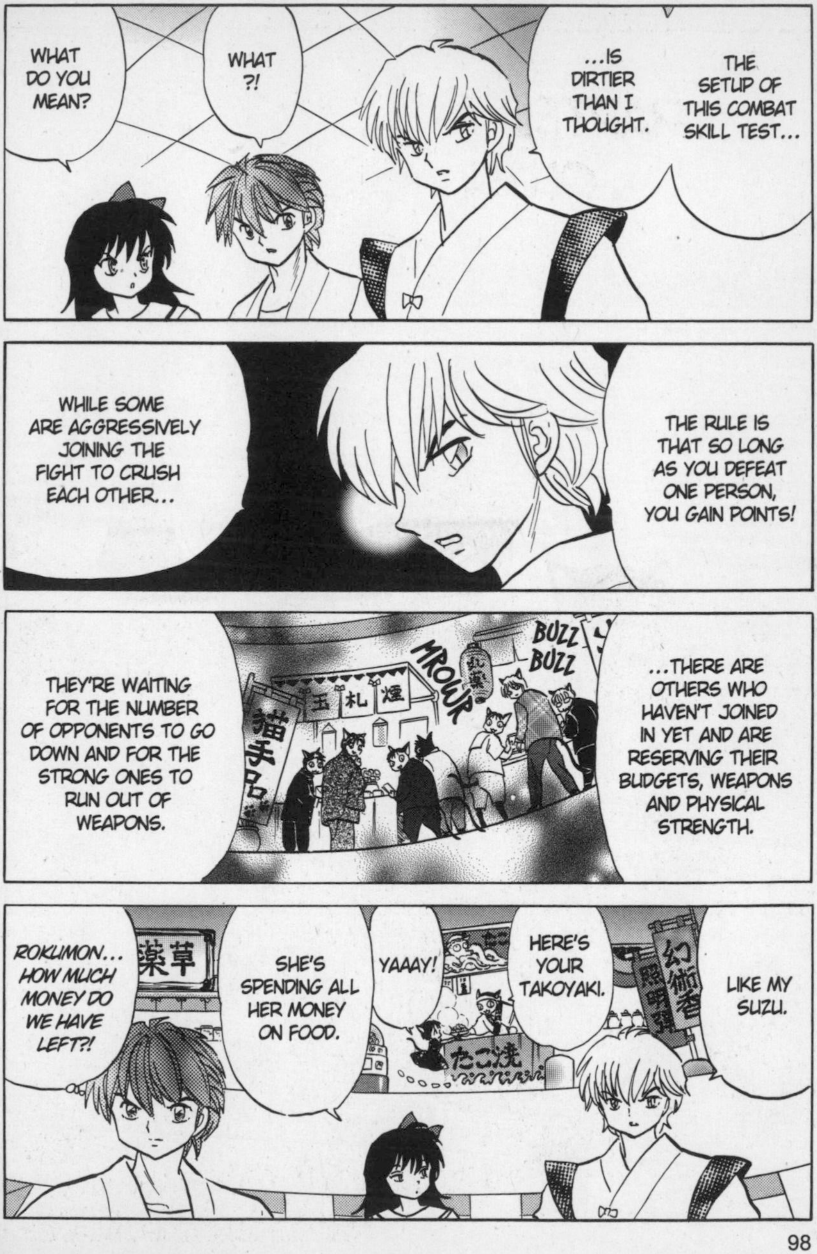
THE SETUP OF THIS COMBAT SKILL TEST...
...IS DIRTIER THAN I THOUGHT.
WHAT ?!
WHAT DO YOU MEAN?
THE RULE IS THAT SO LONG AS YOU DEFEAT ONE PERSON, YOU GAIN POINTS!
WHILE SOME ARE AGGRESSIVELY JOINING THE FIGHT TO CRUSH EACH OTHER...
...THERE ARE OTHERS WHO HAVEN'T JOINED IN YET AND ARE RESERVING THEIR BUDGETS, WEAPONS AND PHYSICAL STRENGTH.
BUZZ BUZZ
MROWR
玉 札 煙
猫手品
THEY'RE WAITING FOR THE NUMBER OF OPPONENTS TO GO DOWN AND FOR THE STRONG ONES TO RUN OUT OF WEAPONS.
幻術香
照明弾
LIKE MY SUZU.
HERE'S YOUR TAKOYAKI.
たこ焼
YAAAY!
SHE'S SPENDING ALL HER MONEY ON FOOD.
薬草
ROKUMON... HOW MUCH MONEY DO WE HAVE LEFT?!

CHAPTER 114: FEARFULLY OUTNUMBERED

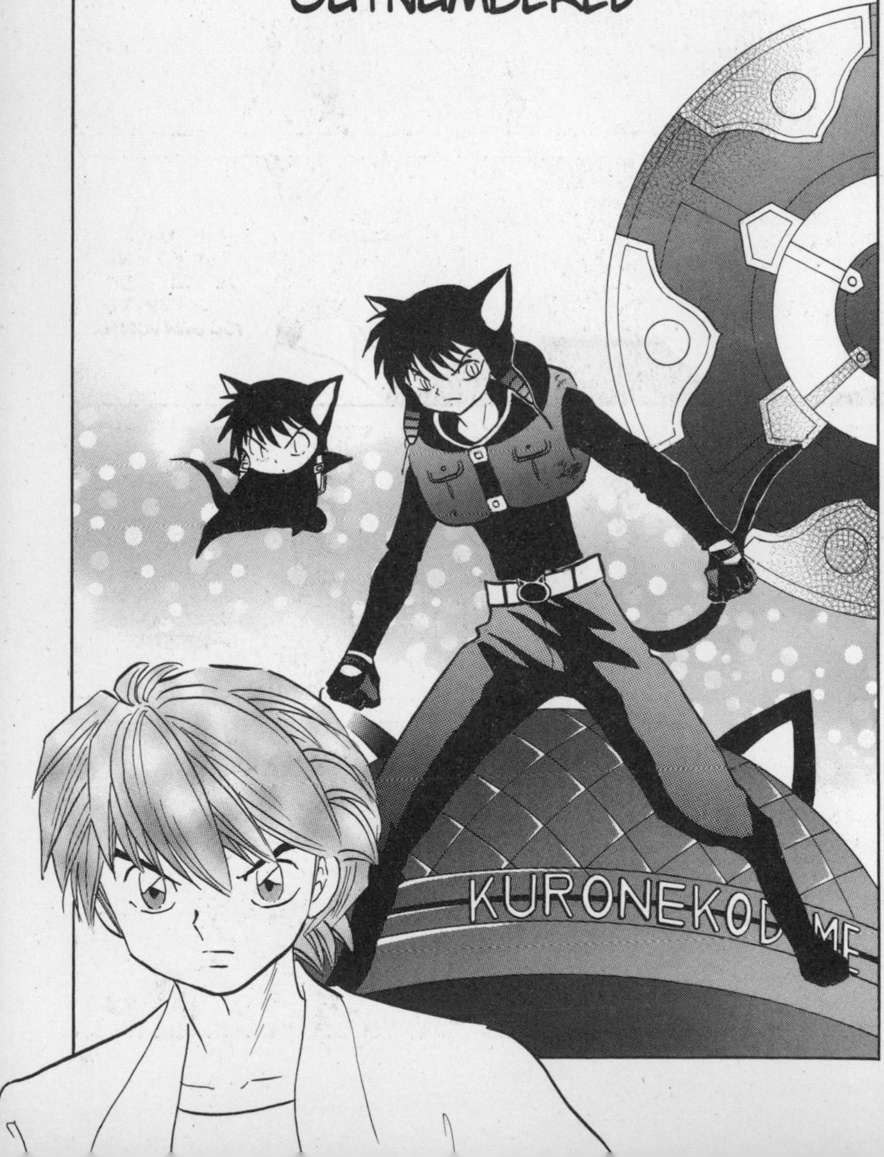
KURONEKOD ME

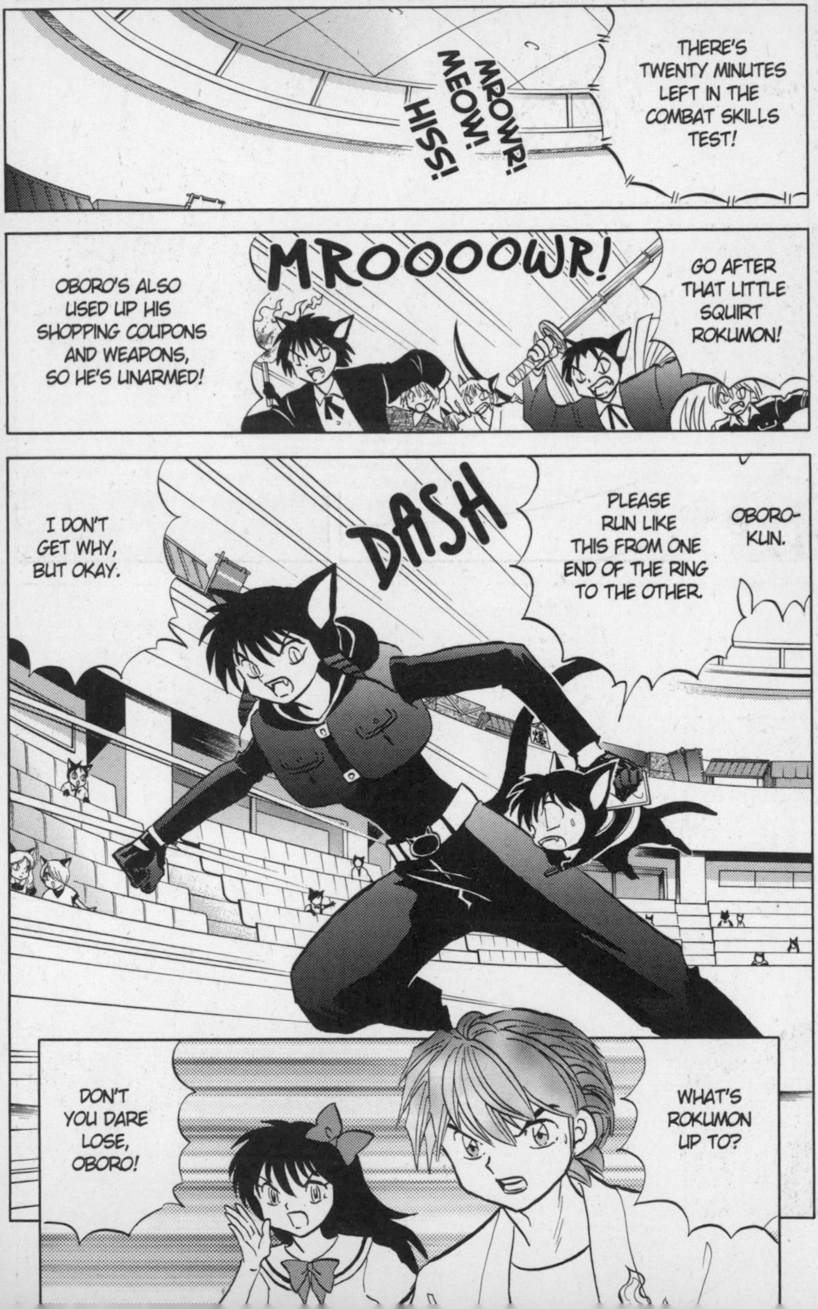
THERE'S TWENTY MINUTES LEFT IN THE COMBAT SKILLS TEST!
MROWR! MEOW! HISS!
GO AFTER THAT LITTLE SQUIRT ROKUMON!
MROOOOWR!
OBORO'S ALSO USED UP HIS SHOPPING COUPONS AND WEAPONS, SO HE'S UNARMED!
OBORO-KUN.
PLEASE RUN LIKE THIS FROM ONE END OF THE RING TO THE OTHER.
DASH
I DON'T GET WHY, BUT OKAY.
WHAT'S ROKUMON UP TO?
DON'T YOU DARE LOSE, OBORO!

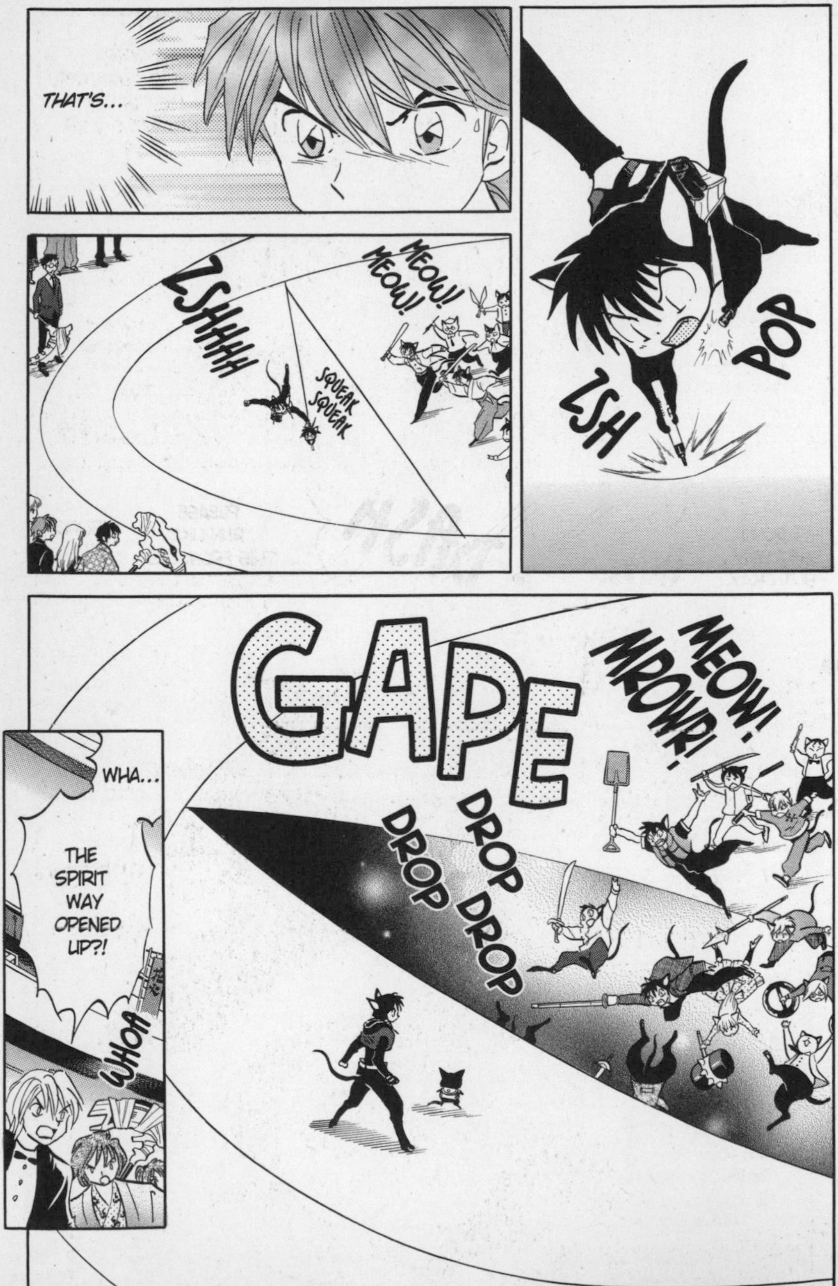
POP
ZSH
THAT'S...
MEOW!! MEOW!!
ZSHHHH
SQUEAK SQUEAK
MEOW! MROWR!
GAPE
DROP DROP DROP
DROP DROP
WHA...
THE SPIRIT WAY OPENED UP?!
WHOA

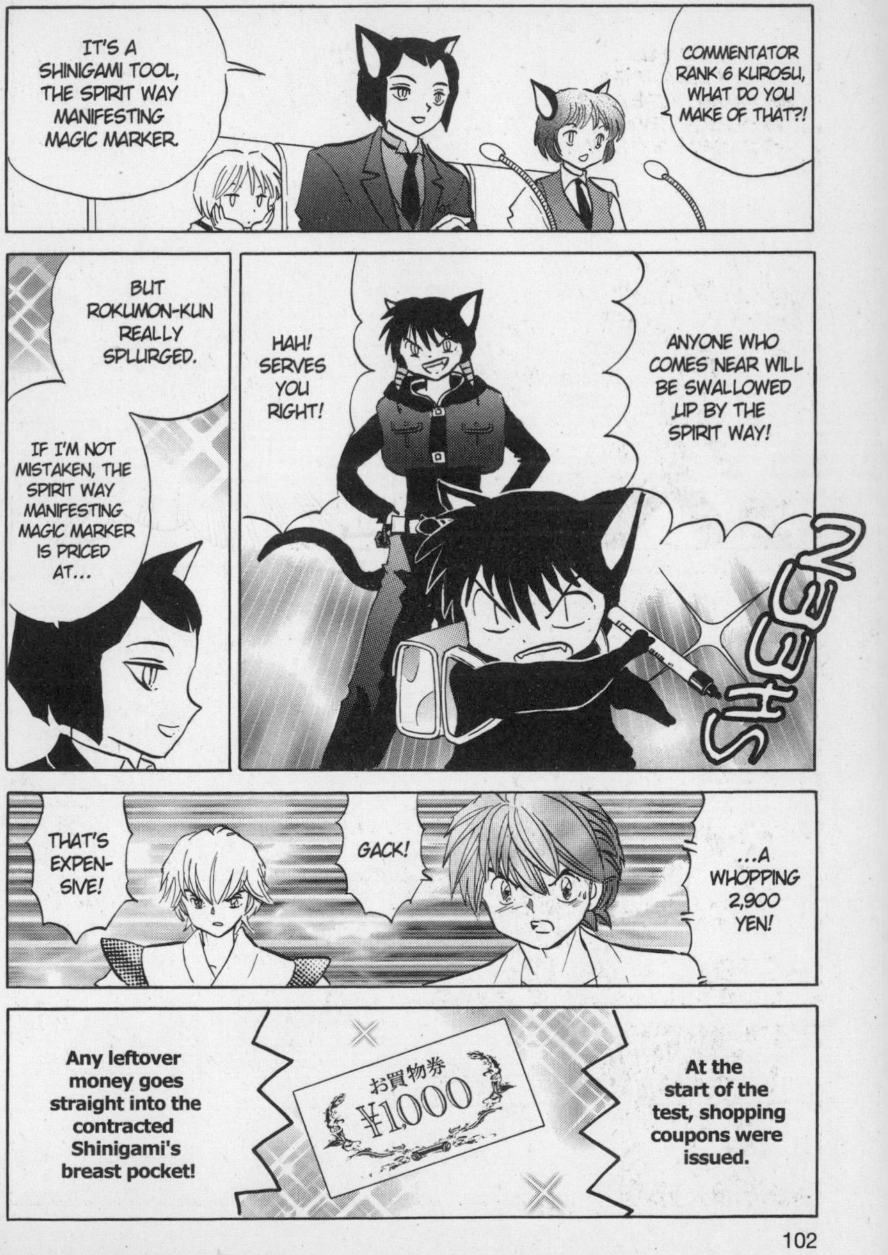
COMMENTATOR RANK 6 KUROSU, WHAT DO YOU MAKE OF THAT?!
IT'S A SHINIGAMI TOOL, THE SPIRIT WAY MANIFESTING MAGIC MARKER.
ANYONE WHO COMES NEAR WILL BE SWALLOWED UP BY THE SPIRIT WAY!
HAH! SERVES YOU RIGHT!
BUT ROKUMON-KUN REALLY SPLURGED.
IF I'M NOT MISTAKEN, THE SPIRIT WAY MANIFESTING MAGIC MARKER IS PRICED AT...
...A WHOPPING 2,900 YEN!
GACK!
THAT'S EXPEN-SIVE!
At the start of the test, shopping coupons were issued.
お買物券
¥1000
Any leftover money goes straight into the contracted Shinigami's breast pocket!

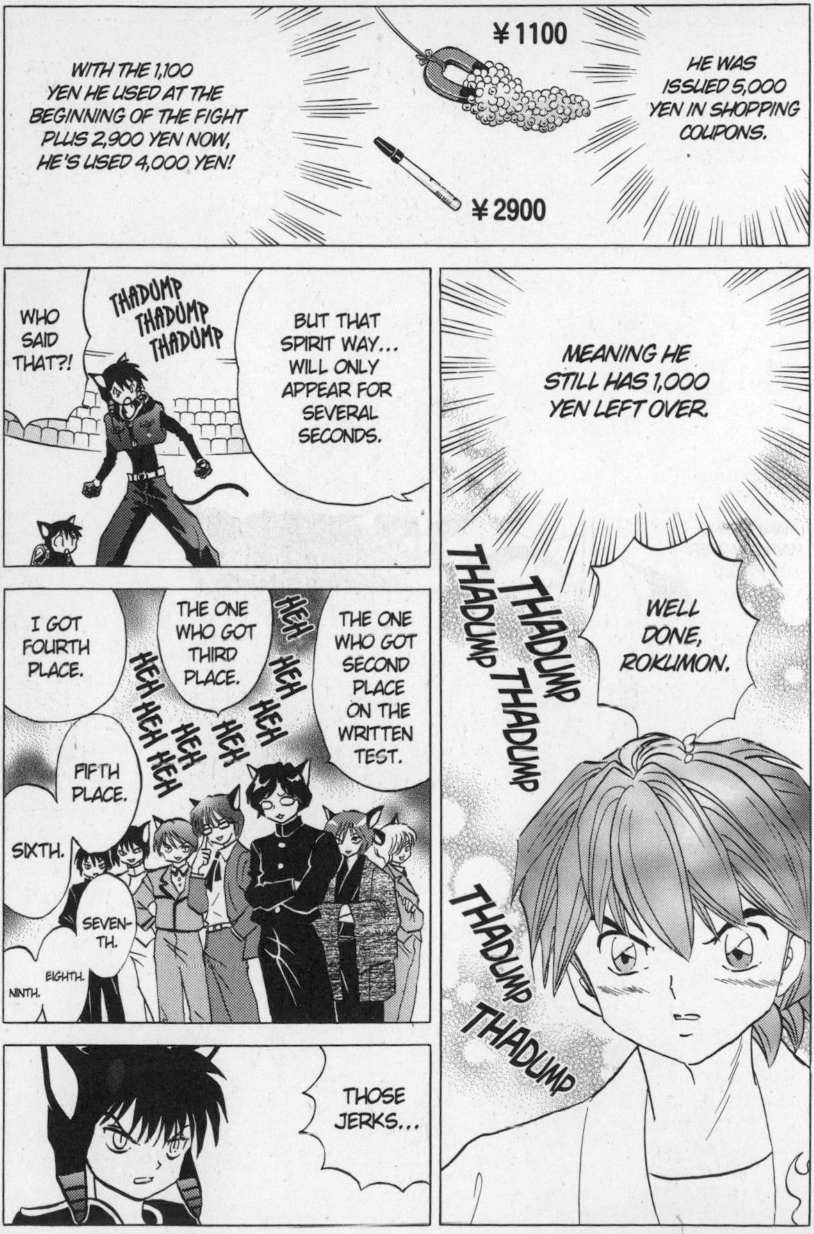
¥1100
HE WAS ISSUED 5,000 YEN IN SHOPPING COUPONS.
WITH THE 1,100 YEN HE USED AT THE BEGINNING OF THE FIGHT PLUS 2,900 YEN NOW, HE'S USED 4,000 YEN!
¥2900
MEANING HE STILL HAS 1,000 YEN LEFT OVER.
WELL DONE, ROKUMON.
THADUMP THADUMP THADUMP
THADUMP THADUMP
BUT THAT SPIRIT WAY... WILL ONLY APPEAR FOR SEVERAL SECONDS.
THADUMP THADUMP THADUMP
WHO SAID THAT?!
THE ONE WHO GOT SECOND PLACE ON THE WRITTEN TEST.
HEH HEH HEH HEH
THE ONE WHO GOT THIRD PLACE.
HEH HEH HEH HEH
I GOT FOURTH PLACE.
FIFTH PLACE.
SIXTH.
SEVEN-TH.
EIGHTH.
NINTH.
THOSE JERKS...

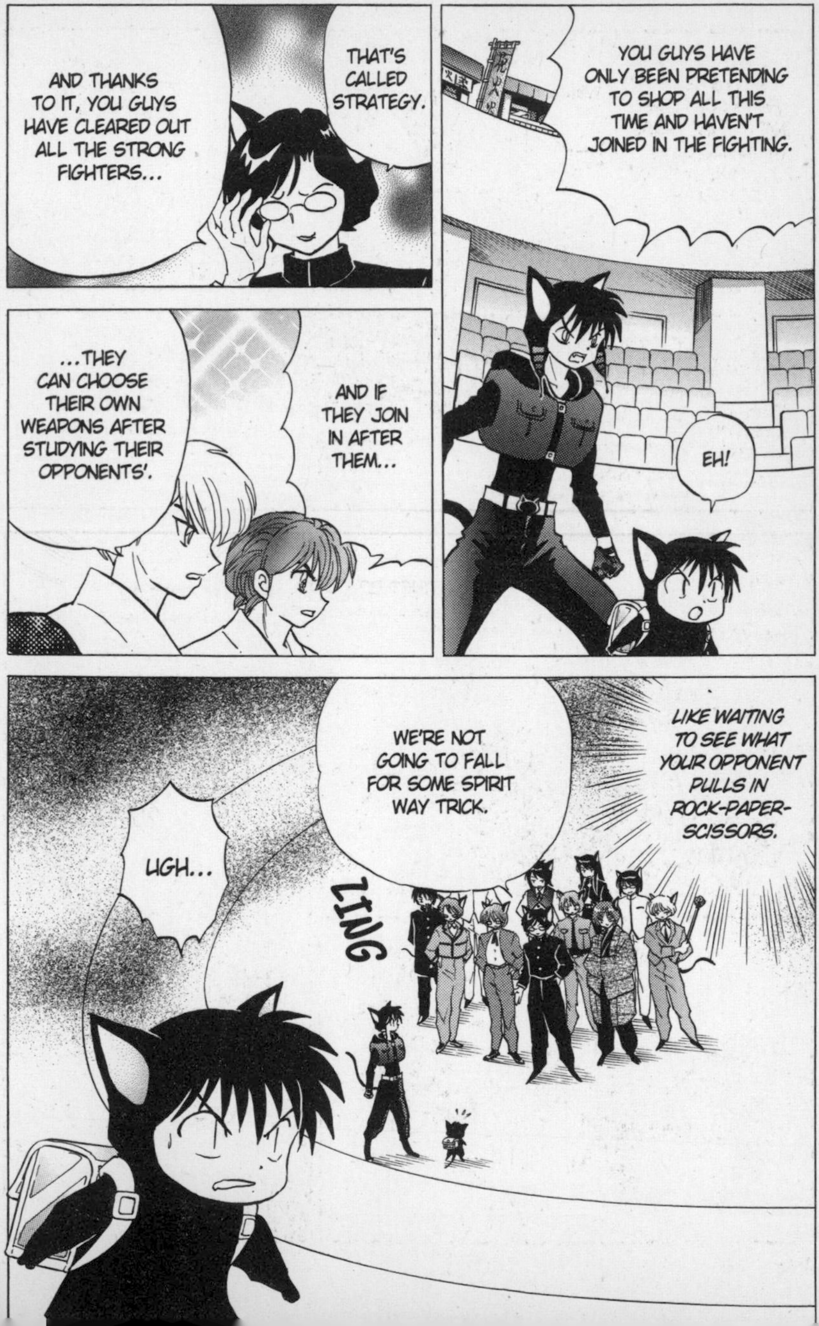
YOU GUYS HAVE ONLY BEEN PRETENDING TO SHOP ALL THIS TIME AND HAVEN'T JOINED IN THE FIGHTING.
EH!
THAT'S CALLED STRATEGY.
AND THANKS TO IT, YOU GUYS HAVE CLEARED OUT ALL THE STRONG FIGHTERS...
AND IF THEY JOIN IN AFTER THEM...
...THEY CAN CHOOSE THEIR OWN WEAPONS AFTER STUDYING THEIR OPPONENTS'.
LIKE WAITING TO SEE WHAT YOUR OPPONENT PULLS IN ROCK-PAPER-SCISSORS.
WE'RE NOT GOING TO FALL FOR SOME SPIRIT WAY TRICK.
ZING
UGH...

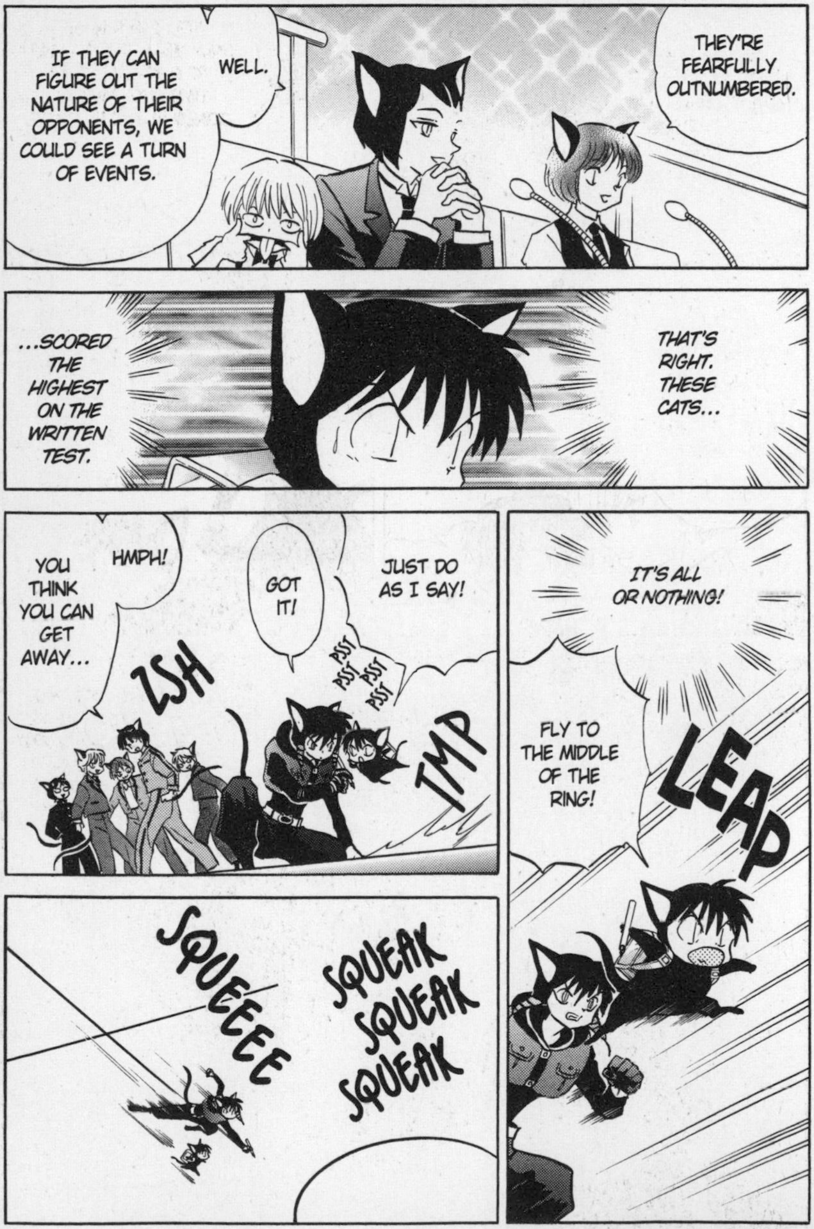
THEY'RE FEARFULLY OUTNUMBERED.
WELL.
IF THEY CAN FIGURE OUT THE NATURE OF THEIR OPPONENTS, WE COULD SEE A TURN OF EVENTS.
THAT'S RIGHT. THESE CATS...
...SCORED THE HIGHEST ON THE WRITTEN TEST.
IT'S ALL OR NOTHING!
LEAP
FLY TO THE MIDDLE OF THE RING!
JUST DO AS I SAY!
PSST PSST PSST PSST
GOT IT!
TMP
HMPH!
YOU THINK YOU CAN GET AWAY...
ZSH
SQUEAK SQUEAK SQUEAK
SQUEEEEE

Sign: Question

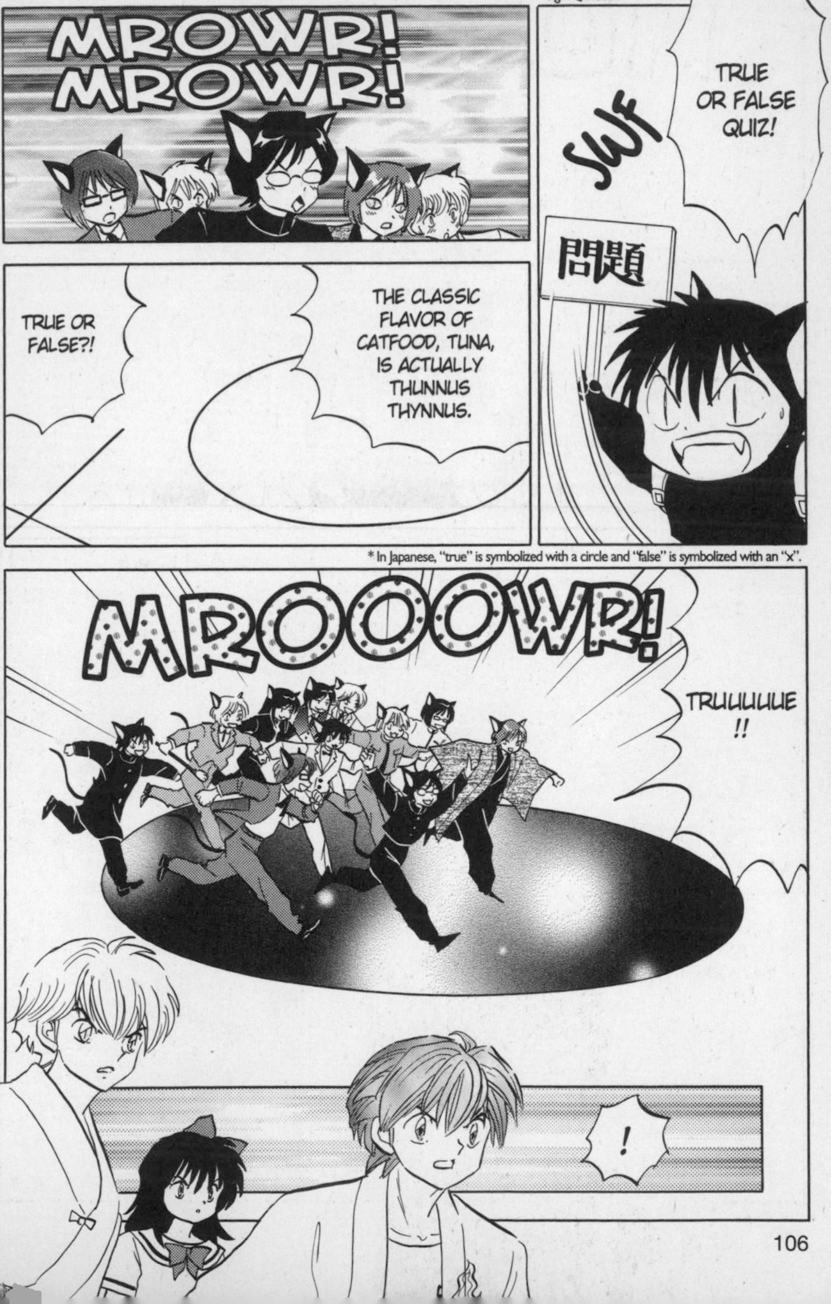

SWF
TRUE OR FALSE QUIZ!
問題
MROWR! MROWR!
THE CLASSIC FLAVOR OF CATFOOD, TUNA, IS ACTUALLY THUNNUS THYNNUS.
TRUE OR FALSE?!
MROOOWR!
TRUUUUUE !!
!

* In Japanese, "true" is symbolized with a circle and "false" is symbolized with an "x".

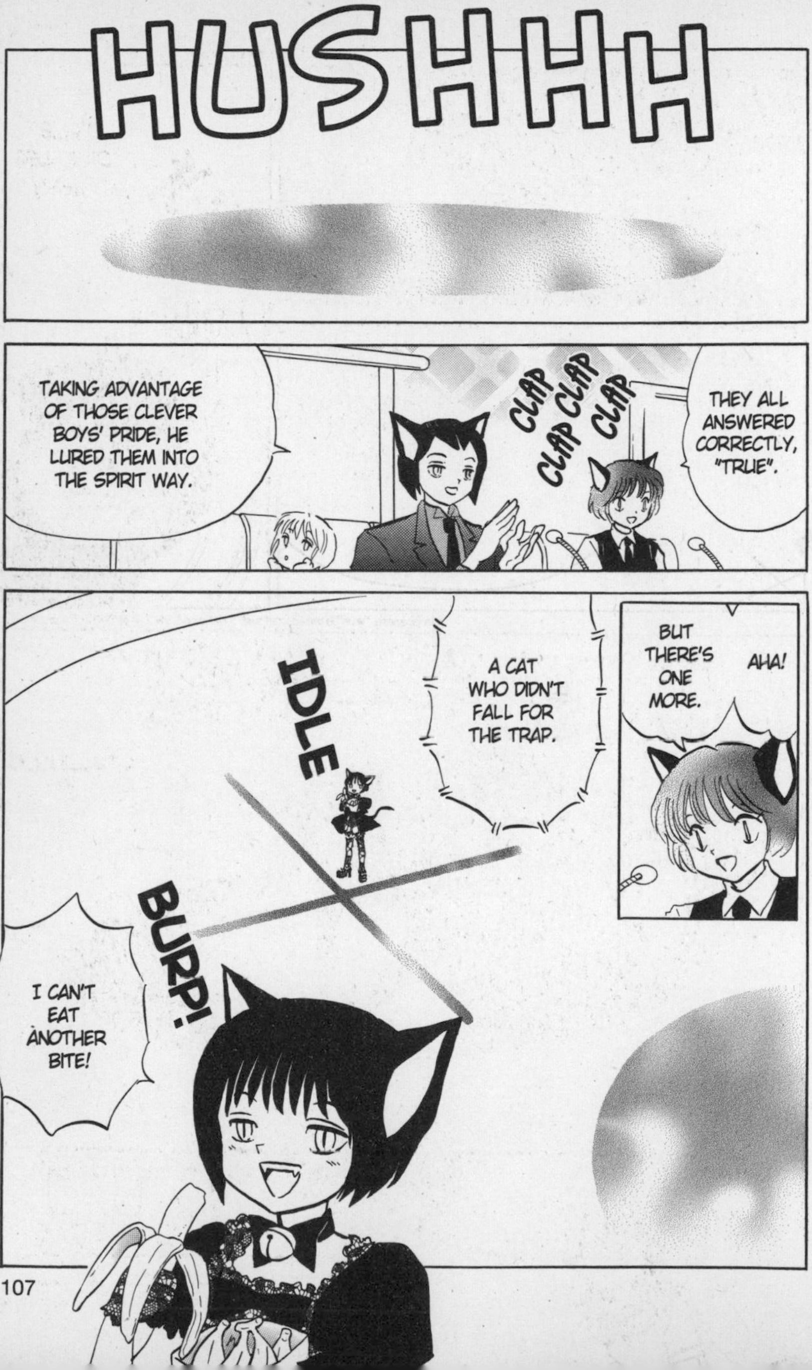
HUSHHH
THEY ALL ANSWERED CORRECTLY, "TRUE".
CLAP CLAP CLAP CLAP
TAKING ADVANTAGE OF THOSE CLEVER BOYS' PRIDE, HE LURED THEM INTO THE SPIRIT WAY.
AHA!
BUT THERE'S ONE MORE.
A CAT WHO DIDN'T FALL FOR THE TRAP.
IDLE
BURP!
I CAN'T EAT ANOTHER BITE!

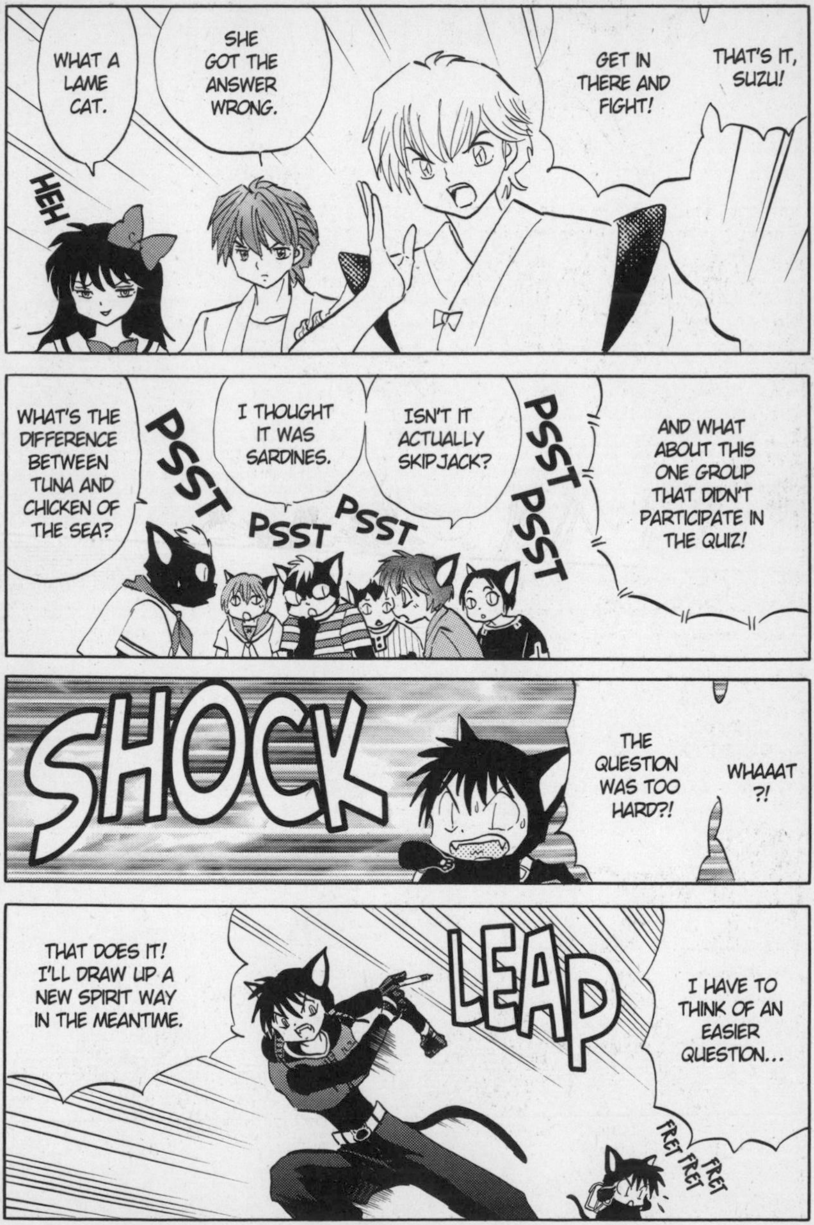
THAT'S IT, SUZU!
GET IN THERE AND FIGHT!
SHE GOT THE ANSWER WRONG.
WHAT A LAME CAT.
HEH
AND WHAT ABOUT THIS ONE GROUP THAT DIDN'T PARTICIPATE IN THE QUIZ!
PSST PSST
ISN'T IT ACTUALLY SKIPJACK?
I THOUGHT IT WAS SARDINES.
PSST PSST
WHAT'S THE DIFFERENCE BETWEEN TUNA AND CHICKEN OF THE SEA?
PSST
WHAAAT ?!
THE QUESTION WAS TOO HARD?!
SHOCK
I HAVE TO THINK OF AN EASIER QUESTION...
FRET FRET FRET
LEAP
THAT DOES IT! I'LL DRAW UP A NEW SPIRIT WAY IN THE MEANTIME.

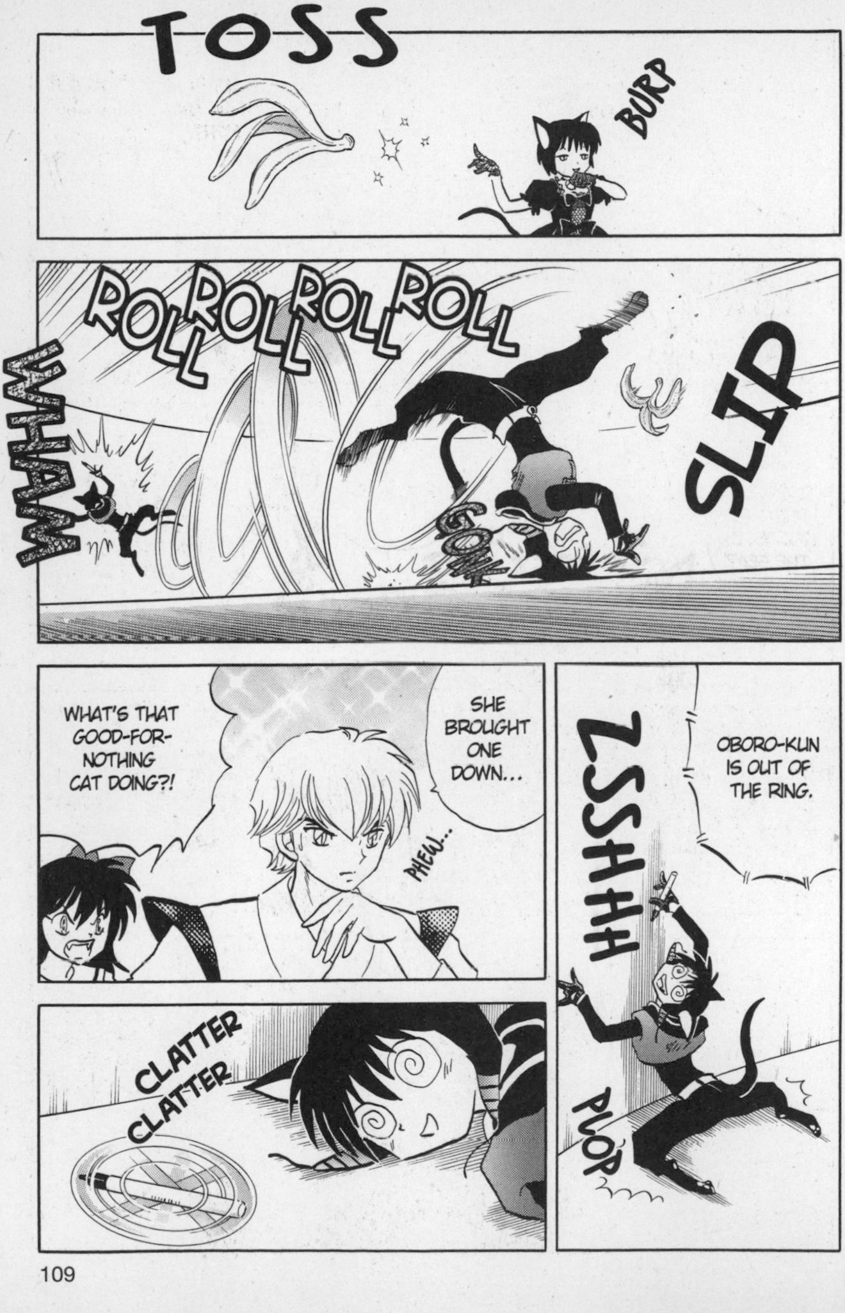
TOSS
BURP
SLIP
ROLL ROLL ROLL ROLL
GONK
WHAM
ZSSHHH
OBORO-KUN IS OUT OF THE RING.
PLOP
SHE BROUGHT ONE DOWN...
PHEW...
WHAT'S THAT GOOD-FOR-NOTHING CAT DOING?!
CLATTER CLATTER

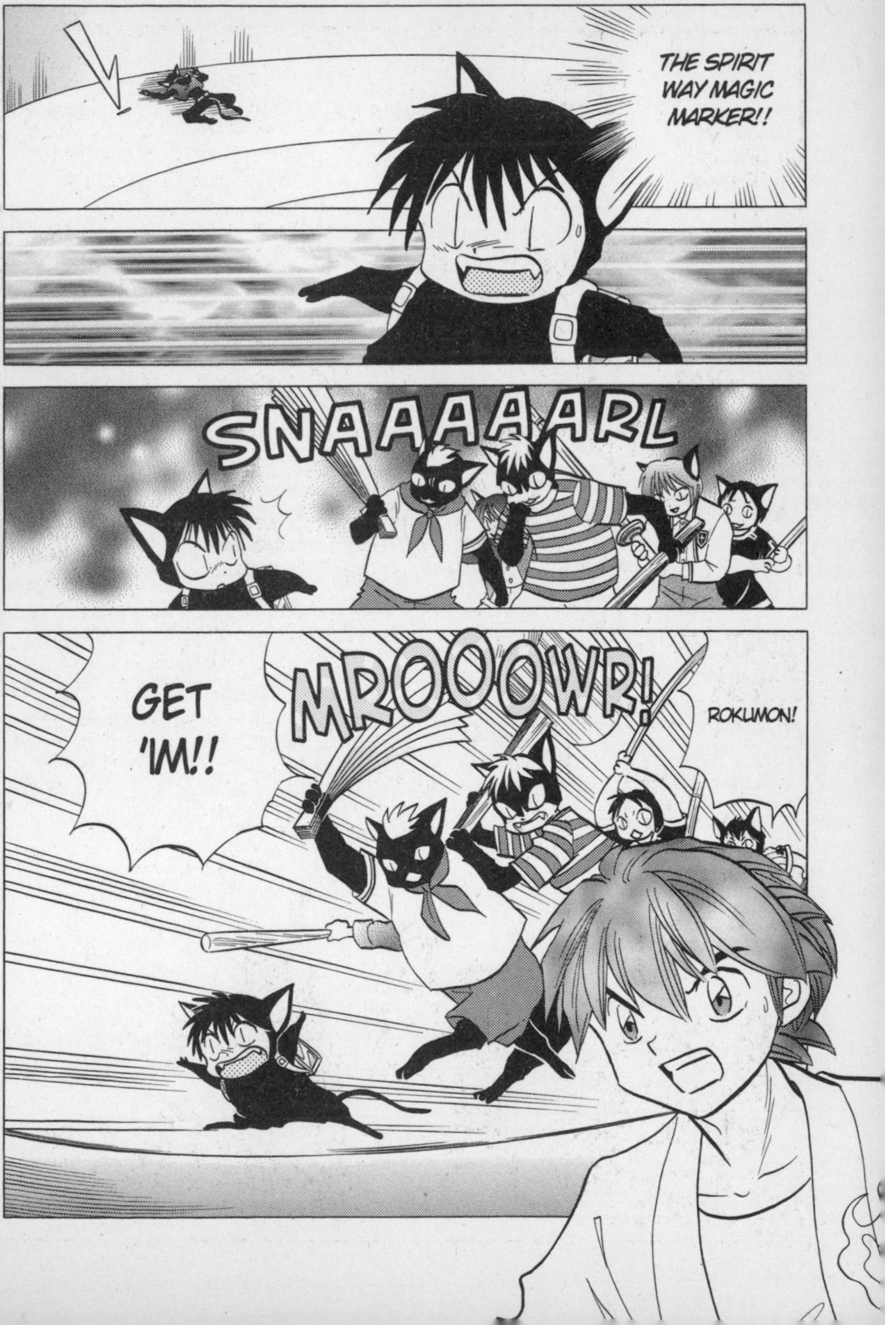
THE SPIRIT WAY MAGIC MARKER!!
SNAAAAARL
ROKUMON!
MROOOWR!
GET 'IM!!

THEY OUT-NUMBER THAT LITTLE KID...
EVEN IF THEY GANG UP ON HIM...
...SO LONG AS ONE OF THEM GETS HIM, THEY'LL ALL SCORE A POINT.
SNORE
IT'S NOT FAIR.
THAT GROUP HASN'T BEAT ONE PERSON.
BEING TARGETED BY WEAKLINGS ...MEANS...
...A LITTLE GIRL LIKE SUZU...
SUZU.
WATCH OUT!
HUH?!
WHY, KAIN-SAMA?
YAWN
SHE STEPPED OUT OF THE RING HERSELF?
SHE'S GIVEN UP?
OKAY, EVERYONE, TEN MINUTES REMAINING.
ACK!
UGH!
WHOMP
THUD

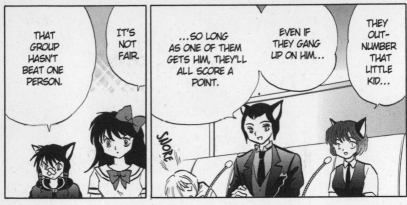

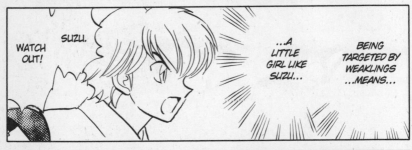

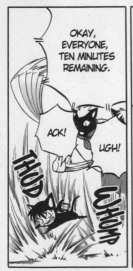

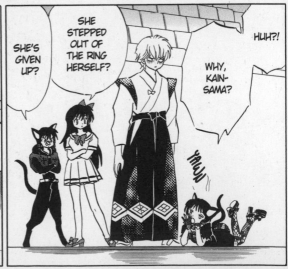

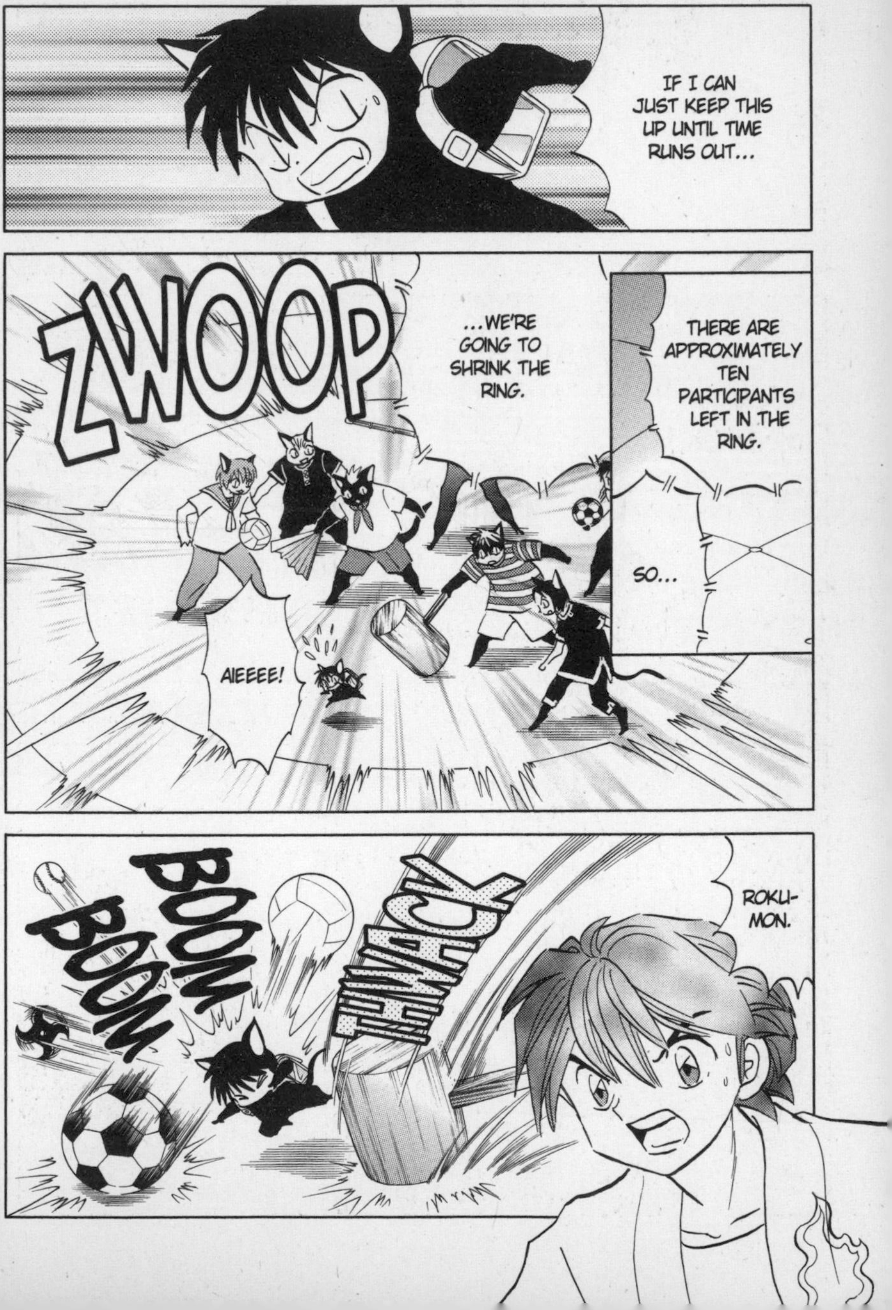
IF I CAN JUST KEEP THIS UP UNTIL TIME RUNS OUT...
THERE ARE APPROXIMATELY TEN PARTICIPANTS LEFT IN THE RING.
SO...
...WE'RE GOING TO SHRINK THE RING.
ZWOOP
AIEEEE!
ROKU-MON.
THWACK
BOOM
BOOM

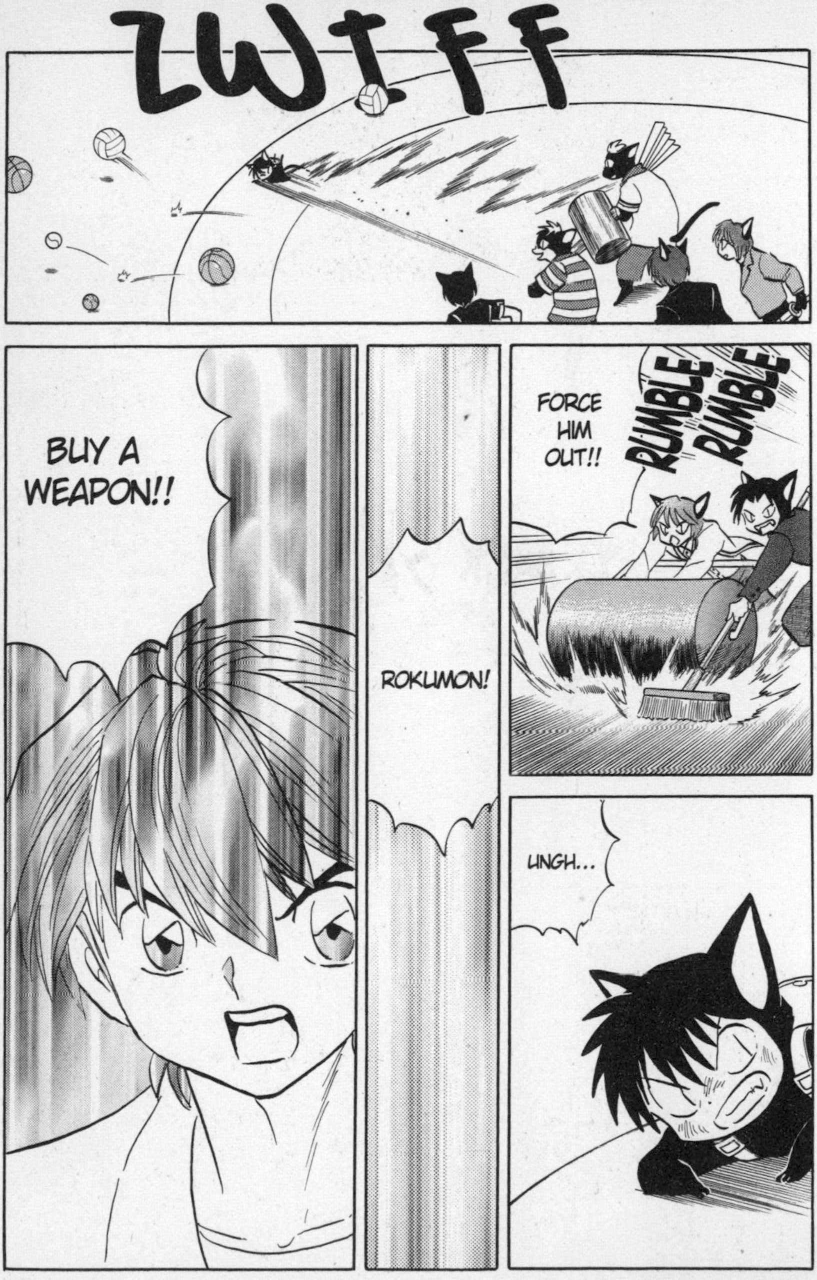
ZWIFF
FORCE HIM OUT!!
RUMBLE RUMBLE
UNGH...
ROKUMON!
BUY A WEAPON!!

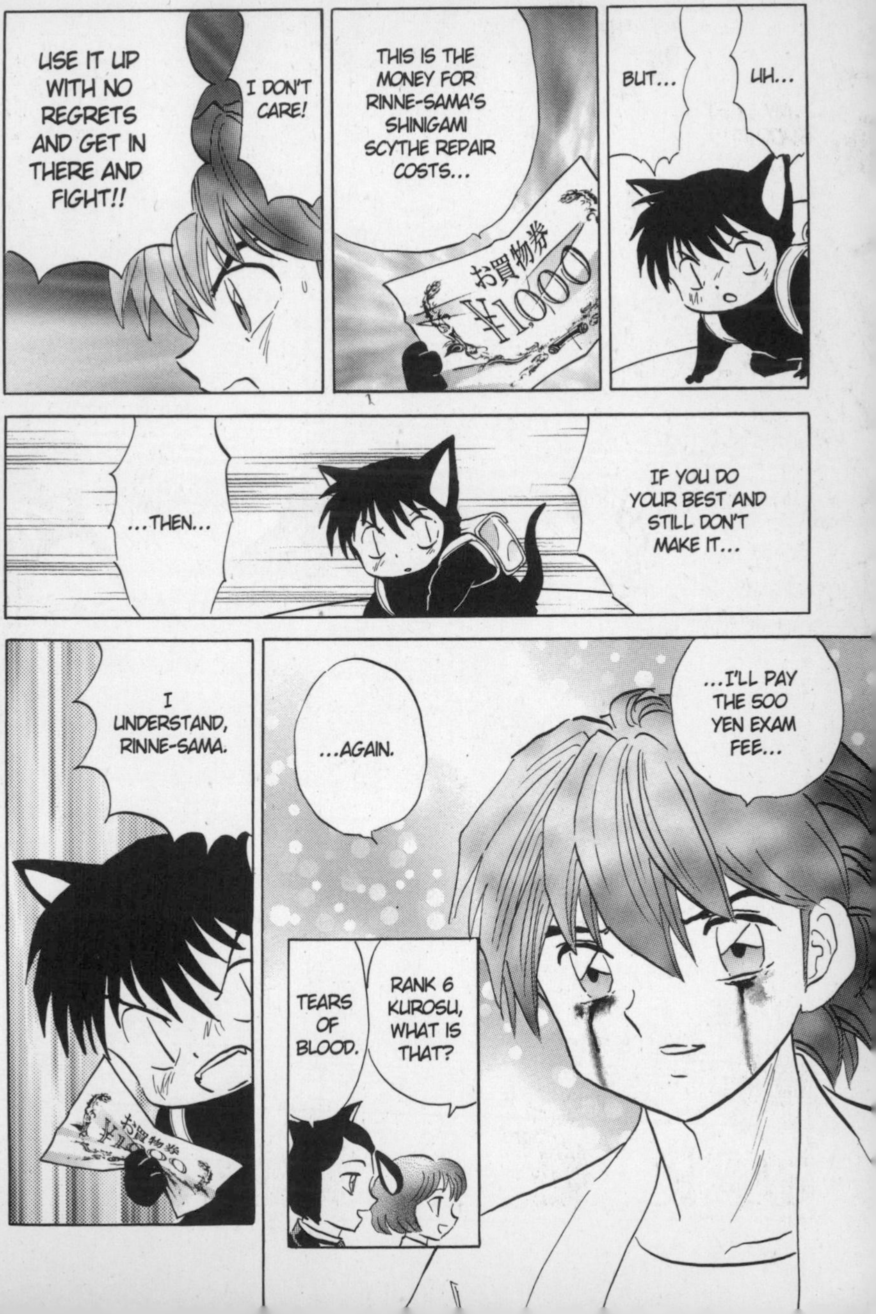
UH...
BUT...
THIS IS THE MONEY FOR RINNE-SAMA'S SHINIGAMI SCYTHE REPAIR COSTS...
お買物券
¥1,000
I DON'T CARE!
USE IT UP WITH NO REGRETS AND GET IN THERE AND FIGHT!!
IF YOU DO YOUR BEST AND STILL DON'T MAKE IT...
...THEN...
...I'LL PAY THE 500 YEN EXAM FEE...
...AGAIN.
I UNDERSTAND, RINNE-SAMA.
RANK 6 KUROSU, WHAT IS THAT?
TEARS OF BLOOD.

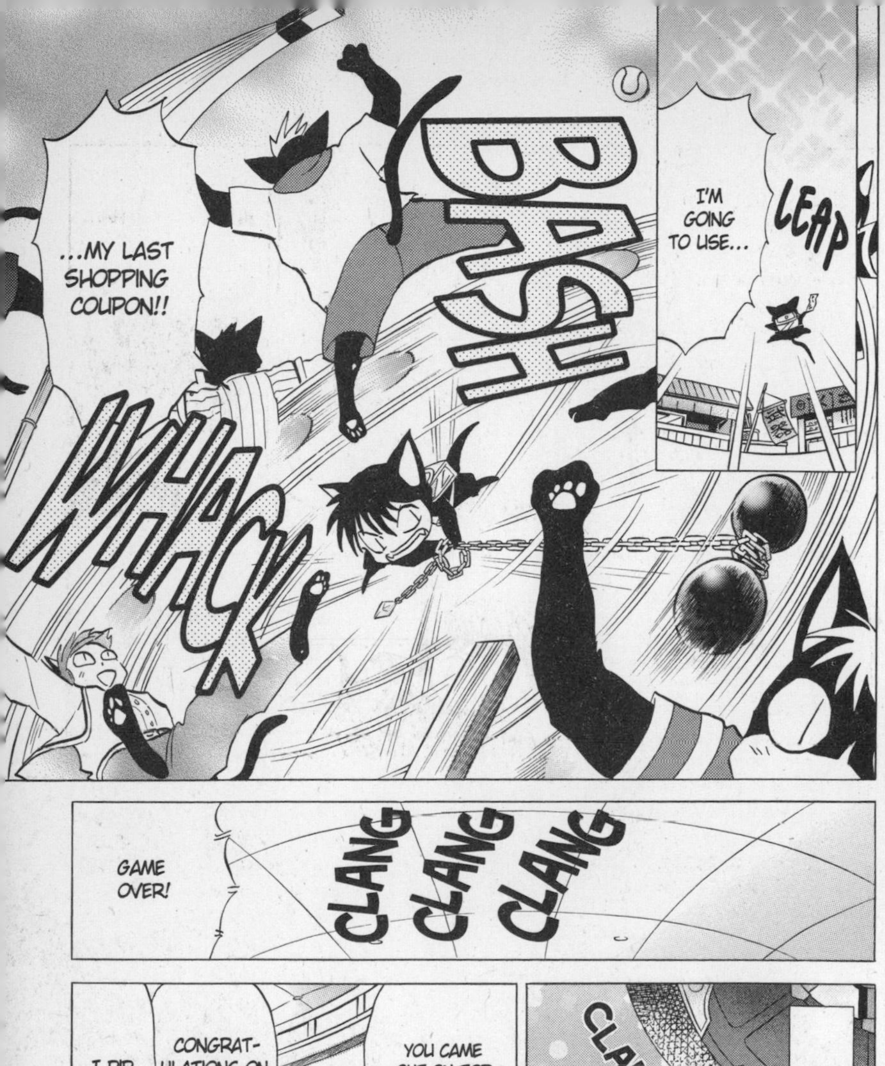
I'M GOING TO USE…
LEAP
…MY LAST SHOPPING COUPON!!
BASH
WHACK
CLANG CLANG CLANG
GAME OVER!
And so…
CLANK
KURONEKO DOME
YOU CAME OUT ON TOP OF THE COMBAT SKILLS TEST, ROKUMON-KUN.
CONGRAT-ULATIONS ON ACHIEVING RANK 1.
I DID IT!
CLAP CLAP CLAP CLAP

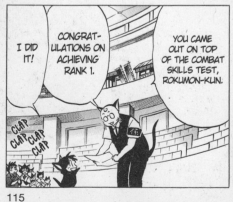

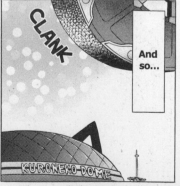

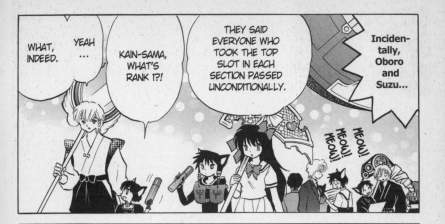

Incidentally, Oboro and Suzu...
MEOW! MEOW! MEOW!
THEY SAID EVERYONE WHO TOOK THE TOP SLOT IN EACH SECTION PASSED UNCONDITIONALLY.
KAIN-SAMA, WHAT'S RANK 1?!
YEAH ...
WHAT, INDEED.
WOW. THAT'S GREAT, ROKUMON-CHAN.
NOT ONLY ARE YOU RANK 1...
...BUT YOU WERE ALSO CHOSEN AS A MVC.
Note: MVC = Most Valuable Cat
IS THIS THE MVC TROPHY?
IT'S A SOUVENIR PIGGY BANK.
I WANTED WHAT GOES INSIDE THAT.

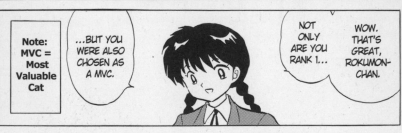

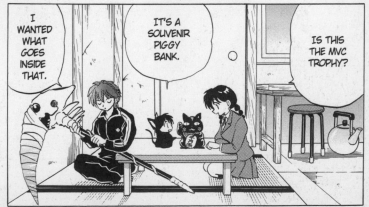

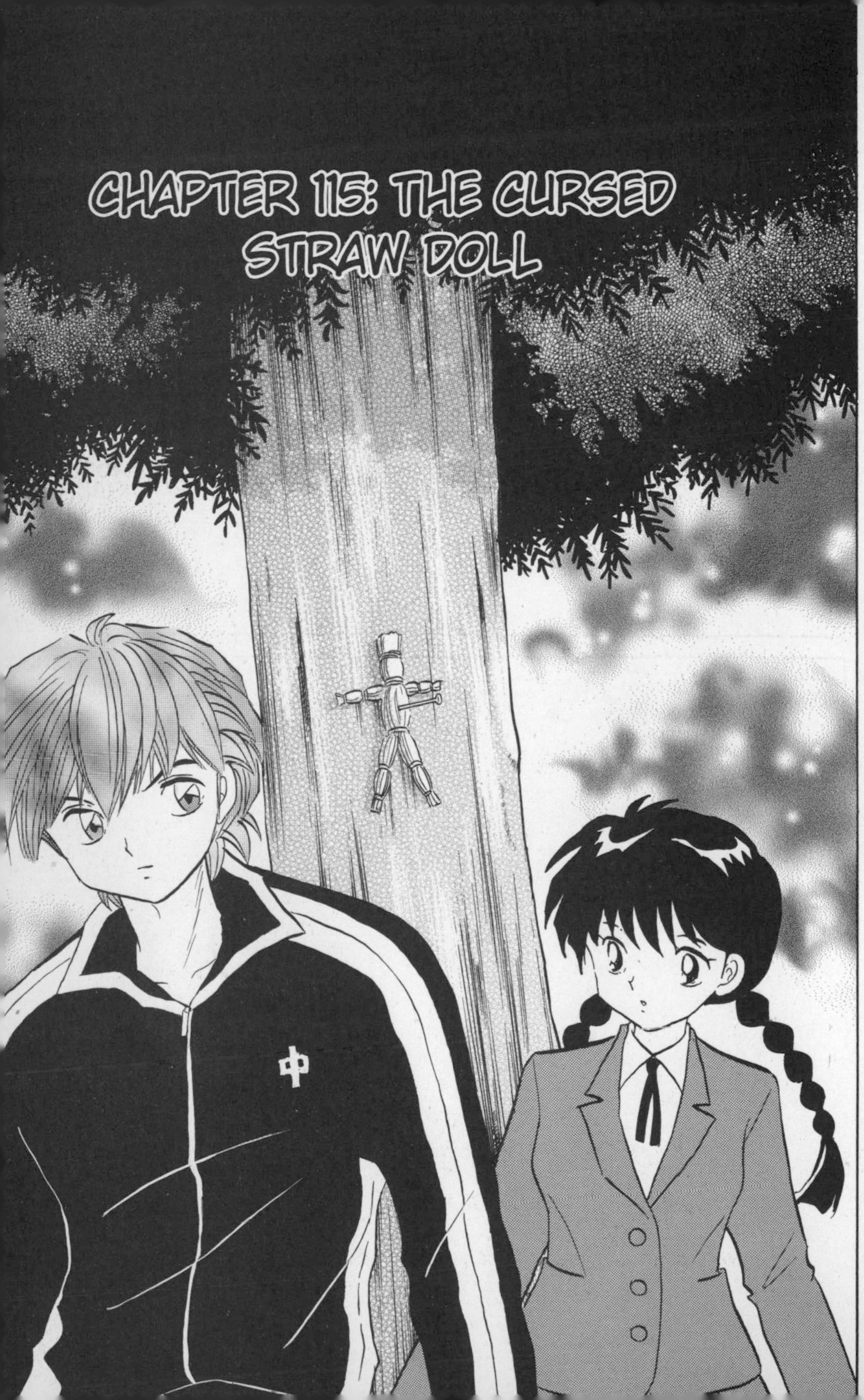
CHAPTER 115: THE CURSED STRAW DOLL
中

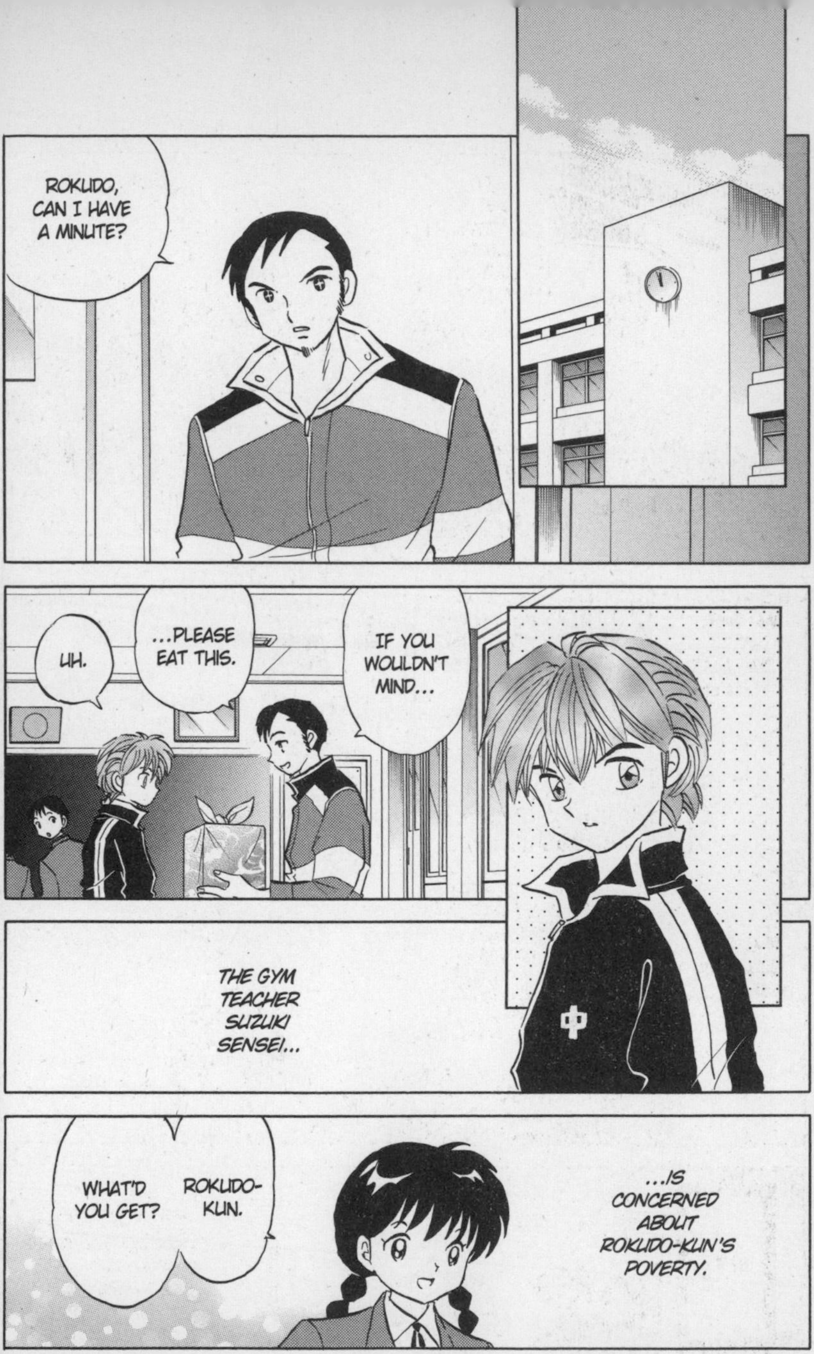
ROKUDO, CAN I HAVE A MINUTE?
IF YOU WOULDN'T MIND...
...PLEASE EAT THIS.
UH.
THE GYM TEACHER SUZUKI SENSEI...
...IS CONCERNED ABOUT ROKUDO-KUN'S POVERTY.
ROKUDO-KUN.
WHAT'D YOU GET?

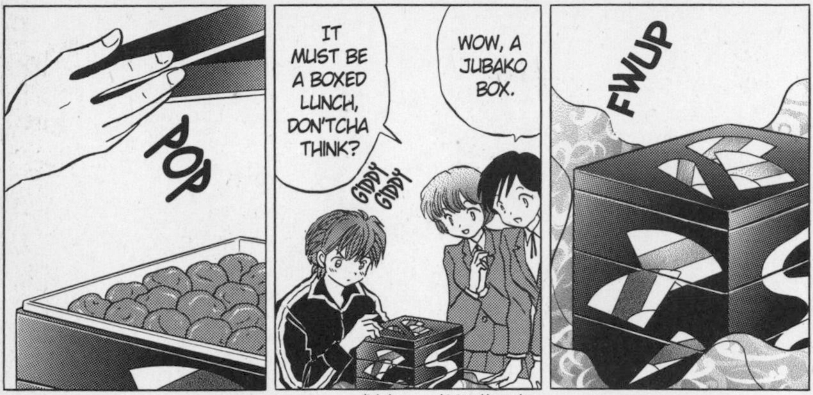
FWUP
WOW, A JUBAKO BOX.
IT MUST BE A BOXED LUNCH, DON'TCHA THINK?
GIDDY GIDDY
POP
*jubako = a multi-tiered bento box

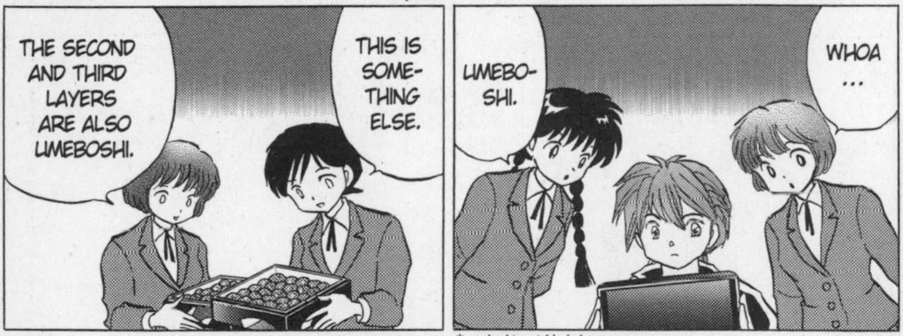
WHOA ...
UMEBOSHI.
THIS IS SOME-THING ELSE.
THE SECOND AND THIRD LAYERS ARE ALSO UMEBOSHI.
*umeboshi = pickled plums

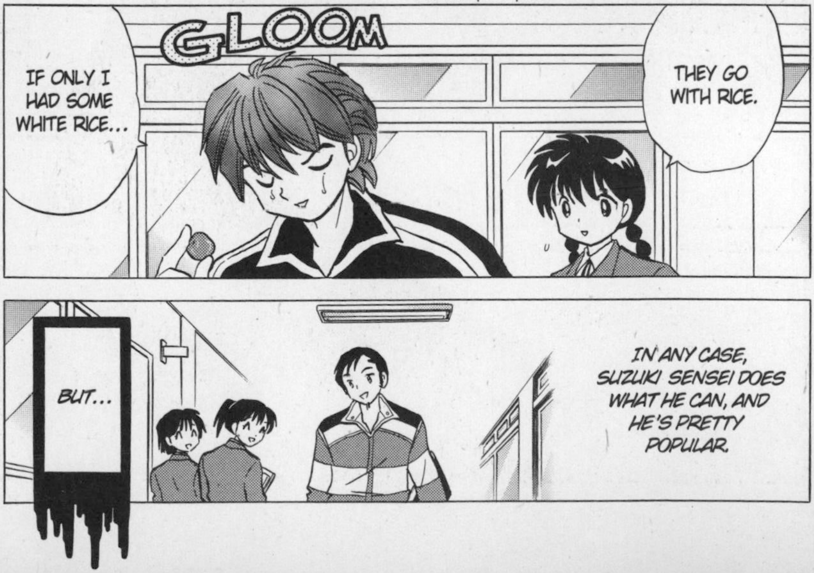
THEY GO WITH RICE.
GLOOM
IF ONLY I HAD SOME WHITE RICE...
IN ANY CASE, SUZUKI SENSEI DOES WHAT HE CAN, AND HE'S PRETTY POPULAR.
BUT...

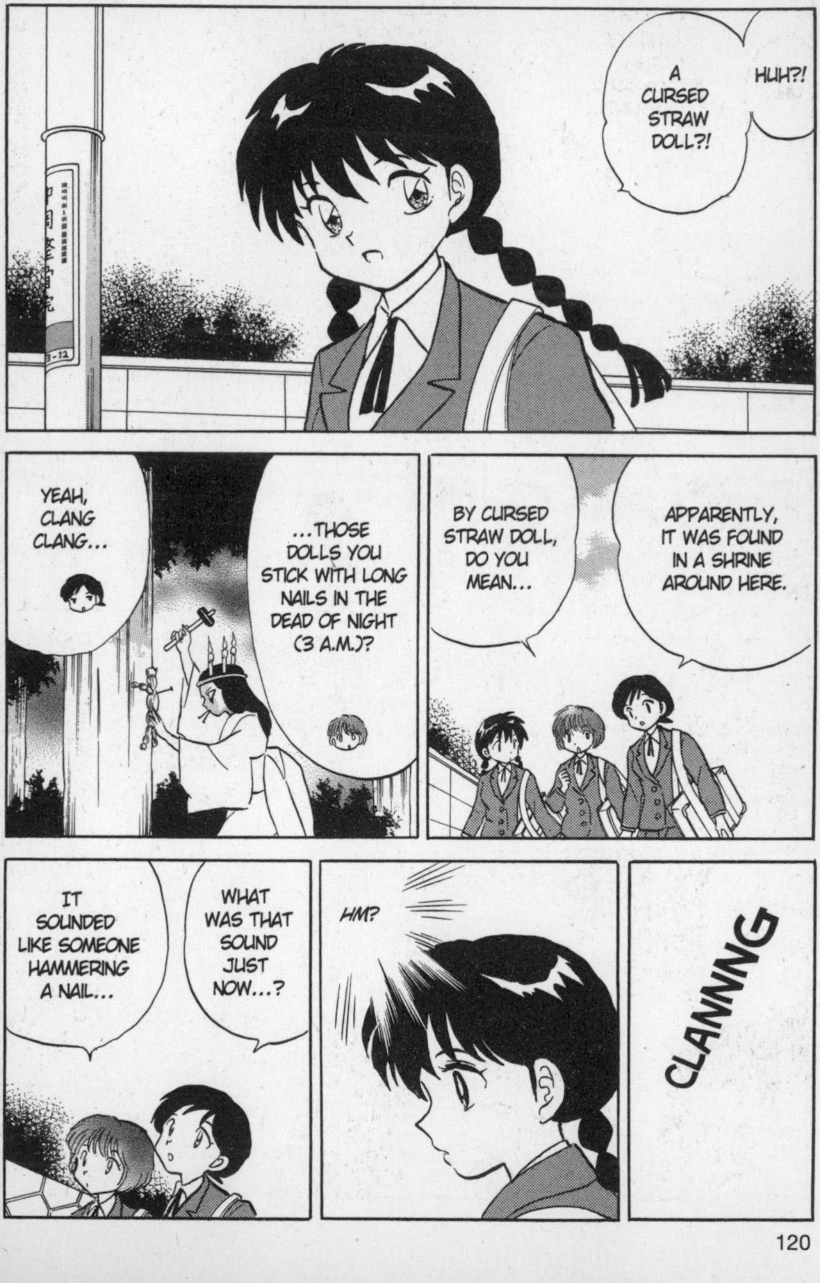
HUH?!
A CURSED STRAW DOLL?!
APPARENTLY, IT WAS FOUND IN A SHRINE AROUND HERE.
BY CURSED STRAW DOLL, DO YOU MEAN...
...THOSE DOLLS YOU STICK WITH LONG NAILS IN THE DEAD OF NIGHT (3 A.M.)?
YEAH, CLANG CLANG...
CLANNNG
HM?
WHAT WAS THAT SOUND JUST NOW...?
IT SOUNDED LIKE SOMEONE HAMMERING A NAIL...

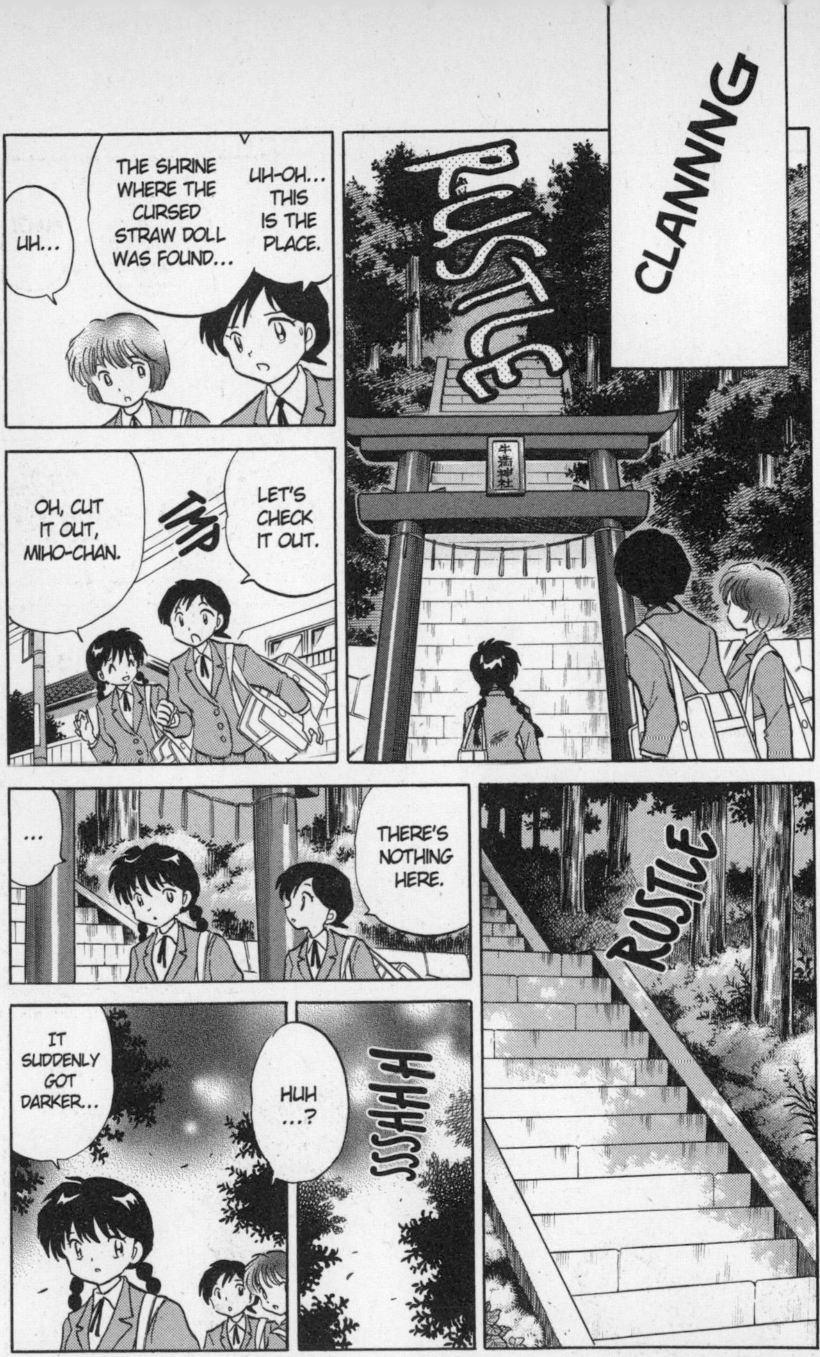
CLANNNG
RUSTLE
UH-OH... THIS IS THE PLACE.
THE SHRINE WHERE THE CURSED STRAW DOLL WAS FOUND...
UH...
LET'S CHECK IT OUT.
TMP
OH, CUT IT OUT, MIHO-CHAN.
RUSTLE
THERE'S NOTHING HERE.
...
HUH ...?
SSSHHH
IT SUDDENLY GOT DARKER...

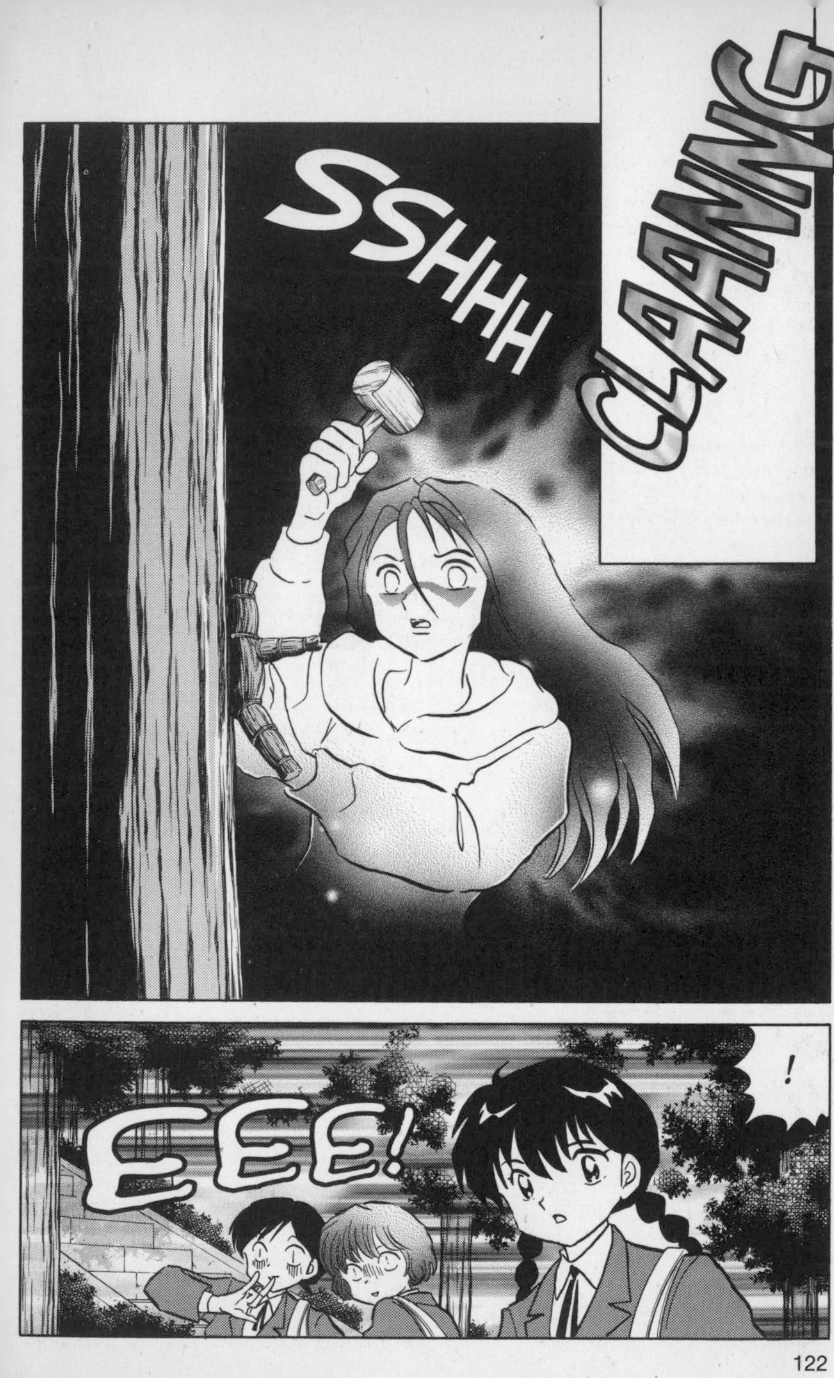
CLANNG
SSHHH
!
EEE!

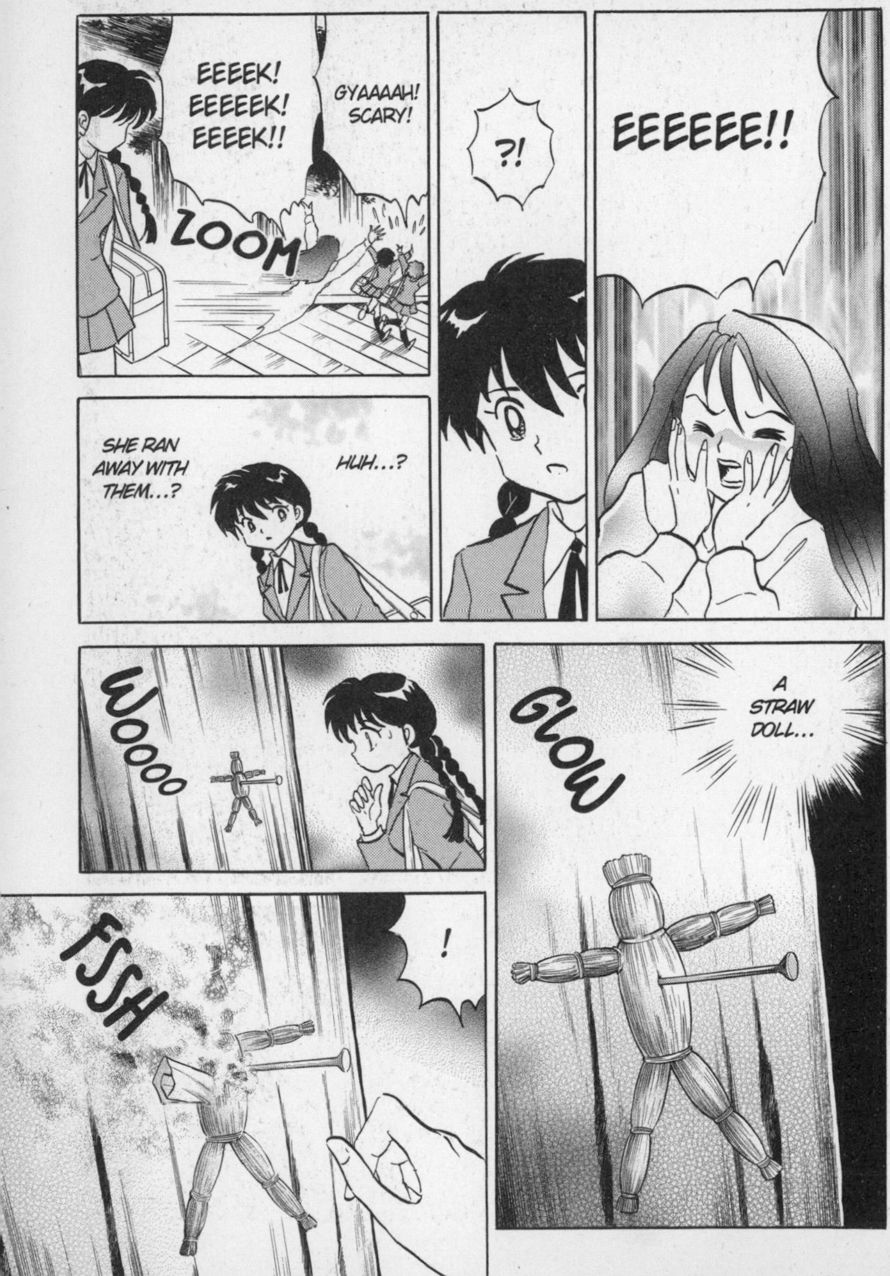
EEEEEE!!
?!
GYAAAAH! SCARY!
EEEEK! EEEEEK! EEEEK!!
ZOOM
HUH...?
SHE RAN AWAY WITH THEM...?
A STRAW DOLL...
GLOW
WOOOO
!
FSSH

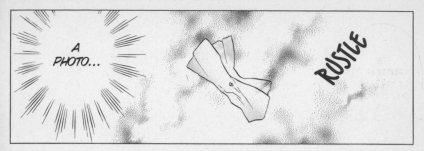

A PHOTO...

RUSTLE

SUZUKI SENSEI?!

HUH...?!

WHAT DOES IT MEAN?!

IT VANISHED...

FZZT

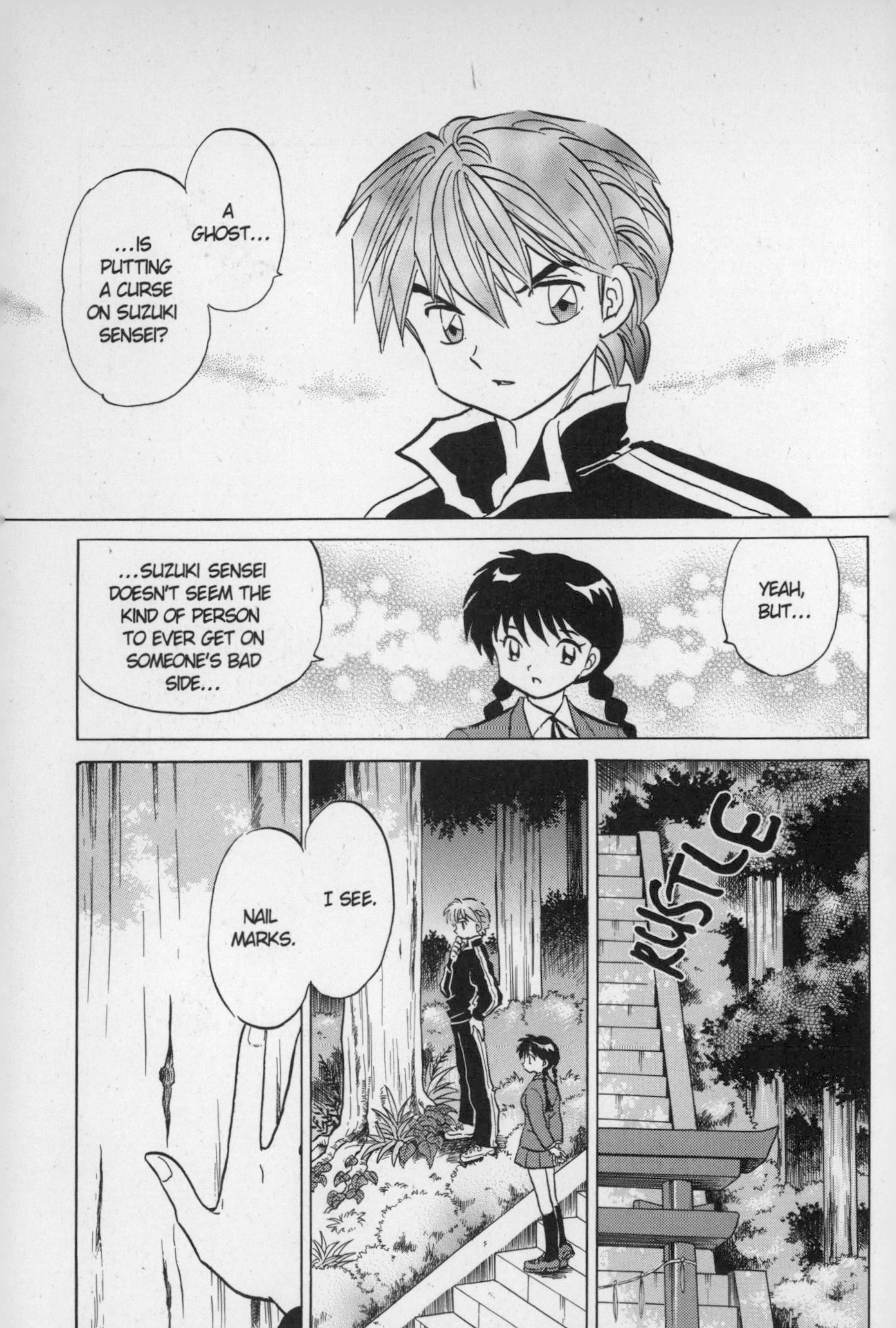
A GHOST…
…IS PUTTING A CURSE ON SUZUKI SENSEI?
YEAH, BUT…
…SUZUKI SENSEI DOESN'T SEEM THE KIND OF PERSON TO EVER GET ON SOMEONE'S BAD SIDE…
RUSTLE
I SEE.
NAIL MARKS.

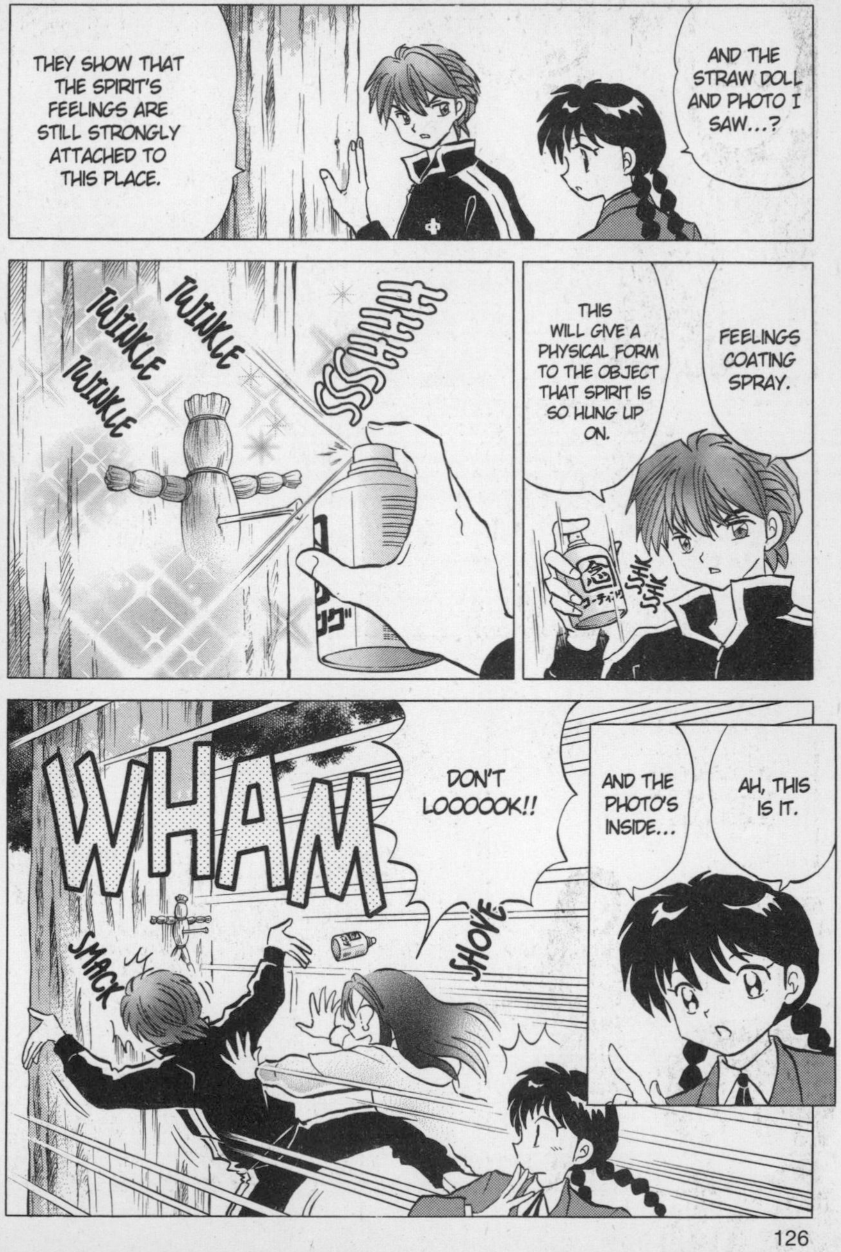
AND THE STRAW DOLL AND PHOTO I SAW...?
THEY SHOW THAT THE SPIRIT'S FEELINGS ARE STILL STRONGLY ATTACHED TO THIS PLACE.
FEELINGS COATING SPRAY.
THIS WILL GIVE A PHYSICAL FORM TO THE OBJECT THAT SPIRIT IS SO HUNG UP ON.
SSHK SSHK
SSSHHH
TWINKLE
TWINKLE
TWINKLE
AH, THIS IS IT.
AND THE PHOTO'S INSIDE...
DON'T LOOOOOK!!
WHAM
SHOVE
SMACK

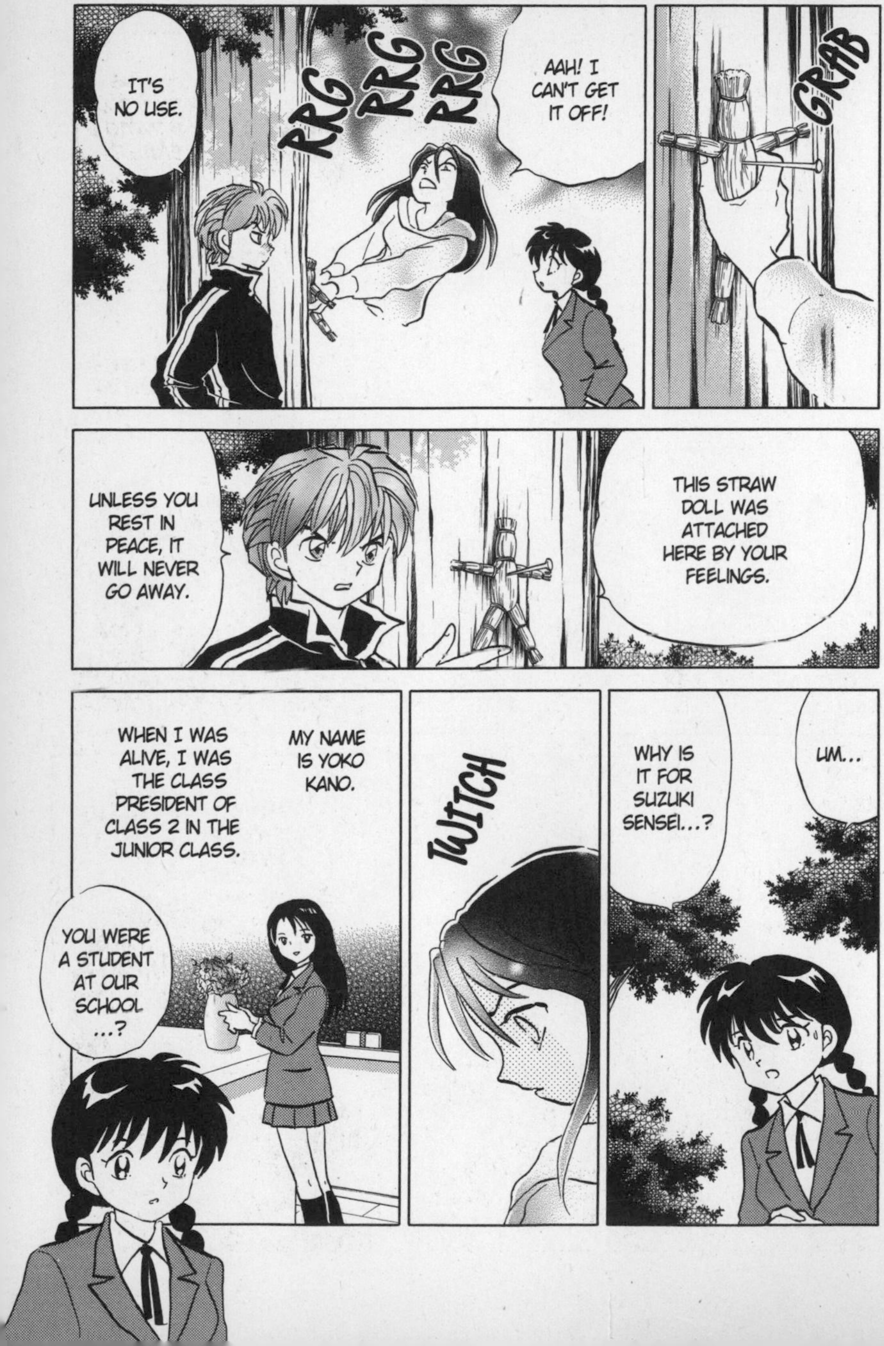
GRAB
AAH! I CAN'T GET IT OFF!
RRG RRG RRG
IT'S NO USE.
THIS STRAW DOLL WAS ATTACHED HERE BY YOUR FEELINGS.
UNLESS YOU REST IN PEACE, IT WILL NEVER GO AWAY.
UM...
WHY IS IT FOR SUZUKI SENSEI...?
TWITCH
MY NAME IS YOKO KANO.
WHEN I WAS ALIVE, I WAS THE CLASS PRESIDENT OF CLASS 2 IN THE JUNIOR CLASS.
YOU WERE A STUDENT AT OUR SCHOOL ...?

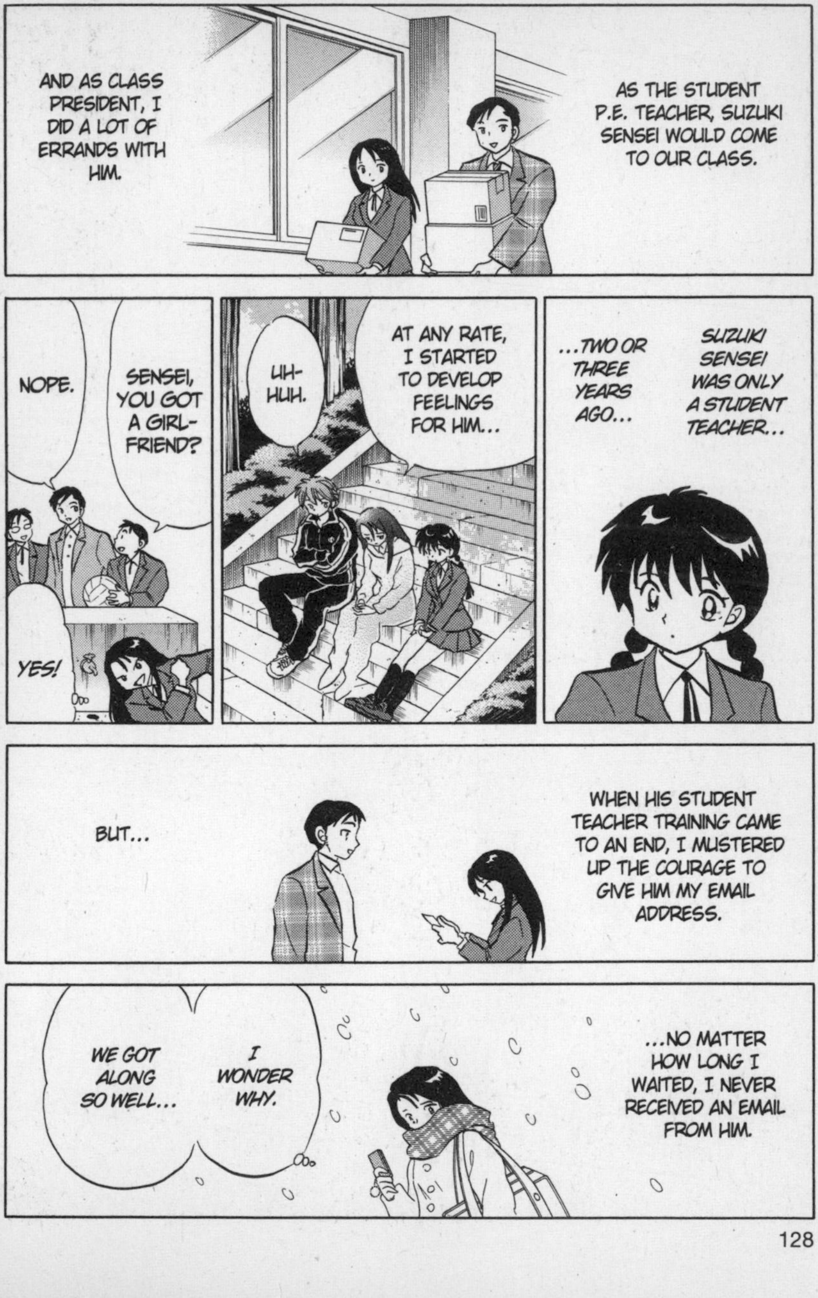
AS THE STUDENT P.E. TEACHER, SUZUKI SENSEI WOULD COME TO OUR CLASS.
AND AS CLASS PRESIDENT, I DID A LOT OF ERRANDS WITH HIM.
SUZUKI SENSEI WAS ONLY A STUDENT TEACHER...
...TWO OR THREE YEARS AGO...
AT ANY RATE, I STARTED TO DEVELOP FEELINGS FOR HIM...
UH-HUH.
SENSEI, YOU GOT A GIRL-FRIEND?
NOPE.
YES!
WHEN HIS STUDENT TEACHER TRAINING CAME TO AN END, I MUSTERED UP THE COURAGE TO GIVE HIM MY EMAIL ADDRESS.
BUT...
...NO MATTER HOW LONG I WAITED, I NEVER RECEIVED AN EMAIL FROM HIM.
I WONDER WHY.
WE GOT ALONG SO WELL...

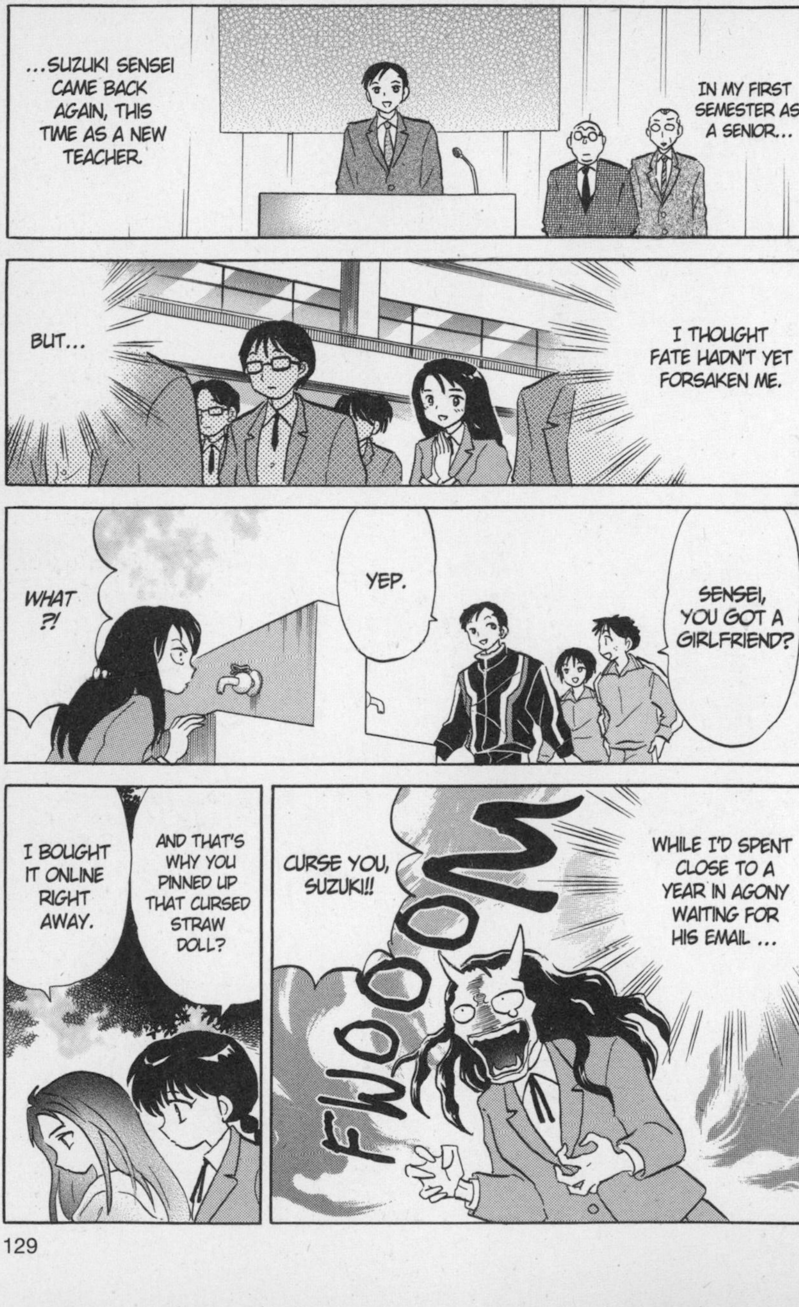
IN MY FIRST SEMESTER AS A SENIOR...
...SUZUKI SENSEI CAME BACK AGAIN, THIS TIME AS A NEW TEACHER.
I THOUGHT FATE HADN'T YET FORSAKEN ME.
BUT...
SENSEI, YOU GOT A GIRLFRIEND?
YEP.
WHAT?!
WHILE I'D SPENT CLOSE TO A YEAR IN AGONY WAITING FOR HIS EMAIL ...
CURSE YOU, SUZUKI!!
FWOOOM
AND THAT'S WHY YOU PINNED UP THAT CURSED STRAW DOLL?
I BOUGHT IT ONLINE RIGHT AWAY.

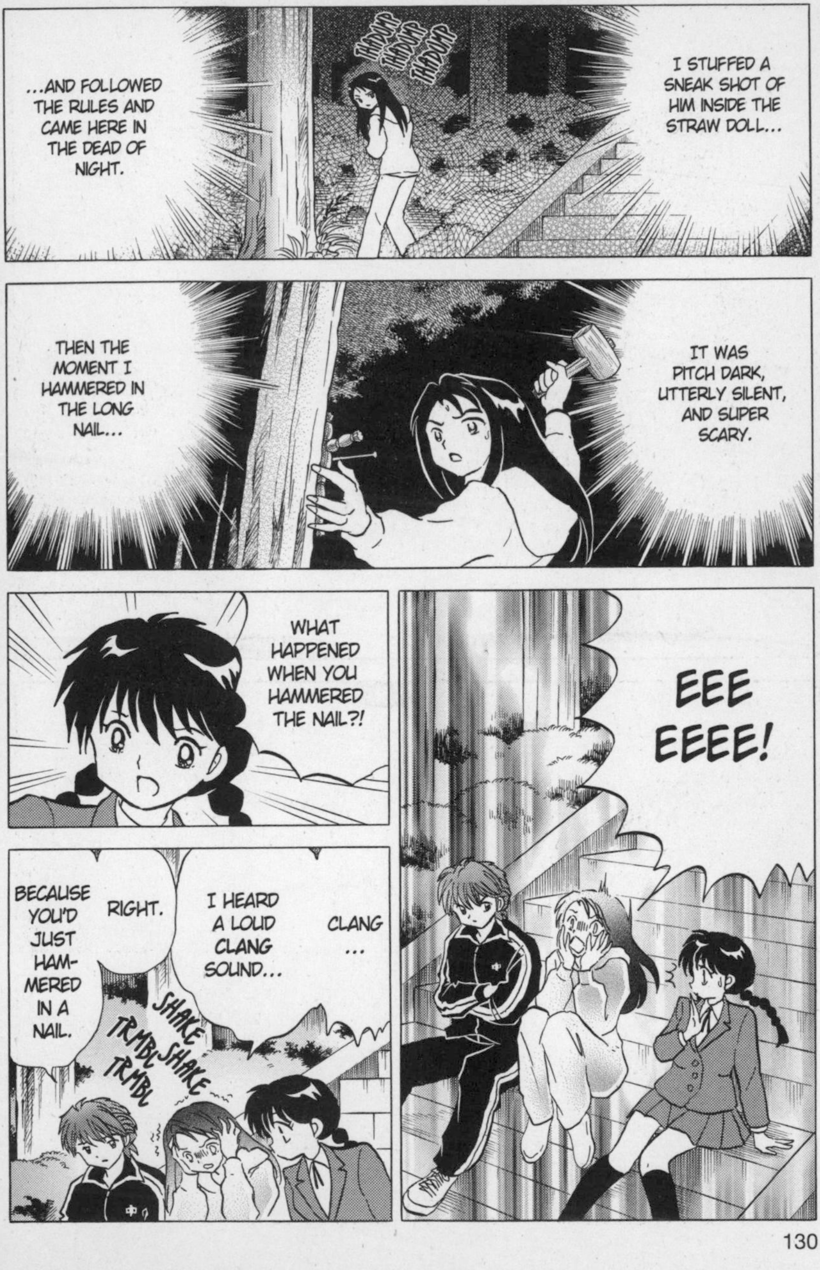
I STUFFED A SNEAK SHOT OF HIM INSIDE THE STRAW DOLL...
THADUMP THADUMP THADUMP
...AND FOLLOWED THE RULES AND CAME HERE IN THE DEAD OF NIGHT.
IT WAS PITCH DARK, UTTERLY SILENT, AND SUPER SCARY.
THEN THE MOMENT I HAMMERED IN THE LONG NAIL...
EEE EEEE!
WHAT HAPPENED WHEN YOU HAMMERED THE NAIL?!
CLANG ...
I HEARD A LOUD CLANG SOUND...
RIGHT.
BECAUSE YOU'D JUST HAM-MERED IN A NAIL.
SHAKE SHAKE
TRMBL TRMBL

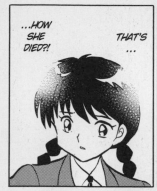

I RAN AWAY AND LEFT THE STRAW DOLL LIKE THAT.
THEN I SLIPPED ON A STEP...
THAT'S ...
...HOW SHE DIED?!
I FELL DOWN THE REST OF THE STAIRS, BUT I COULD TAKE IT.
TOTTER
OW OW...
ON THE WAY HOME, I ALMOST GOT HIT BY A CAR, AND DOGS BARKED AT ME, BUT I MADE IT HOME AND FELL ASLEEP.
SHAKE SHAKE
TRMBL TRMBL
THE NEXT MORNING, I FELT PERFECTLY CALM.
WHAT I DID WAS STUPID ...
AH! THE STRAW DOLL.
I HAVE TO GO GET IT AND EXORCISE IT.
BUT THAT MORNING I GOT FOOD POISONING FROM WHAT I ATE...

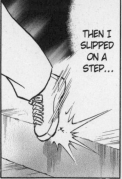

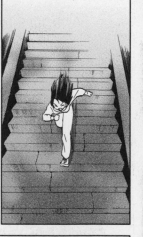

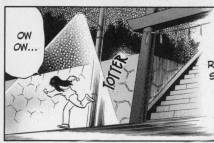

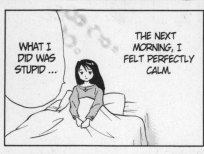

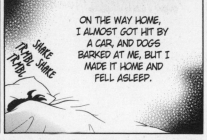

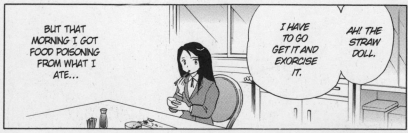

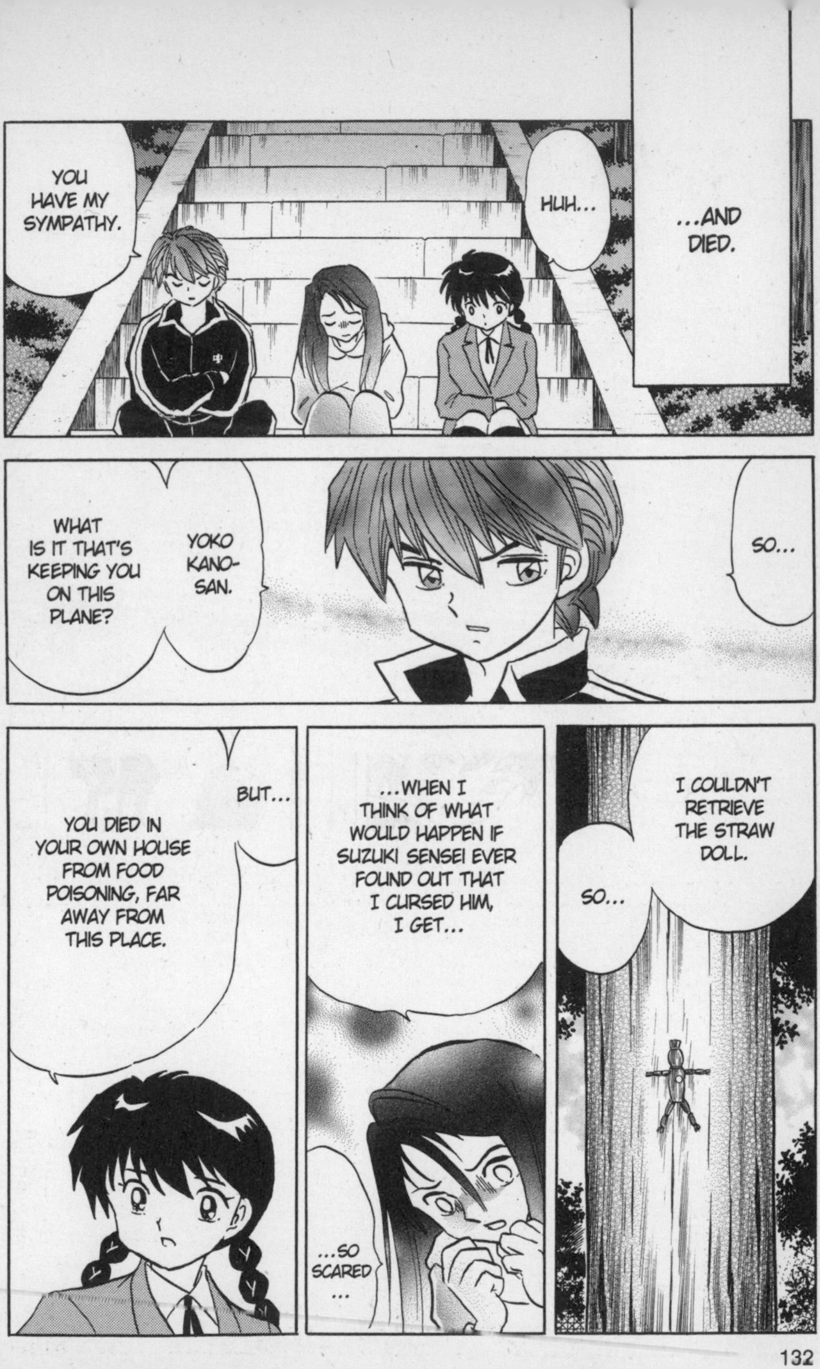
...AND DIED.
HUH...
YOU HAVE MY SYMPATHY.
SO...
YOKO KANO-SAN.
WHAT IS IT THAT'S KEEPING YOU ON THIS PLANE?
I COULDN'T RETRIEVE THE STRAW DOLL.
SO...
...WHEN I THINK OF WHAT WOULD HAPPEN IF SUZUKI SENSEI EVER FOUND OUT THAT I CURSED HIM, I GET...
...SO SCARED...
BUT...
YOU DIED IN YOUR OWN HOUSE FROM FOOD POISONING, FAR AWAY FROM THIS PLACE.

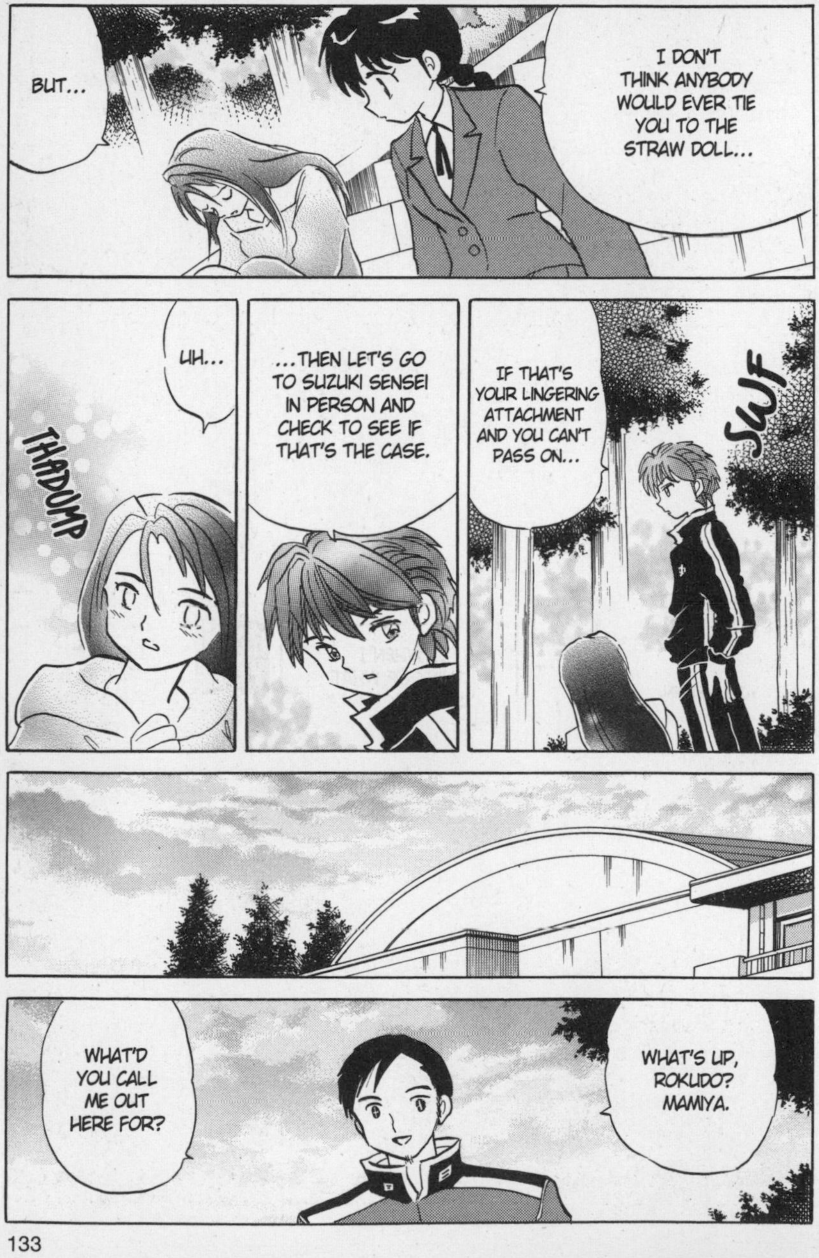
I DON'T THINK ANYBODY WOULD EVER TIE YOU TO THE STRAW DOLL...
BUT...
IF THAT'S YOUR LINGERING ATTACHMENT AND YOU CAN'T PASS ON...
SWF
...THEN LET'S GO TO SUZUKI SENSEI IN PERSON AND CHECK TO SEE IF THAT'S THE CASE.
UH...
THADUMP
WHAT'S UP, ROKUDO? MAMIYA.
WHAT'D YOU CALL ME OUT HERE FOR?

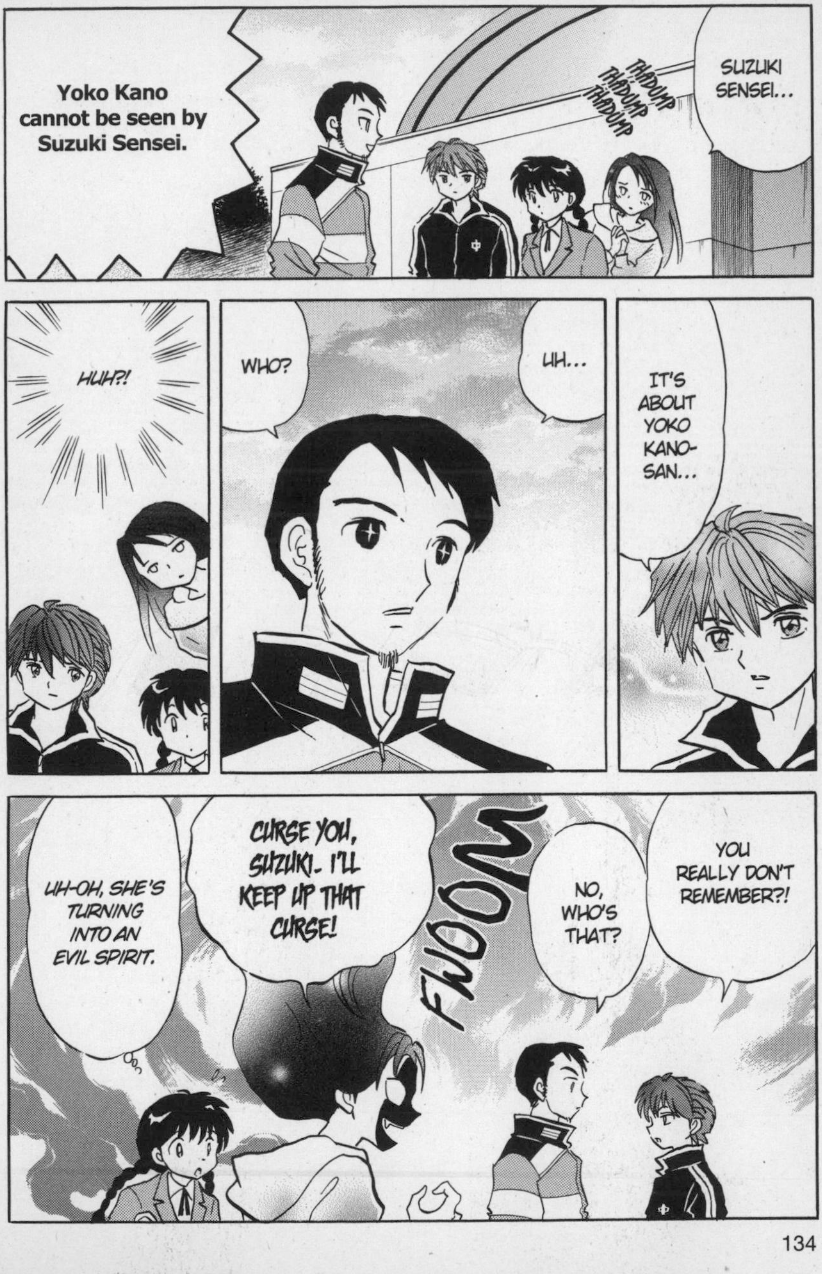
SUZUKI SENSEI...
THADUMP THADUMP THADUMP
Yoko Kano cannot be seen by Suzuki Sensei.
IT'S ABOUT YOKO KANO-SAN...
UH...
WHO?
HUH?!
YOU REALLY DON'T REMEMBER?!
NO, WHO'S THAT?
FWOOM
CURSE YOU, SUZUKI. I'LL KEEP UP THAT CURSE!
UH-OH, SHE'S TURNING INTO AN EVIL SPIRIT.

CHAPTER 116: LET'S TALK IT OUT

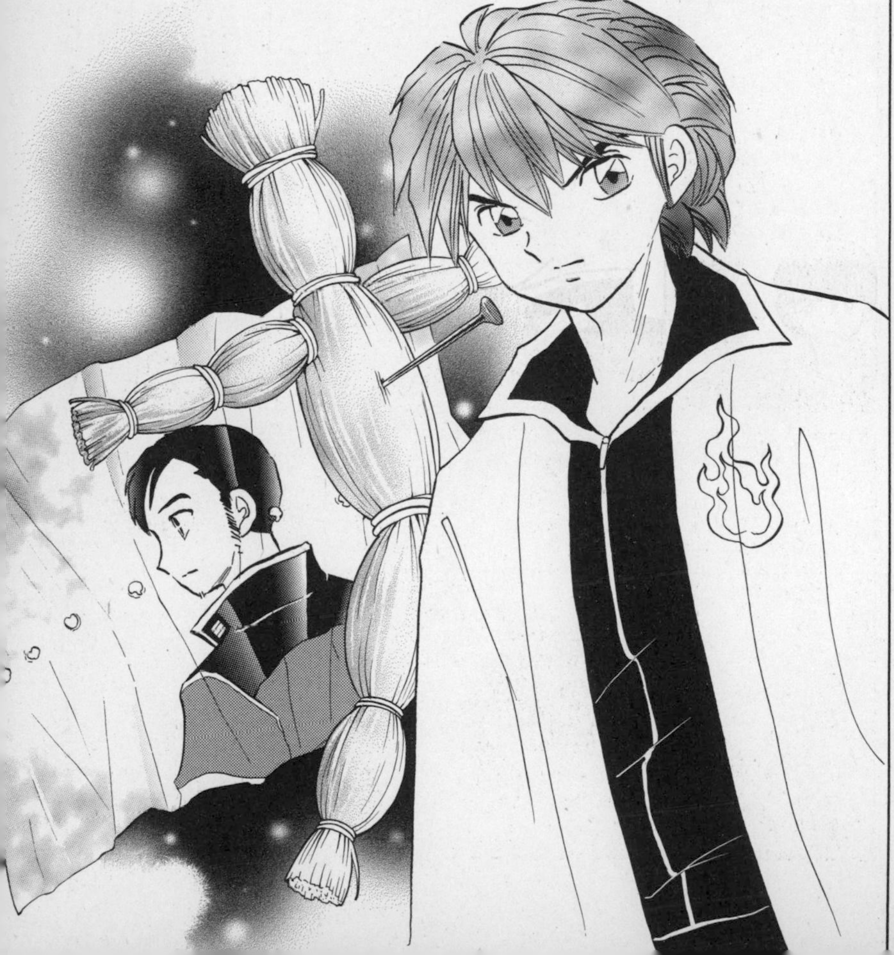

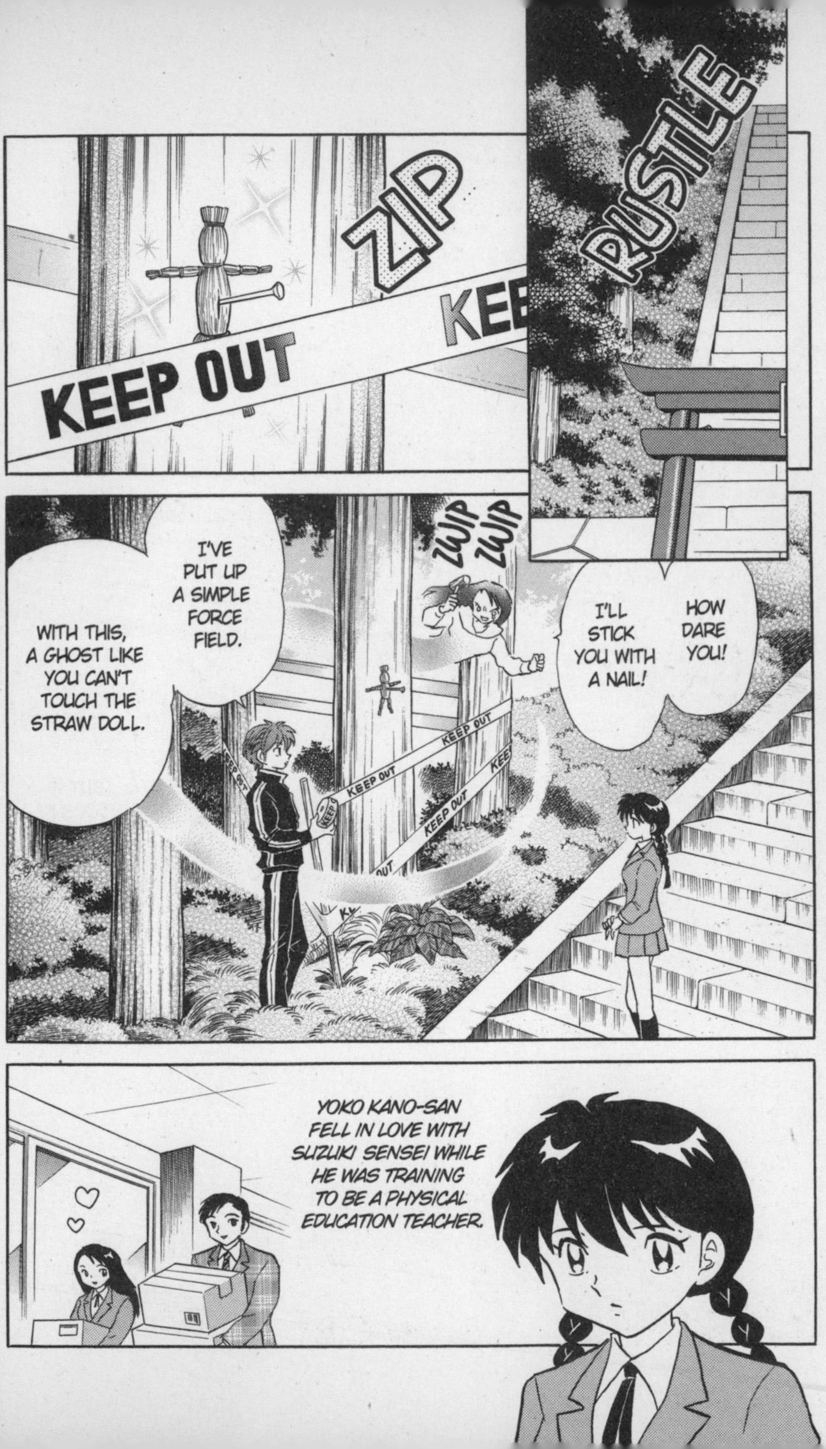
RUSTLE
ZIP
KEE
KEEP OUT
ZWIP ZWIP
HOW DARE YOU!
I'LL STICK YOU WITH A NAIL!
I'VE PUT UP A SIMPLE FORCE FIELD.
WITH THIS, A GHOST LIKE YOU CAN'T TOUCH THE STRAW DOLL.
YOKO KANO-SAN FELL IN LOVE WITH SUZUKI SENSEI WHILE HE WAS TRAINING TO BE A PHYSICAL EDUCATION TEACHER.

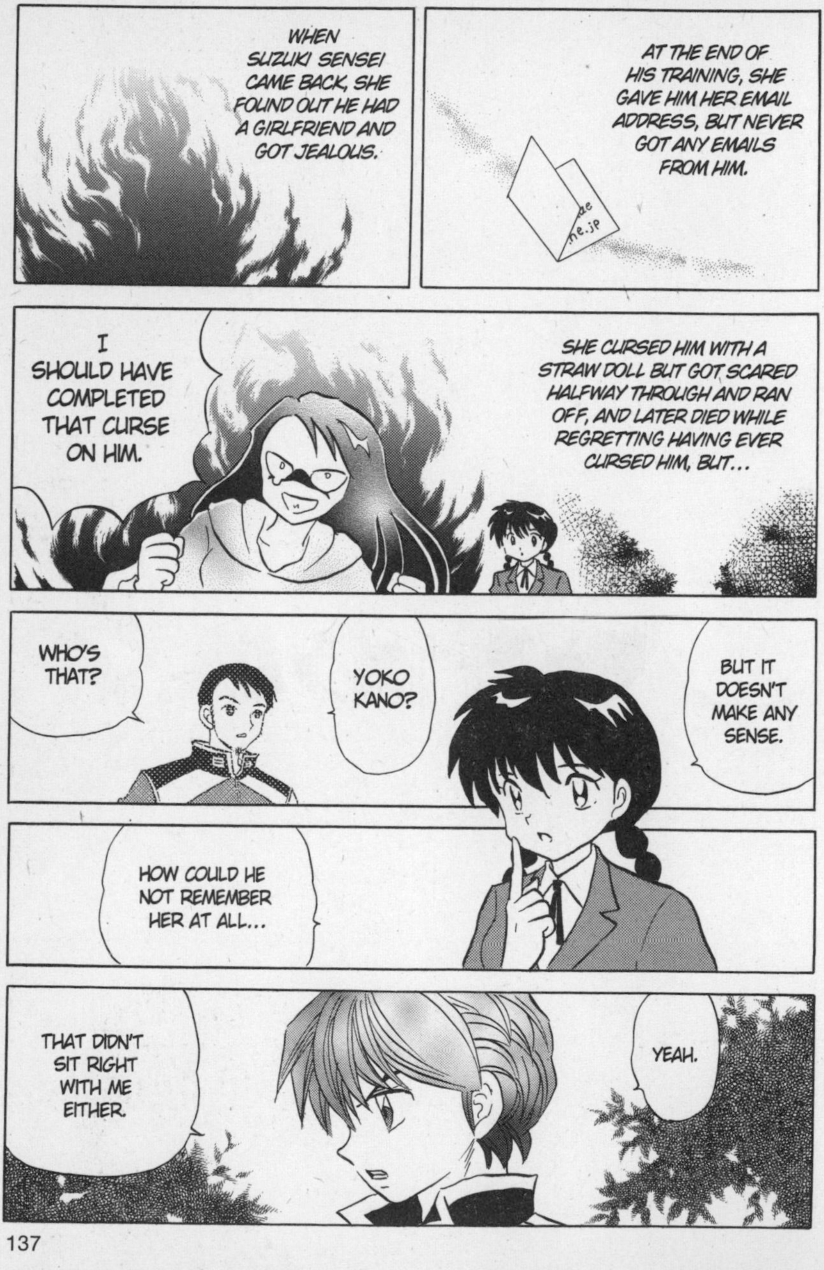
AT THE END OF HIS TRAINING, SHE GAVE HIM HER EMAIL ADDRESS, BUT NEVER GOT ANY EMAILS FROM HIM.
WHEN SUZUKI SENSEI CAME BACK, SHE FOUND OUT HE HAD A GIRLFRIEND AND GOT JEALOUS.
SHE CURSED HIM WITH A STRAW DOLL BUT GOT SCARED HALFWAY THROUGH AND RAN OFF, AND LATER DIED WHILE REGRETTING HAVING EVER CURSED HIM, BUT...
I SHOULD HAVE COMPLETED THAT CURSE ON HIM.
BUT IT DOESN'T MAKE ANY SENSE.
YOKO KANO?
WHO'S THAT?
HOW COULD HE NOT REMEMBER HER AT ALL...
YEAH.
THAT DIDN'T SIT RIGHT WITH ME EITHER.

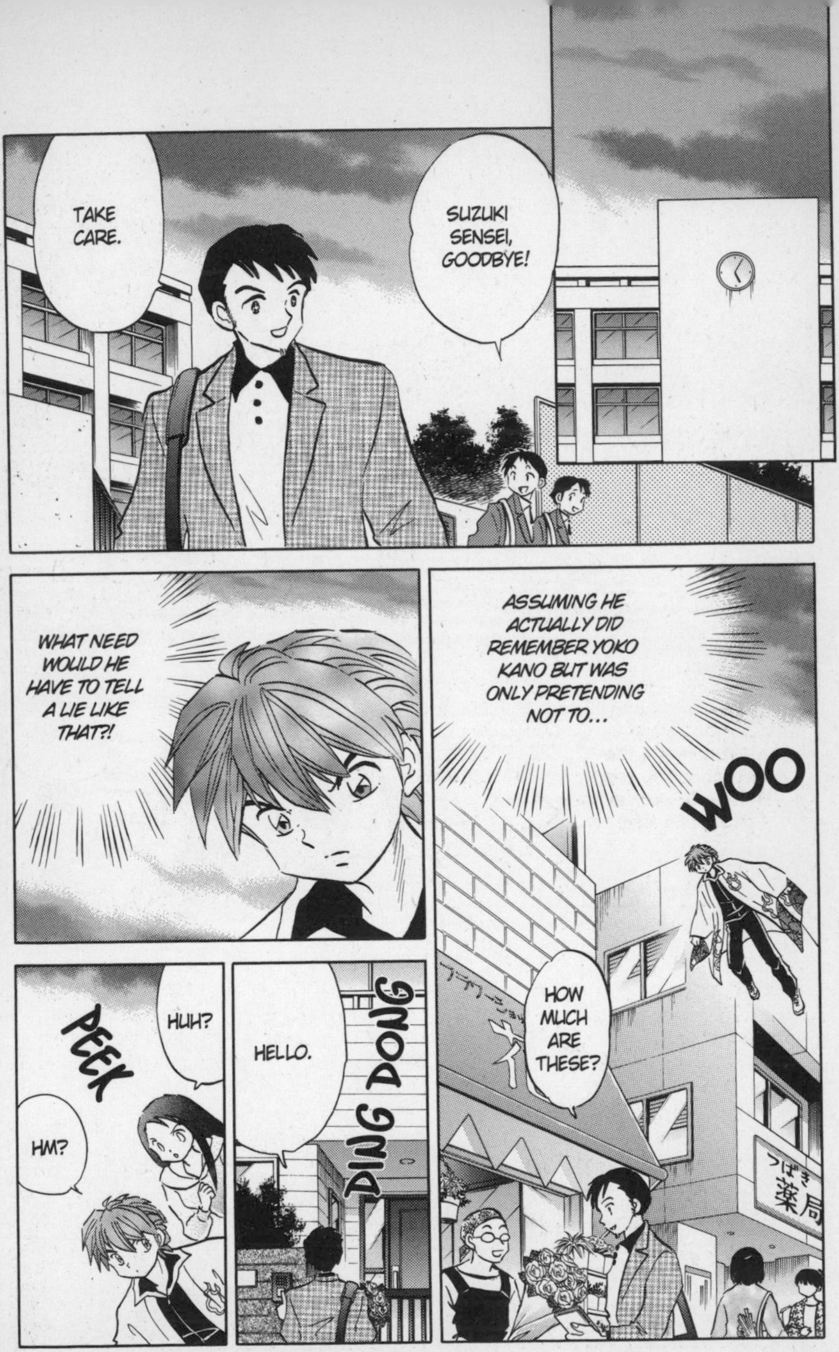
SUZUKI SENSEI, GOODBYE!
TAKE CARE.
ASSUMING HE ACTUALLY DID REMEMBER YOKO KANO BUT WAS ONLY PRETENDING NOT TO...
WOO
HOW MUCH ARE THESE?
つばき 薬局
WHAT NEED WOULD HE HAVE TO TELL A LIE LIKE THAT?!
DING DONG
HELLO.
HUH?
PEEK
HM?

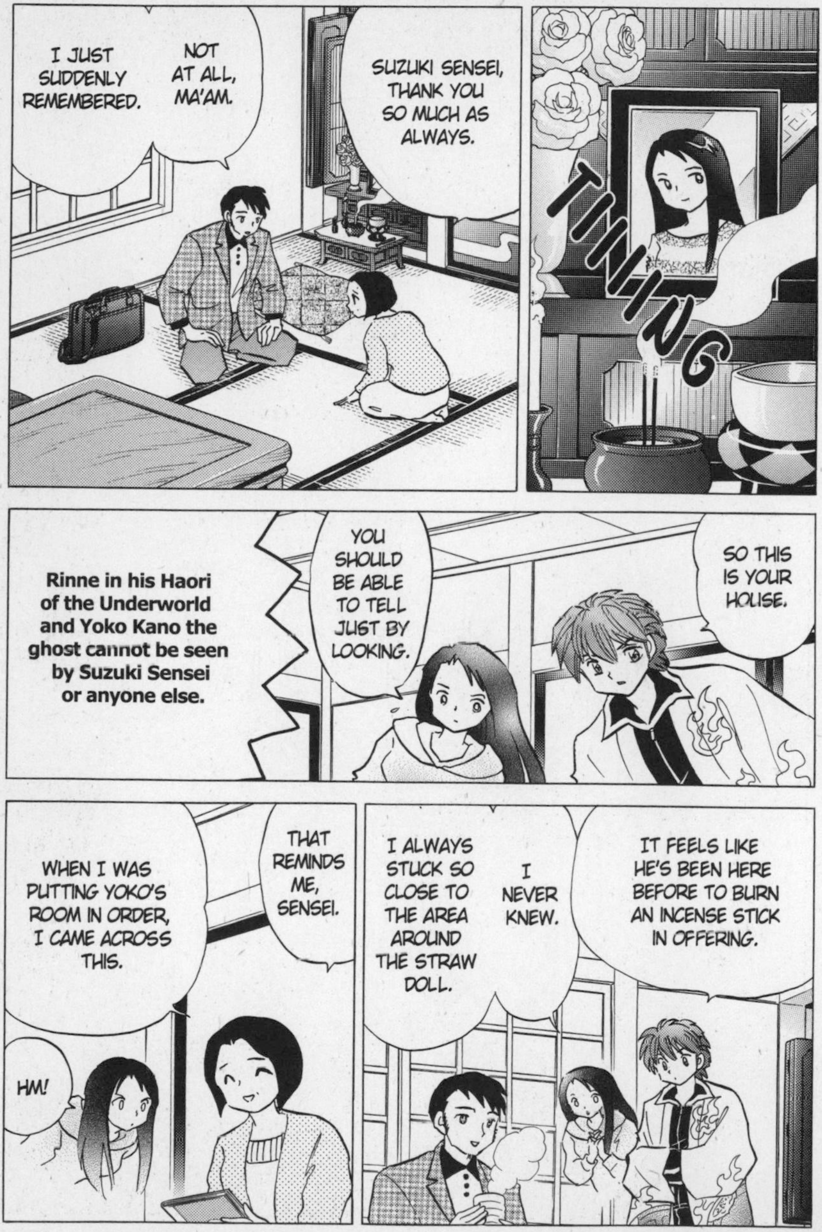
TINNING
SUZUKI SENSEI, THANK YOU SO MUCH AS ALWAYS.
NOT AT ALL, MA'AM.
I JUST SUDDENLY REMEMBERED.
SO THIS IS YOUR HOUSE.
YOU SHOULD BE ABLE TO TELL JUST BY LOOKING.
Rinne in his Haori of the Underworld and Yoko Kano the ghost cannot be seen by Suzuki Sensei or anyone else.
IT FEELS LIKE HE'S BEEN HERE BEFORE TO BURN AN INCENSE STICK IN OFFERING.
I NEVER KNEW.
I ALWAYS STUCK SO CLOSE TO THE AREA AROUND THE STRAW DOLL.
THAT REMINDS ME, SENSEI.
WHEN I WAS PUTTING YOKO'S ROOM IN ORDER, I CAME ACROSS THIS.
HM!

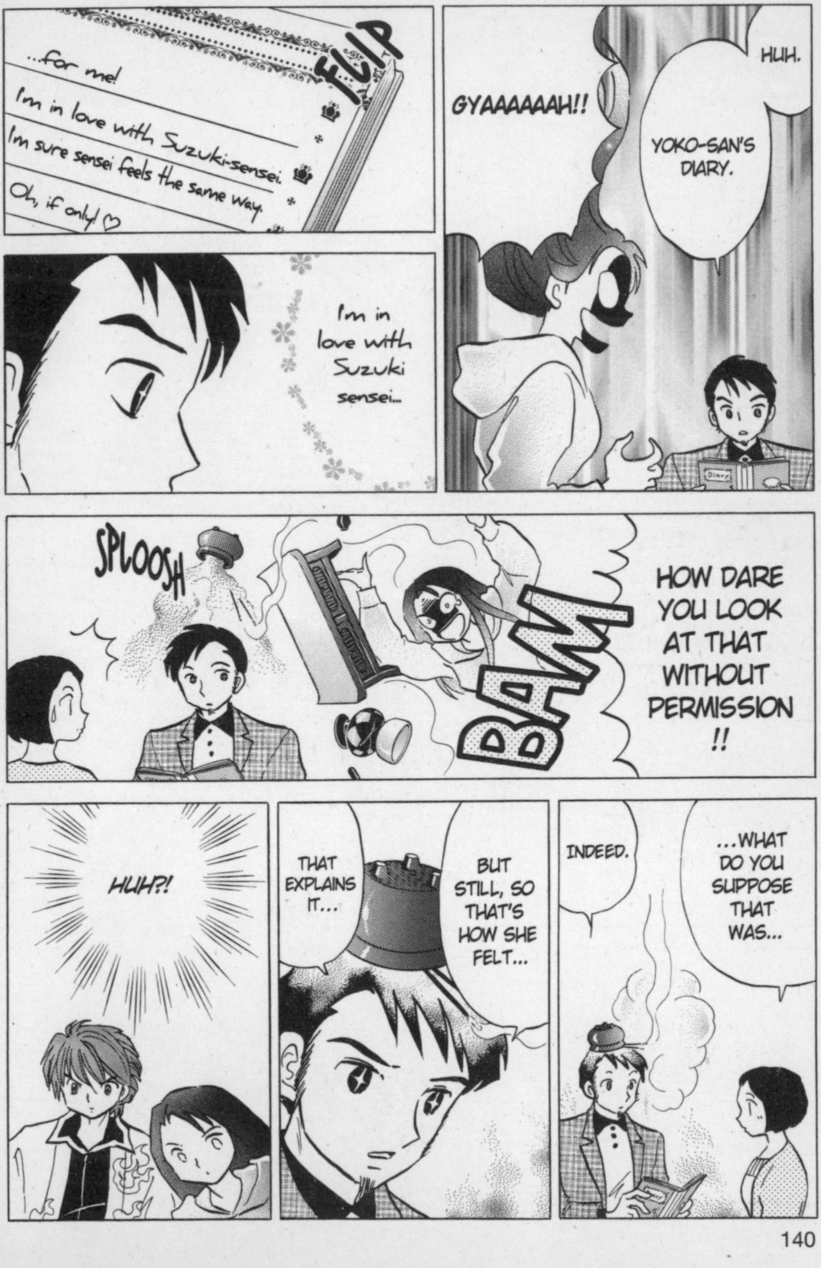
HUH.
YOKO-SAN'S DIARY.
GYAAAAAAH!!
FLIP
...for me!
I'm in love with Suzuki-sensei.
I'm sure sensei feels the same way.
Oh, if only! ♡
I'm in love with Suzuki sensei...
HOW DARE YOU LOOK AT THAT WITHOUT PERMISSION !!
BAM
SPLOOSH
...WHAT DO YOU SUPPOSE THAT WAS...
INDEED.
BUT STILL, SO THAT'S HOW SHE FELT...
THAT EXPLAINS IT...
HUH?!

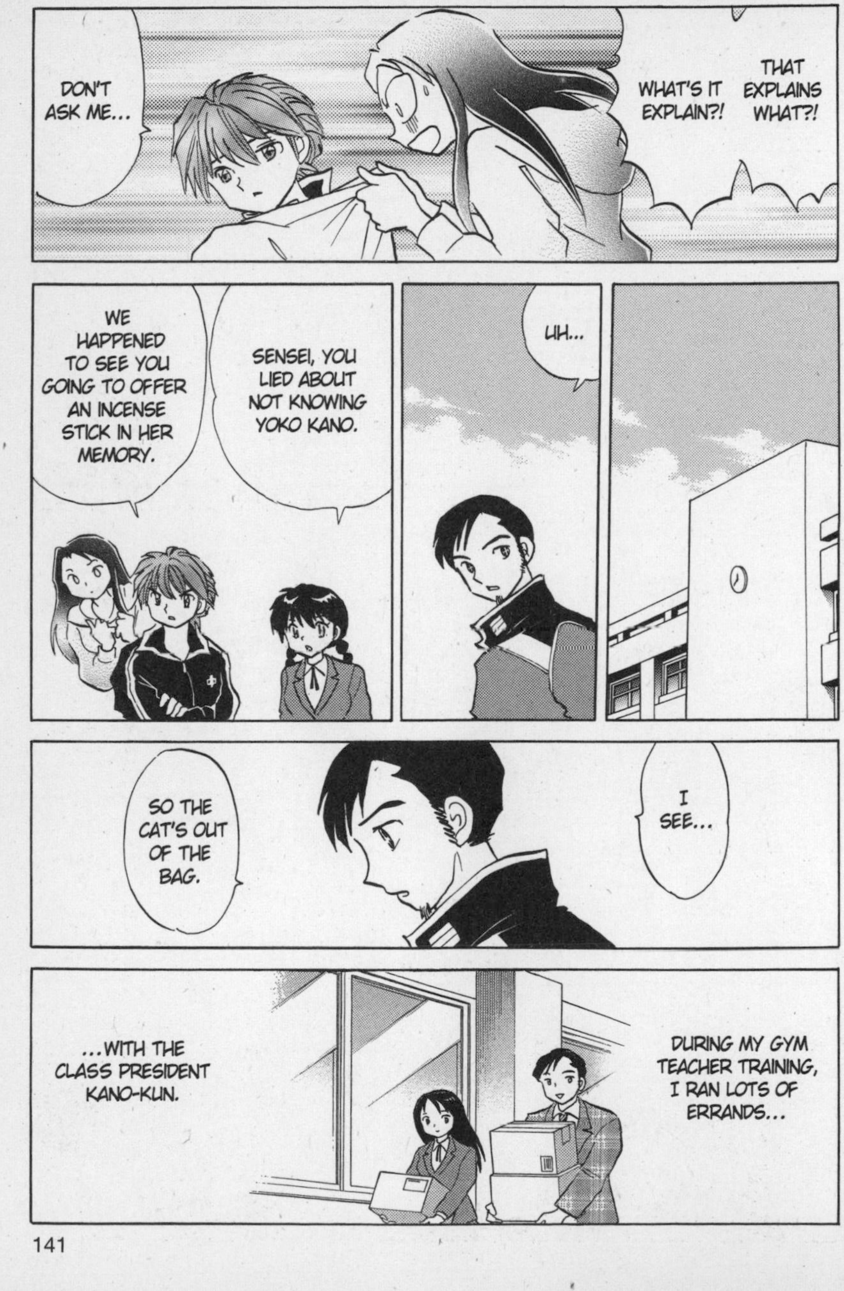
THAT EXPLAINS WHAT?!
WHAT'S IT EXPLAIN?!
DON'T ASK ME...
UH...
SENSEI, YOU LIED ABOUT NOT KNOWING YOKO KANO.
WE HAPPENED TO SEE YOU GOING TO OFFER AN INCENSE STICK IN HER MEMORY.
I SEE...
SO THE CAT'S OUT OF THE BAG.
DURING MY GYM TEACHER TRAINING, I RAN LOTS OF ERRANDS...
...WITH THE CLASS PRESIDENT KANO-KUN.

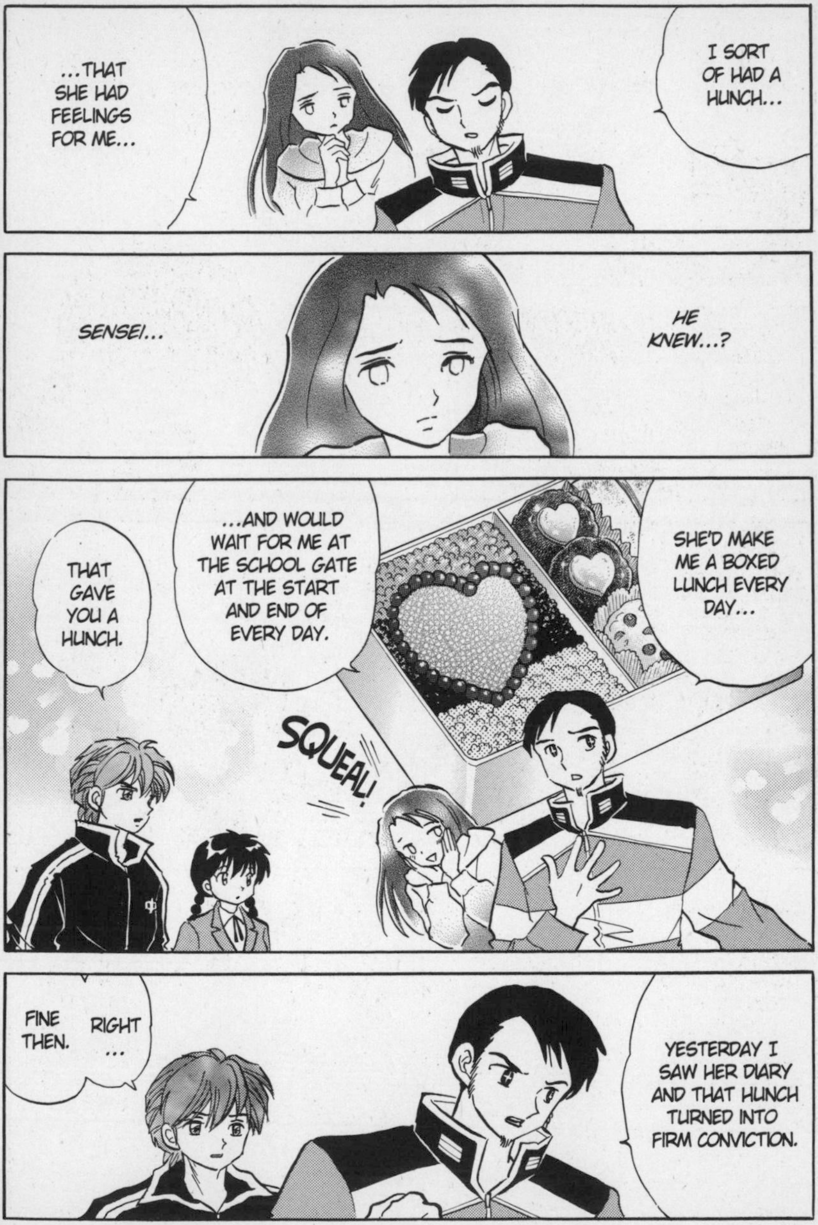
I SORT OF HAD A HUNCH...
...THAT SHE HAD FEELINGS FOR ME...
HE KNEW...?
SENSEI...
SHE'D MAKE ME A BOXED LUNCH EVERY DAY...
...AND WOULD WAIT FOR ME AT THE SCHOOL GATE AT THE START AND END OF EVERY DAY.
SQUEAL!
THAT GAVE YOU A HUNCH.
YESTERDAY I SAW HER DIARY AND THAT HUNCH TURNED INTO FIRM CONVICTION.
RIGHT ...
FINE THEN.

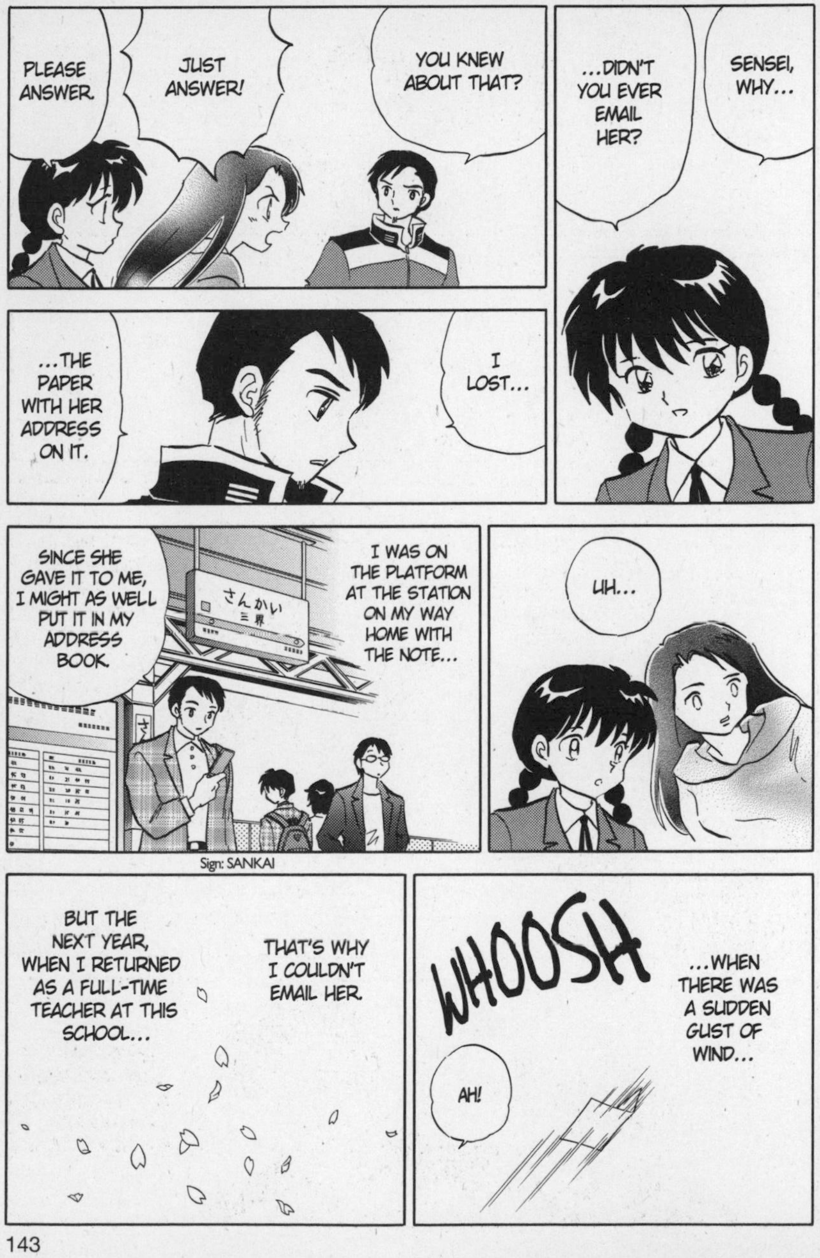
SENSEI, WHY...
...DIDN'T YOU EVER EMAIL HER?
YOU KNEW ABOUT THAT?
JUST ANSWER!
PLEASE ANSWER.
I LOST...
...THE PAPER WITH HER ADDRESS ON IT.
UH...
I WAS ON THE PLATFORM AT THE STATION ON MY WAY HOME WITH THE NOTE...
SINCE SHE GAVE IT TO ME, I MIGHT AS WELL PUT IT IN MY ADDRESS BOOK.
さんかい
三界
Sign: SANKAI
...WHEN THERE WAS A SUDDEN GUST OF WIND...
WHOOSH
AH!
THAT'S WHY I COULDN'T EMAIL HER.
BUT THE NEXT YEAR, WHEN I RETURNED AS A FULL-TIME TEACHER AT THIS SCHOOL...

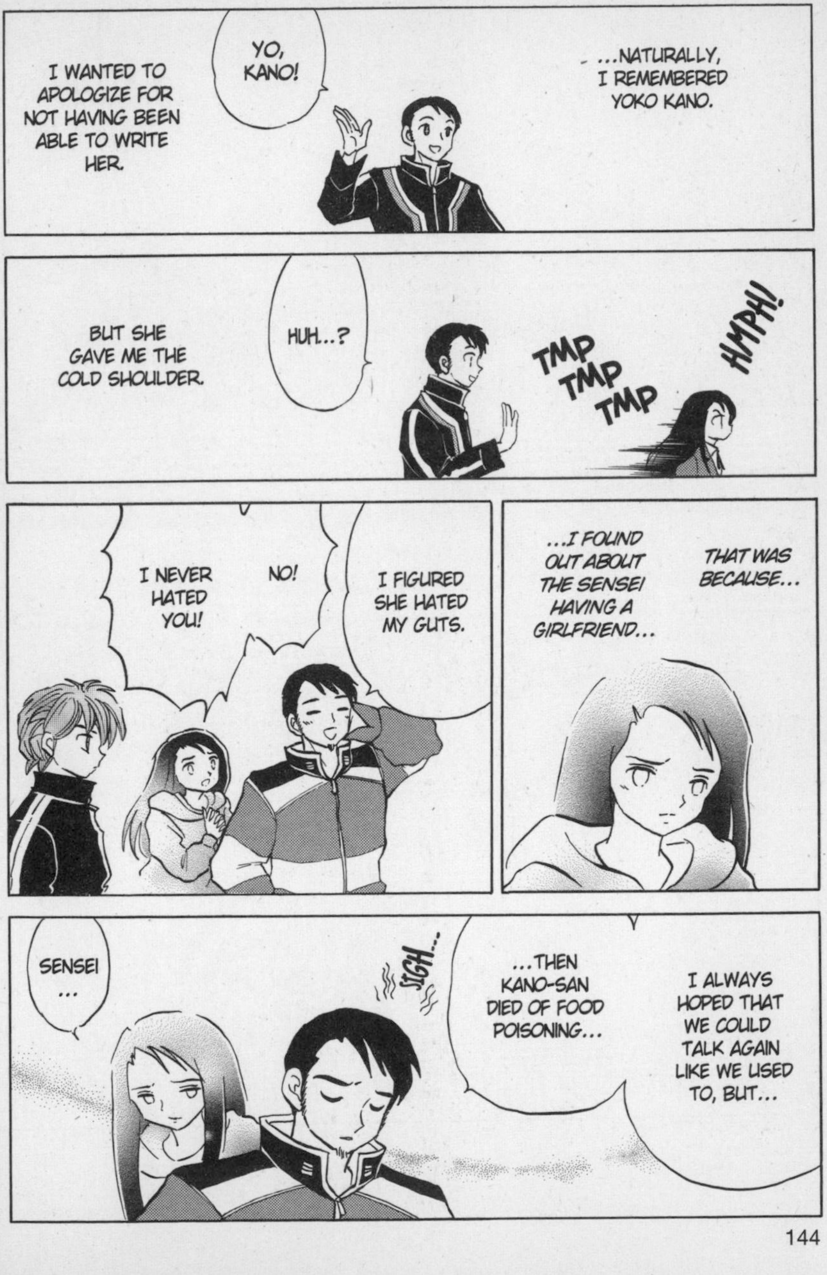
...NATURALLY, I REMEMBERED YOKO KANO.
YO, KANO!
I WANTED TO APOLOGIZE FOR NOT HAVING BEEN ABLE TO WRITE HER.
HMPH!
TMP TMP TMP
HUH...?
BUT SHE GAVE ME THE COLD SHOULDER.
THAT WAS BECAUSE...
...I FOUND OUT ABOUT THE SENSEI HAVING A GIRLFRIEND...
I FIGURED SHE HATED MY GUTS.
NO!
I NEVER HATED YOU!
I ALWAYS HOPED THAT WE COULD TALK AGAIN LIKE WE USED TO, BUT...
...THEN KANO-SAN DIED OF FOOD POISONING...
SIGH...
SENSEI ...

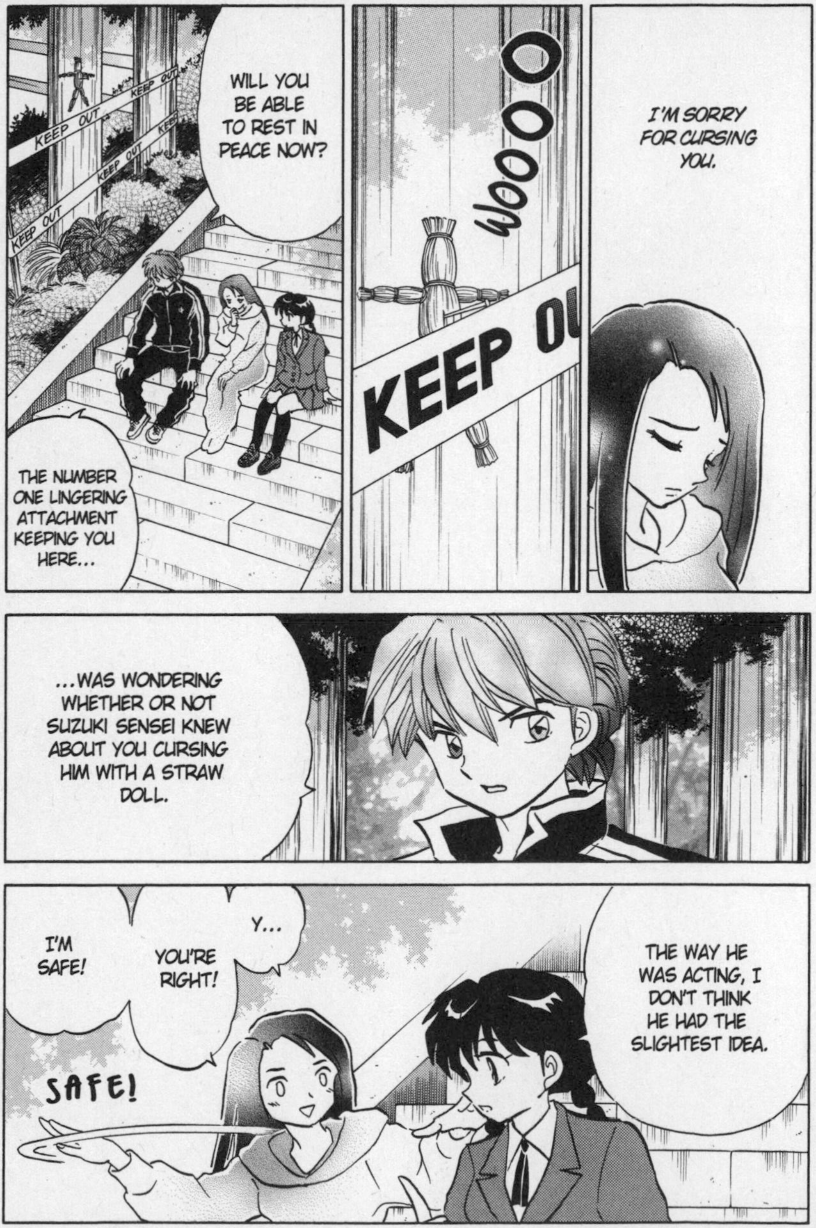
I'M SORRY FOR CURSING YOU.
WOOOO
KEEP OU
WILL YOU BE ABLE TO REST IN PEACE NOW?
THE NUMBER ONE LINGERING ATTACHMENT KEEPING YOU HERE...
...WAS WONDERING WHETHER OR NOT SUZUKI SENSEI KNEW ABOUT YOU CURSING HIM WITH A STRAW DOLL.
THE WAY HE WAS ACTING, I DON'T THINK HE HAD THE SLIGHTEST IDEA.
Y... YOU'RE RIGHT!
I'M SAFE!
SAFE!

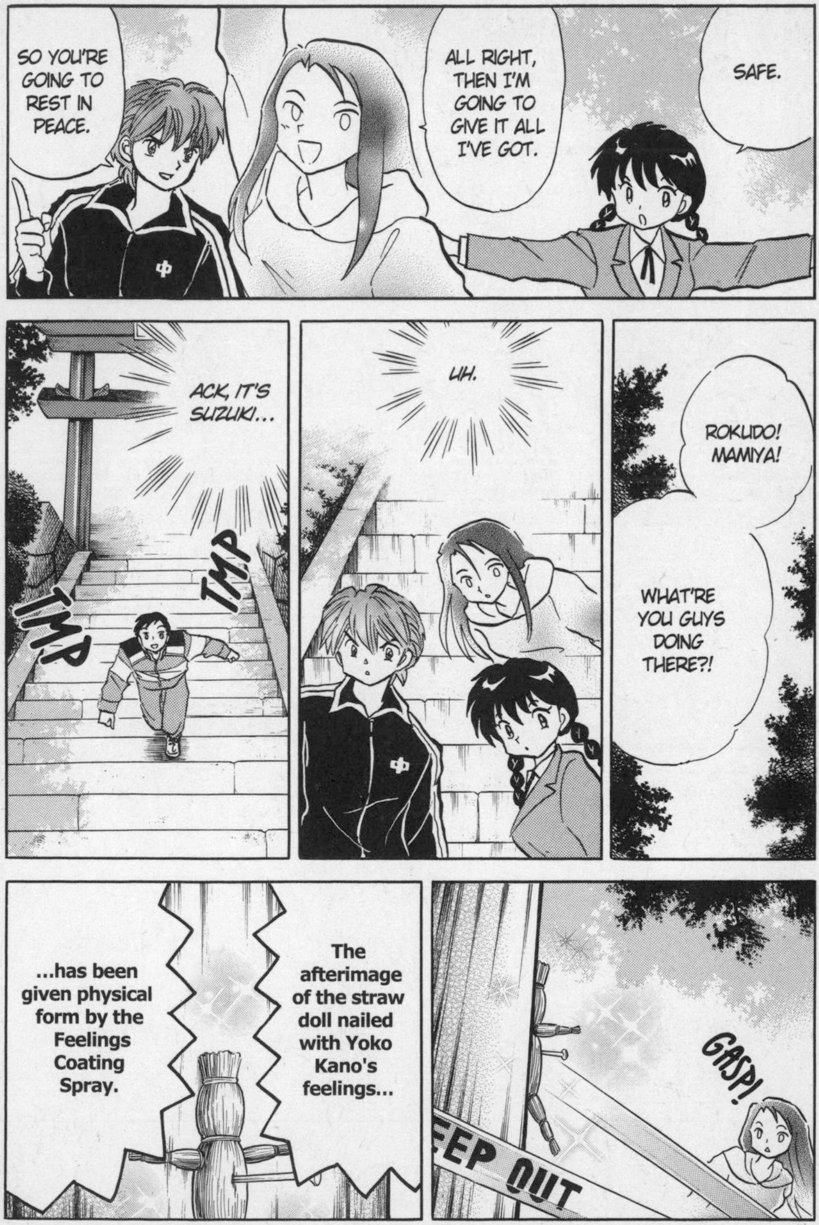
SAFE.
ALL RIGHT, THEN I'M GOING TO GIVE IT ALL I'VE GOT.
SO YOU'RE GOING TO REST IN PEACE.
ROKUDO! MAMIYA!
WHAT'RE YOU GUYS DOING THERE?!
UH.
ACK, IT'S SUZUKI...
TMP
TMP
GASP!
EEP OUT
The afterimage of the straw doll nailed with Yoko Kano's feelings...
...has been given physical form by the Feelings Coating Spray.

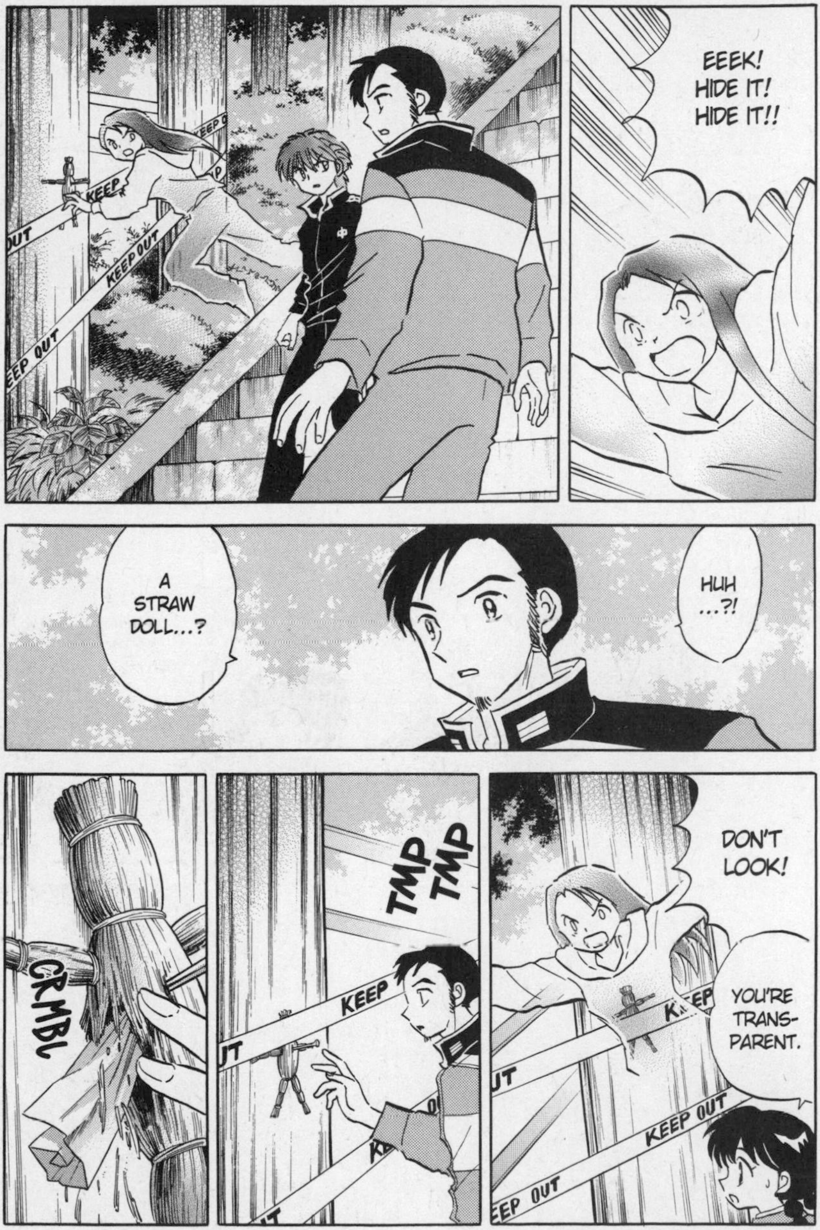
EEEK! HIDE IT! HIDE IT!!
HUH ...?!
A STRAW DOLL...?
DON'T LOOK!
YOU'RE TRANS-PARENT.
TMP TMP
CRMBL

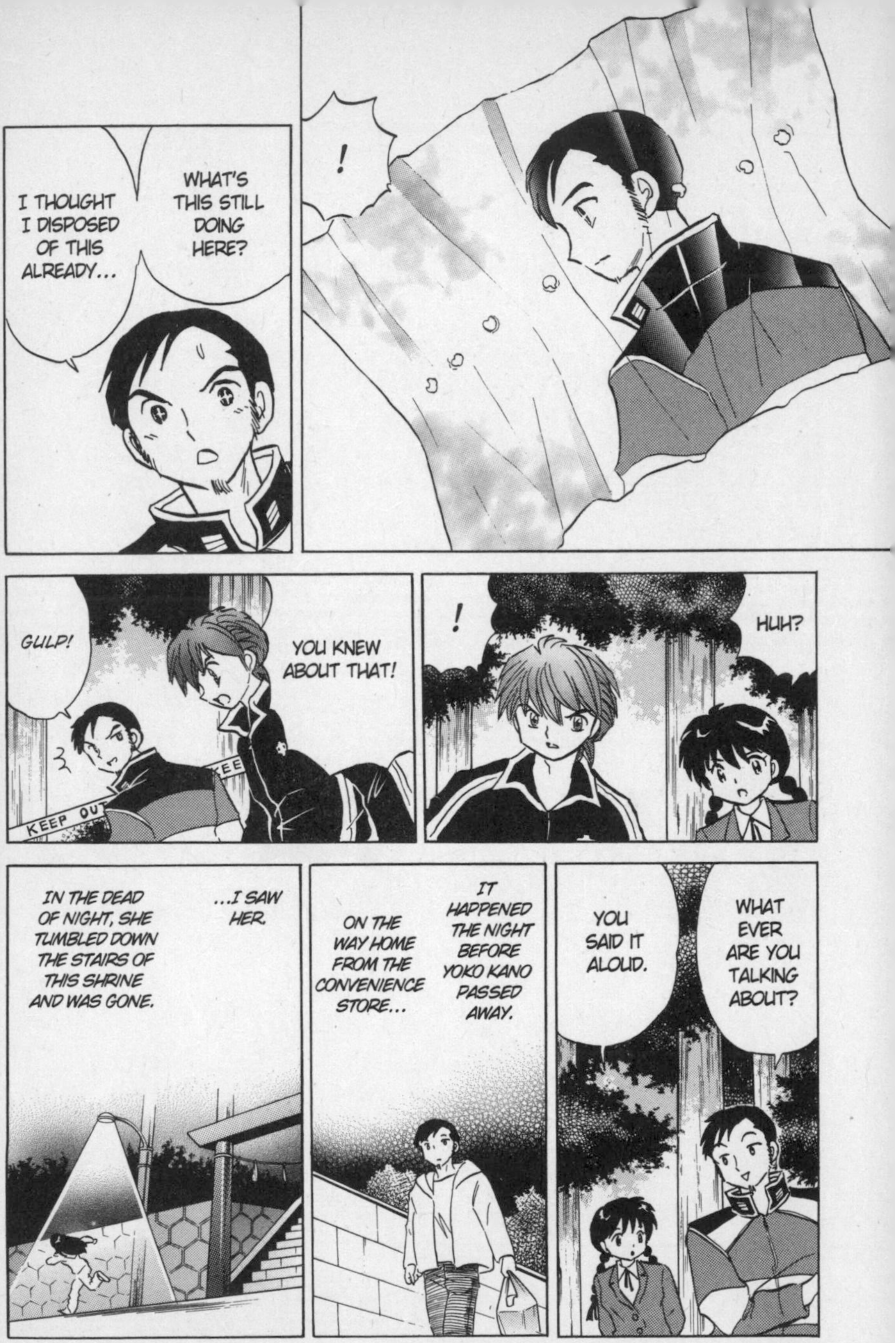
!
WHAT'S THIS STILL DOING HERE?
I THOUGHT I DISPOSED OF THIS ALREADY...
HUH?
!
YOU KNEW ABOUT THAT!
GULP!
KEEP OUT
WHAT EVER ARE YOU TALKING ABOUT?
YOU SAID IT ALOUD.
IT HAPPENED THE NIGHT BEFORE YOKO KANO PASSED AWAY.
ON THE WAY HOME FROM THE CONVENIENCE STORE...
...I SAW HER.
IN THE DEAD OF NIGHT, SHE TUMBLED DOWN THE STAIRS OF THIS SHRINE AND WAS GONE.

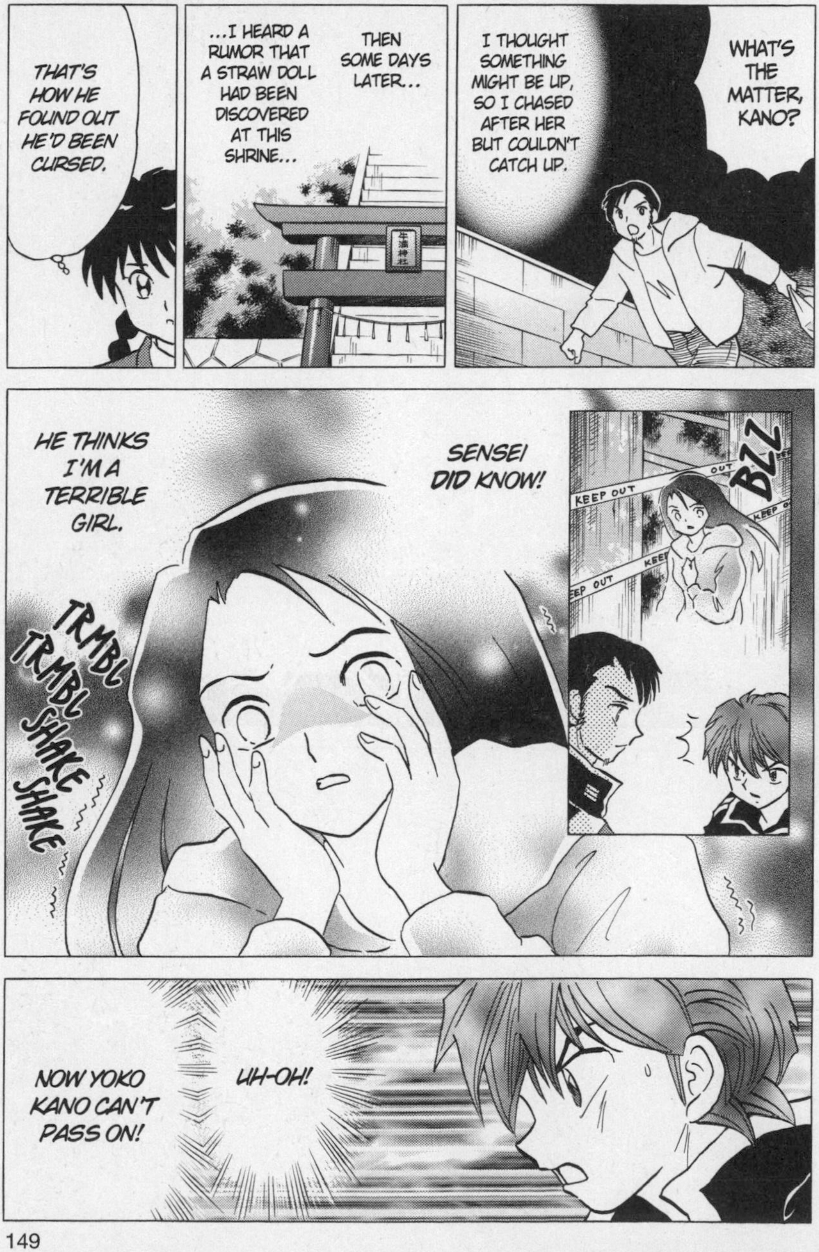
WHAT'S THE MATTER, KANO?
I THOUGHT SOMETHING MIGHT BE UP, SO I CHASED AFTER HER BUT COULDN'T CATCH UP.
THEN SOME DAYS LATER...
...I HEARD A RUMOR THAT A STRAW DOLL HAD BEEN DISCOVERED AT THIS SHRINE...
THAT'S HOW HE FOUND OUT HE'D BEEN CURSED.
BZZ
KEEP OUT
KEEP OUT
SENSEI DID KNOW!
HE THINKS I'M A TERRIBLE GIRL.
TRMBL TRMBL SHAKE SHAKE
UH-OH!
NOW YOKO KANO CAN'T PASS ON!

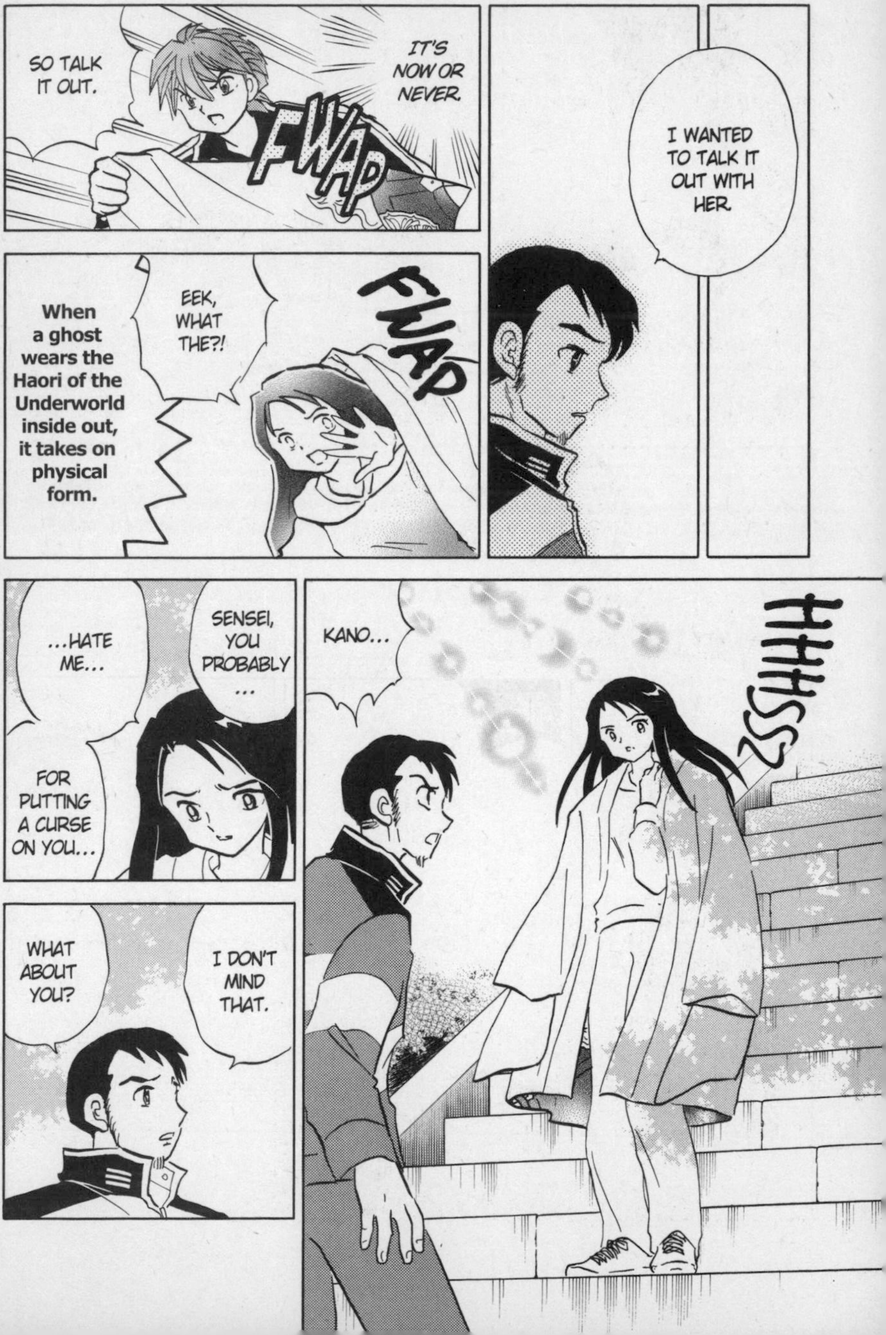
I WANTED TO TALK IT OUT WITH HER.
IT'S NOW OR NEVER.
FWAP
SO TALK IT OUT.
FWAP
EEK, WHAT THE?!
When a ghost wears the Haori of the Underworld inside out, it takes on physical form.
HHHSSS
KANO...
SENSEI, YOU PROBABLY...
...HATE ME...
FOR PUTTING A CURSE ON YOU...
I DON'T MIND THAT.
WHAT ABOUT YOU?

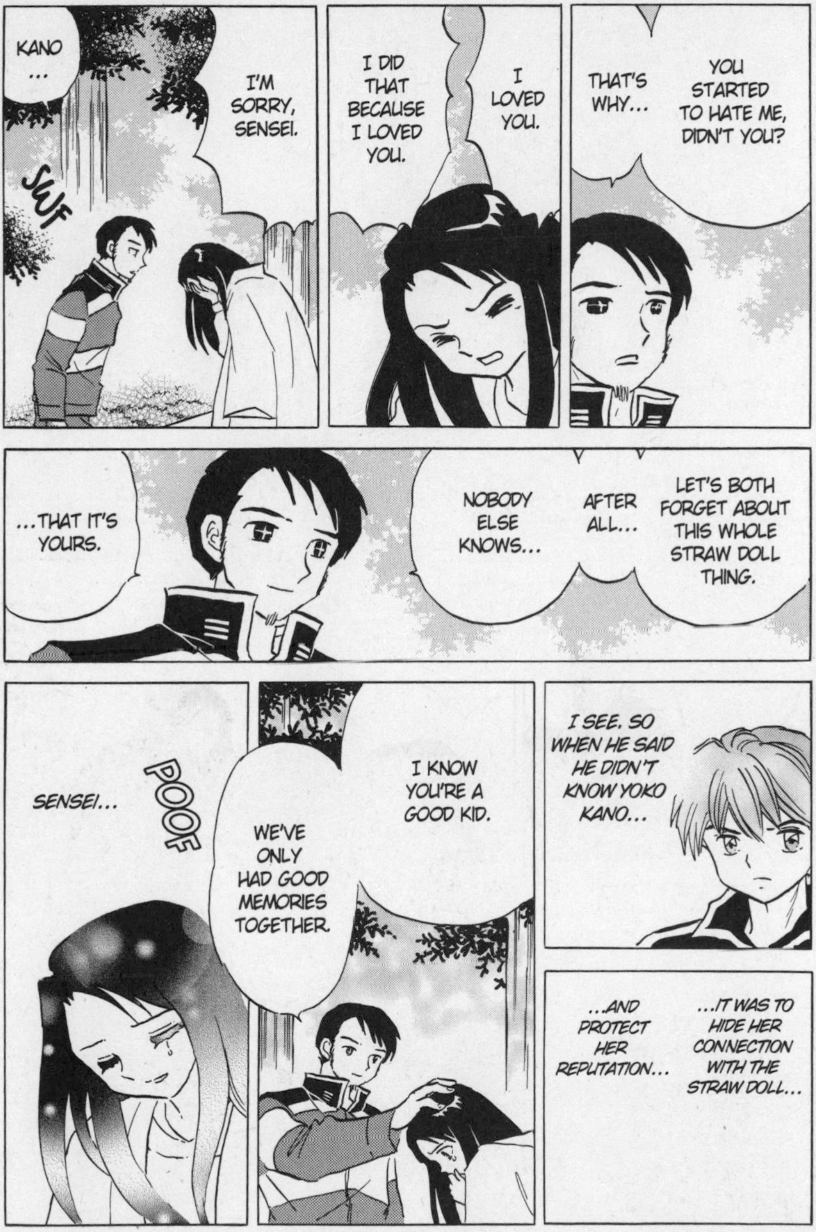
YOU STARTED TO HATE ME, DIDN'T YOU?
THAT'S WHY...
I LOVED YOU.
I DID THAT BECAUSE I LOVED YOU.
I'M SORRY, SENSEI.
KANO...
SWF
LET'S BOTH FORGET ABOUT THIS WHOLE STRAW DOLL THING.
AFTER ALL...
NOBODY ELSE KNOWS...
...THAT IT'S YOURS.
I SEE. SO WHEN HE SAID HE DIDN'T KNOW YOKO KANO...
...IT WAS TO HIDE HER CONNECTION WITH THE STRAW DOLL...
...AND PROTECT HER REPUTATION...
I KNOW YOU'RE A GOOD KID.
WE'VE ONLY HAD GOOD MEMORIES TOGETHER.
POOF
SENSEI...

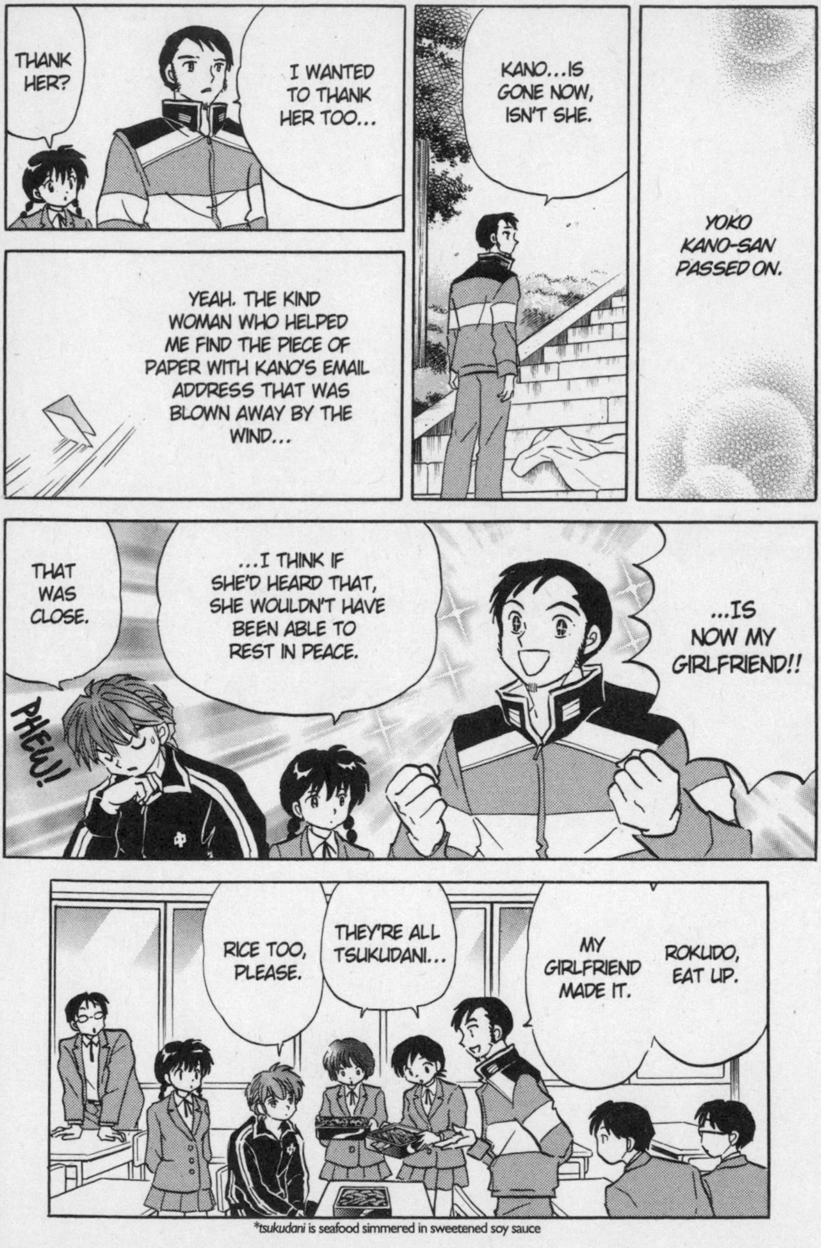
YOKO KANO-SAN PASSED ON.
KANO…IS GONE NOW, ISN'T SHE.
I WANTED TO THANK HER TOO…
THANK HER?
YEAH. THE KIND WOMAN WHO HELPED ME FIND THE PIECE OF PAPER WITH KANO'S EMAIL ADDRESS THAT WAS BLOWN AWAY BY THE WIND…
...IS NOW MY GIRLFRIEND!!
…I THINK IF SHE'D HEARD THAT, SHE WOULDN'T HAVE BEEN ABLE TO REST IN PEACE.
THAT WAS CLOSE.
PHEW!
ROKUDO, EAT UP.
MY GIRLFRIEND MADE IT.
THEY'RE ALL TSUKUDANI…
RICE TOO, PLEASE.

tsukudani is seafood simmered in sweetened soy sauce

CHAPTER 117: THE WANDERING POWER STONE

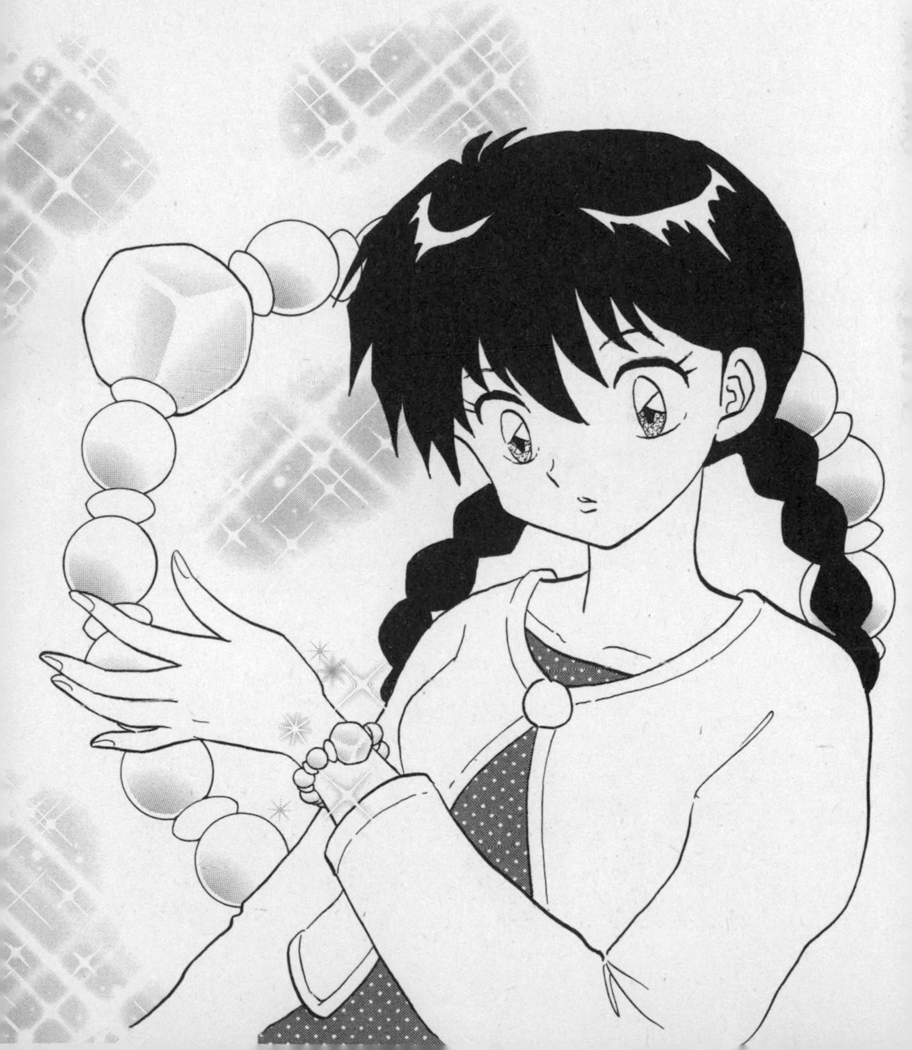

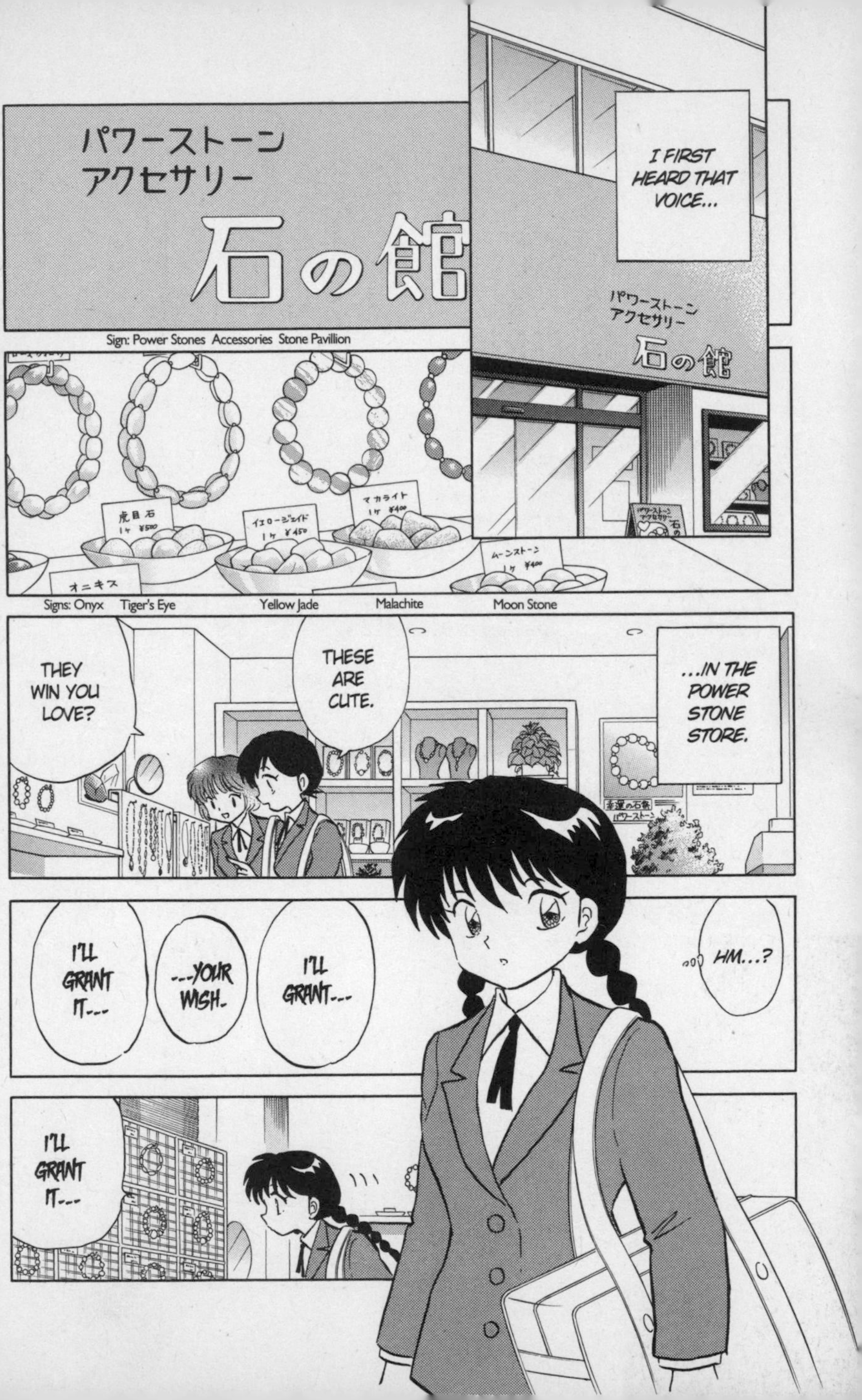
I FIRST HEARD THAT VOICE...
パワーストーン
アクセサリー
石の館
パワーストーン
アクセサリー
石の館
Sign: Power Stones Accessories Stone Pavillion
マカライト 1ケ ¥400
イエロージェイド 1ケ ¥450
虎目石 1ケ ¥500
ムーンストーン 1ケ ¥400
オニキス
Signs: Onyx Tiger's Eye Yellow Jade Malachite Moon Stone
...IN THE POWER STONE STORE.
THESE ARE CUTE.
THEY WIN YOU LOVE?
HM...?
I'LL GRANT...
...YOUR WISH.
I'LL GRANT IT...
I'LL GRANT IT...

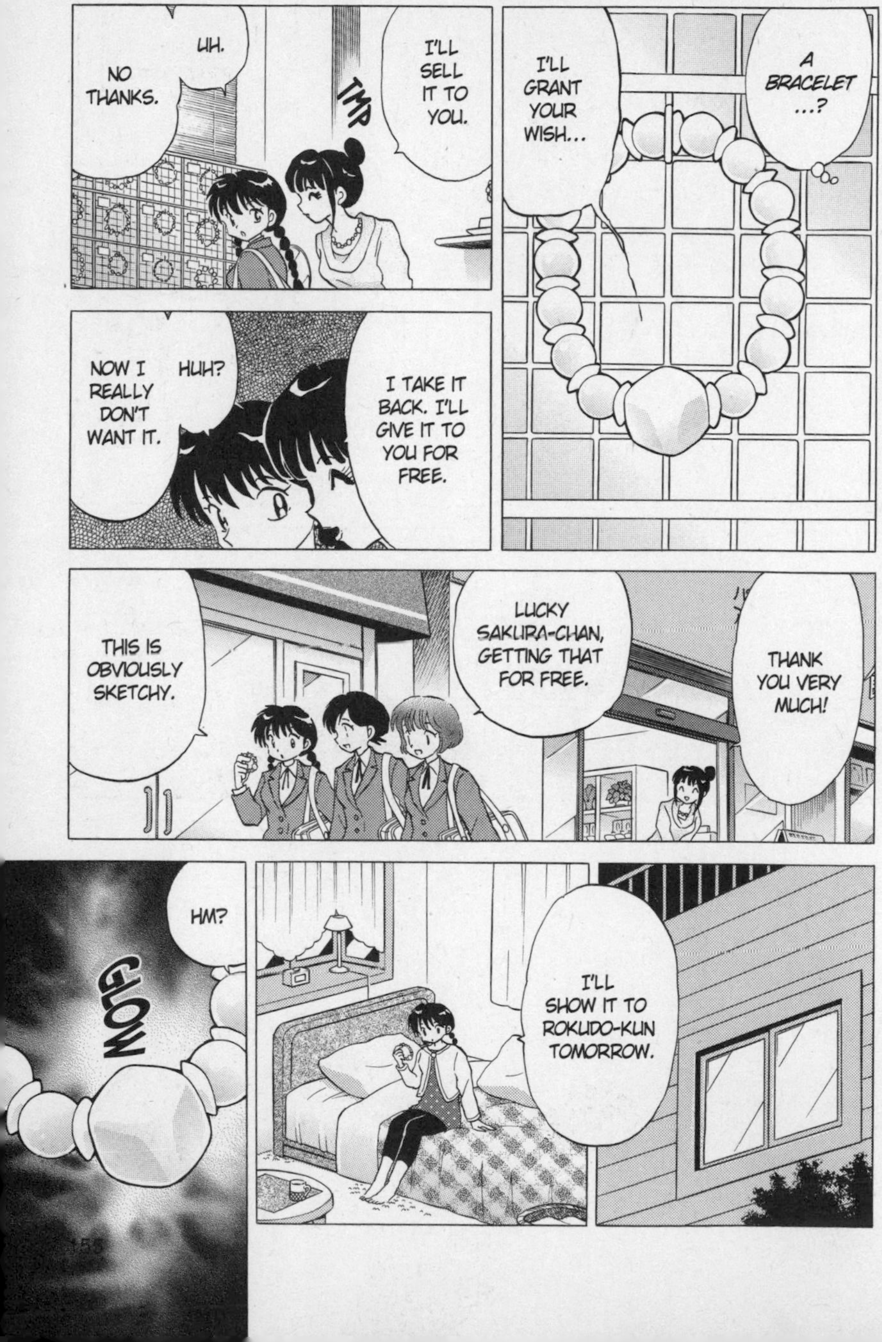
A BRACELET …?
I'LL GRANT YOUR WISH…
I'LL SELL IT TO YOU.
TMP
UH.
NO THANKS.
I TAKE IT BACK. I'LL GIVE IT TO YOU FOR FREE.
HUH?
NOW I REALLY DON'T WANT IT.
THANK YOU VERY MUCH!
LUCKY SAKURA-CHAN, GETTING THAT FOR FREE.
THIS IS OBVIOUSLY SKETCHY.
I'LL SHOW IT TO ROKUDO-KUN TOMORROW.
HM?
GLOW

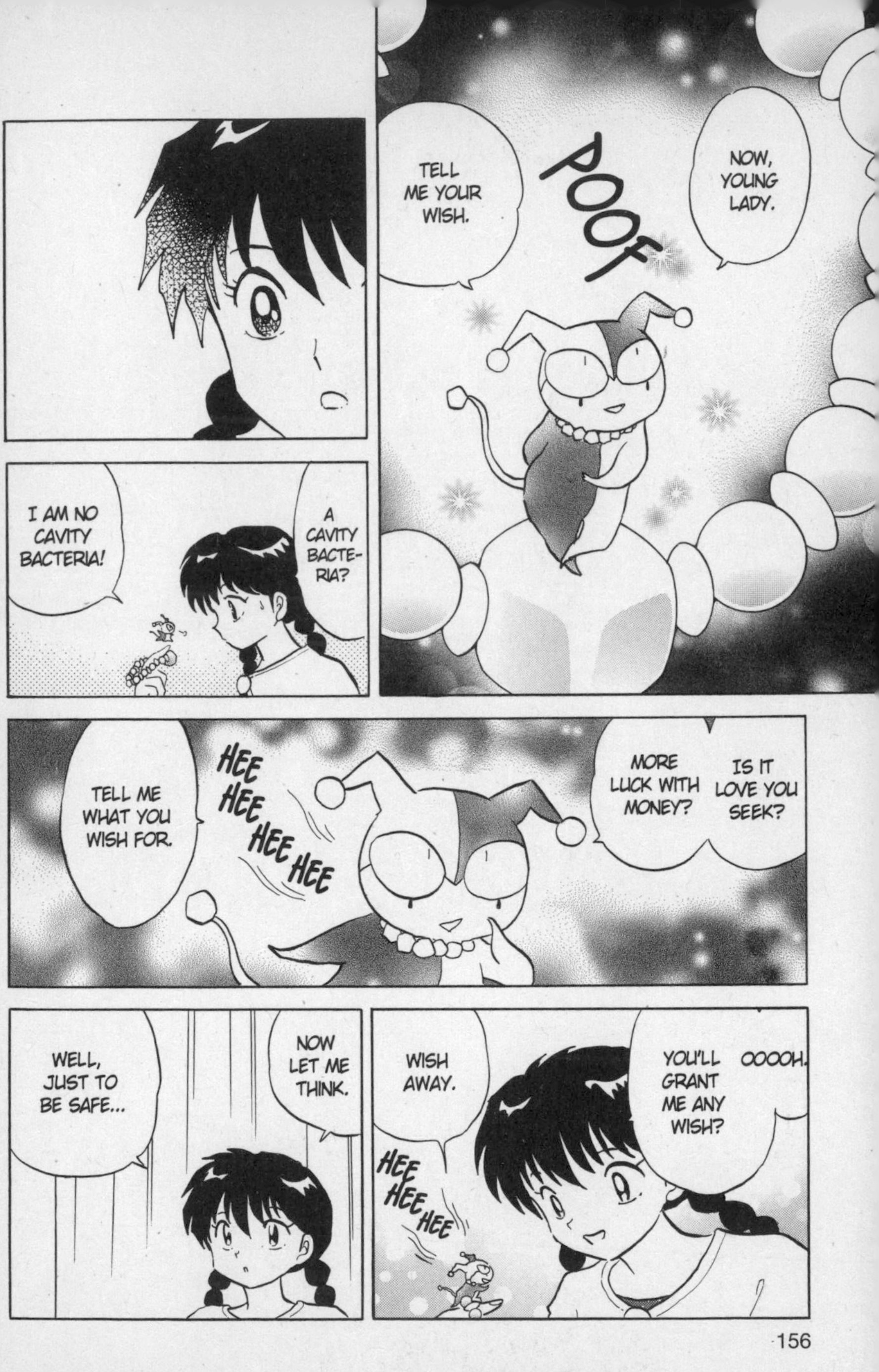
NOW, YOUNG LADY.
POOF
TELL ME YOUR WISH.
A CAVITY BACTERIA?
I AM NO CAVITY BACTERIA!
IS IT LOVE YOU SEEK?
MORE LUCK WITH MONEY?
HEE HEE HEE HEE
TELL ME WHAT YOU WISH FOR.
OOOOH.
YOU'LL GRANT ME ANY WISH?
WISH AWAY.
HEE HEE HEE
NOW LET ME THINK.
WELL, JUST TO BE SAFE...

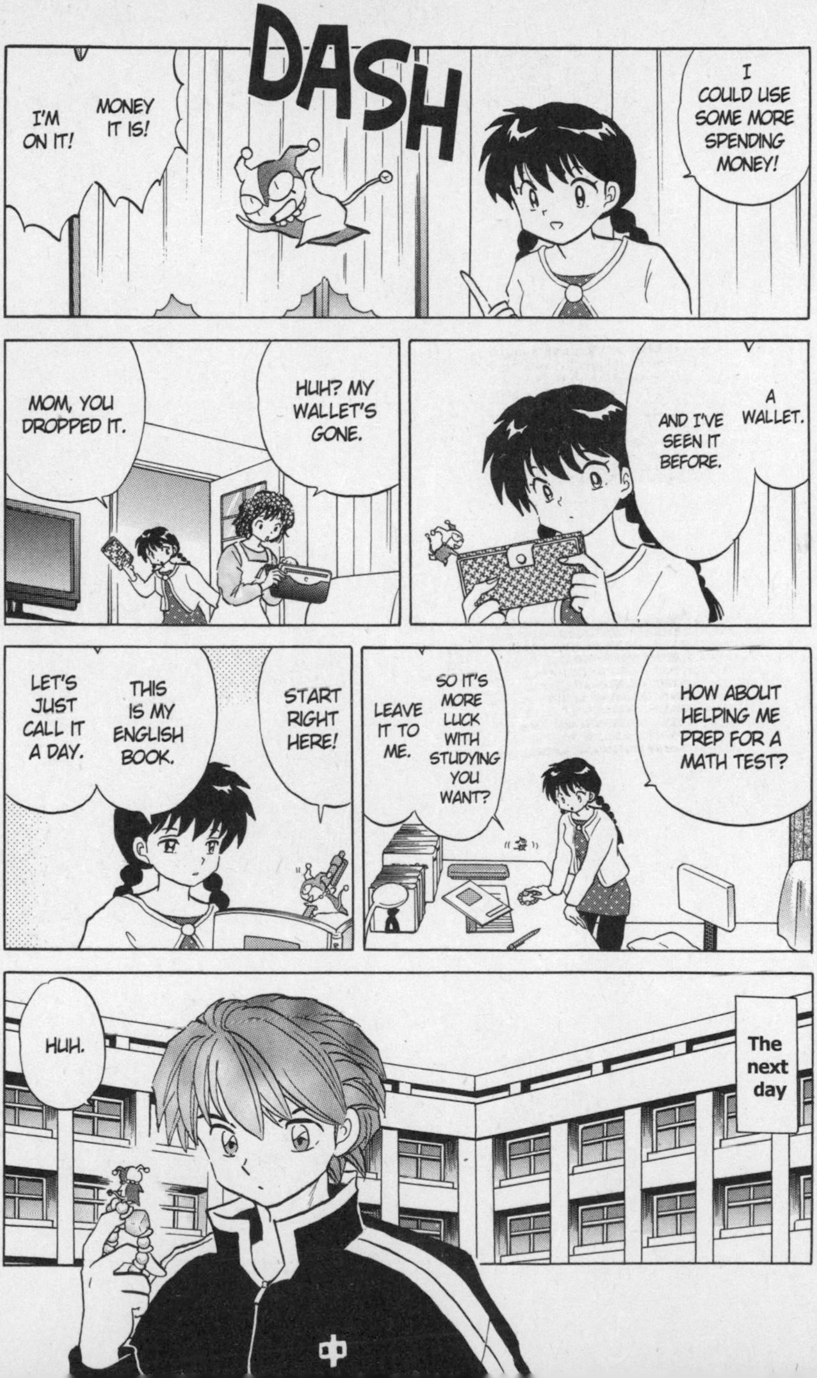
I COULD USE SOME MORE SPENDING MONEY!
DASH
MONEY IT IS!
I'M ON IT!
A WALLET.
AND I'VE SEEN IT BEFORE.
HUH? MY WALLET'S GONE.
MOM, YOU DROPPED IT.
HOW ABOUT HELPING ME PREP FOR A MATH TEST?
SO IT'S MORE LUCK WITH STUDYING YOU WANT?
LEAVE IT TO ME.
START RIGHT HERE!
THIS IS MY ENGLISH BOOK.
LET'S JUST CALL IT A DAY.
The next day
HUH.

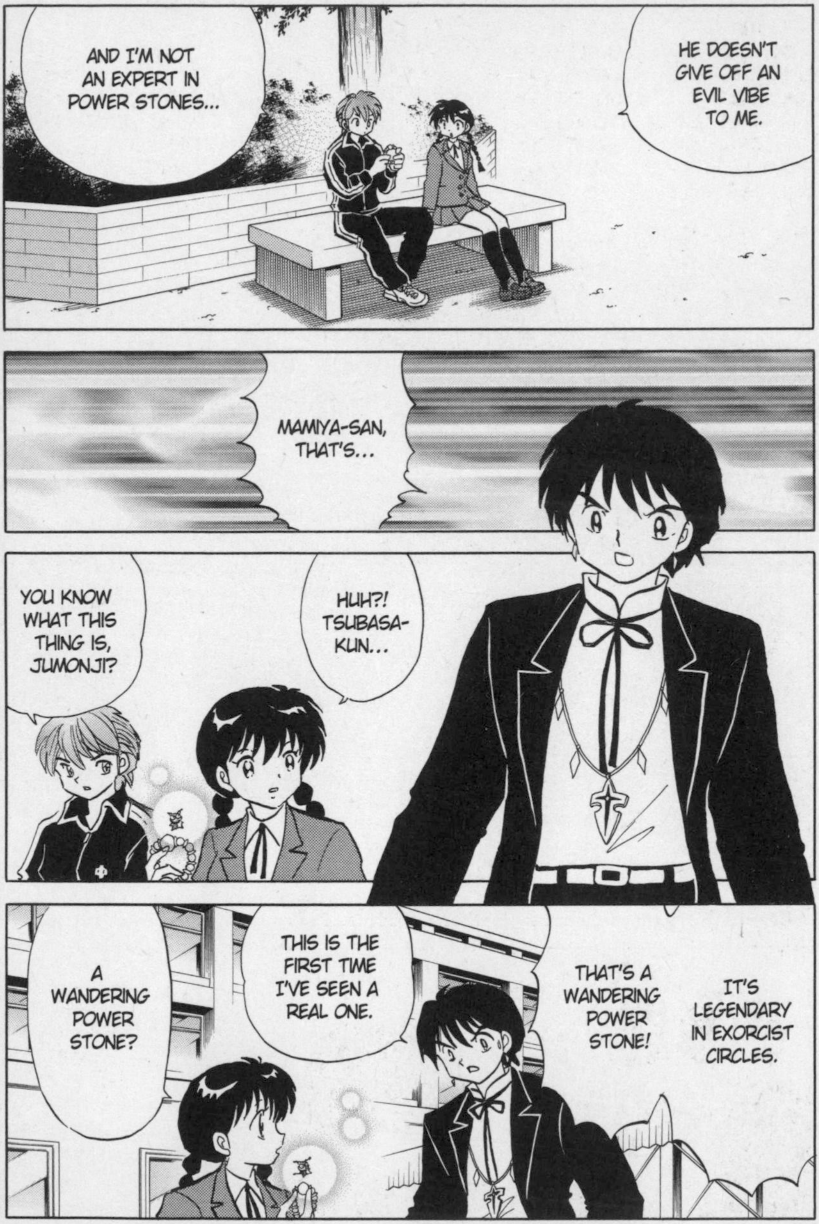
HE DOESN'T GIVE OFF AN EVIL VIBE TO ME.
AND I'M NOT AN EXPERT IN POWER STONES...
MAMIYA-SAN, THAT'S...
HUH?! TSUBASA-KUN...
YOU KNOW WHAT THIS THING IS, JUMONJI?
THAT'S A WANDERING POWER STONE!
IT'S LEGENDARY IN EXORCIST CIRCLES.
THIS IS THE FIRST TIME I'VE SEEN A REAL ONE.
A WANDERING POWER STONE?

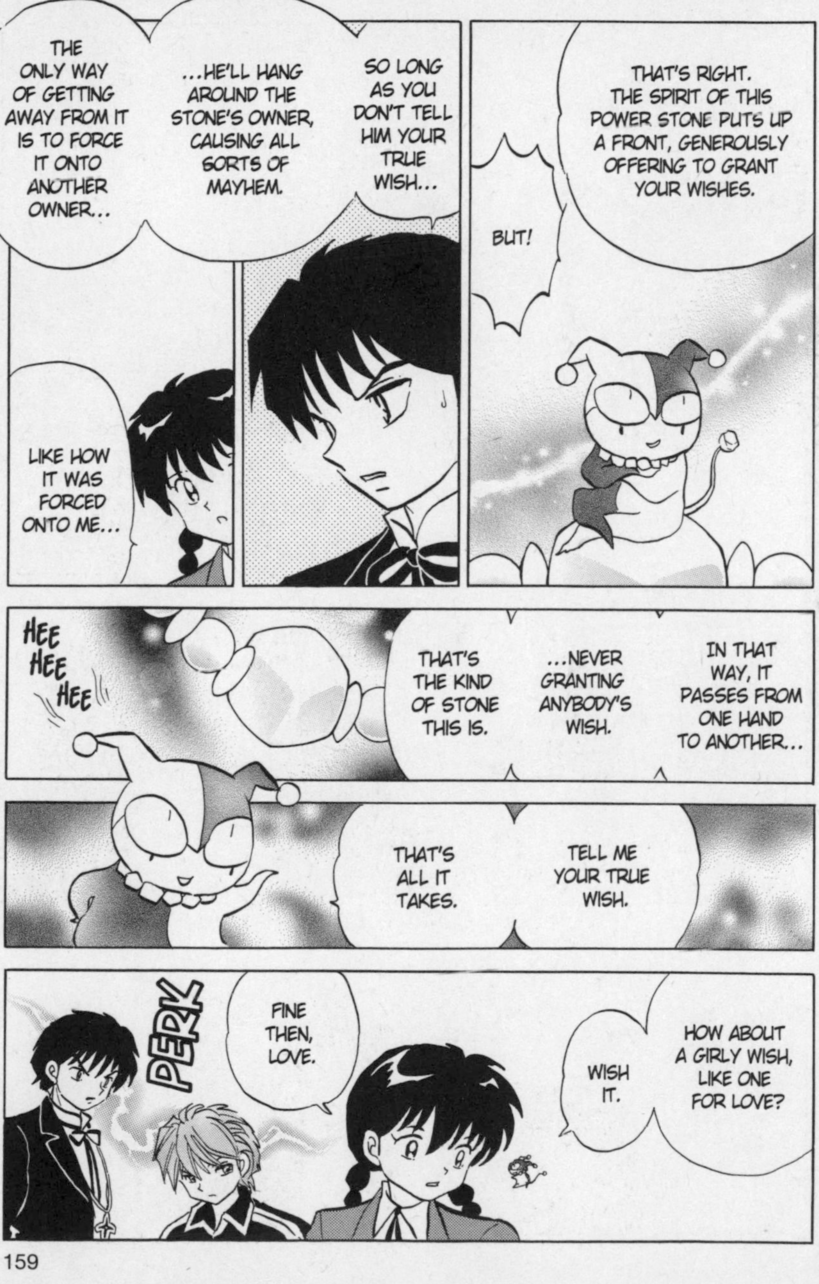

THAT'S RIGHT. THE SPIRIT OF THIS POWER STONE PUTS UP A FRONT, GENEROUSLY OFFERING TO GRANT YOUR WISHES.
BUT!
SO LONG AS YOU DON'T TELL HIM YOUR TRUE WISH...
...HE'LL HANG AROUND THE STONE'S OWNER, CAUSING ALL SORTS OF MAYHEM.
THE ONLY WAY OF GETTING AWAY FROM IT IS TO FORCE IT ONTO ANOTHER OWNER...
LIKE HOW IT WAS FORCED ONTO ME...
IN THAT WAY, IT PASSES FROM ONE HAND TO ANOTHER...
...NEVER GRANTING ANYBODY'S WISH.
THAT'S THE KIND OF STONE THIS IS.
HEE HEE HEE
TELL ME YOUR TRUE WISH.
THAT'S ALL IT TAKES.
HOW ABOUT A GIRLY WISH, LIKE ONE FOR LOVE?
WISH IT.
FINE THEN, LOVE.
PERK

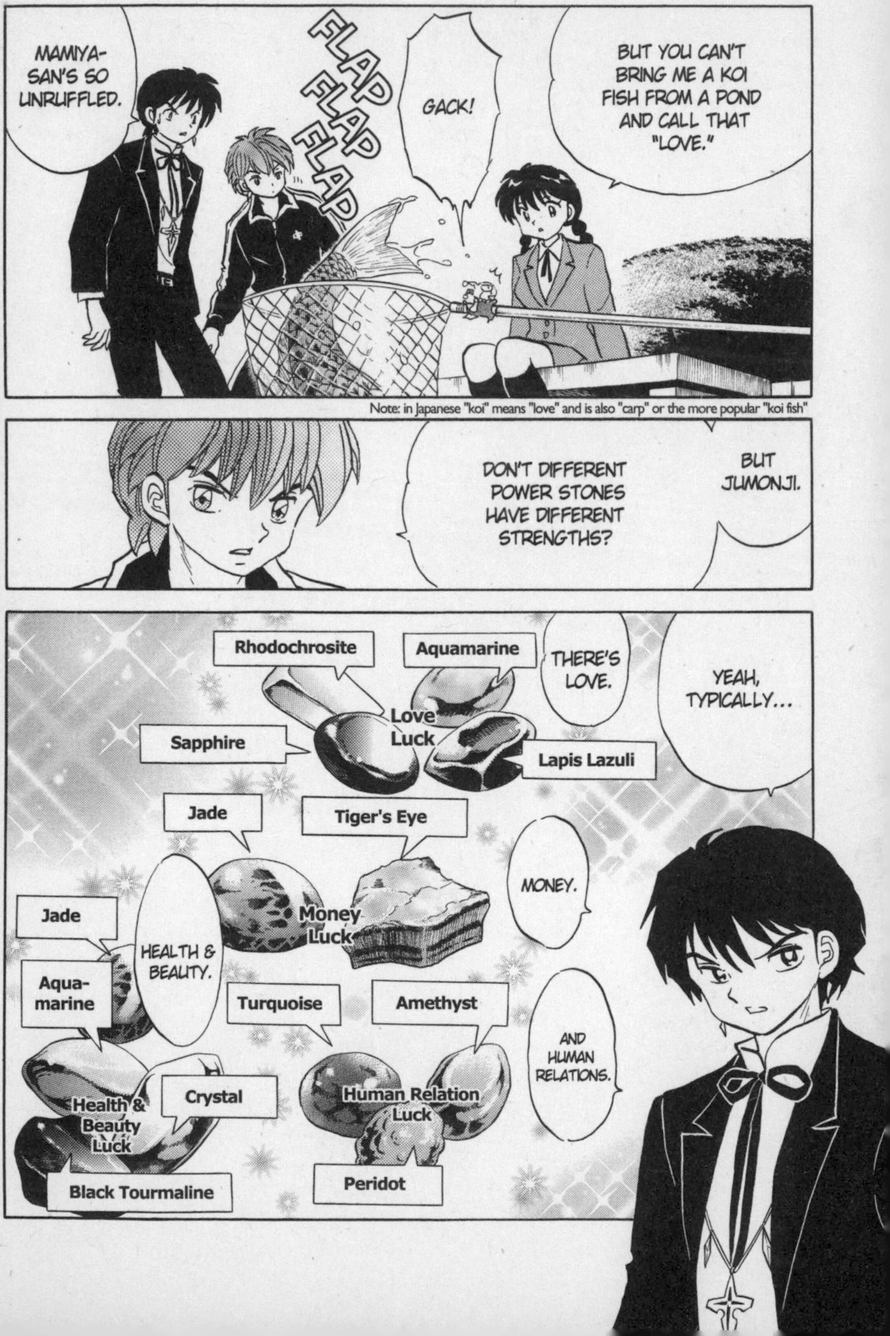
BUT YOU CAN'T BRING ME A KOI FISH FROM A POND AND CALL THAT "LOVE."
GACK!
FLAP FLAP FLAP
MAMIYA-SAN'S SO UNRUFFLED.
Note: in Japanese "koi" means "love" and is also "carp" or the more popular "koi fish"
BUT JUMONJI.
DON'T DIFFERENT POWER STONES HAVE DIFFERENT STRENGTHS?
YEAH, TYPICALLY...
THERE'S LOVE.
Aquamarine
Rhodochrosite
Love Luck
Sapphire
Lapis Lazuli
Tiger's Eye
Jade
MONEY.
Money Luck
HEALTH & BEAUTY.
Jade
Aqua-marine
AND HUMAN RELATIONS.
Amethyst
Turquoise
Human Relation Luck
Peridot
Crystal
Health & Beauty Luck
Black Tourmaline

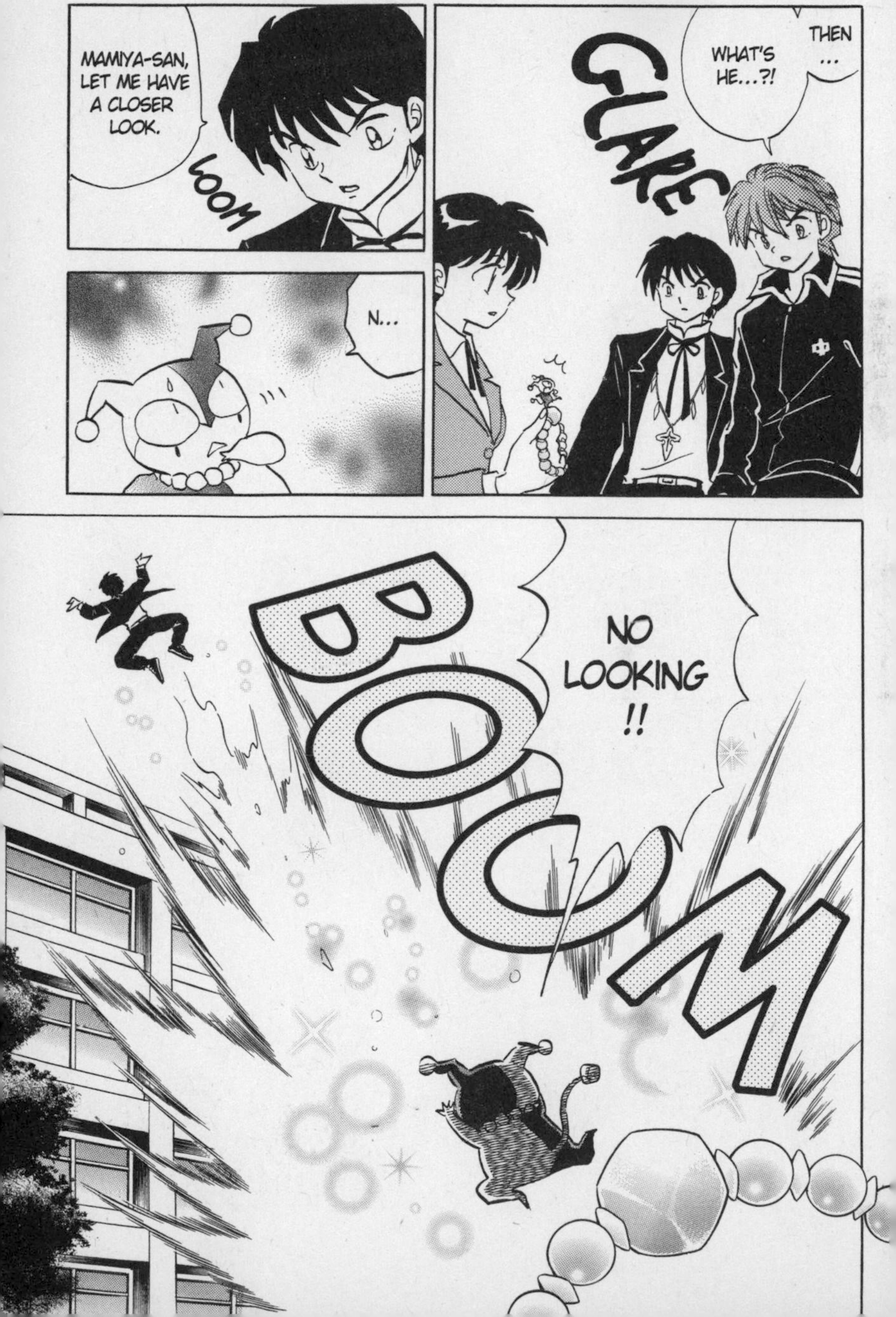
THEN ...
WHAT'S HE...?!
GLARE
MAMIYA-SAN, LET ME HAVE A CLOSER LOOK.
LOOM
N...
NO LOOKING !!
BOOM

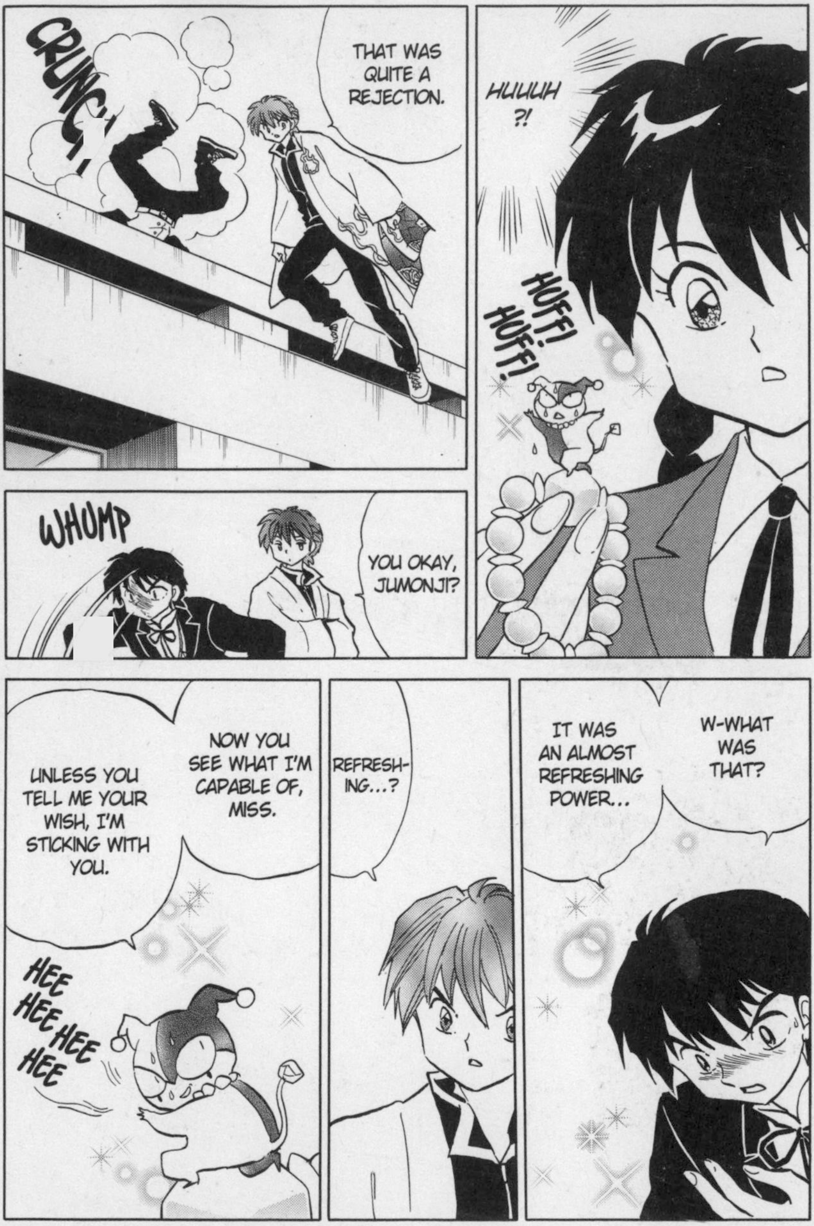
HUUUH ?!
HUFF! HUFF!
CRUNCH!
THAT WAS QUITE A REJECTION.
WHUMP
YOU OKAY, JUMONJI?
W-WHAT WAS THAT?
IT WAS AN ALMOST REFRESHING POWER...
REFRESH-ING...?
NOW YOU SEE WHAT I'M CAPABLE OF, MISS.
UNLESS YOU TELL ME YOUR WISH, I'M STICKING WITH YOU.
HEE HEE HEE HEE

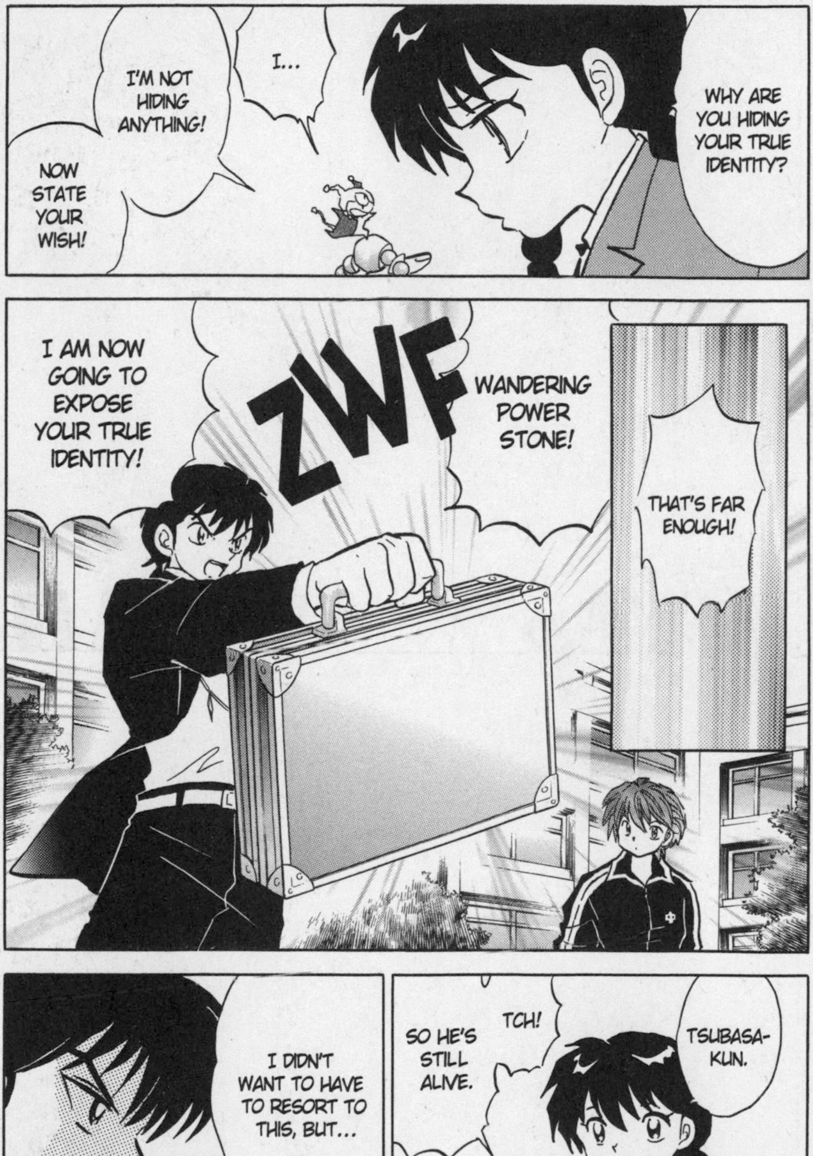
WHY ARE YOU HIDING YOUR TRUE IDENTITY?
I...
I'M NOT HIDING ANYTHING!
NOW STATE YOUR WISH!
I AM NOW GOING TO EXPOSE YOUR TRUE IDENTITY!
ZWF
WANDERING POWER STONE!
THAT'S FAR ENOUGH!
TSUBASA-KUN.
TCH!
SO HE'S STILL ALIVE.
I DIDN'T WANT TO HAVE TO RESORT TO THIS, BUT...

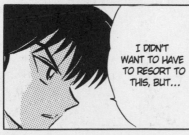

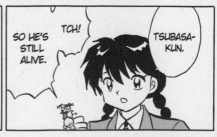

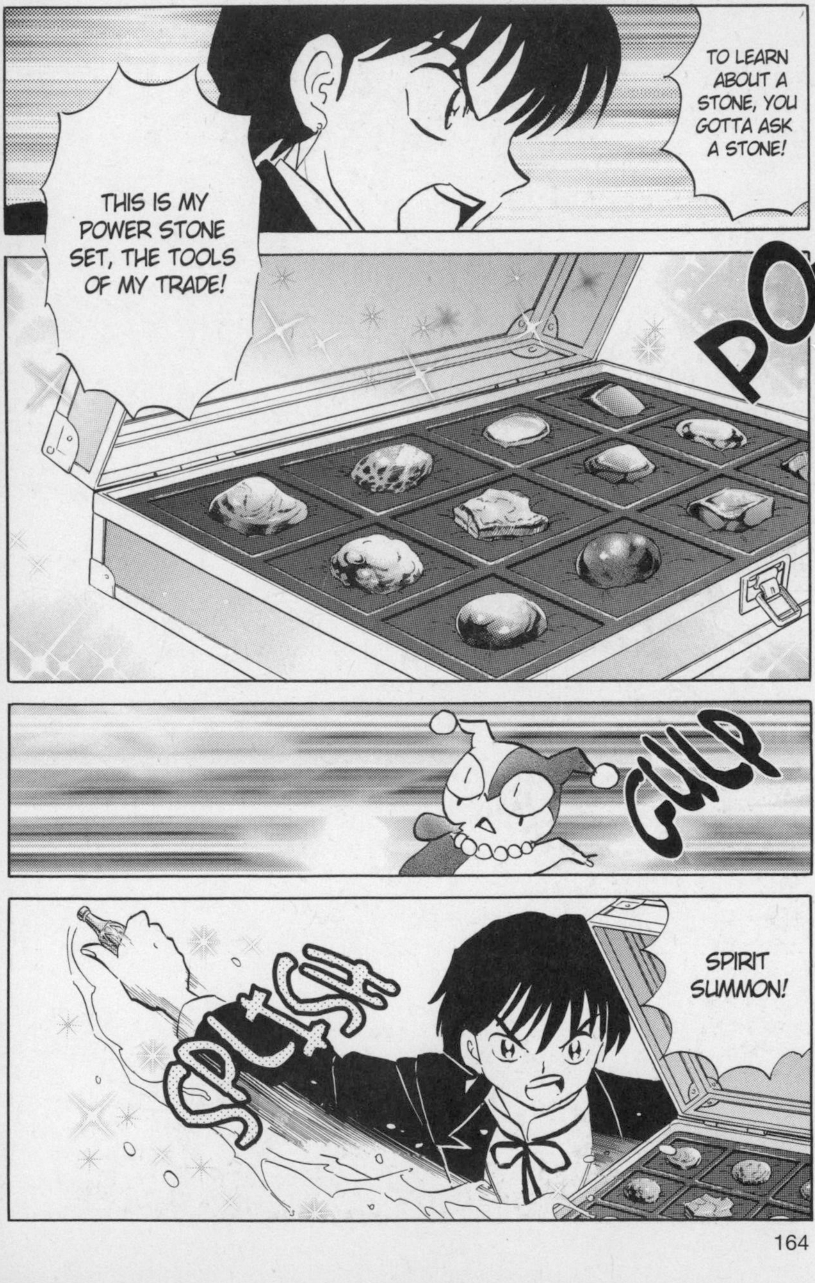
TO LEARN ABOUT A STONE, YOU GOTTA ASK A STONE!
THIS IS MY POWER STONE SET, THE TOOLS OF MY TRADE!
POP
GULP
SPIRIT SUMMON!
SPLISH

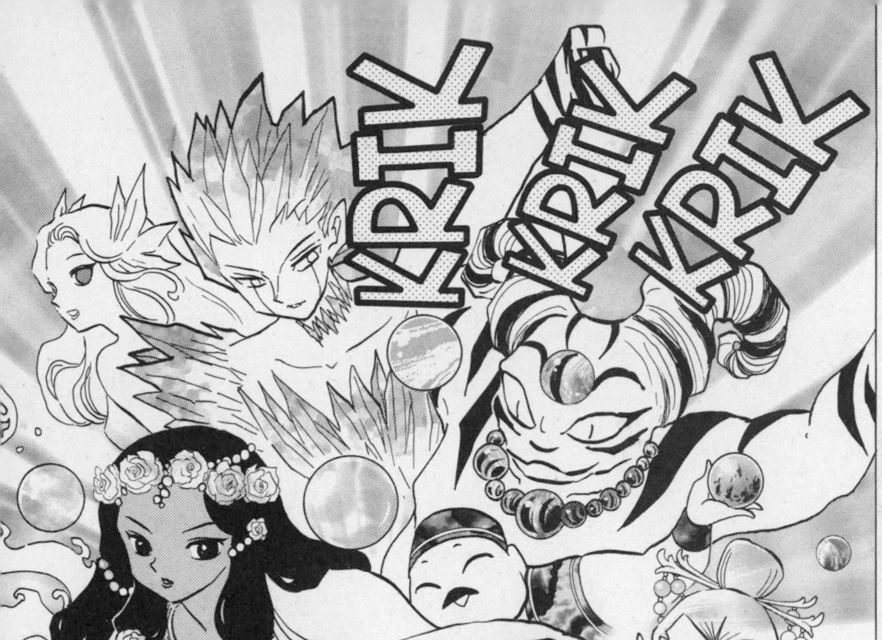
KRILK
KRILK
KRILK
VWOOOO

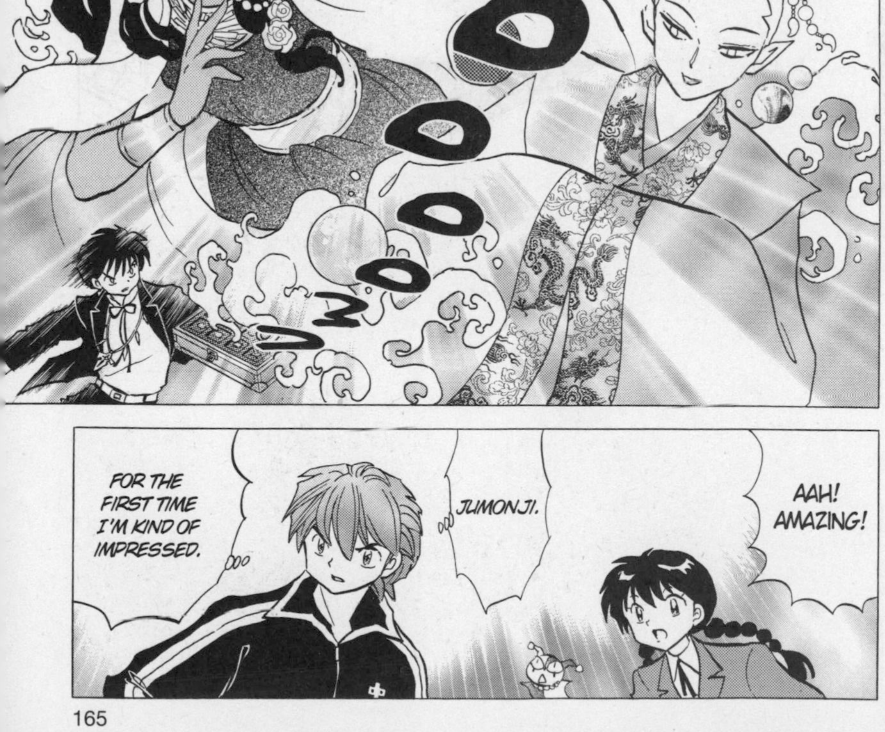
AAH! AMAZING!
JUMONJI.
FOR THE FIRST TIME I'M KIND OF IMPRESSED.

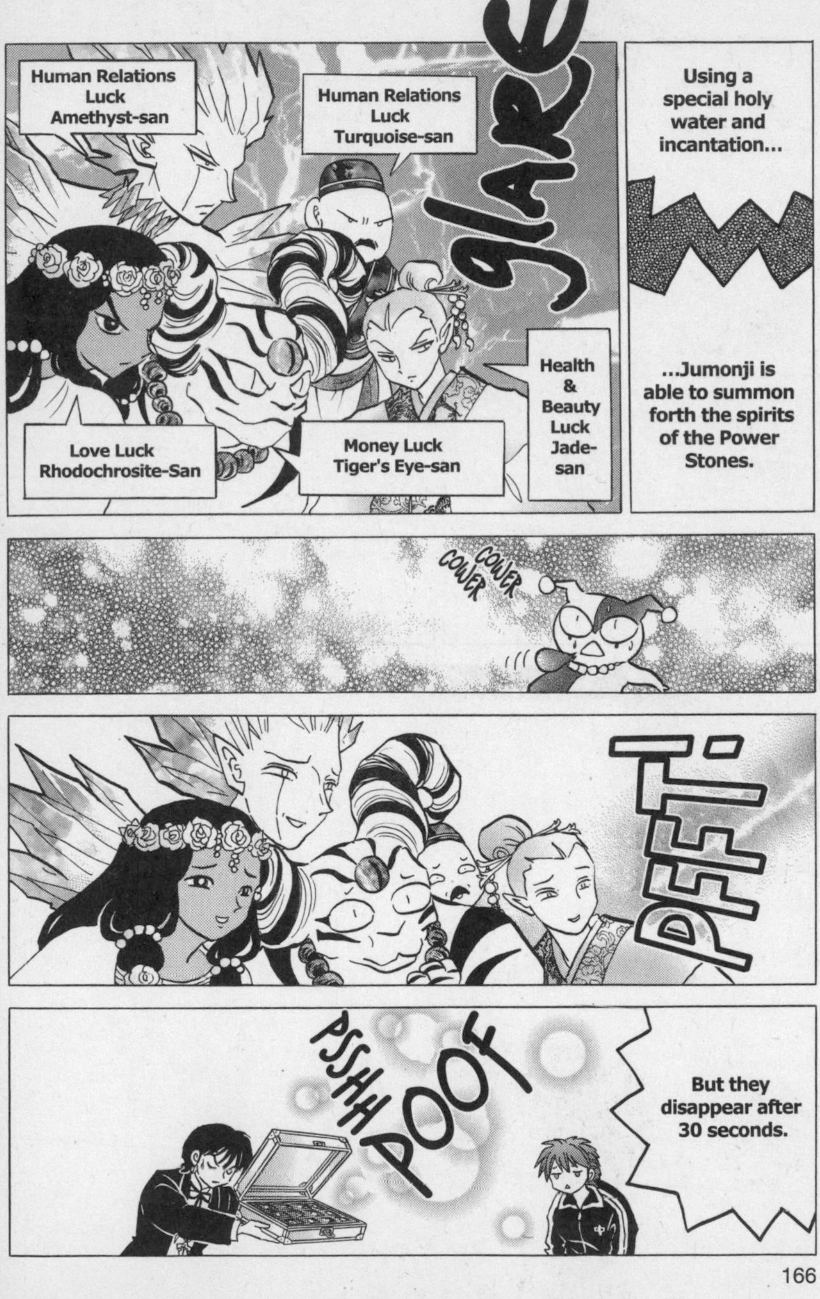

Using a special holy water and incantation...
...Jumonji is able to summon forth the spirits of the Power Stones.
GLARE
Human Relations Luck Turquoise-san
Human Relations Luck Amethyst-san
Health & Beauty Luck Jade-san
Money Luck Tiger's Eye-san
Love Luck Rhodochrosite-San
COWER COWER
PFFT
But they disappear after 30 seconds.
PSSHH POOF

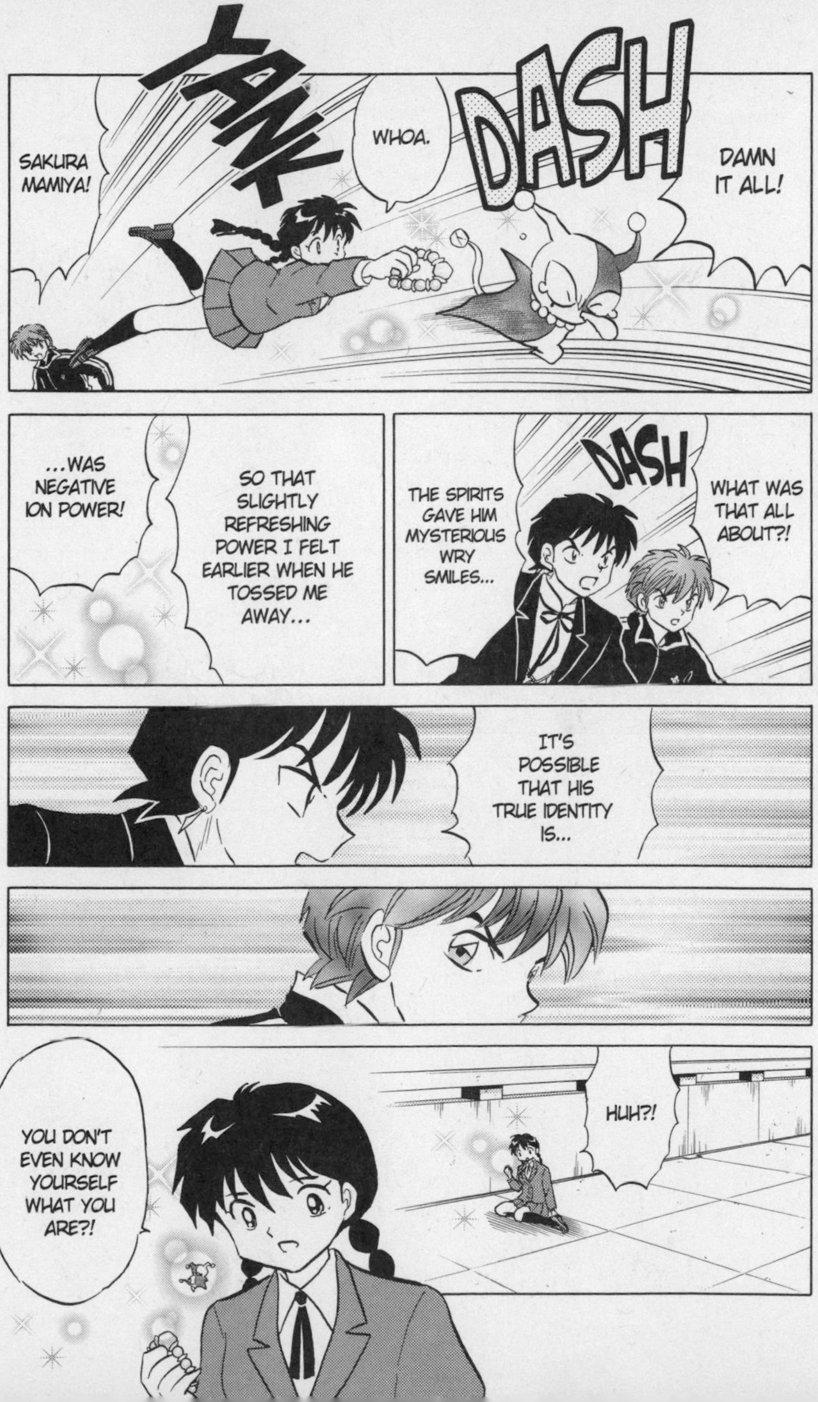
DAMN IT ALL!
DASH
WHOA.
YANK
SAKURA MAMIYA!
WHAT WAS THAT ALL ABOUT?!
DASH
THE SPIRITS GAVE HIM MYSTERIOUS WRY SMILES...
SO THAT SLIGHTLY REFRESHING POWER I FELT EARLIER WHEN HE TOSSED ME AWAY...
...WAS NEGATIVE ION POWER!
IT'S POSSIBLE THAT HIS TRUE IDENTITY IS...
HUH?!
YOU DON'T EVEN KNOW YOURSELF WHAT YOU ARE?!

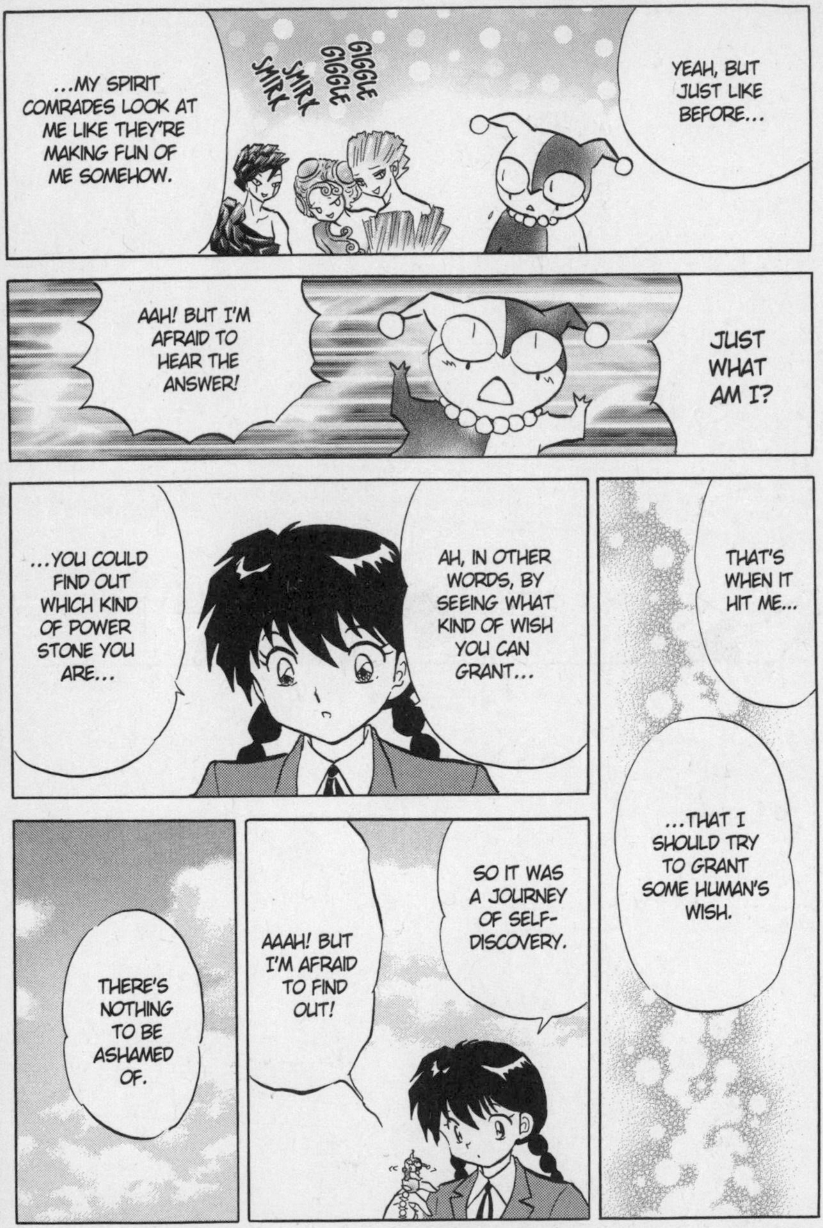
YEAH, BUT JUST LIKE BEFORE...
GIGGLE GIGGLE
SMIRK SMIRK
...MY SPIRIT COMRADES LOOK AT ME LIKE THEY'RE MAKING FUN OF ME SOMEHOW.
JUST WHAT AM I?
AAH! BUT I'M AFRAID TO HEAR THE ANSWER!
THAT'S WHEN IT HIT ME...
...THAT I SHOULD TRY TO GRANT SOME HUMAN'S WISH.
AH, IN OTHER WORDS, BY SEEING WHAT KIND OF WISH YOU CAN GRANT...
...YOU COULD FIND OUT WHICH KIND OF POWER STONE YOU ARE...
SO IT WAS A JOURNEY OF SELF-DISCOVERY.
AAAH! BUT I'M AFRAID TO FIND OUT!
THERE'S NOTHING TO BE ASHAMED OF.

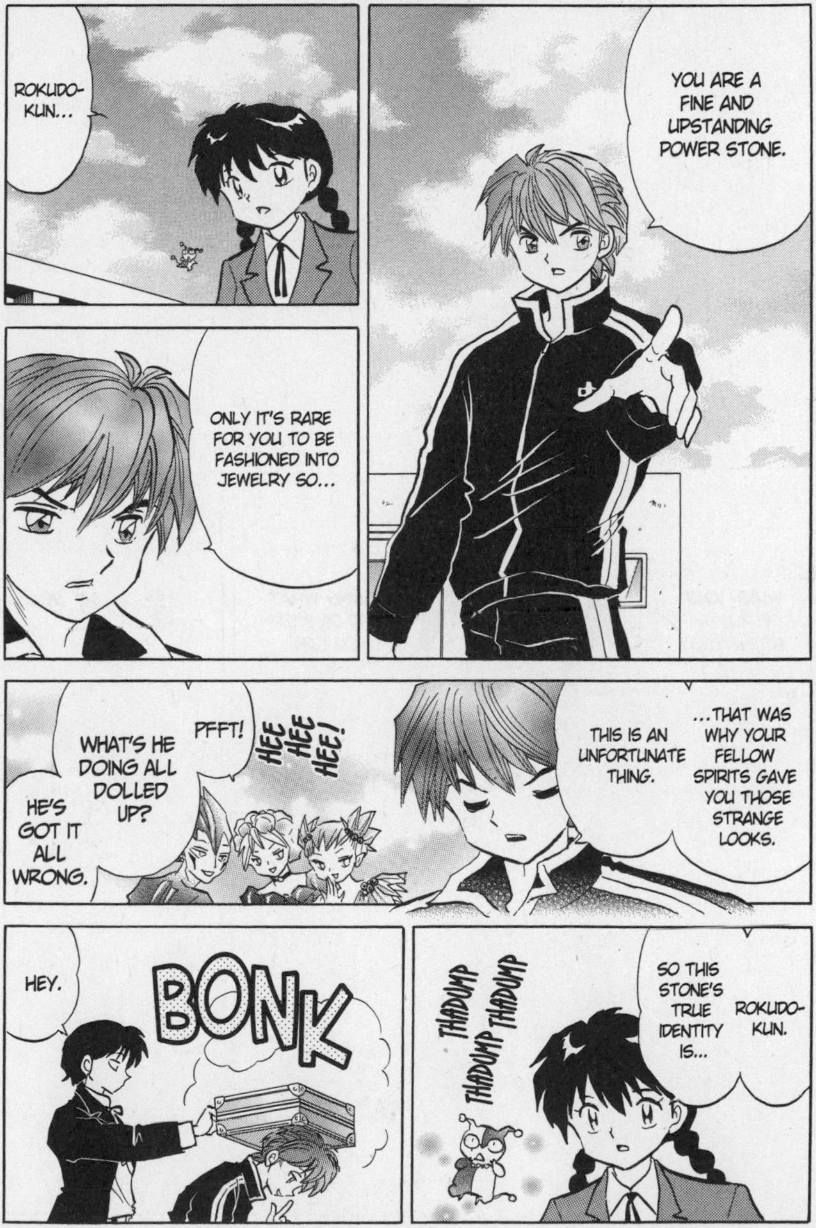
YOU ARE A FINE AND UPSTANDING POWER STONE.
ROKUDO-KUN...
ONLY IT'S RARE FOR YOU TO BE FASHIONED INTO JEWELRY SO...
...THAT WAS WHY YOUR FELLOW SPIRITS GAVE YOU THOSE STRANGE LOOKS.
THIS IS AN UNFORTUNATE THING.
HEE HEE HEE!
PFFT!
WHAT'S HE DOING ALL DOLLED UP?
HE'S GOT IT ALL WRONG.
ROKUDO-KUN.
SO THIS STONE'S TRUE IDENTITY IS...
THADUMP THADUMP THADUMP
BONK
HEY.

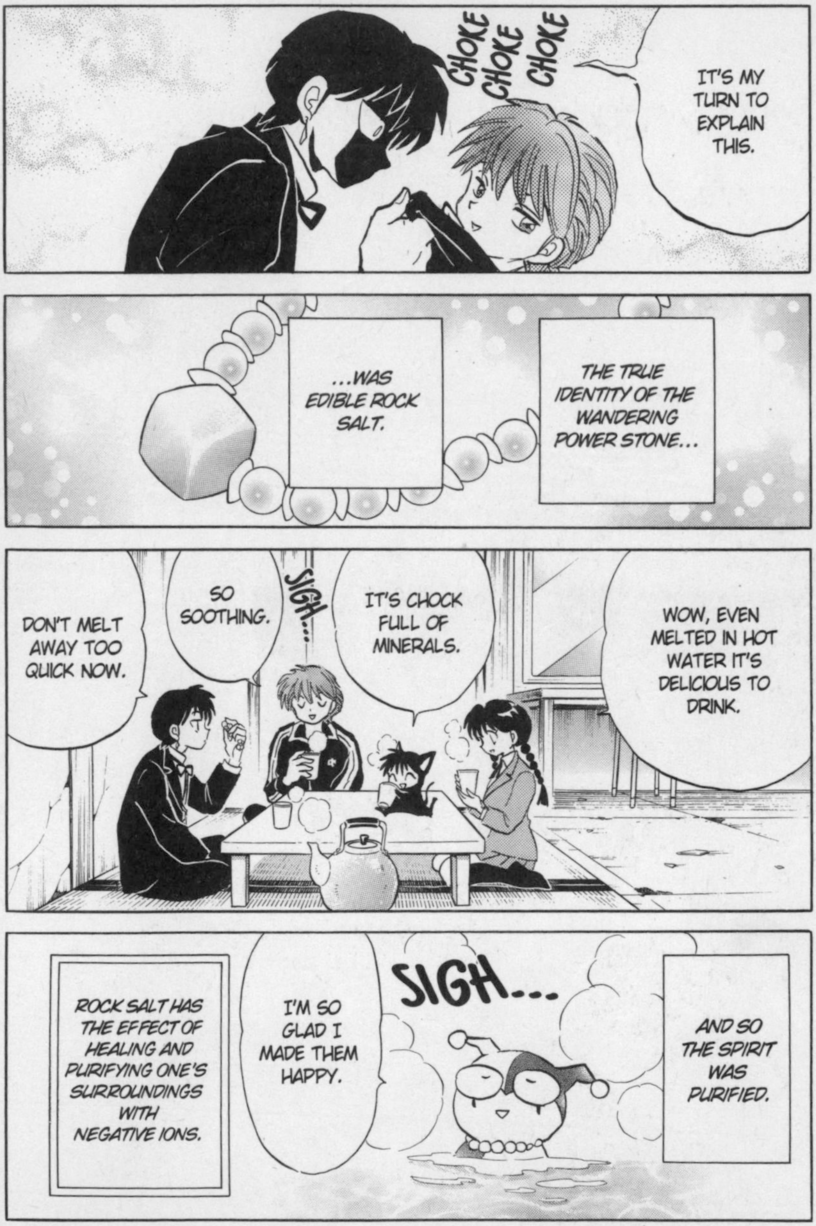
IT'S MY TURN TO EXPLAIN THIS.
CHOKE CHOKE CHOKE
THE TRUE IDENTITY OF THE WANDERING POWER STONE...
...WAS EDIBLE ROCK SALT.
WOW, EVEN MELTED IN HOT WATER IT'S DELICIOUS TO DRINK.
IT'S CHOCK FULL OF MINERALS.
SIGH...
SO SOOTHING.
DON'T MELT AWAY TOO QUICK NOW.
AND SO THE SPIRIT WAS PURIFIED.
SIGH...
I'M SO GLAD I MADE THEM HAPPY.
ROCK SALT HAS THE EFFECT OF HEALING AND PURIFYING ONE'S SURROUNDINGS WITH NEGATIVE IONS.

CHAPTER 118: THE MATSUTAKE MUSHROOM COMMOTION

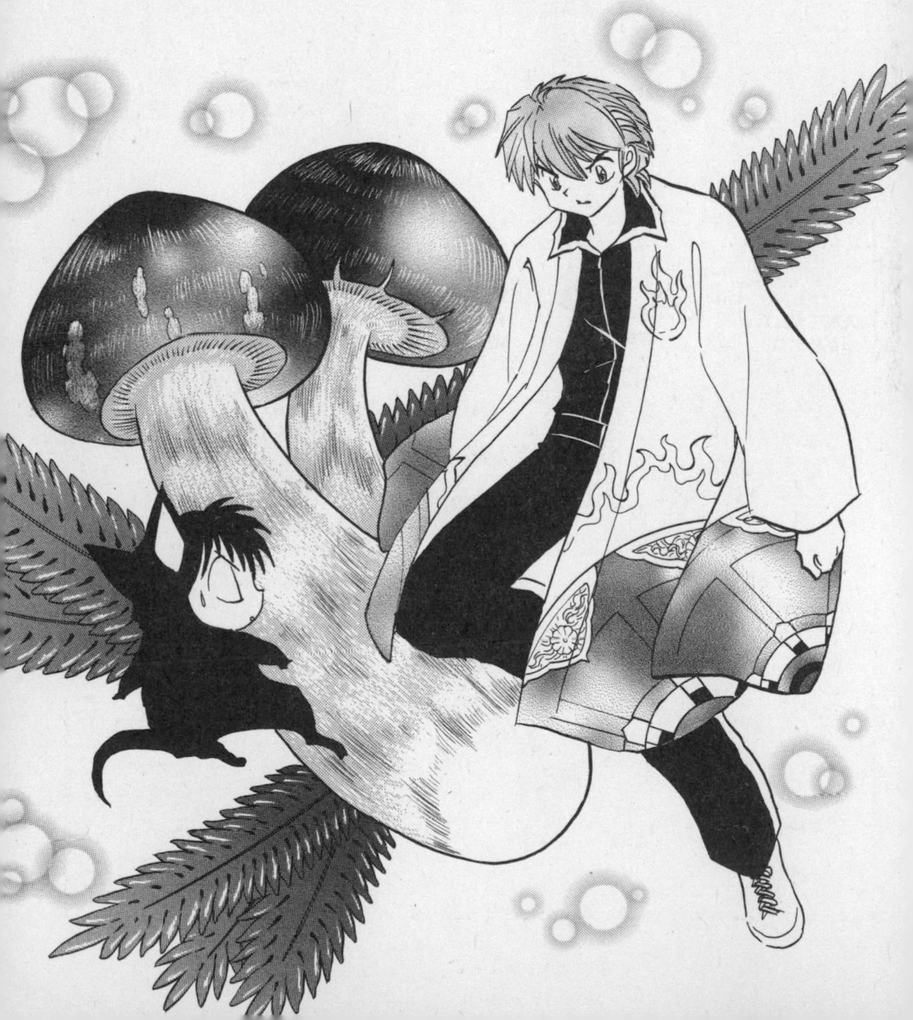

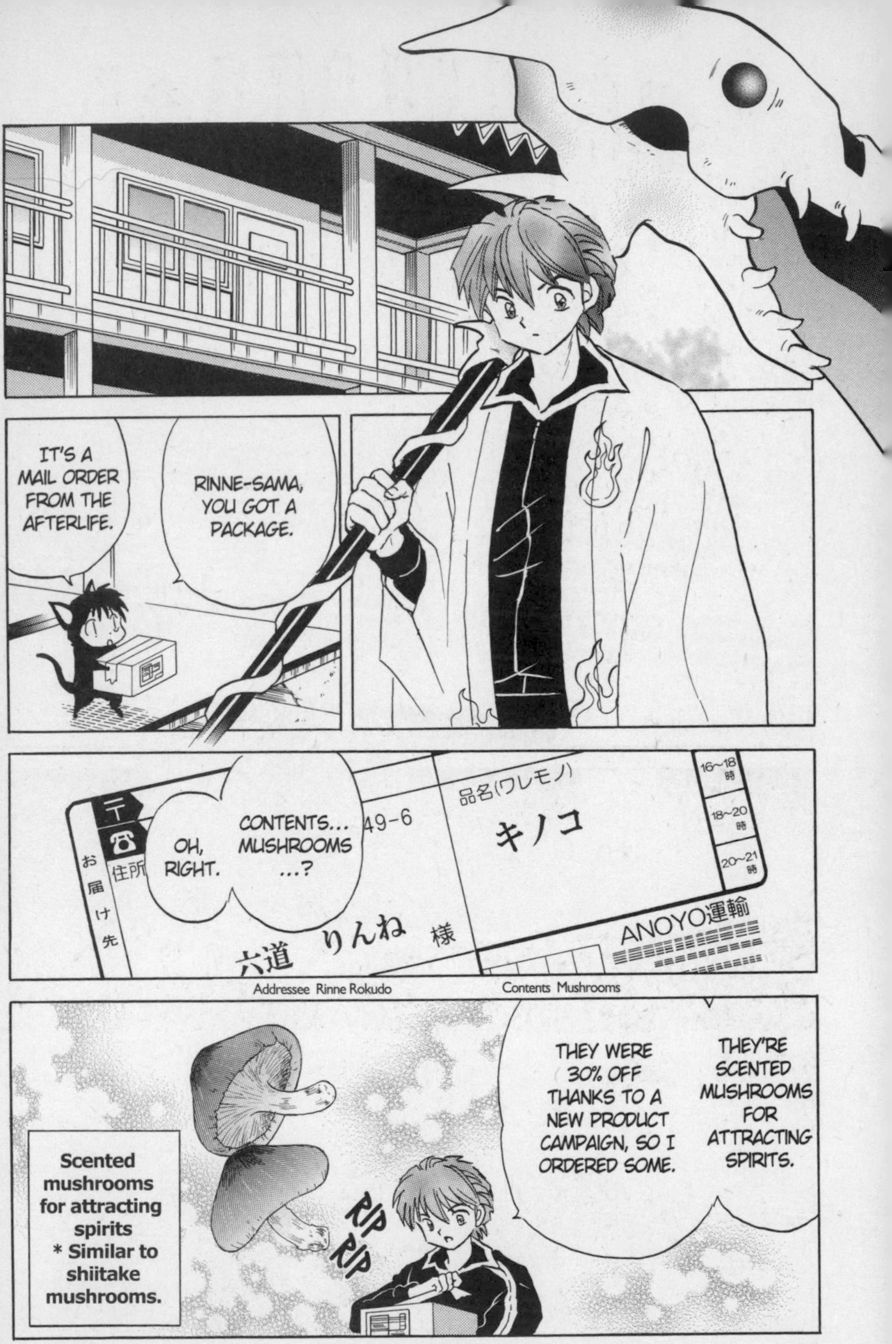
RINNE-SAMA, YOU GOT A PACKAGE.
IT'S A MAIL ORDER FROM THE AFTERLIFE.
品名(ワレモノ)
キノコ
16~18時
18~20時
20~21時
49-6
〒
住所
お届け先
六道 りんね 様
ANOYO運輸
CONTENTS... MUSHROOMS ...?
OH, RIGHT.
Addressee Rinne Rokudo
Contents Mushrooms
THEY'RE SCENTED MUSHROOMS FOR ATTRACTING SPIRITS.
THEY WERE 30% OFF THANKS TO A NEW PRODUCT CAMPAIGN, SO I ORDERED SOME.
RIP RIP
Scented mushrooms for attracting spirits
* Similar to shiitake mushrooms.

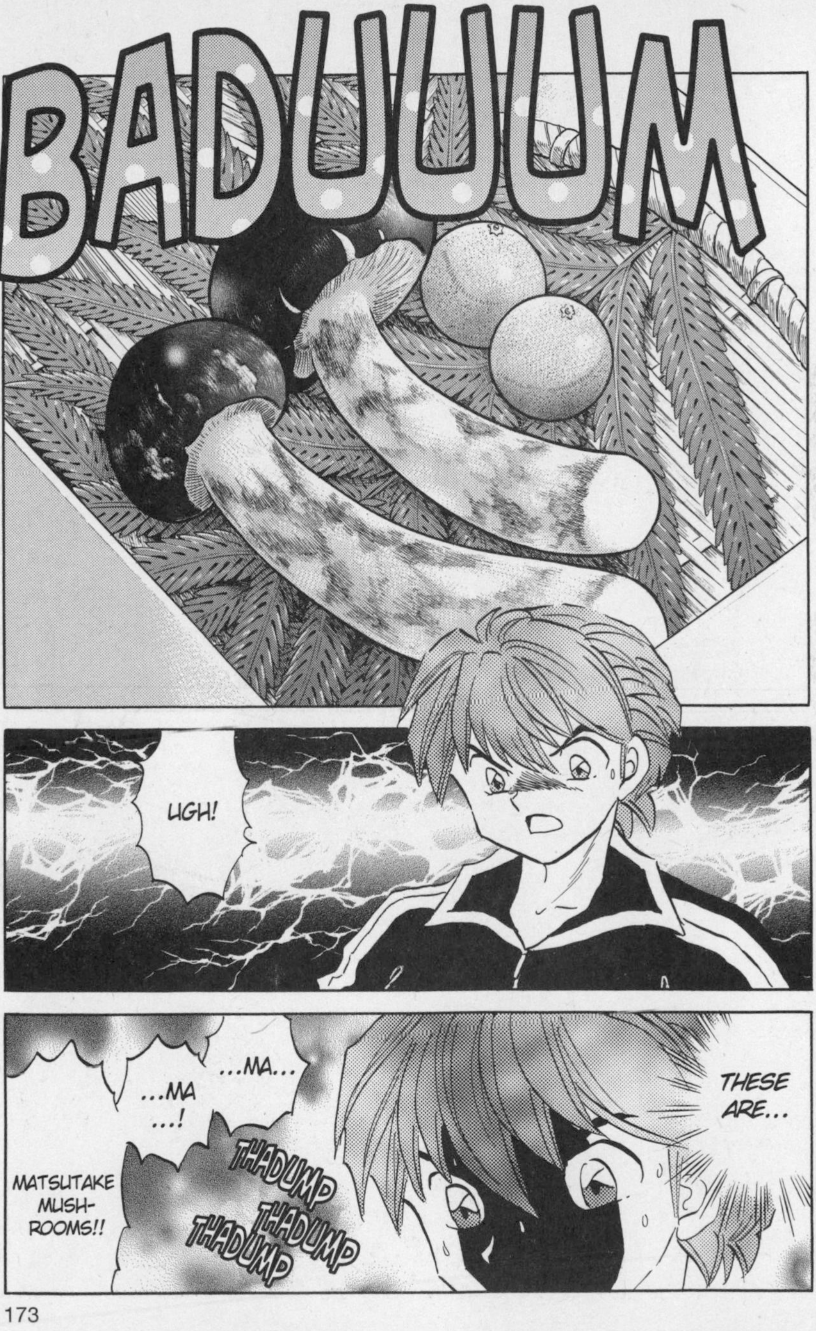
BADUUUM
UGH!
THESE ARE...
...MA...
...MA ...!
THADUMP THADUMP THADUMP
MATSUTAKE MUSHROOMS!!

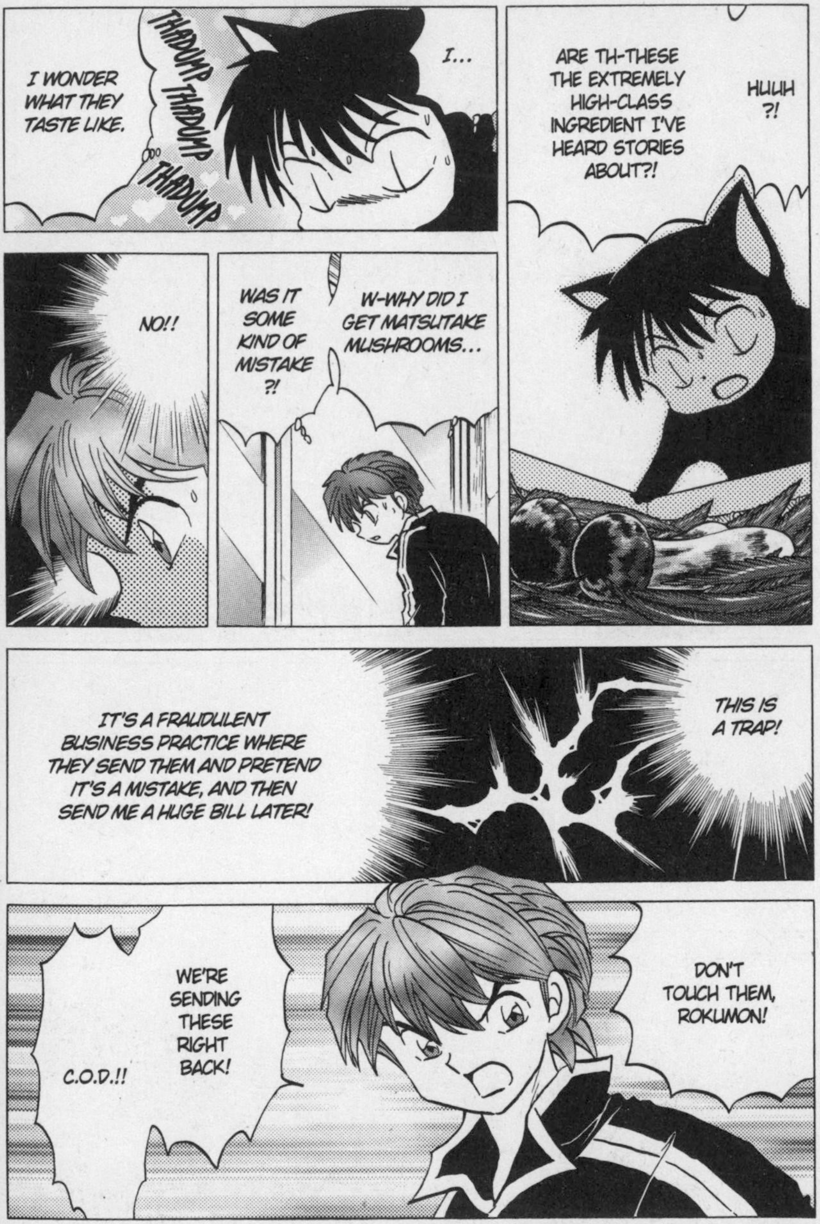
HUUH ?!
ARE TH-THESE THE EXTREMELY HIGH-CLASS INGREDIENT I'VE HEARD STORIES ABOUT?!
I...
THADUMP THADUMP THADUMP
I WONDER WHAT THEY TASTE LIKE.
W-WHY DID I GET MATSUTAKE MUSHROOMS...
WAS IT SOME KIND OF MISTAKE ?!
NO!!
THIS IS A TRAP!
IT'S A FRAUDULENT BUSINESS PRACTICE WHERE THEY SEND THEM AND PRETEND IT'S A MISTAKE, AND THEN SEND ME A HUGE BILL LATER!
DON'T TOUCH THEM, ROKUMON!
WE'RE SENDING THESE RIGHT BACK!
C.O.D.!!

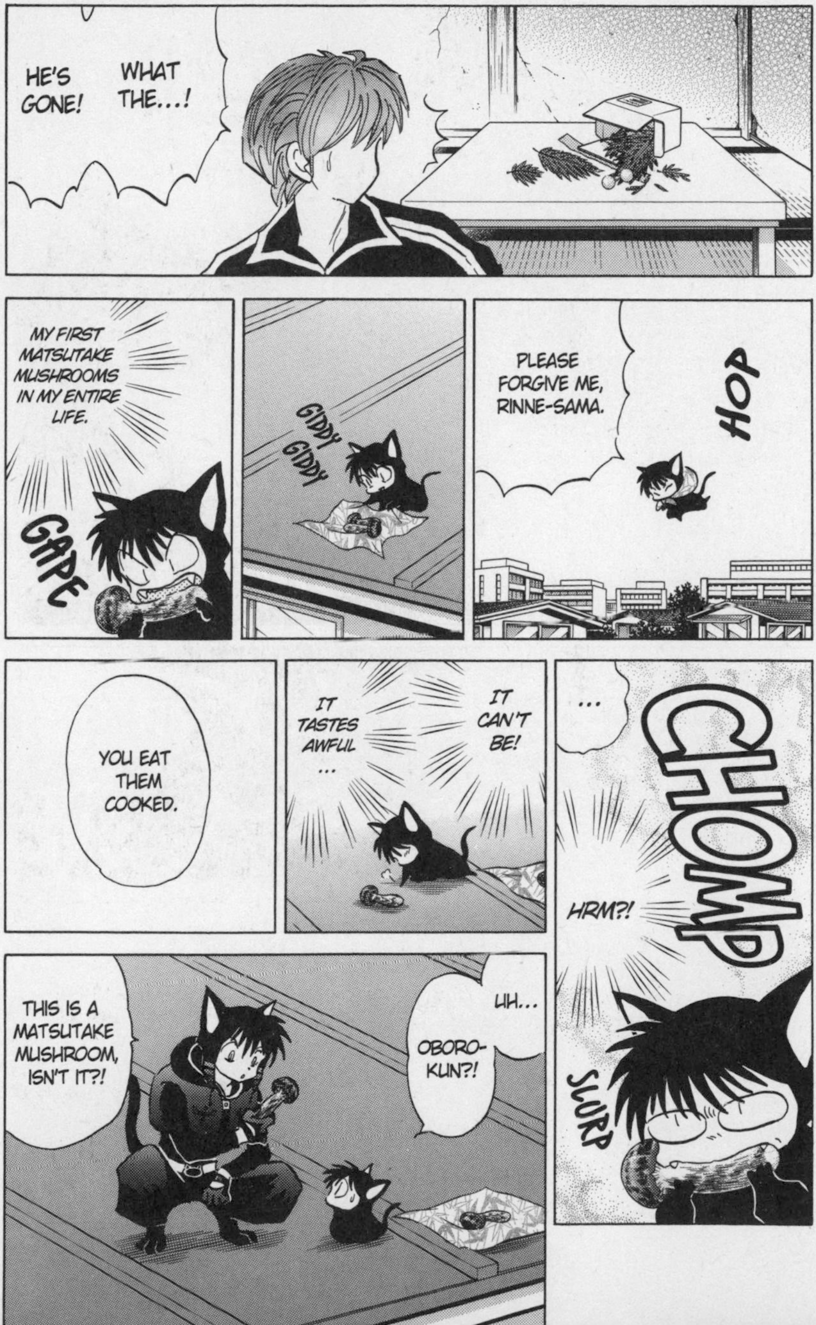
WHAT THE...!
HE'S GONE!
HOP
PLEASE FORGIVE ME, RINNE-SAMA.
GIDDY GIDDY
MY FIRST MATSUTAKE MUSHROOMS IN MY ENTIRE LIFE.
GAPE
...
CHOMP
HRM?!
SLURP
IT CAN'T BE!
IT TASTES AWFUL...
YOU EAT THEM COOKED.
UH...
OBORO-KUN?!
THIS IS A MATSUTAKE MUSHROOM, ISN'T IT?!

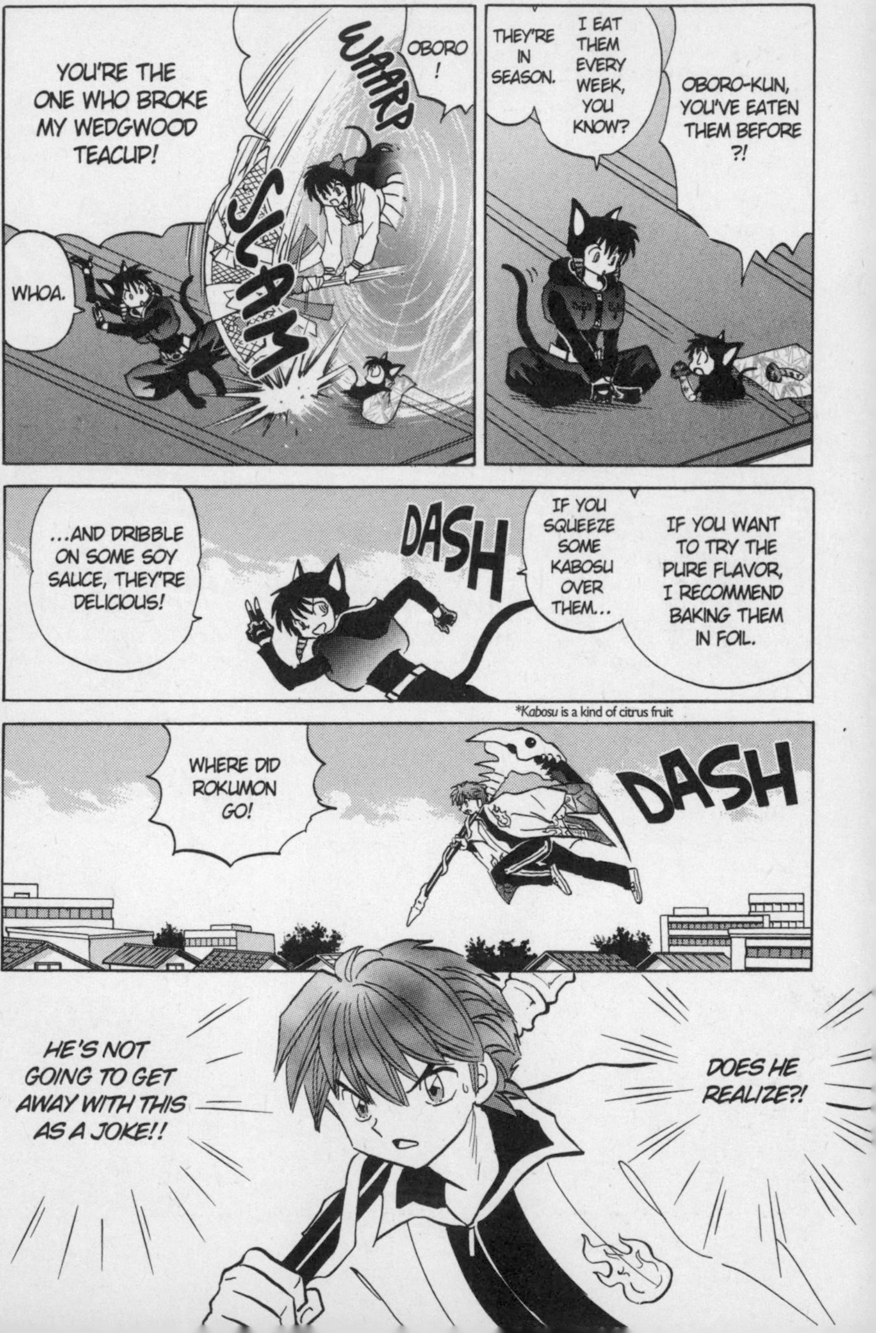
OBORO-KUN, YOU'VE EATEN THEM BEFORE?!
I EAT THEM EVERY WEEK, YOU KNOW?
THEY'RE IN SEASON.
OBORO!
WAARP
YOU'RE THE ONE WHO BROKE MY WEDGWOOD TEACUP!
SLAM
WHOA.
IF YOU WANT TO TRY THE PURE FLAVOR, I RECOMMEND BAKING THEM IN FOIL.
IF YOU SQUEEZE SOME KABOSU OVER THEM...
DASH
...AND DRIBBLE ON SOME SOY SAUCE, THEY'RE DELICIOUS!
DASH
WHERE DID ROKUMON GO!
DOES HE REALIZE?!
HE'S NOT GOING TO GET AWAY WITH THIS AS A JOKE!!

*Kabosu is a kind of citrus fruit

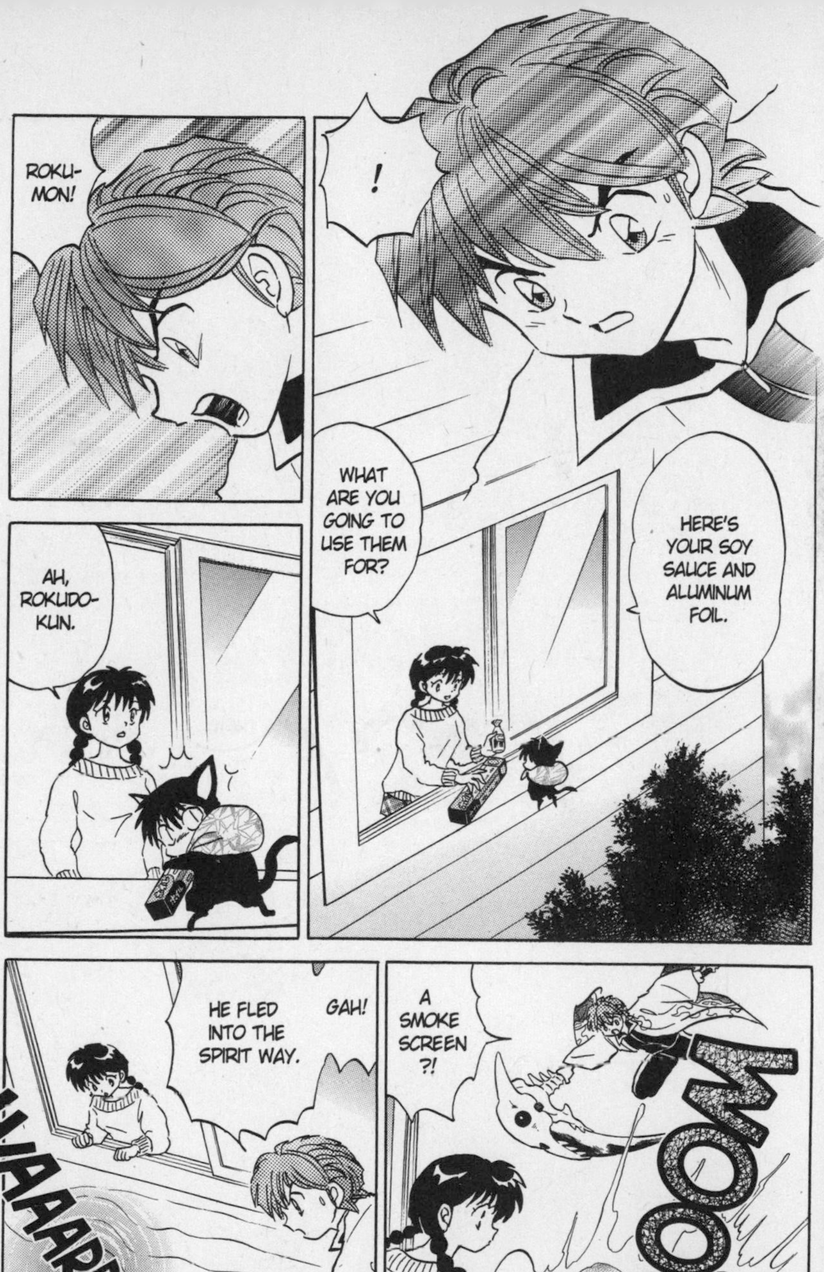
!
ROKU-MON!
HERE'S YOUR SOY SAUCE AND ALUMINUM FOIL.
WHAT ARE YOU GOING TO USE THEM FOR?
AH, ROKUDO-KUN.
BOOM
A SMOKE SCREEN ?!
GAH!
HE FLED INTO THE SPIRIT WAY.
WAAARP

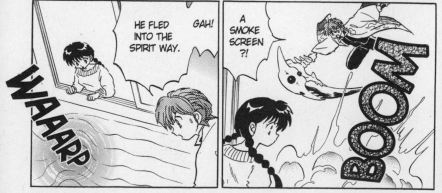

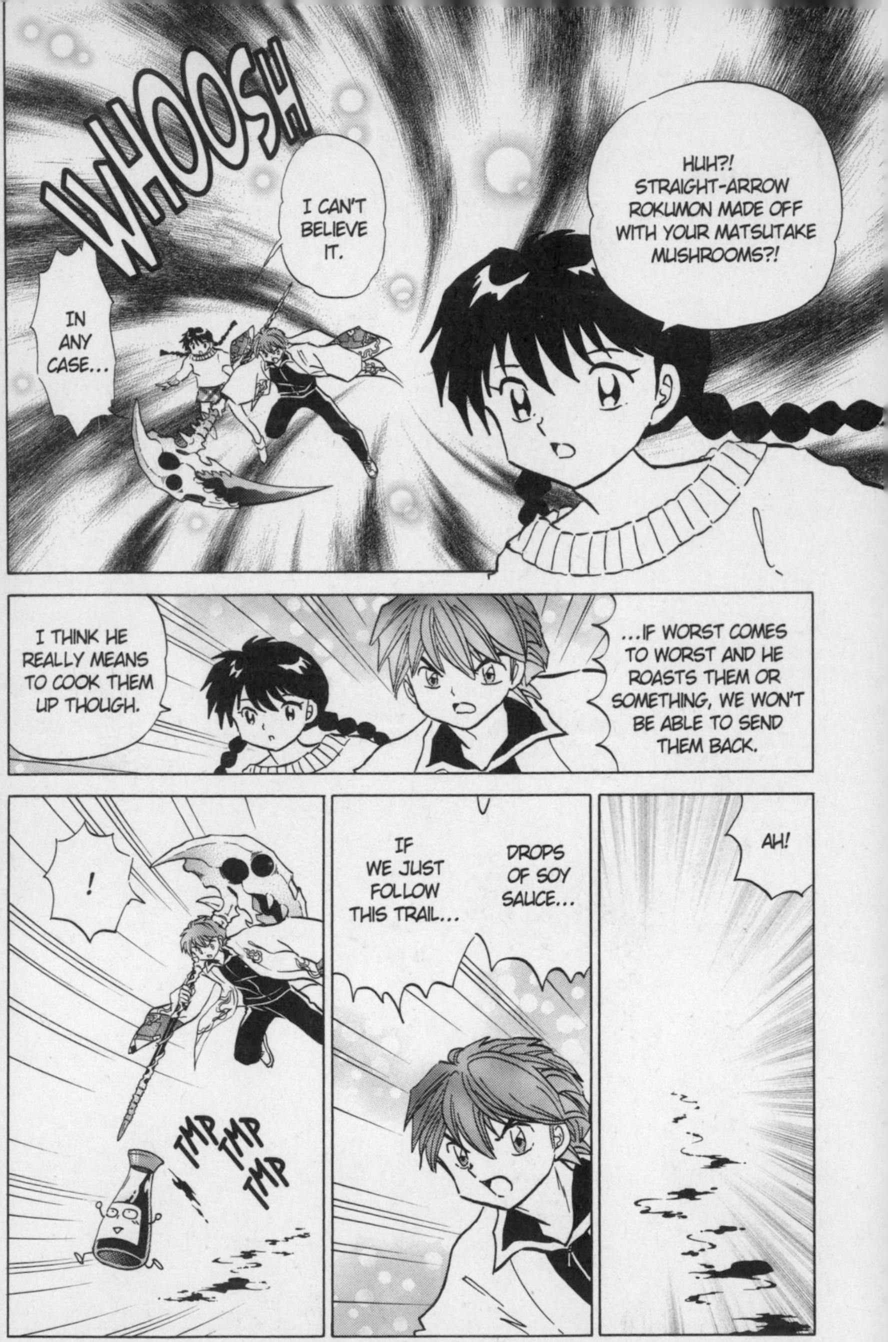
HUH?! STRAIGHT-ARROW ROKUMON MADE OFF WITH YOUR MATSUTAKE MUSHROOMS?!
I CAN'T BELIEVE IT.
WHOOSH!
IN ANY CASE…
…IF WORST COMES TO WORST AND HE ROASTS THEM OR SOMETHING, WE WON'T BE ABLE TO SEND THEM BACK.
I THINK HE REALLY MEANS TO COOK THEM UP THOUGH.
AH!
DROPS OF SOY SAUCE…
IF WE JUST FOLLOW THIS TRAIL…
!
TMP TMP TMP

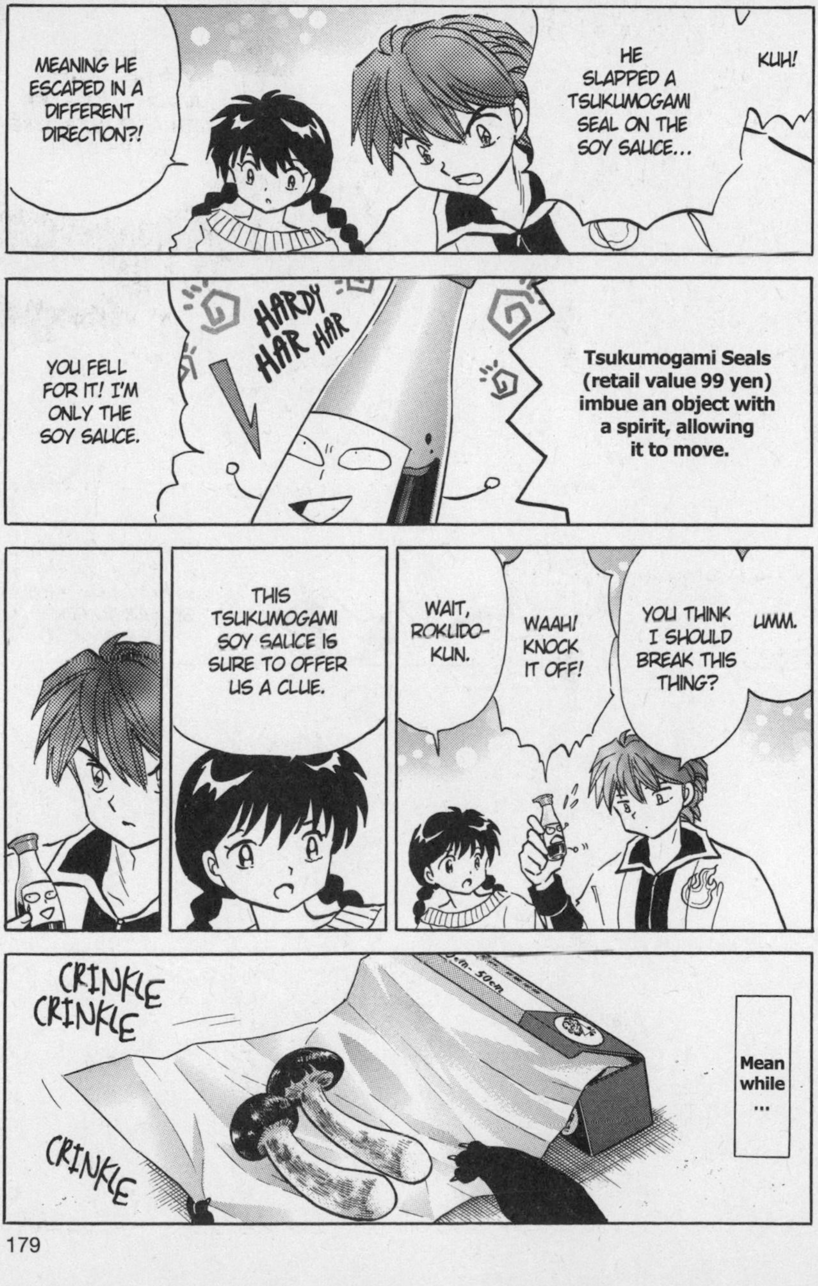
KUH!
HE SLAPPED A TSUKUMOGAMI SEAL ON THE SOY SAUCE...
MEANING HE ESCAPED IN A DIFFERENT DIRECTION?!
Tsukumogami Seals (retail value 99 yen) imbue an object with a spirit, allowing it to move.
HARDY HAR HAR
YOU FELL FOR IT! I'M ONLY THE SOY SAUCE.
UMM.
YOU THINK I SHOULD BREAK THIS THING?
WAAH! KNOCK IT OFF!
WAIT, ROKUDO-KUN.
THIS TSUKUMOGAMI SOY SAUCE IS SURE TO OFFER US A CLUE.
Mean while ...
CRINKLE CRINKLE
CRINKLE

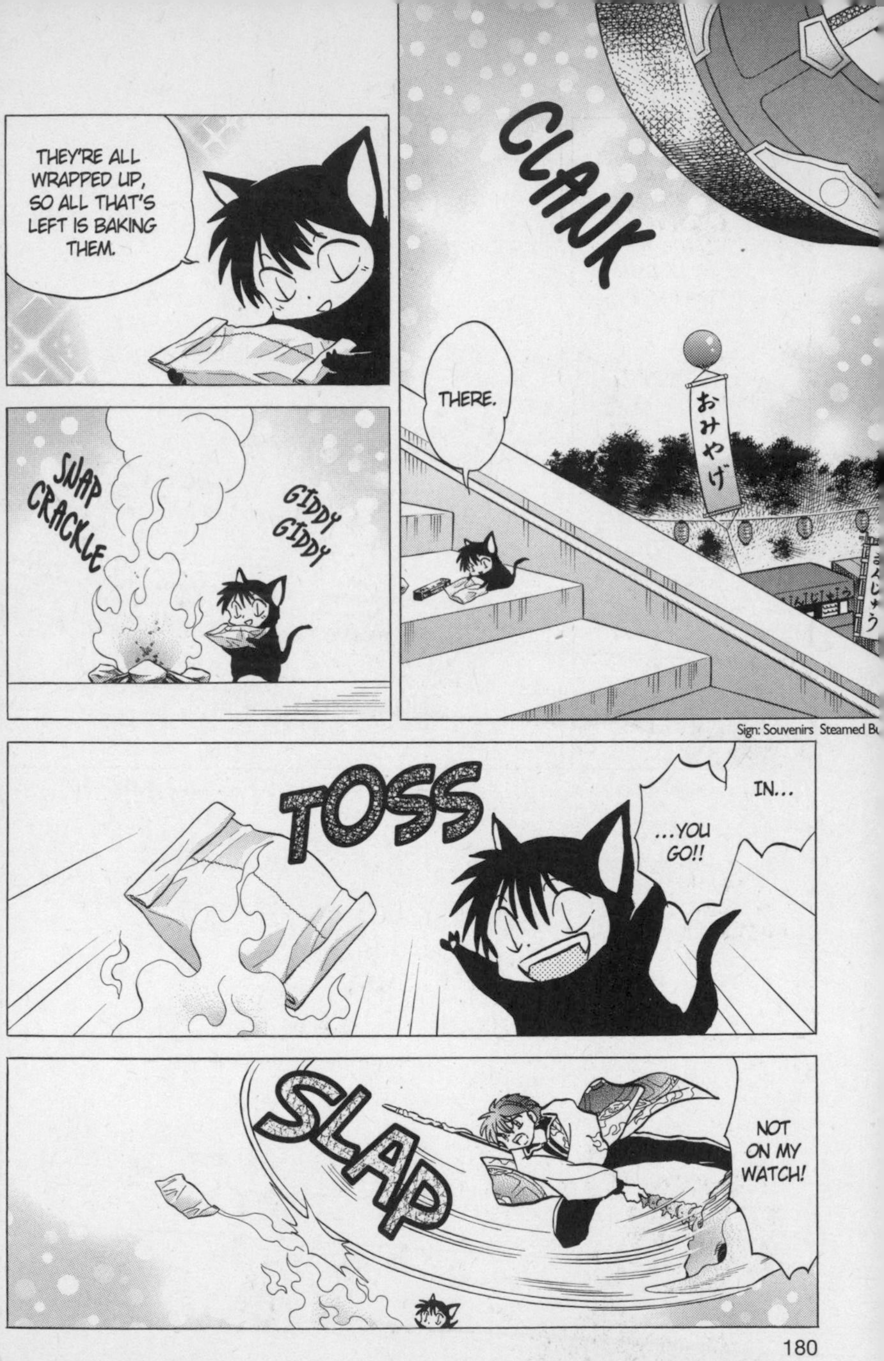
CLANK
THERE.
おみやげ
Sign: Souvenirs Steamed Bu
THEY'RE ALL WRAPPED UP, SO ALL THAT'S LEFT IS BAKING THEM.
GIDDY GIDDY
SNAP CRACKLE
IN...
...YOU GO!!
TOSS
NOT ON MY WATCH!
SLAP

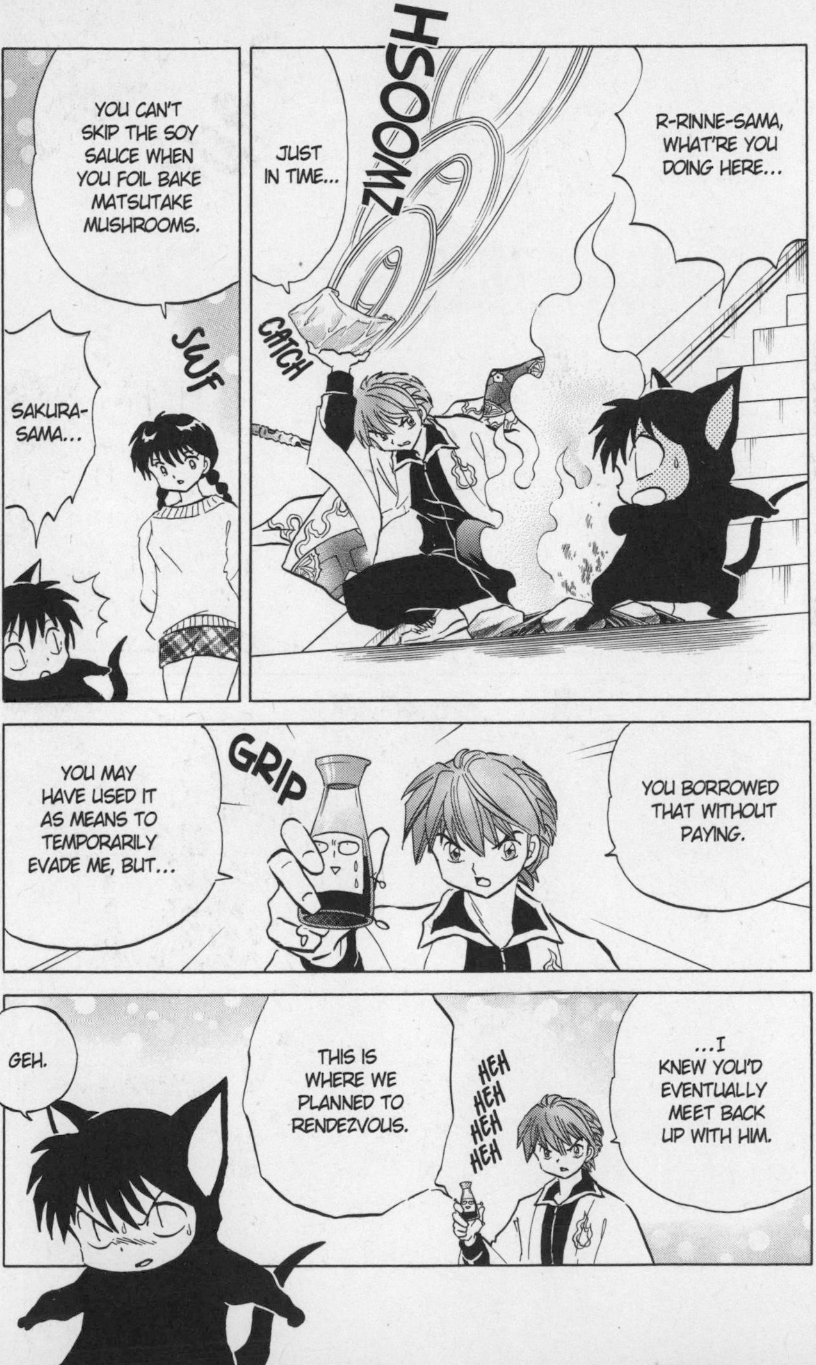
R-RINNE-SAMA, WHAT'RE YOU DOING HERE...
ZWOOSH
JUST IN TIME...
CATCH
YOU CAN'T SKIP THE SOY SAUCE WHEN YOU FOIL BAKE MATSUTAKE MUSHROOMS.
SWF
SAKURA-SAMA...
YOU BORROWED THAT WITHOUT PAYING.
GRIP
YOU MAY HAVE USED IT AS MEANS TO TEMPORARILY EVADE ME, BUT...
...I KNEW YOU'D EVENTUALLY MEET BACK UP WITH HIM.
HEH HEH HEH HEH
THIS IS WHERE WE PLANNED TO RENDEZVOUS.
GEH.

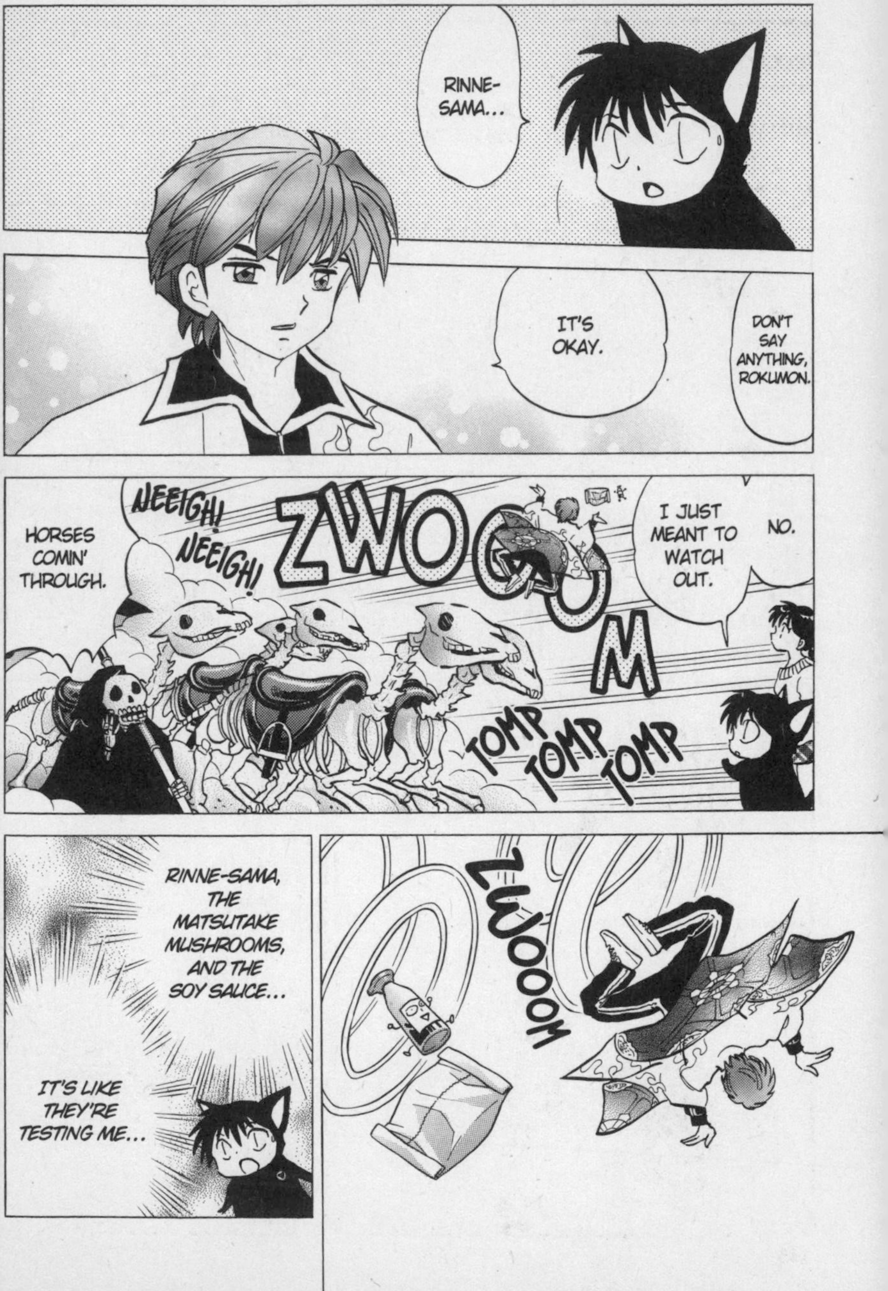
RINNE-SAMA...
DON'T SAY ANYTHING, ROKUMON.
IT'S OKAY.
NO.
I JUST MEANT TO WATCH OUT.
ZWOOOM
NEEIGH! NEEIGH!
HORSES COMIN' THROUGH.
TOMP TOMP TOMP
ZWOOOOM
RINNE-SAMA, THE MATSUTAKE MUSHROOMS, AND THE SOY SAUCE...
IT'S LIKE THEY'RE TESTING ME...

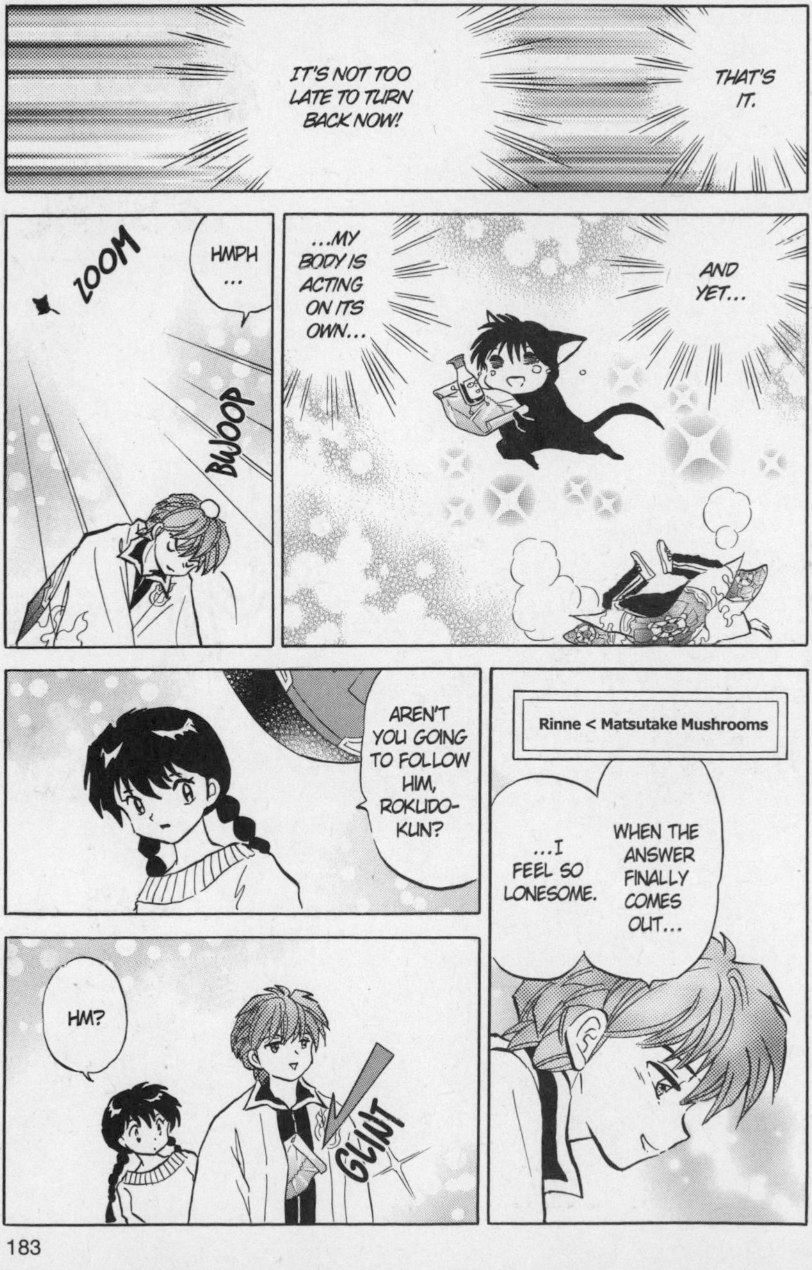
THAT'S IT.
IT'S NOT TOO LATE TO TURN BACK NOW!
AND YET...
...MY BODY IS ACTING ON ITS OWN...
HMPH...
ZOOM
BWOOP
Rinne < Matsutake Mushrooms
WHEN THE ANSWER FINALLY COMES OUT...
...I FEEL SO LONESOME.
AREN'T YOU GOING TO FOLLOW HIM, ROKUDO-KUN?
HM?
GLINT

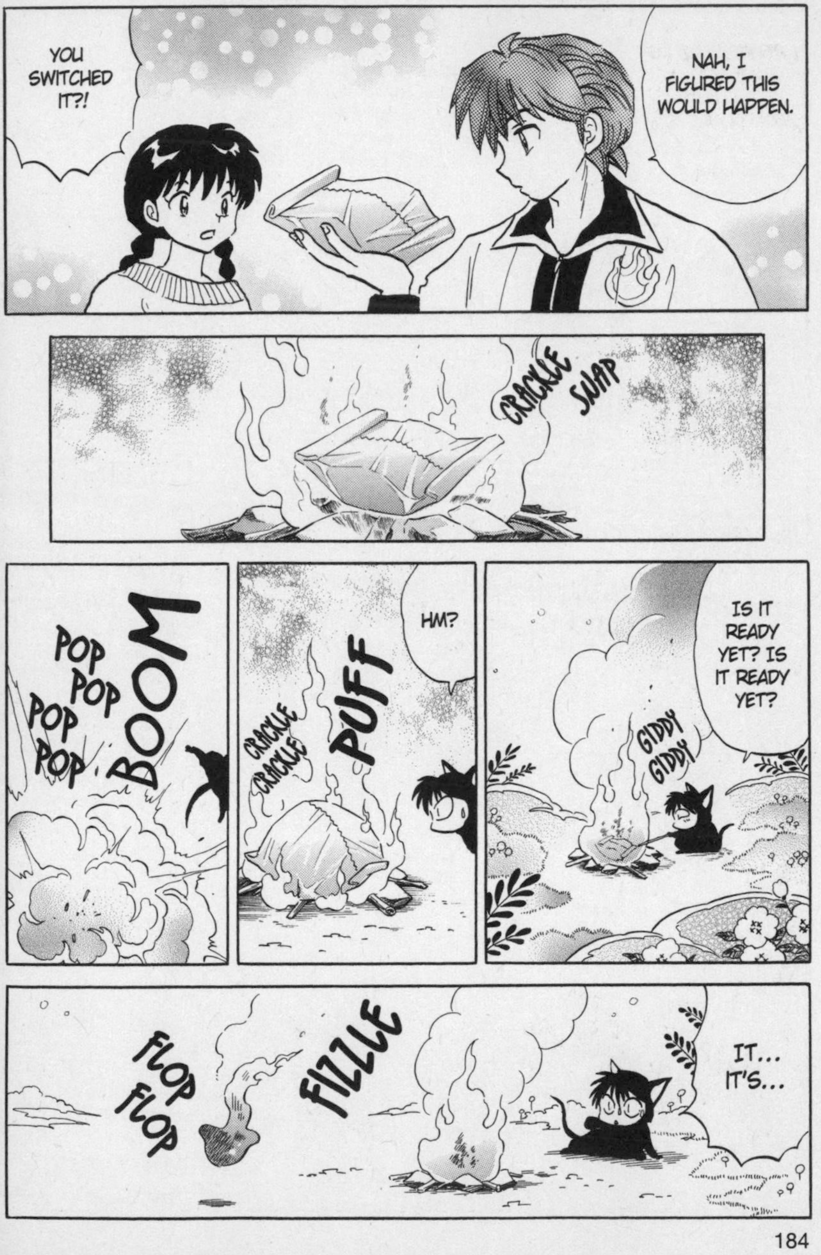
NAH, I FIGURED THIS WOULD HAPPEN.
YOU SWITCHED IT?!
CRACKLE SNAP
IS IT READY YET? IS IT READY YET?
GIDDY GIDDY
HM?
PUFF
CRACKLE CRACKLE
BOOM
POP POP POP POP
IT... IT'S...
FIZZLE
FLOP FLOP

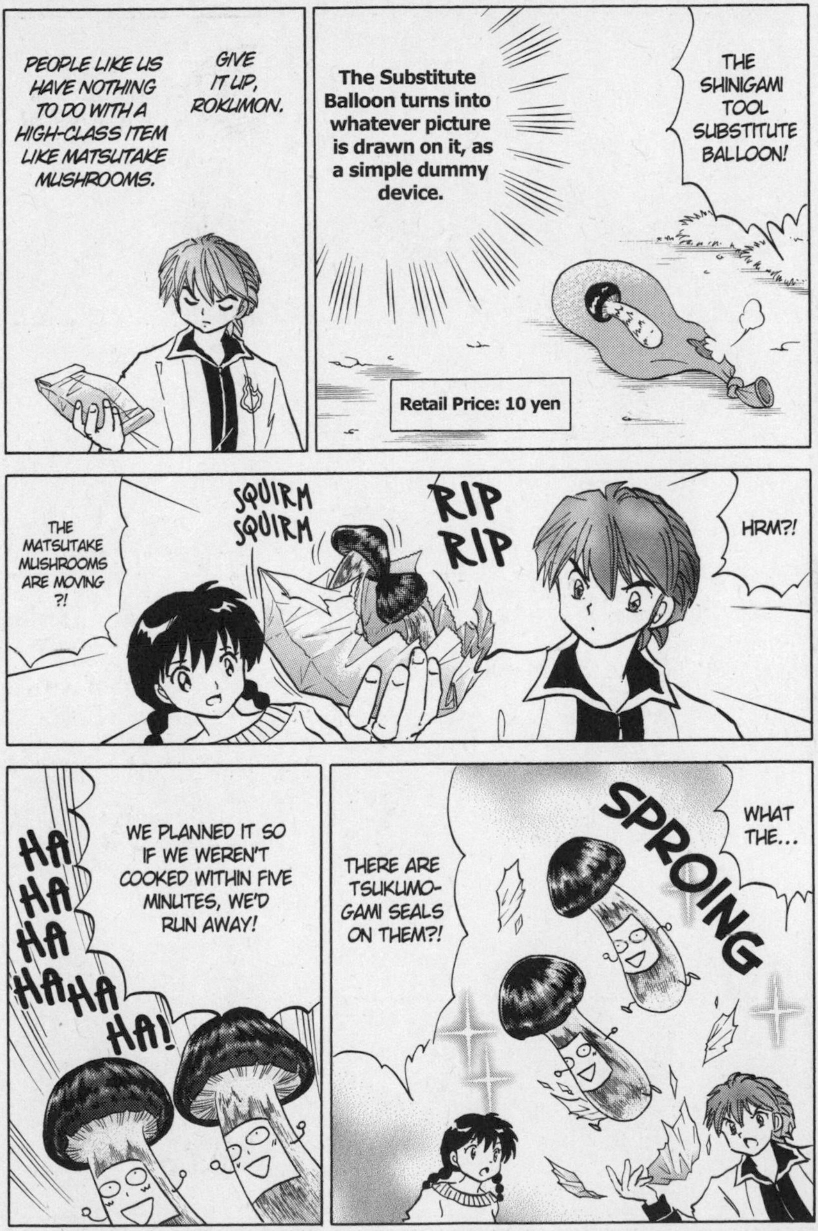

THE SHINIGAMI TOOL SUBSTITUTE BALLOON!
The Substitute Balloon turns into whatever picture is drawn on it, as a simple dummy device.
Retail Price: 10 yen
GIVE IT UP, ROKUMON.
PEOPLE LIKE US HAVE NOTHING TO DO WITH A HIGH-CLASS ITEM LIKE MATSUTAKE MUSHROOMS.
HRM?!
RIP RIP
SQUIRM SQUIRM
THE MATSUTAKE MUSHROOMS ARE MOVING?!
WHAT THE...
SPROING
THERE ARE TSUKUMO-GAMI SEALS ON THEM?!
WE PLANNED IT SO IF WE WEREN'T COOKED WITHIN FIVE MINUTES, WE'D RUN AWAY!
HA HA HA HA HA HA HA!

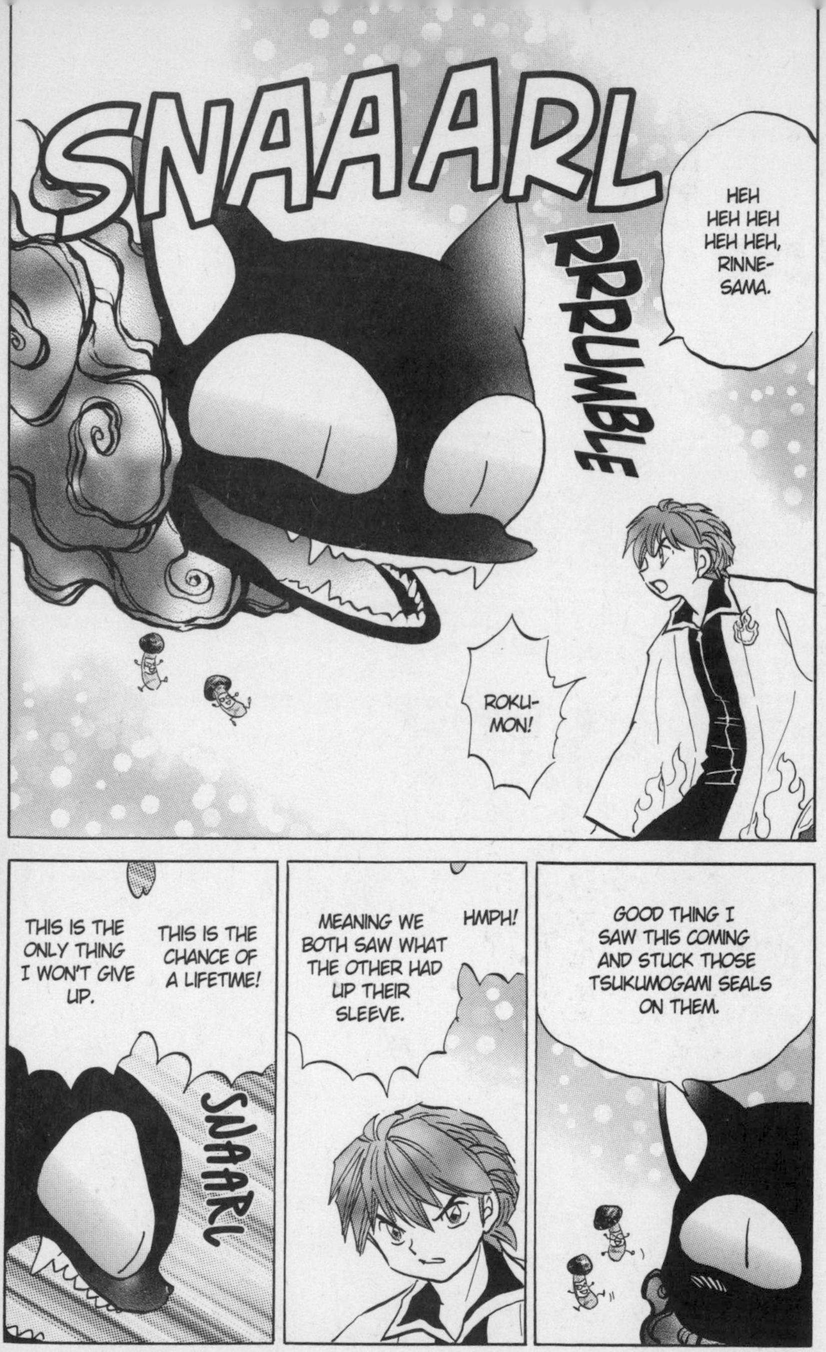
HEH HEH HEH HEH HEH, RINNE-SAMA.
SNAAARL
RRRUMBLE
ROKU-MON!
GOOD THING I SAW THIS COMING AND STUCK THOSE TSUKUMOGAMI SEALS ON THEM.
HMPH!
MEANING WE BOTH SAW WHAT THE OTHER HAD UP THEIR SLEEVE.
THIS IS THE CHANCE OF A LIFETIME!
THIS IS THE ONLY THING I WON'T GIVE UP.
SNAARL

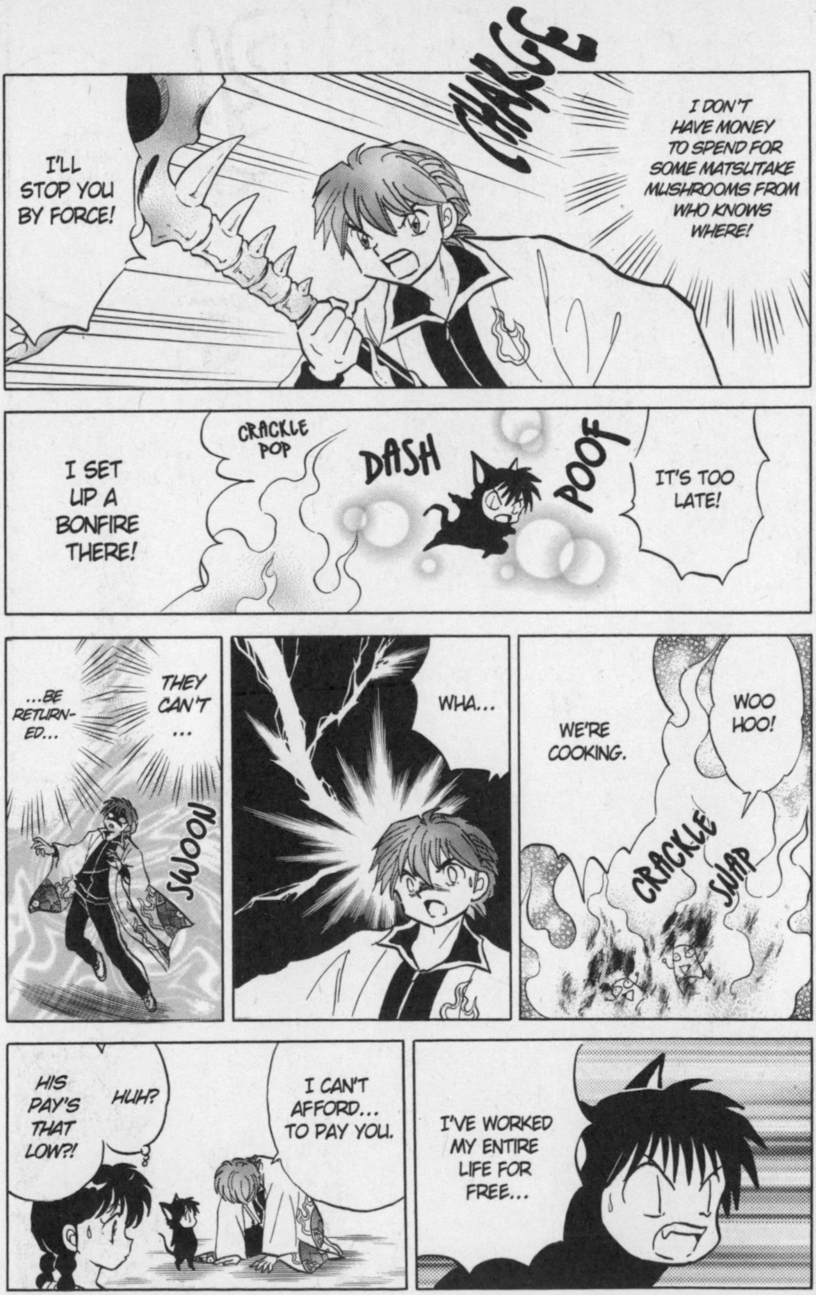
CHARGE
I DON'T HAVE MONEY TO SPEND FOR SOME MATSUTAKE MUSHROOMS FROM WHO KNOWS WHERE!
I'LL STOP YOU BY FORCE!
IT'S TOO LATE!
POOF
DASH
CRACKLE POP
I SET UP A BONFIRE THERE!
WOO HOO!
WE'RE COOKING.
CRACKLE SNAP
WHA...
THEY CAN'T ...
...BE RETURN-ED...
SWOON
I'VE WORKED MY ENTIRE LIFE FOR FREE...
I CAN'T AFFORD... TO PAY YOU.
HUH?
HIS PAY'S THAT LOW?!

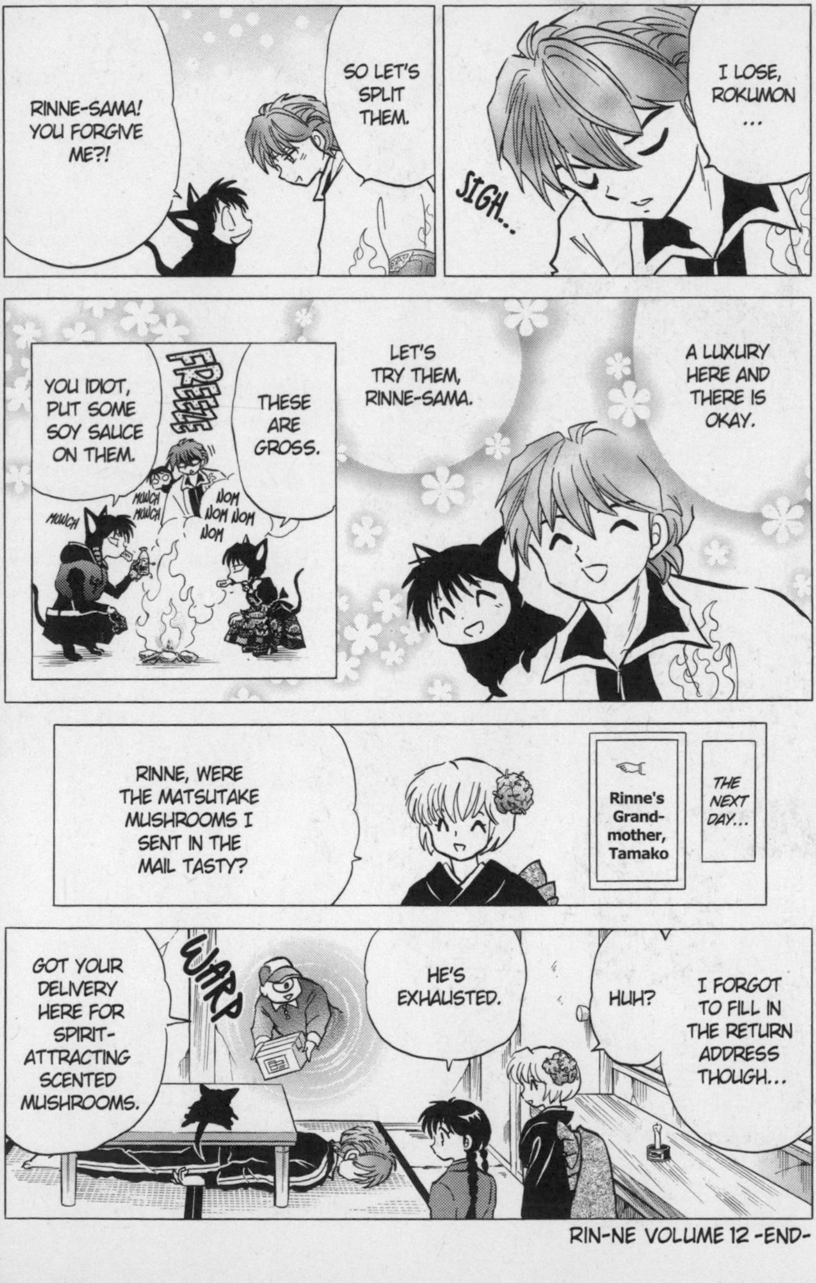
I LOSE, ROKUMON ...
SIGH...
SO LET'S SPLIT THEM.
RINNE-SAMA! YOU FORGIVE ME?!
A LUXURY HERE AND THERE IS OKAY.
LET'S TRY THEM, RINNE-SAMA.
THESE ARE GROSS.
FREEZE
YOU IDIOT, PUT SOME SOY SAUCE ON THEM.
NOM NOM NOM NOM
MUNCH MUNCH
MUNCH
THE NEXT DAY...
Rinne's Grand-mother, Tamako
RINNE, WERE THE MATSUTAKE MUSHROOMS I SENT IN THE MAIL TASTY?
I FORGOT TO FILL IN THE RETURN ADDRESS THOUGH...
HUH?
HE'S EXHAUSTED.
WARP
GOT YOUR DELIVERY HERE FOR SPIRIT-ATTRACTING SCENTED MUSHROOMS.

RIN-NE VOLUME 12 -END-

Hey! You're Reading in the Wrong Direction!

This is the end of this graphic novel!

To properly enjoy this VIZ graphic novel, please turn it around and begin reading from right to left. Unlike English, Japanese is read right to left, so Japanese comics are read in reverse order from the way English comics are typically read.

This book has been printed in the original Japanese format in order to preserve the orientation of the original artwork. Have fun with it!

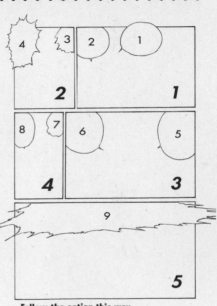

Follow the action this way